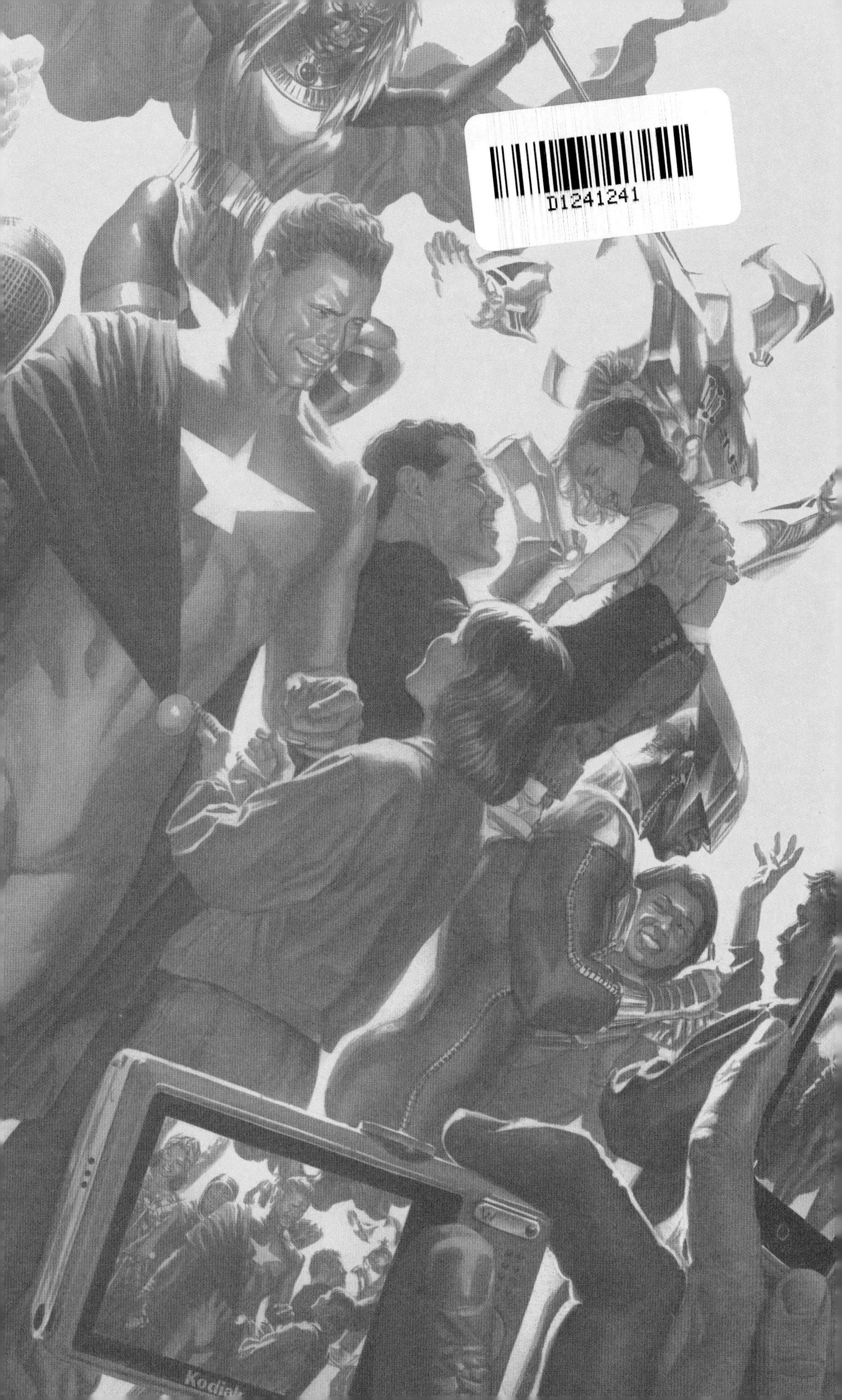

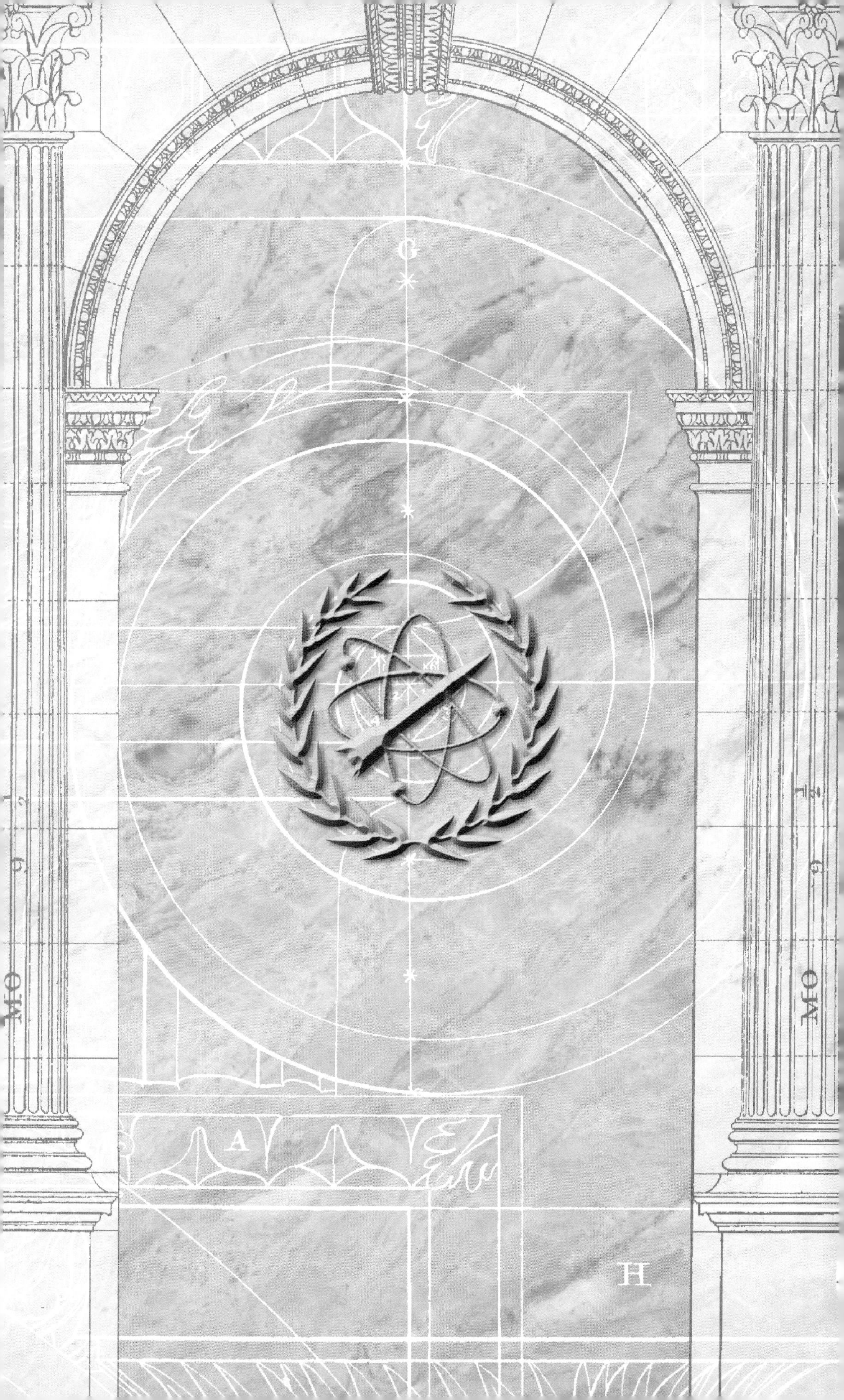
G
A
H

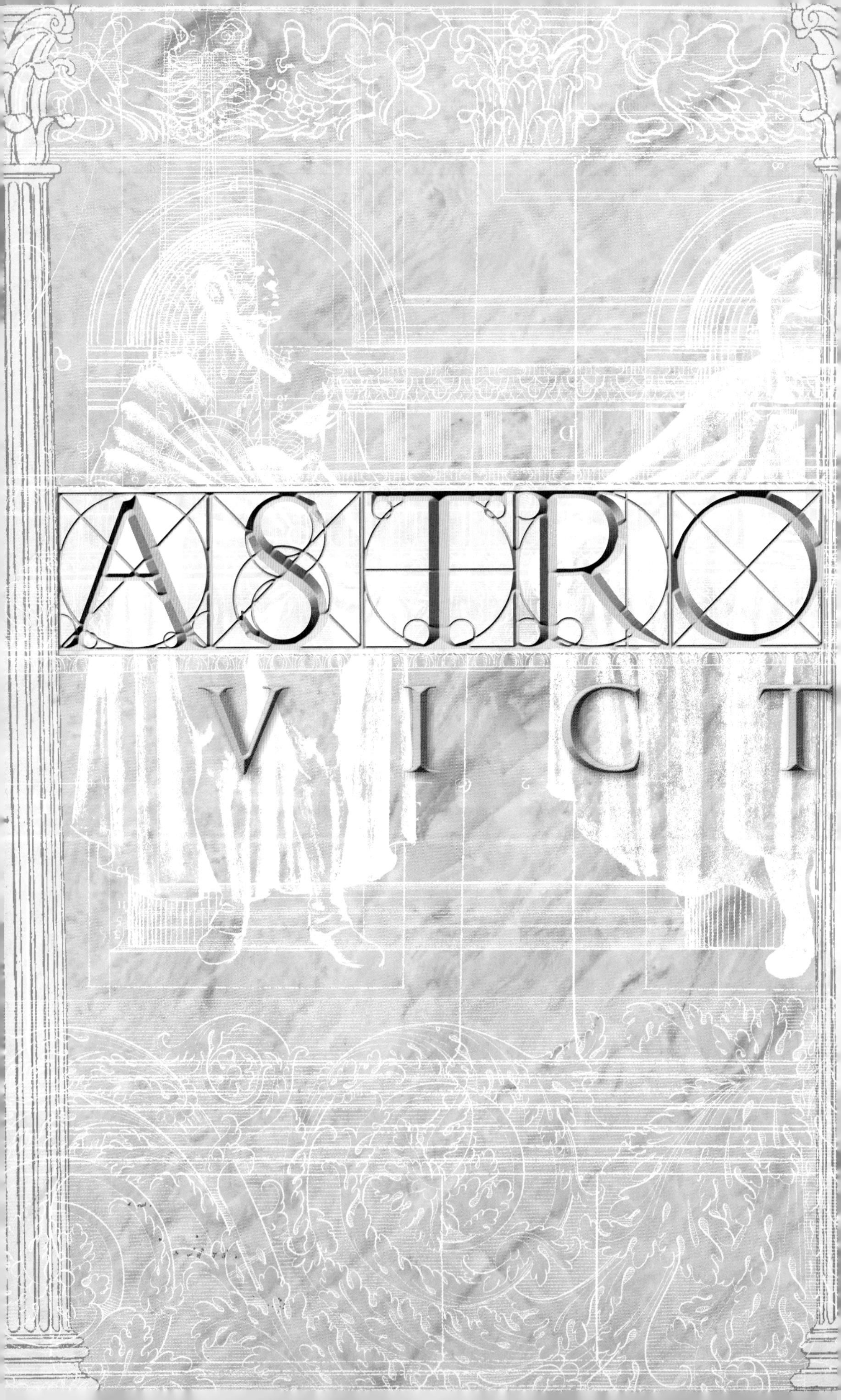
ASTRO
VICT

CITY
ORY

KURT BUSIEK
WRITER

BRENT ERIC ANDERSON
ARTIST

ALEX ROSS
COVER ART

ALEX SINCLAIR & WENDY BROOME
COLORS

BEN OLIVER
FINISHED ART & COLOR ON "HAVING A WONDERFUL TIME"

COMICRAFT'S JOHN ROSHELL & JIMMY BETANCOURT
LETTERING & DESIGN

ASTRO CITY CREATED BY
BUSIEK, ANDERSON & ROSS

39999002261269

Little Elm Public Library
214-975-0430

RICHARD STARKINGS
ART DIRECTOR

VERTIGO

KRISTY QUINN EDITOR
JESSICA CHEN ASSISTANT EDITOR
BEN ABERNATHY SERIES EDITOR, "A VISITORS GUIDE"
ROBBIN BROSTERMAN DESIGN DIRECTOR – BOOKS

SHELLY BOND EXECUTIVE EDITOR – VERTIGO
HANK KANALZ SENIOR VP – VERTIGO &
INTEGRATED PUBLISHING

DIANE NELSON PRESIDENT
DAN DIDIO AND JIM LEE CO-PUBLISHERS
GEOFF JOHNS CHIEF CREATIVE OFFICER
AMIT DESAI SENIOR VP – MARKETING &
FRANCHISE MANAGEMENT
AMY GENKINS SENIOR VP – BUSINESS & LEGAL AFFAIRS
NAIRI GARDINER SENIOR VP – FINANCE
JEFF BOISON VP – PUBLISHING PLANNING
MARK CHIARELLO VP – ART DIRECTION & DESIGN
JOHN CUNNINGHAM VP – MARKETING
TERRI CUNNINGHAM VP – EDITORIAL ADMINISTRATION
LARRY GANEM VP – TALENT RELATIONS & SERVICES
ALISON GILL SENIOR VP – MANUFACTURING & OPERATIONS
JAY KOGAN VP – BUSINESS & LEGAL AFFAIRS, PUBLISHING
JACK MAHAN VP – BUSINESS AFFAIRS, TALENT
NICK NAPOLITANO VP – MANUFACTURING ADMINISTRATION
SUE POHJA VP – BOOK SALES
FRED RUIZ VP – MANUFACTURING OPERATIONS
COURTNEY SIMMONS SENIOR VP – PUBLICITY
BOB WAYNE SENIOR VP – SALES

SUSTAINABLE
FORESTRY
INITIATIVE

Certified Chain of Custody
20% Certified Forest Content,
80% Certified Sourcing
www.sfiprogram.org
SFI-01042
APPLIES TO TEXT STOCK ONLY

LIBRARY OF CONGRESS
CATALOGING-IN-PUBLICATION DATA

BUSIEK, KURT, AUTHOR.
ASTRO CITY : VICTORY / KURT BUSIEK,
BRENT ANDERSON.
PAGES CM
SUMMARY: "A MAJOR NEW EPIC BEGINS
FEATURING WINGED VICTORY, SAMARITAN,
AND THE CONFESSOR, THREE OF ASTRO
CITY'S MOST POPULAR HEROES. WHEN
CRIMINAL CHARGES ARE BROUGHT AGAINST
WINGED VICTORY, THE CONFESSOR MUST
INVESTIGATE AND IT LEADS TO OPEN
COMBAT WITH SAMARITAN! CAN ASTRO
CITY'S THREE GREATEST HEROES FIND A WAY
TO WORK TOGETHER AGAINST THIS MYSTERY
THREAT? PLUS, WINGED VICTORY'S ORIGIN
IS REVEALED AT LAST! COLLECTS ASTRO CITY
NOS.7-10 AND ASTRO CITY VISITOR'S GUIDE
NO.1"-- PROVIDED BY PUBLISHER.
ISBN 978-1-4012-5057-7 (HARDBACK)
1. GRAPHIC NOVELS. I. ANDERSON, BRENT
ERIC. ILLUSTRATOR. II. TITLE.
PN6728.A79B89 2014
741.5'973--DC23
2014011632

ASTRO CITY: VICTORY, PUBLISHED BY
DC COMICS, 1700 BROADWAY, NEW YORK, NY 10019.

COVER, SKETCHES AND COMPILATION
COPYRIGHT © 2014 JUKE BOX PRODUCTIONS.

ORIGINALLY PUBLISHED AS ASTRO CITY NOS. 7-10 ©
2013 AND ASTRO CITY: A VISITOR'S GUIDE © 1998. ALL
RIGHTS RESERVED. ASTRO CITY, ITS LOGOS, SYMBOLS,
PROMINENT CHARACTERS FEATURED IN THIS
VOLUME AND THE DISTINCTIVE LIKENESSES THEREOF
ARE TRADEMARKS OF JUKE BOX PRODUCTIONS.
VERTIGO IS A TRADEMARK OF DC COMICS. ANY
SIMILIARITY TO INSTITUTIONS OR PERSONS
LIVING OR DEAD IS UNINTENTIONAL AND
PURELY COINCIDENTAL.

PRINTED ON RECYCLABLE PAPER. DC COMICS DOES
NOT READ OR ACCEPT UNSOLICITED SUBMISSIONS
OF IDEAS, STORIES OR ARTWORK.

PRINTED BY RR DONNELLEY, SALEM, VA, USA. 8/15/2014.
FIRST PRINTING

DC COMICS, A WARNER BROS. ENTERTAINMENT
COMPANY.

ISBN: 978-1-4012-5057-7

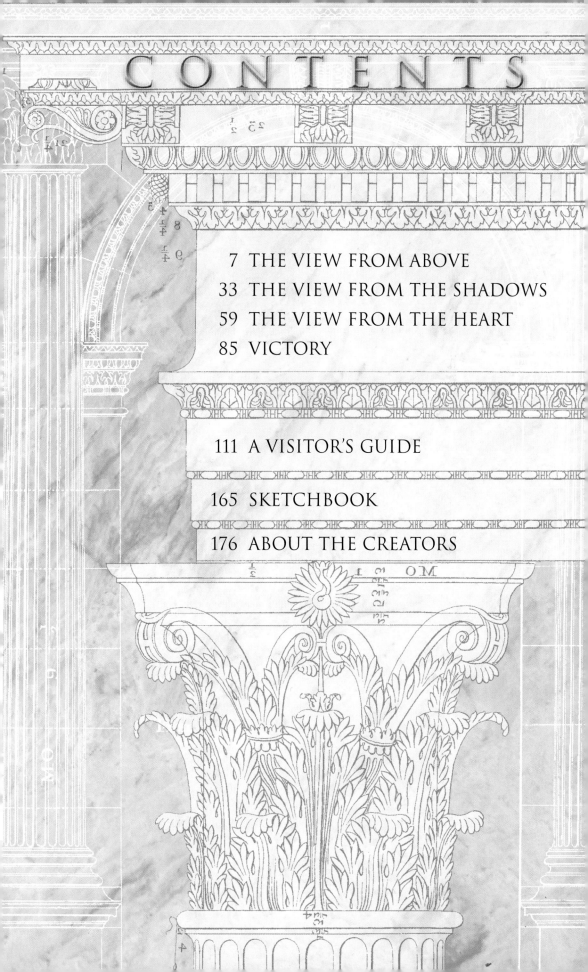

CONTENTS

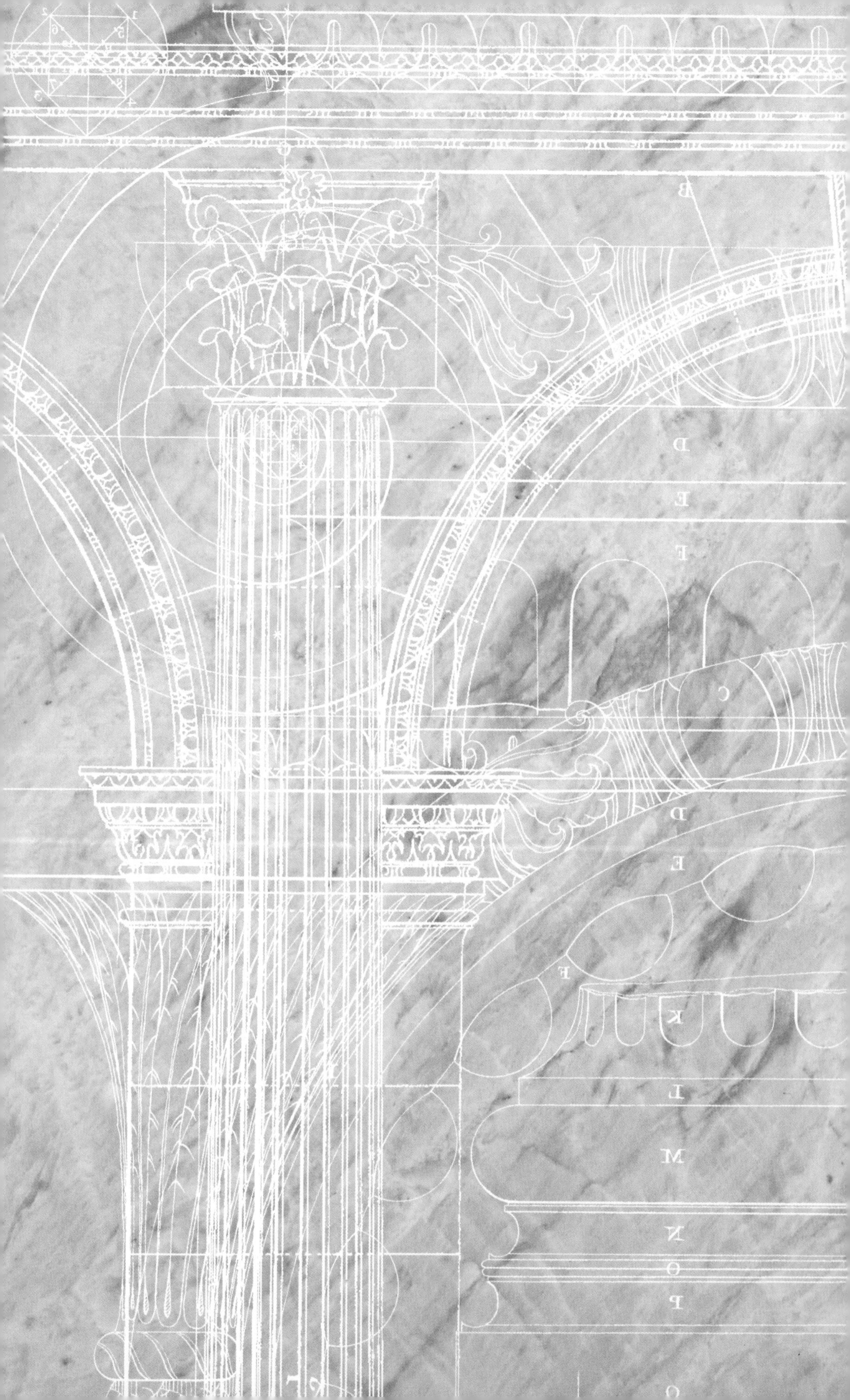

ONE

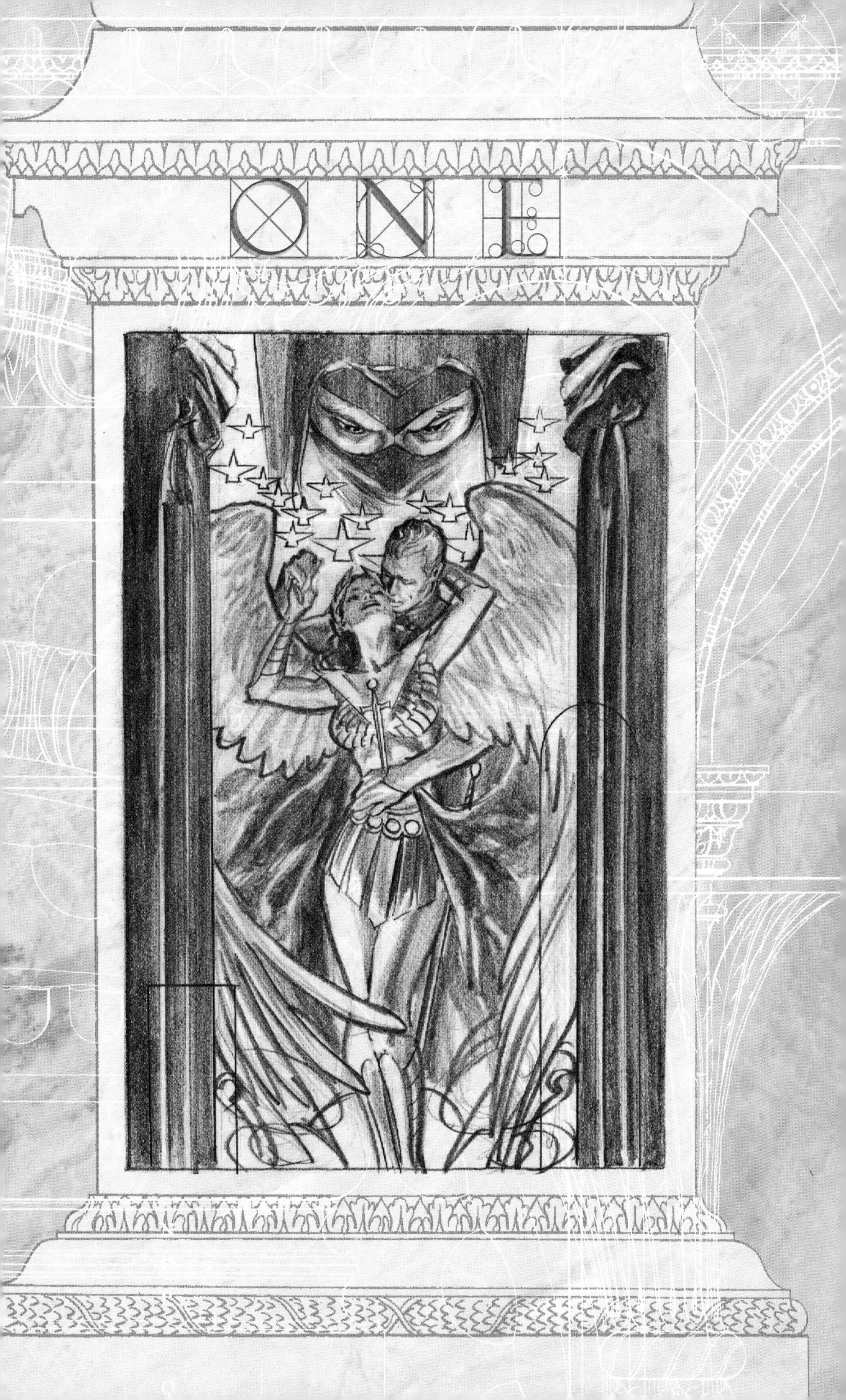

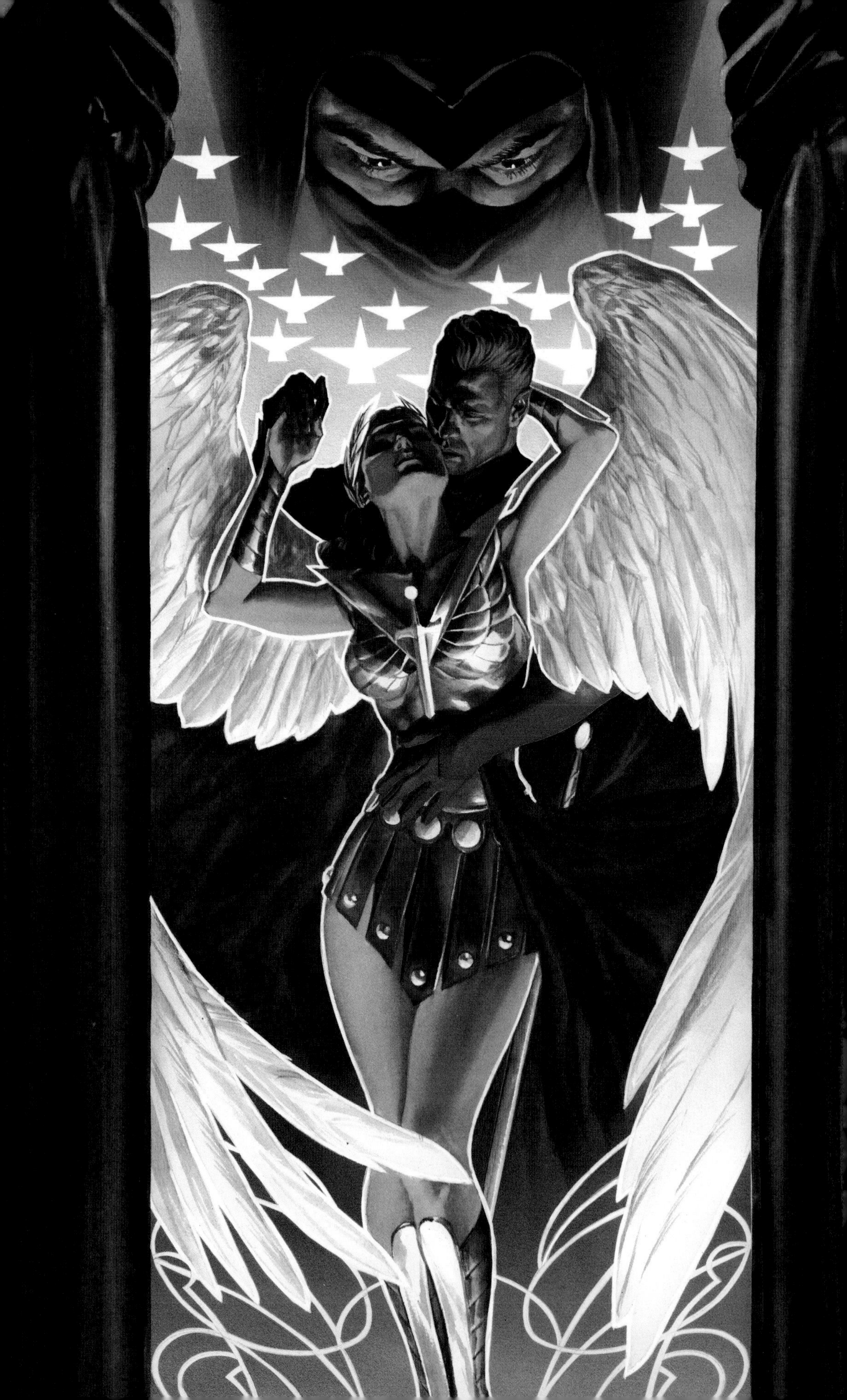

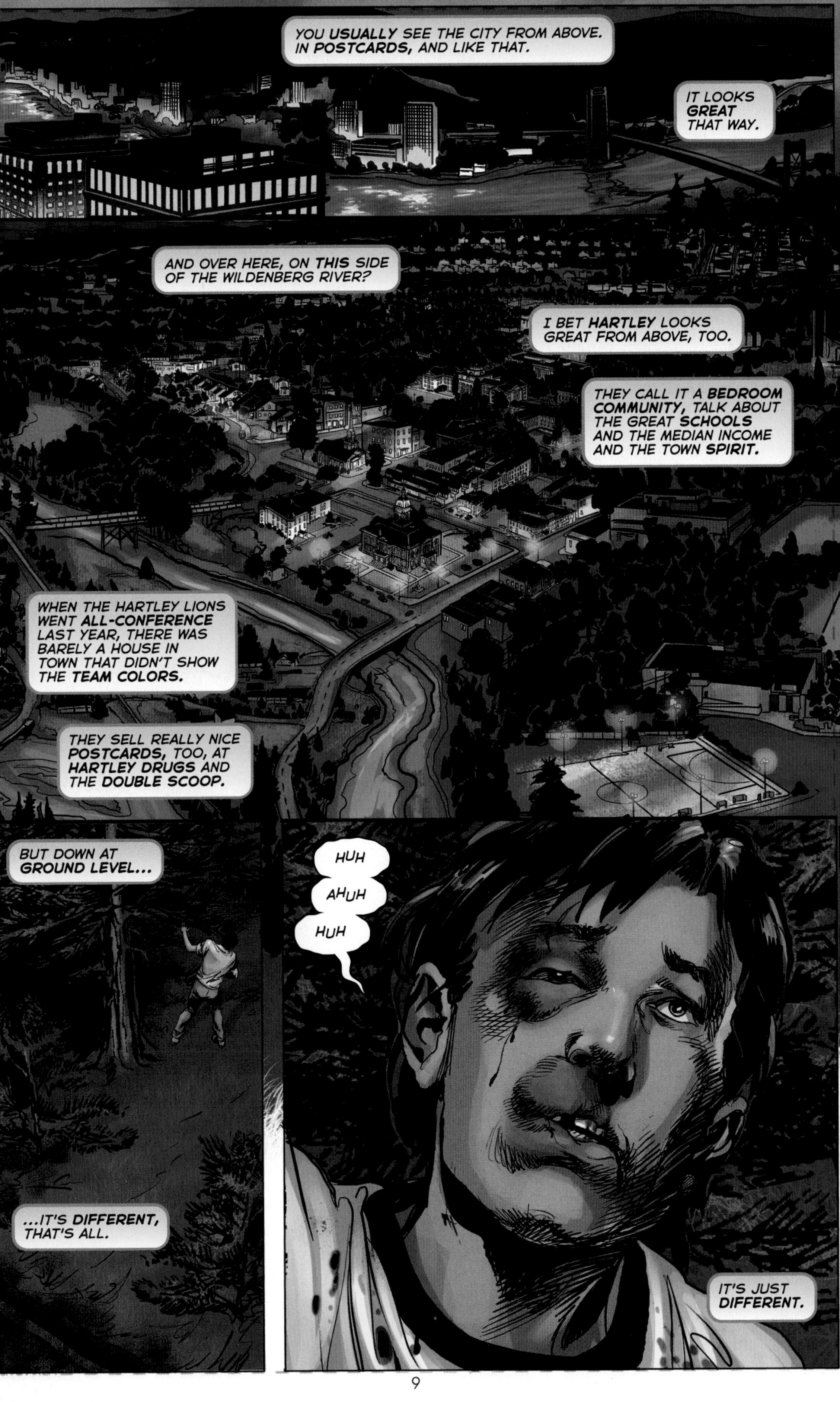

YOU USUALLY SEE THE CITY FROM ABOVE. IN POSTCARDS, AND LIKE THAT.
IT LOOKS GREAT THAT WAY.
AND OVER HERE, ON THIS SIDE OF THE WILDENBERG RIVER?
I BET HARTLEY LOOKS GREAT FROM ABOVE, TOO.
THEY CALL IT A BEDROOM COMMUNITY, TALK ABOUT THE GREAT SCHOOLS AND THE MEDIAN INCOME AND THE TOWN SPIRIT.
WHEN THE HARTLEY LIONS WENT ALL-CONFERENCE LAST YEAR, THERE WAS BARELY A HOUSE IN TOWN THAT DIDN'T SHOW THE TEAM COLORS.
THEY SELL REALLY NICE POSTCARDS, TOO, AT HARTLEY DRUGS AND THE DOUBLE SCOOP.
BUT DOWN AT GROUND LEVEL...
...IT'S DIFFERENT, THAT'S ALL.
HUH
AHUH
HUH
IT'S JUST DIFFERENT.

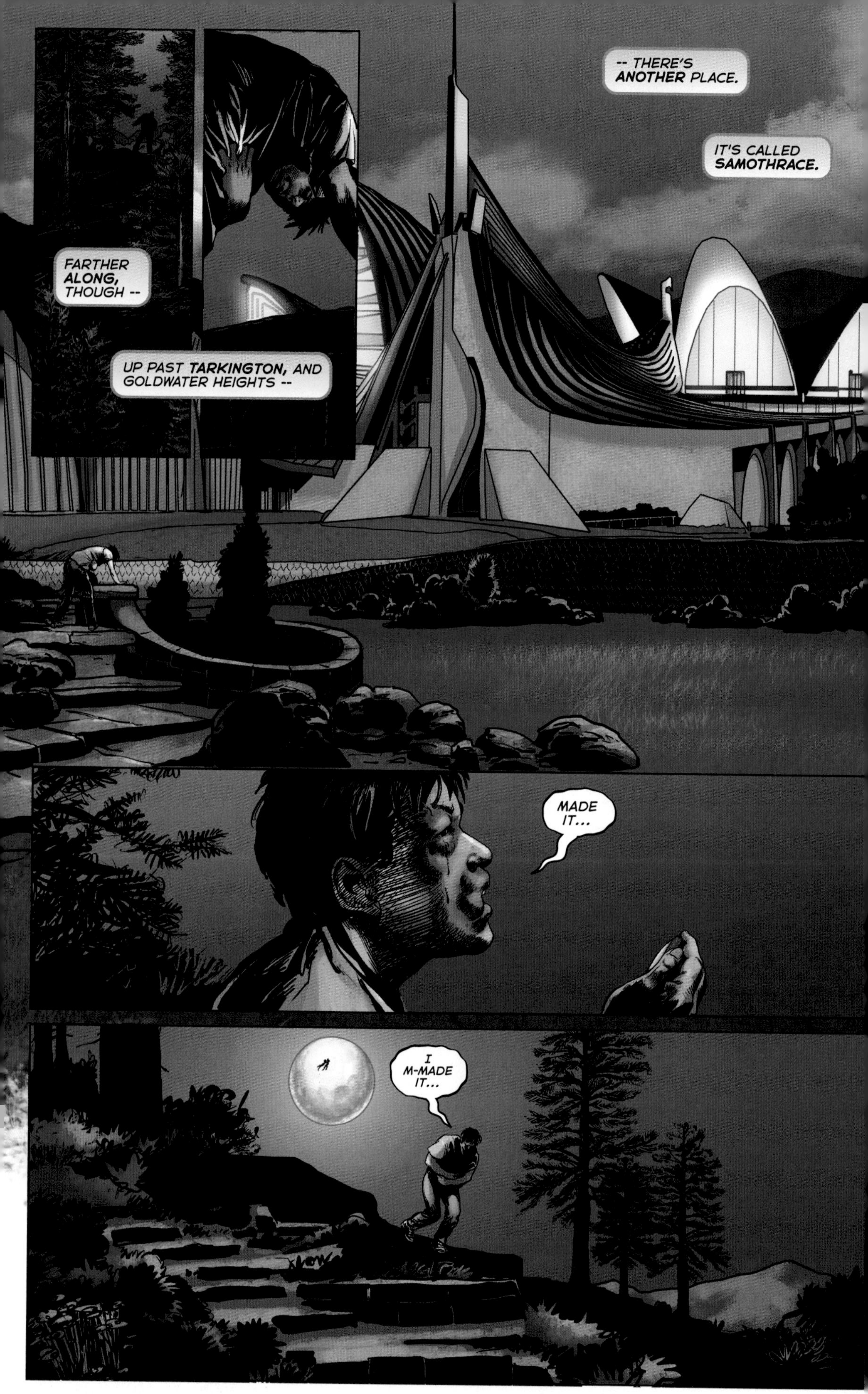
FARTHER ALONG, THOUGH --
UP PAST TARKINGTON, AND GOLDWATER HEIGHTS --
-- THERE'S ANOTHER PLACE.
IT'S CALLED SAMOTHRACE.
MADE IT...
I M-MADE IT...

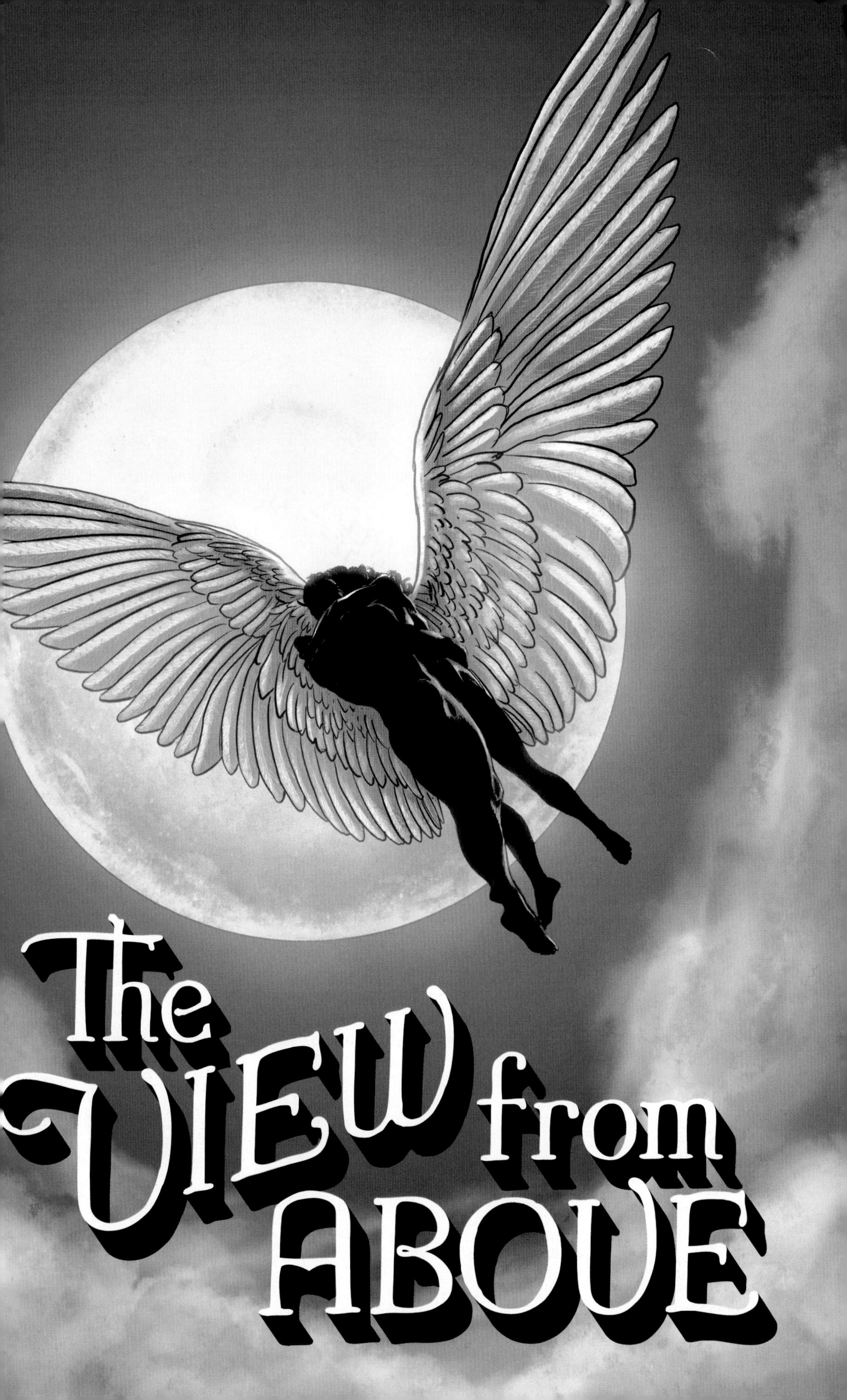
The VIEW from ABOVE

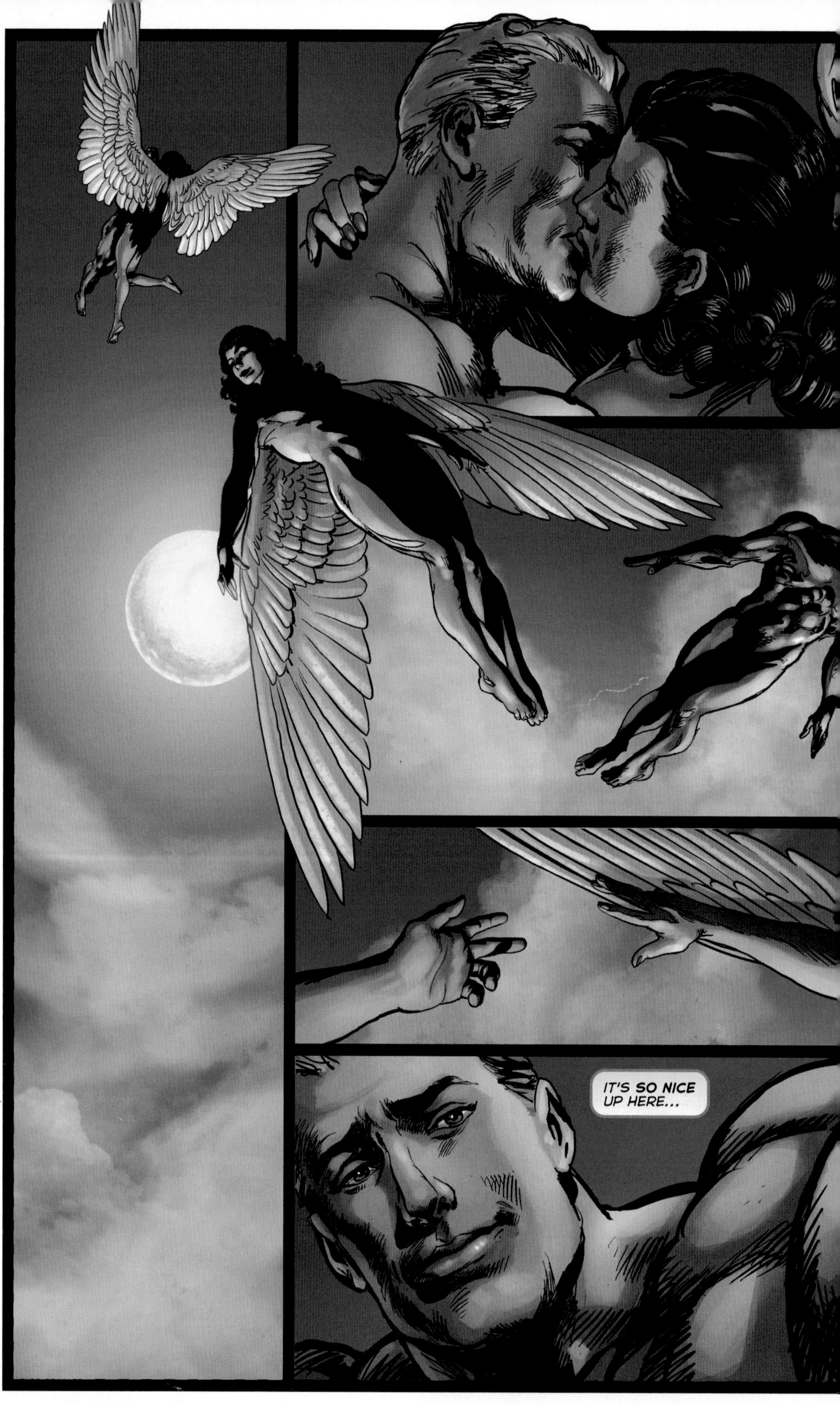
IT'S SO NICE
UP HERE...

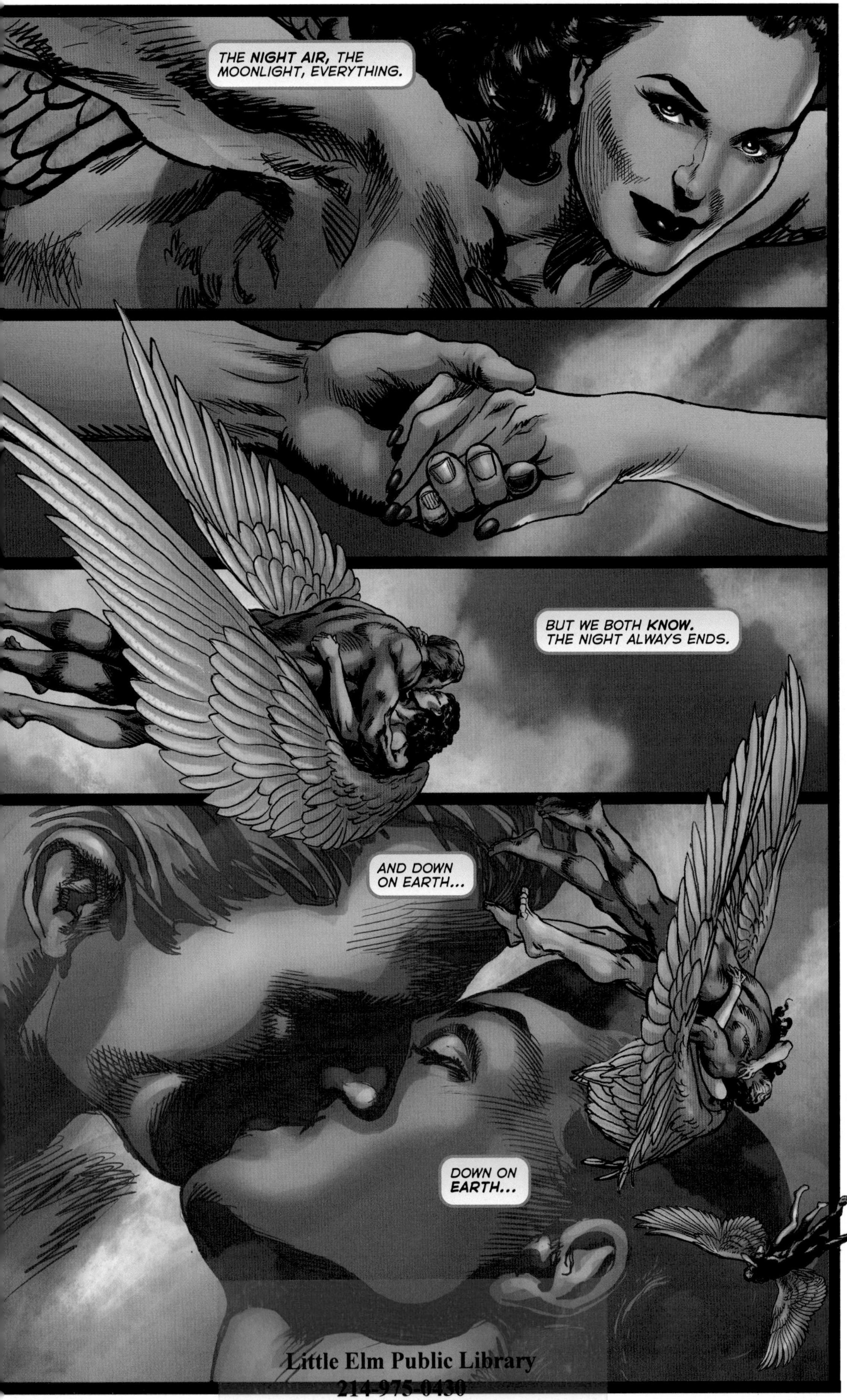
THE NIGHT AIR, THE MOONLIGHT, EVERYTHING.
BUT WE BOTH KNOW. THE NIGHT ALWAYS ENDS.
AND DOWN ON EARTH...
DOWN ON EARTH...

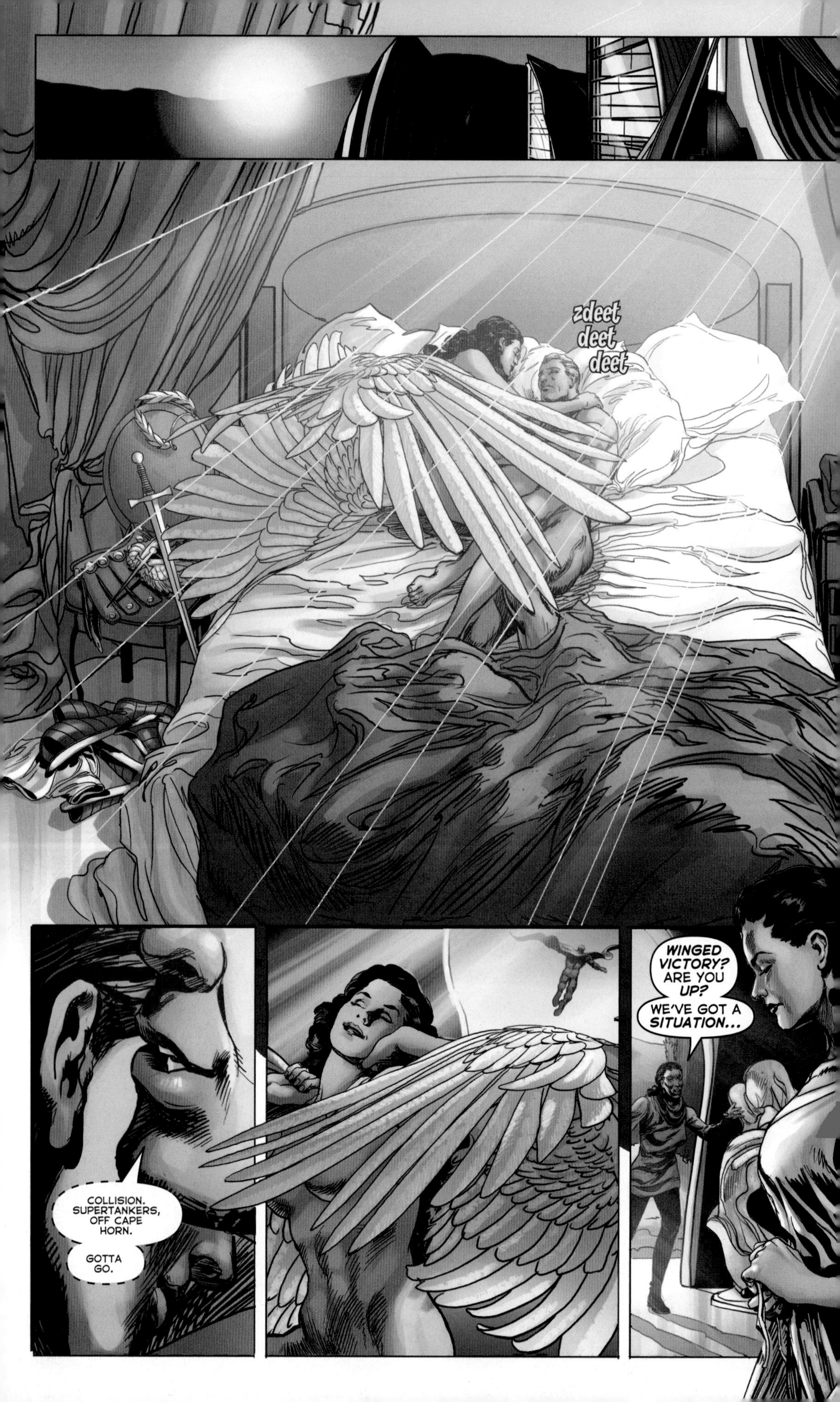
zdeet
deet
deet
COLLISION. SUPERTANKERS, OFF CAPE HORN.
GOTTA GO.
WINGED VICTORY? ARE YOU UP?
WE'VE GOT A SITUATION...

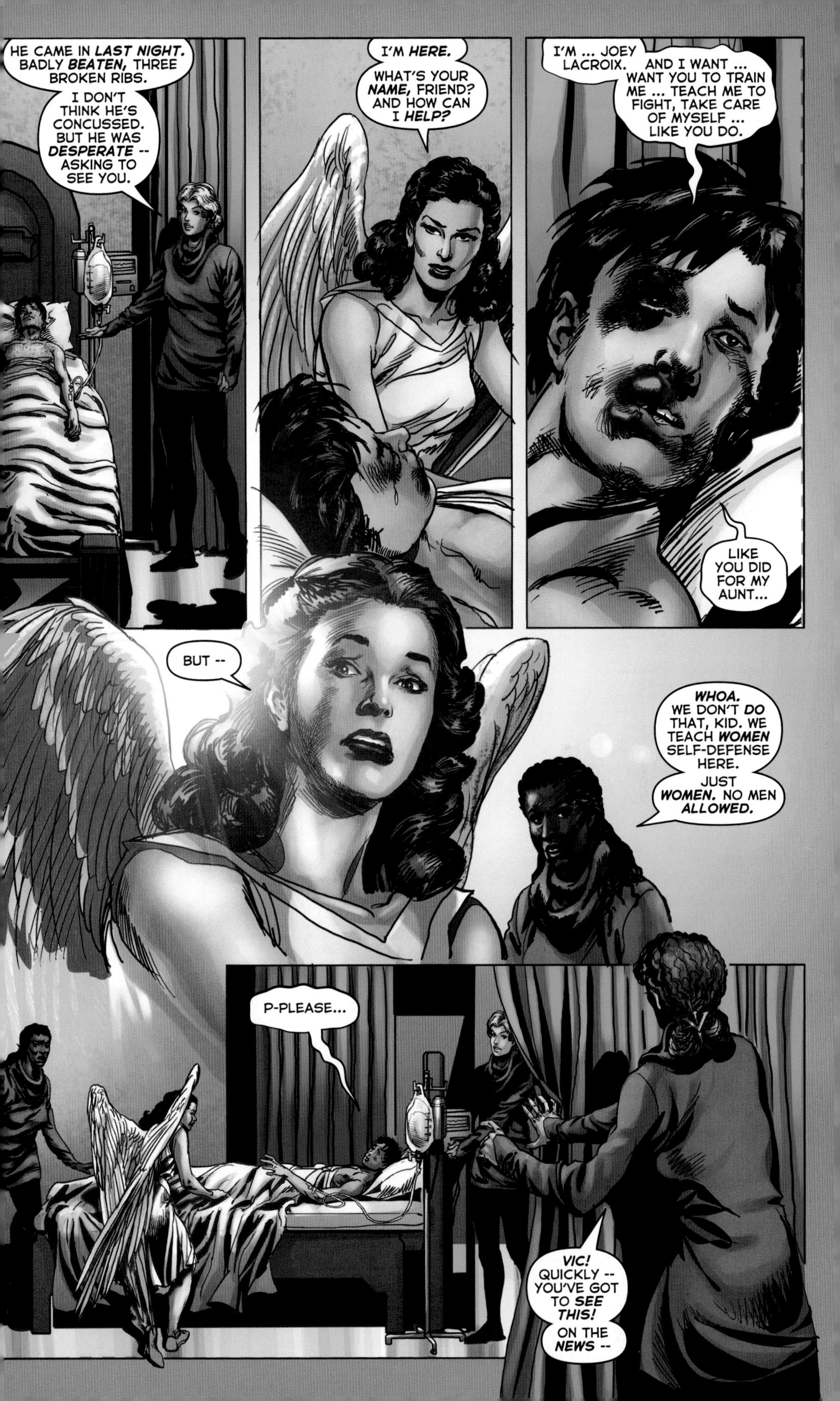
HE CAME IN LAST NIGHT. BADLY BEATEN, THREE BROKEN RIBS.
I DON'T THINK HE'S CONCUSSED. BUT HE WAS DESPERATE -- ASKING TO SEE YOU.
I'M HERE.
WHAT'S YOUR NAME, FRIEND? AND HOW CAN I HELP?
I'M ... JOEY LACROIX.
AND I WANT ... WANT YOU TO TRAIN ME ... TEACH ME TO FIGHT, TAKE CARE OF MYSELF ... LIKE YOU DO.
LIKE YOU DID FOR MY AUNT...
BUT --
WHOA. WE DON'T DO THAT, KID. WE TEACH WOMEN SELF-DEFENSE HERE.
JUST WOMEN. NO MEN ALLOWED.
P-PLEASE...
VIC! QUICKLY -- YOU'VE GOT TO SEE THIS!
ON THE NEWS --

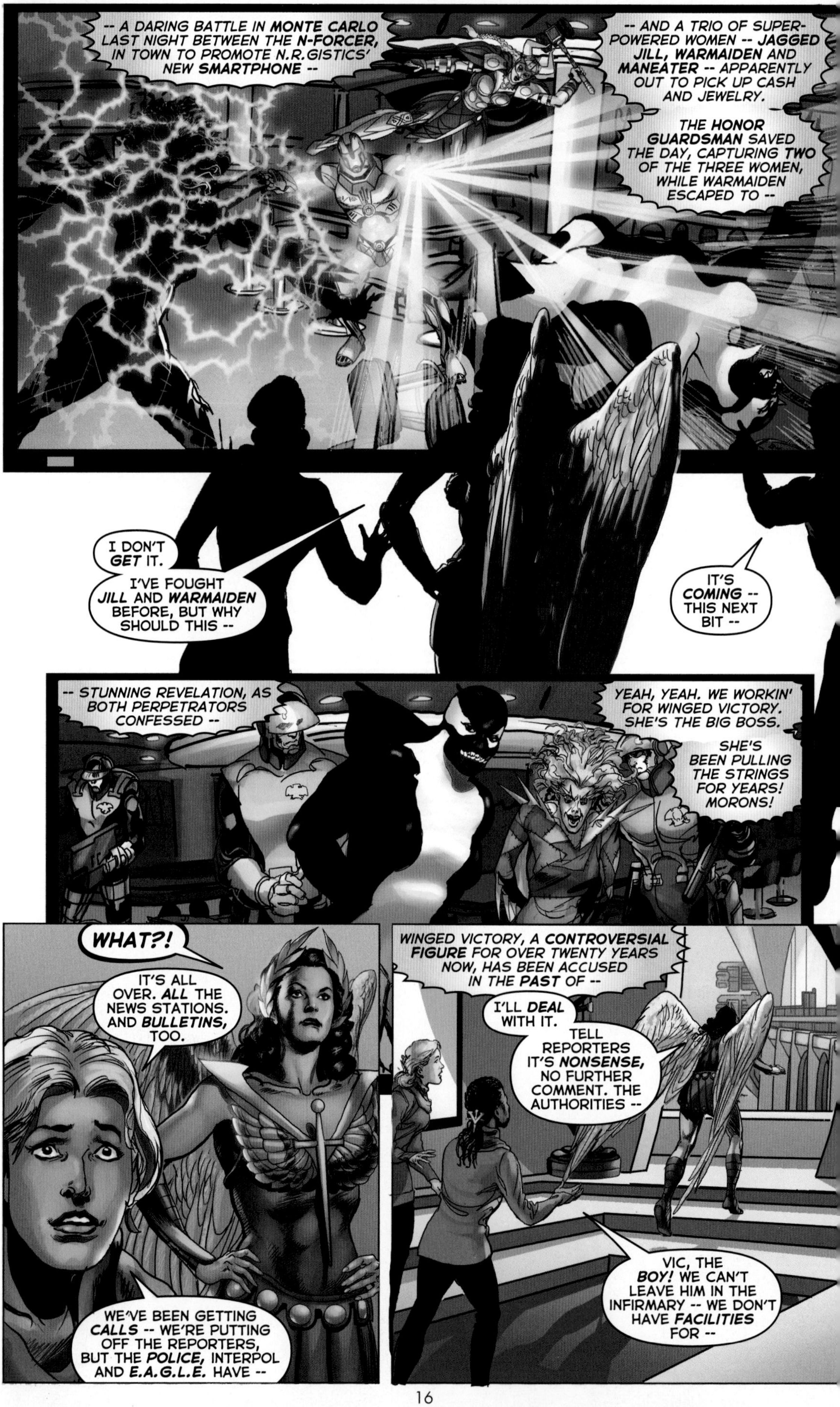

-- A DARING BATTLE IN MONTE CARLO LAST NIGHT BETWEEN THE N-FORCER, IN TOWN TO PROMOTE N.R.GISTICS' NEW SMARTPHONE --
-- AND A TRIO OF SUPER-POWERED WOMEN -- JAGGED JILL, WARMAIDEN AND MANEATER -- APPARENTLY OUT TO PICK UP CASH AND JEWELRY.
THE HONOR GUARDSMAN SAVED THE DAY, CAPTURING TWO OF THE THREE WOMEN, WHILE WARMAIDEN ESCAPED TO --
I DON'T GET IT.
I'VE FOUGHT JILL AND WARMAIDEN BEFORE, BUT WHY SHOULD THIS --
IT'S COMING -- THIS NEXT BIT --
-- STUNNING REVELATION, AS BOTH PERPETRATORS CONFESSED --
YEAH, YEAH. WE WORKIN' FOR WINGED VICTORY. SHE'S THE BIG BOSS.
SHE'S BEEN PULLING THE STRINGS FOR YEARS! MORONS!
WHAT?!
IT'S ALL OVER. ALL THE NEWS STATIONS. AND BULLETINS, TOO.
WE'VE BEEN GETTING CALLS -- WE'RE PUTTING OFF THE REPORTERS, BUT THE POLICE, INTERPOL AND E.A.G.L.E. HAVE --
WINGED VICTORY, A CONTROVERSIAL FIGURE FOR OVER TWENTY YEARS NOW, HAS BEEN ACCUSED IN THE PAST OF --
I'LL DEAL WITH IT.
TELL REPORTERS IT'S NONSENSE, NO FURTHER COMMENT. THE AUTHORITIES --
VIC, THE BOY! WE CAN'T LEAVE HIM IN THE INFIRMARY -- WE DON'T HAVE FACILITIES FOR --

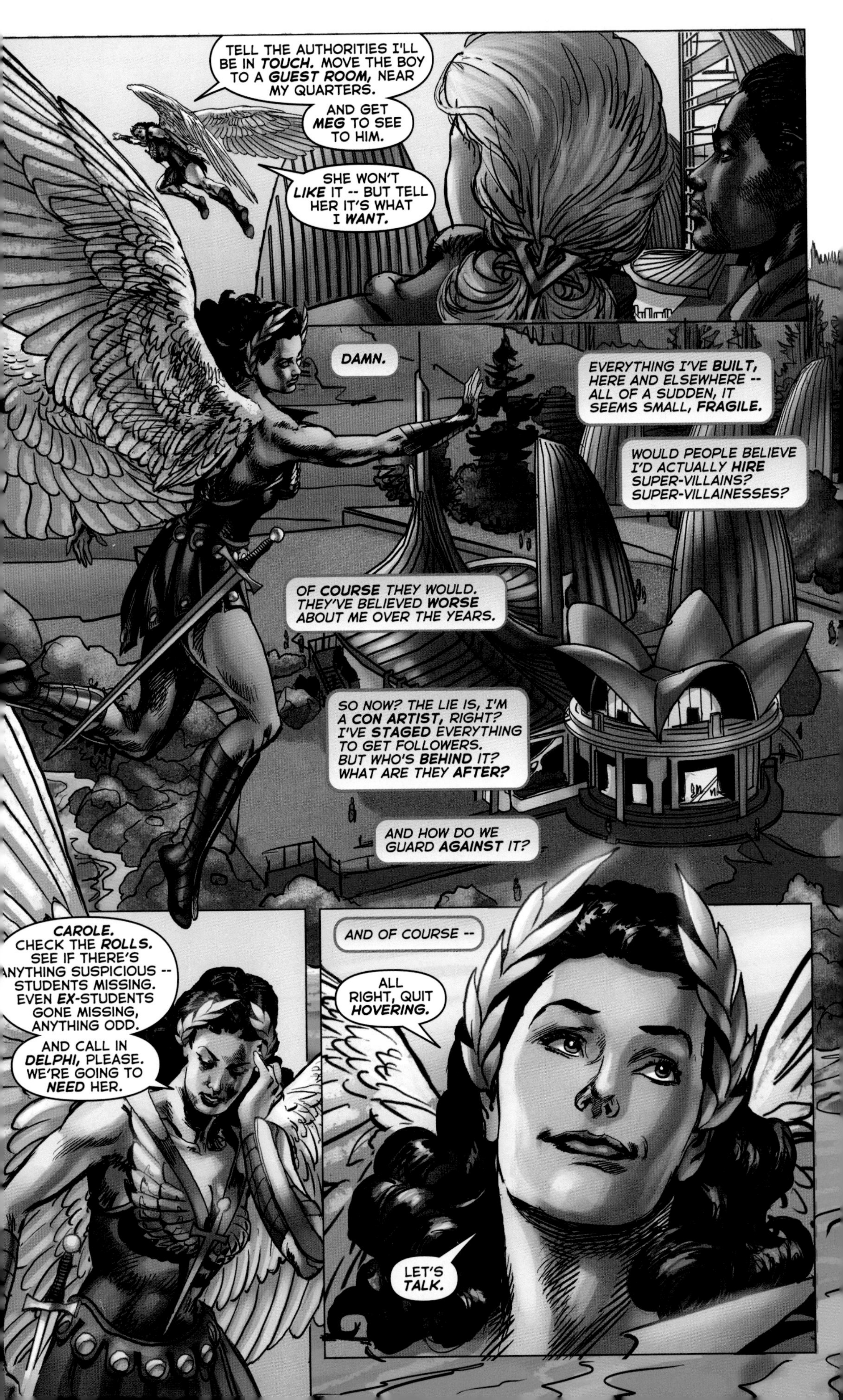

TELL THE AUTHORITIES I'LL BE IN TOUCH. MOVE THE BOY TO A GUEST ROOM, NEAR MY QUARTERS.
AND GET MEG TO SEE TO HIM.
SHE WON'T LIKE IT -- BUT TELL HER IT'S WHAT I WANT.
DAMN.
EVERYTHING I'VE BUILT, HERE AND ELSEWHERE -- ALL OF A SUDDEN, IT SEEMS SMALL, FRAGILE.
WOULD PEOPLE BELIEVE I'D ACTUALLY HIRE SUPER-VILLAINS? SUPER-VILLAINESSES?
OF COURSE THEY WOULD. THEY'VE BELIEVED WORSE ABOUT ME OVER THE YEARS.
SO NOW? THE LIE IS, I'M A CON ARTIST, RIGHT? I'VE STAGED EVERYTHING TO GET FOLLOWERS. BUT WHO'S BEHIND IT? WHAT ARE THEY AFTER?
AND HOW DO WE GUARD AGAINST IT?
CAROLE. CHECK THE ROLLS. SEE IF THERE'S ANYTHING SUSPICIOUS -- STUDENTS MISSING. EVEN EX-STUDENTS GONE MISSING, ANYTHING ODD.
AND CALL IN DELPHI, PLEASE. WE'RE GOING TO NEED HER.
AND OF COURSE --
ALL RIGHT, QUIT HOVERING.
LET'S TALK.

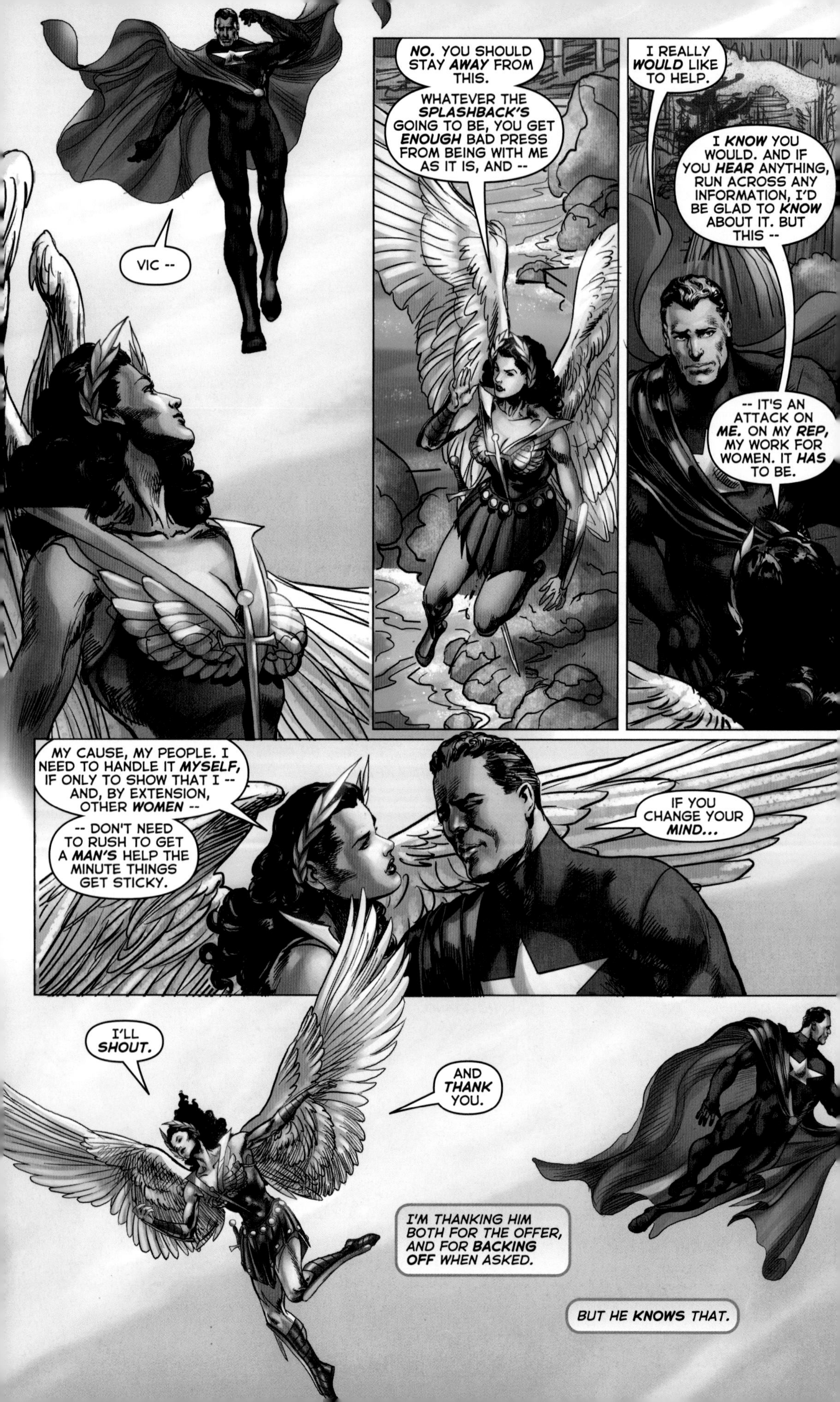

VIC --
NO. YOU SHOULD STAY AWAY FROM THIS.
WHATEVER THE SPLASHBACK'S GOING TO BE, YOU GET ENOUGH BAD PRESS FROM BEING WITH ME AS IT IS, AND --
I REALLY WOULD LIKE TO HELP.
I KNOW YOU WOULD. AND IF YOU HEAR ANYTHING, RUN ACROSS ANY INFORMATION, I'D BE GLAD TO KNOW ABOUT IT. BUT THIS --
-- IT'S AN ATTACK ON ME. ON MY REP, MY WORK FOR WOMEN. IT HAS TO BE.
MY CAUSE, MY PEOPLE. I NEED TO HANDLE IT MYSELF, IF ONLY TO SHOW THAT I -- AND, BY EXTENSION, OTHER WOMEN --
-- DON'T NEED TO RUSH TO GET A MAN'S HELP THE MINUTE THINGS GET STICKY.
IF YOU CHANGE YOUR MIND...
I'LL SHOUT.
AND THANK YOU.
I'M THANKING HIM BOTH FOR THE OFFER, AND FOR BACKING OFF WHEN ASKED.
BUT HE KNOWS THAT.

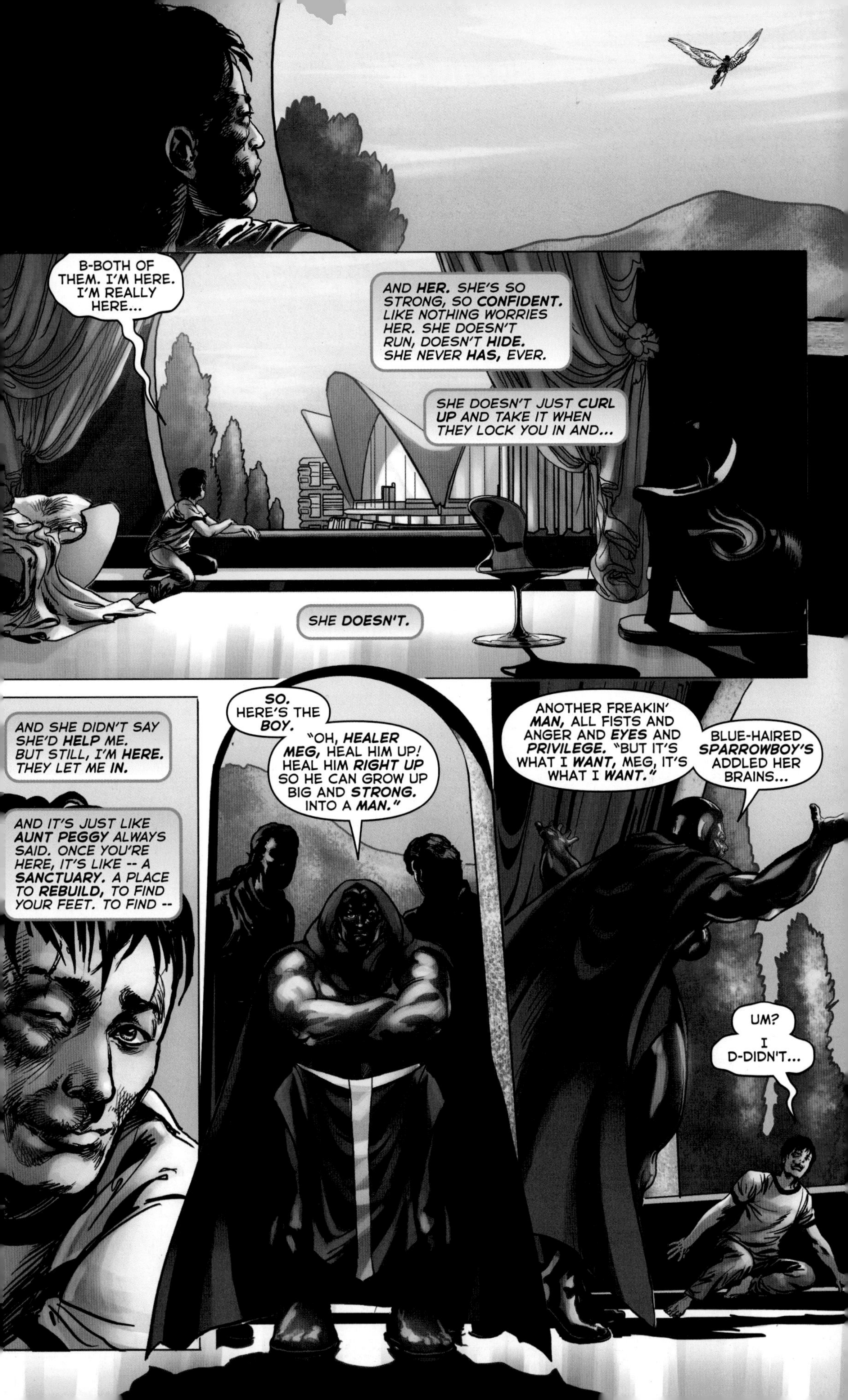

B-BOTH OF THEM. I'M HERE. I'M REALLY HERE...
AND HER. SHE'S SO STRONG, SO CONFIDENT. LIKE NOTHING WORRIES HER. SHE DOESN'T RUN, DOESN'T HIDE. SHE NEVER HAS, EVER.
SHE DOESN'T JUST CURL UP AND TAKE IT WHEN THEY LOCK YOU IN AND...
SHE DOESN'T.
AND SHE DIDN'T SAY SHE'D HELP ME. BUT STILL, I'M HERE. THEY LET ME IN.
AND IT'S JUST LIKE AUNT PEGGY ALWAYS SAID. ONCE YOU'RE HERE, IT'S LIKE -- A SANCTUARY. A PLACE TO REBUILD, TO FIND YOUR FEET. TO FIND --
SO. HERE'S THE BOY.
"OH, HEALER MEG, HEAL HIM UP! HEAL HIM RIGHT UP SO HE CAN GROW UP BIG AND STRONG. INTO A MAN."
ANOTHER FREAKIN' MAN, ALL FISTS AND ANGER AND EYES AND PRIVILEGE. "BUT IT'S WHAT I WANT, MEG, IT'S WHAT I WANT."
BLUE-HAIRED SPARROWBOY'S ADDLED HER BRAINS...
UM? I D-DIDN'T...

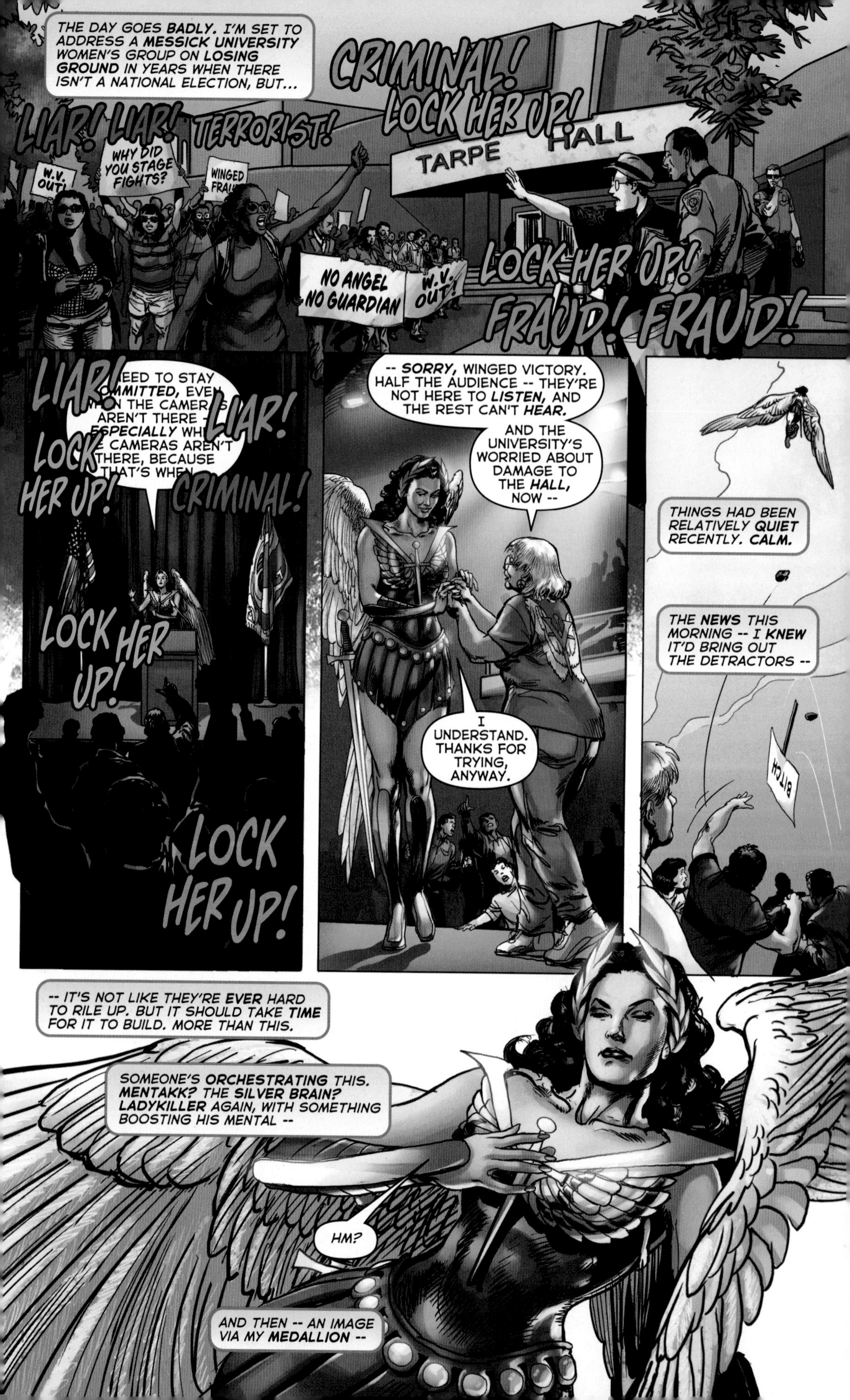

THE DAY GOES BADLY. I'M SET TO ADDRESS A MESSICK UNIVERSITY WOMEN'S GROUP ON LOSING GROUND IN YEARS WHEN THERE ISN'T A NATIONAL ELECTION, BUT...
LIAR! LIAR!
TERRORIST!
CRIMINAL! LOCK HER UP!
W.V. OUT!
WHY DID YOU STAGE FIGHTS?
WINGED FRAU
TARPE HALL
NO ANGEL NO GUARDIAN
W.V. OUT!
LOCK HER UP!
FRAUD! FRAUD!
LIAR!
EED TO STAY OMMITTED, EVE HEN THE CAMERA AREN'T THERE -- ESPECIALLY WH E CAMERAS AREN'T THERE, BECAUSE THAT'S WHEN...
LIAR!
LOCK HER UP!
CRIMINAL!
LOCK HER UP!
LOCK HER UP!
-- SORRY, WINGED VICTORY. HALF THE AUDIENCE -- THEY'RE NOT HERE TO LISTEN, AND THE REST CAN'T HEAR.
AND THE UNIVERSITY'S WORRIED ABOUT DAMAGE TO THE HALL, NOW --
I UNDERSTAND. THANKS FOR TRYING, ANYWAY.
THINGS HAD BEEN RELATIVELY QUIET RECENTLY. CALM.
THE NEWS THIS MORNING -- I KNEW IT'D BRING OUT THE DETRACTORS --
BITCH
-- IT'S NOT LIKE THEY'RE EVER HARD TO RILE UP. BUT IT SHOULD TAKE TIME FOR IT TO BUILD. MORE THAN THIS.
SOMEONE'S ORCHESTRATING THIS. MENTAKK? THE SILVER BRAIN? LADYKILLER AGAIN, WITH SOMETHING BOOSTING HIS MENTAL --
HM?
AND THEN -- AN IMAGE VIA MY MEDALLION --

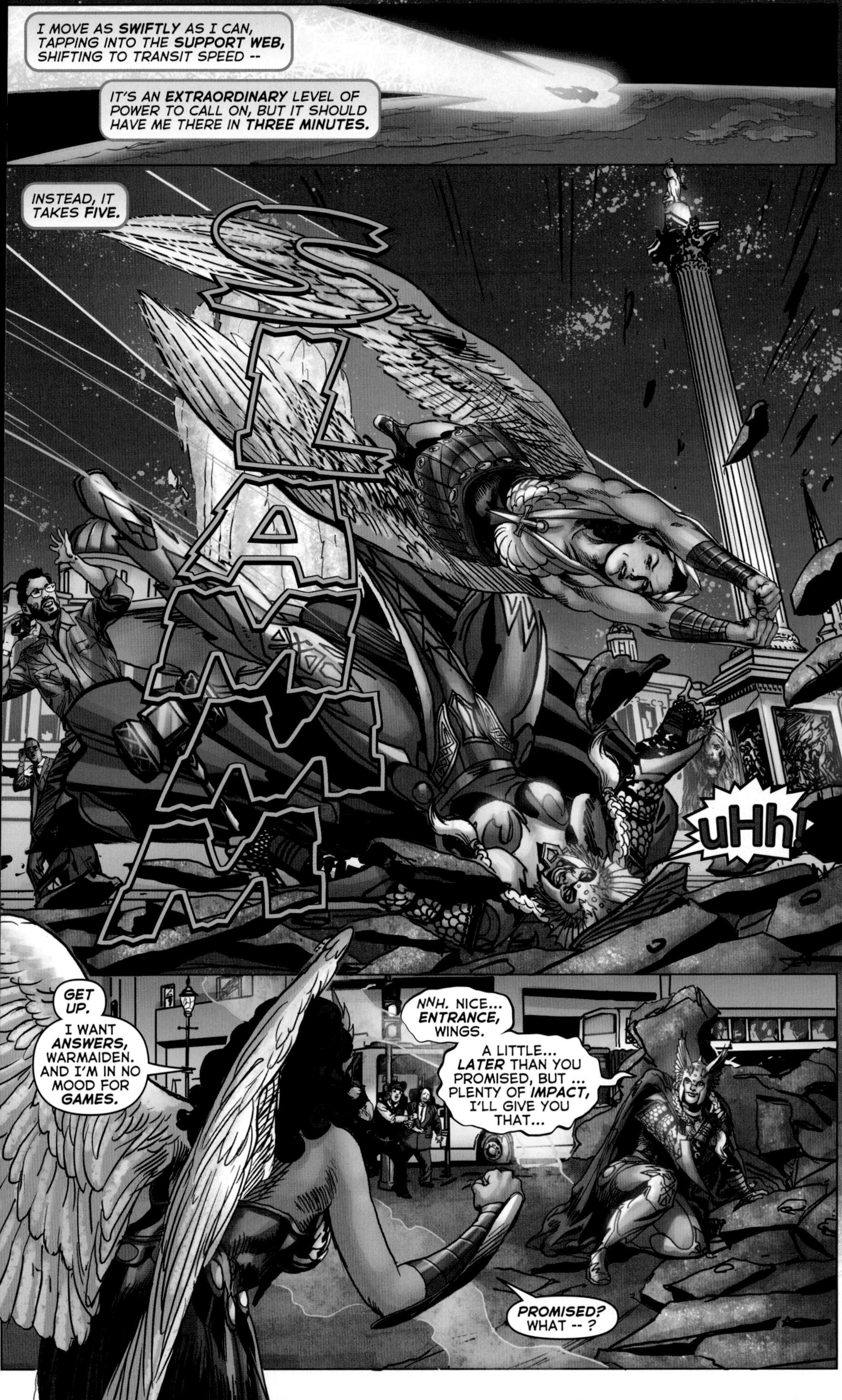
I MOVE AS SWIFTLY AS I CAN, TAPPING INTO THE SUPPORT WEB, SHIFTING TO TRANSIT SPEED --
IT'S AN EXTRAORDINARY LEVEL OF POWER TO CALL ON, BUT IT SHOULD HAVE ME THERE IN THREE MINUTES.
INSTEAD, IT TAKES FIVE.
SLAMMM
uHh!
GET UP.
I WANT ANSWERS, WARMAIDEN. AND I'M IN NO MOOD FOR GAMES.
NNH. NICE... ENTRANCE, WINGS.
A LITTLE... LATER THAN YOU PROMISED, BUT ... PLENTY OF IMPACT, I'LL GIVE YOU THAT...
PROMISED? WHAT -- ?

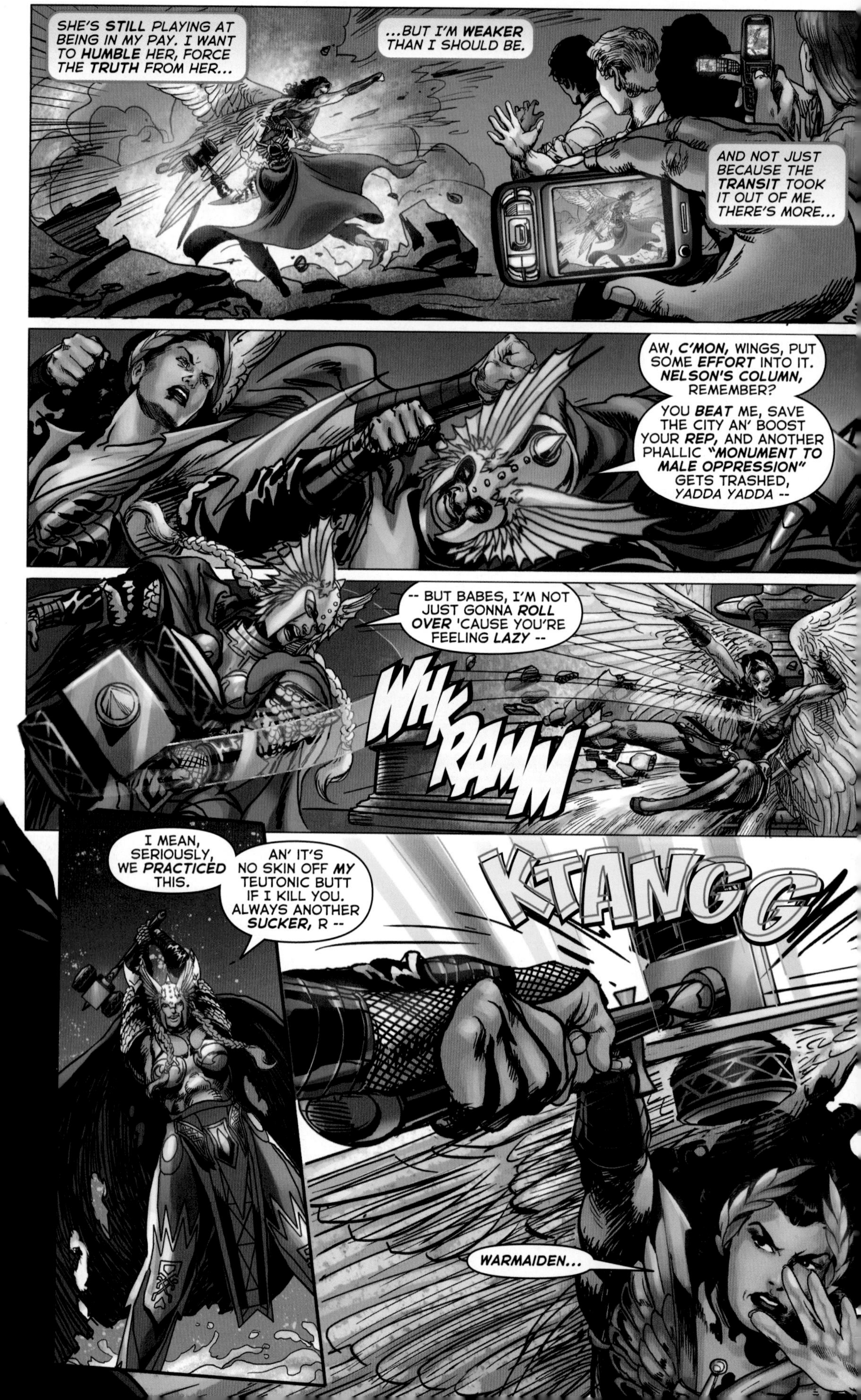

SHE'S STILL PLAYING AT BEING IN MY PAY. I WANT TO HUMBLE HER, FORCE THE TRUTH FROM HER...
...BUT I'M WEAKER THAN I SHOULD BE.
AND NOT JUST BECAUSE THE TRANSIT TOOK IT OUT OF ME. THERE'S MORE...
AW, C'MON, WINGS, PUT SOME EFFORT INTO IT. NELSON'S COLUMN, REMEMBER?
YOU BEAT ME, SAVE THE CITY AN' BOOST YOUR REP, AND ANOTHER PHALLIC "MONUMENT TO MALE OPPRESSION" GETS TRASHED, YADDA YADDA --
-- BUT BABES, I'M NOT JUST GONNA ROLL OVER 'CAUSE YOU'RE FEELING LAZY --
WHKRAMM
I MEAN, SERIOUSLY, WE PRACTICED THIS.
AN' IT'S NO SKIN OFF MY TEUTONIC BUTT IF I KILL YOU. ALWAYS ANOTHER SUCKER, R --
KTANGG
WARMAIDEN...

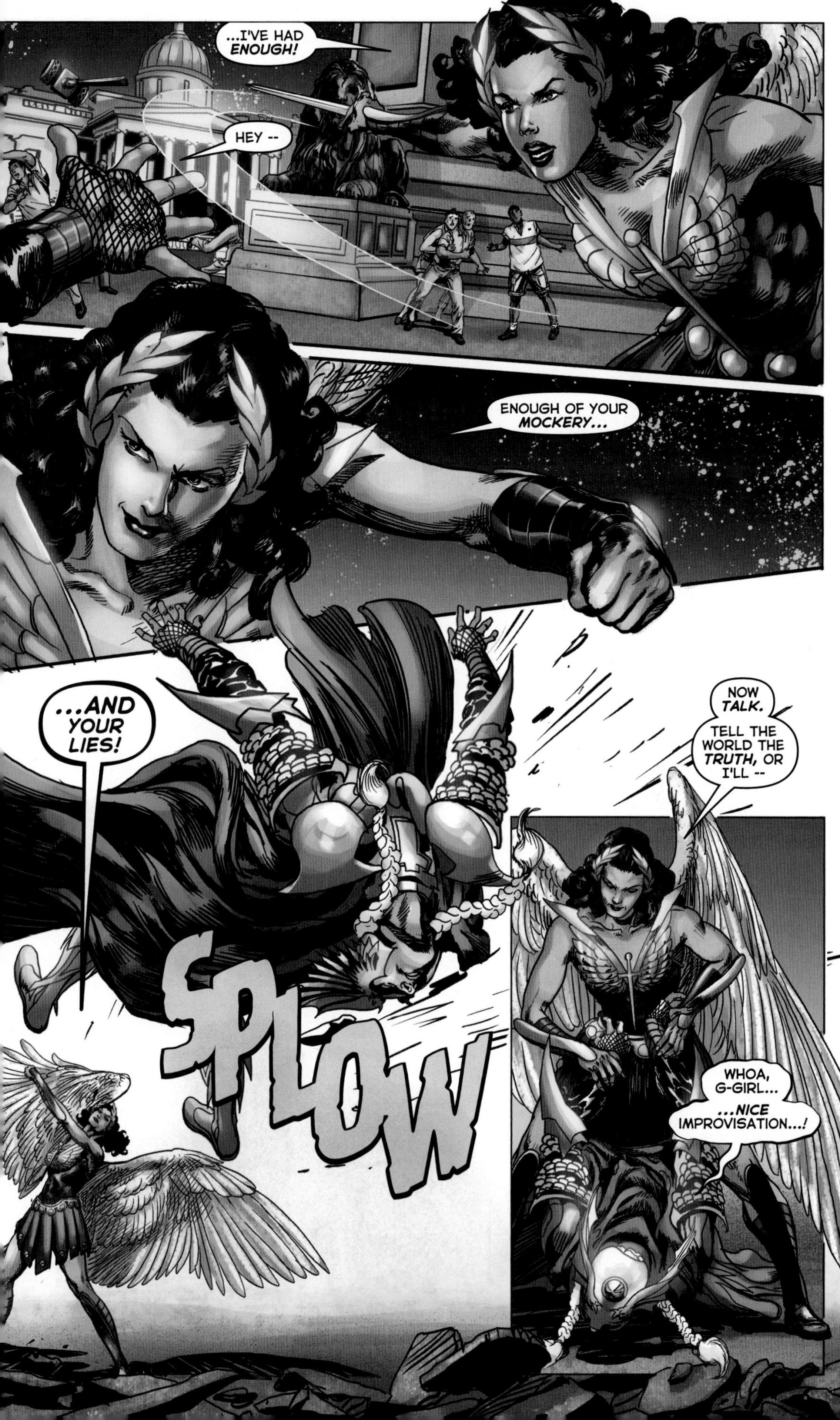

...I'VE HAD ENOUGH!
HEY --
ENOUGH OF YOUR MOCKERY...
...AND YOUR LIES!
SPLOW
NOW TALK.
TELL THE WORLD THE TRUTH, OR I'LL --
WHOA, G-GIRL...
...NICE IMPROVISATION...!

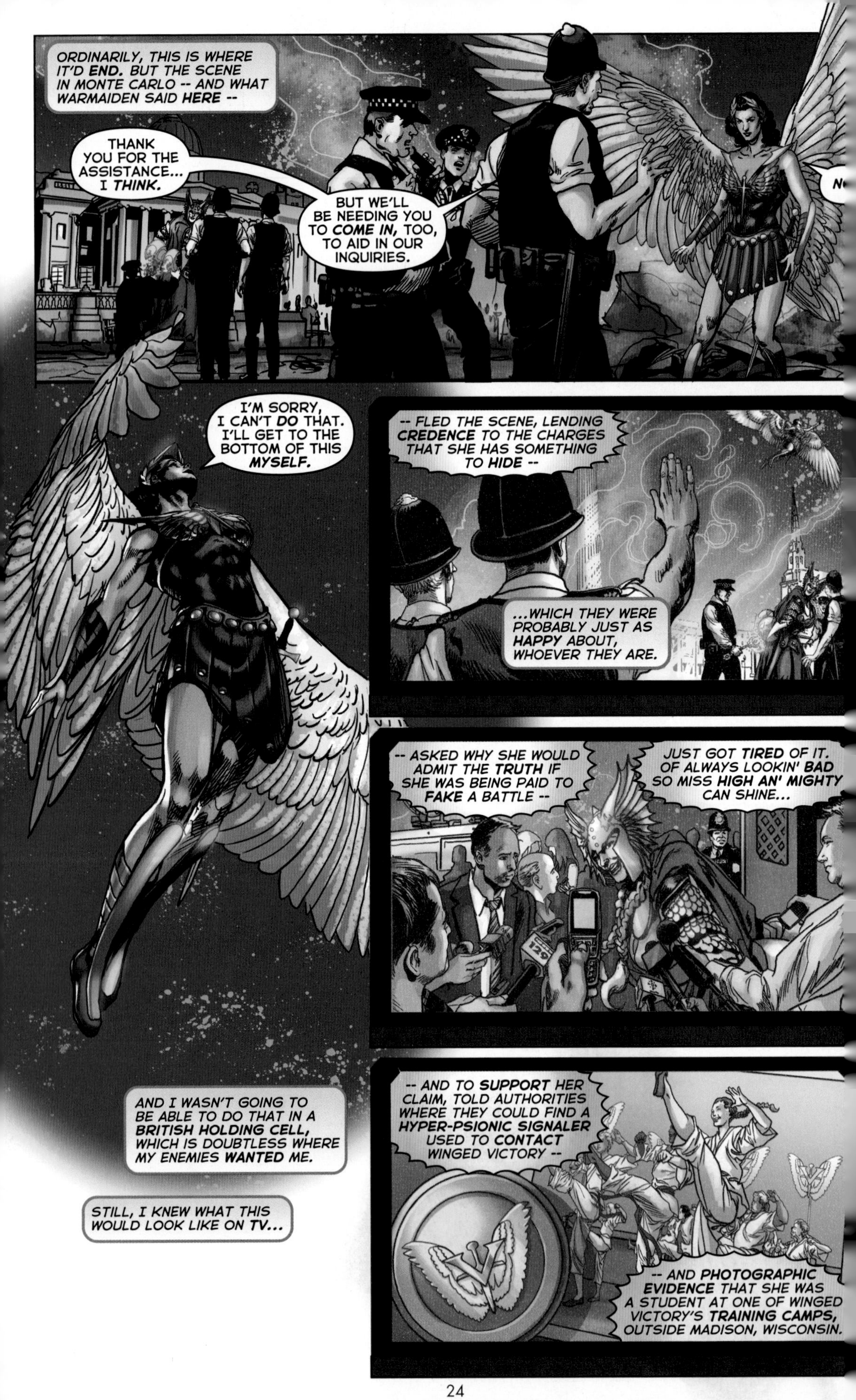
ORDINARILY, THIS IS WHERE IT'D END. BUT THE SCENE IN MONTE CARLO -- AND WHAT WARMAIDEN SAID HERE --
THANK YOU FOR THE ASSISTANCE... I THINK.
BUT WE'LL BE NEEDING YOU TO COME IN, TOO, TO AID IN OUR INQUIRIES.
I'M SORRY, I CAN'T DO THAT. I'LL GET TO THE BOTTOM OF THIS MYSELF.
-- FLED THE SCENE, LENDING CREDENCE TO THE CHARGES THAT SHE HAS SOMETHING TO HIDE --
...WHICH THEY WERE PROBABLY JUST AS HAPPY ABOUT, WHOEVER THEY ARE.
-- ASKED WHY SHE WOULD ADMIT THE TRUTH IF SHE WAS BEING PAID TO FAKE A BATTLE --
JUST GOT TIRED OF IT. OF ALWAYS LOOKIN' BAD SO MISS HIGH AN' MIGHTY CAN SHINE...
AND I WASN'T GOING TO BE ABLE TO DO THAT IN A BRITISH HOLDING CELL, WHICH IS DOUBTLESS WHERE MY ENEMIES WANTED ME.
STILL, I KNEW WHAT THIS WOULD LOOK LIKE ON TV...
-- AND TO SUPPORT HER CLAIM, TOLD AUTHORITIES WHERE THEY COULD FIND A HYPER-PSIONIC SIGNALER USED TO CONTACT WINGED VICTORY --
-- AND PHOTOGRAPHIC EVIDENCE THAT SHE WAS A STUDENT AT ONE OF WINGED VICTORY'S TRAINING CAMPS, OUTSIDE MADISON, WISCONSIN.

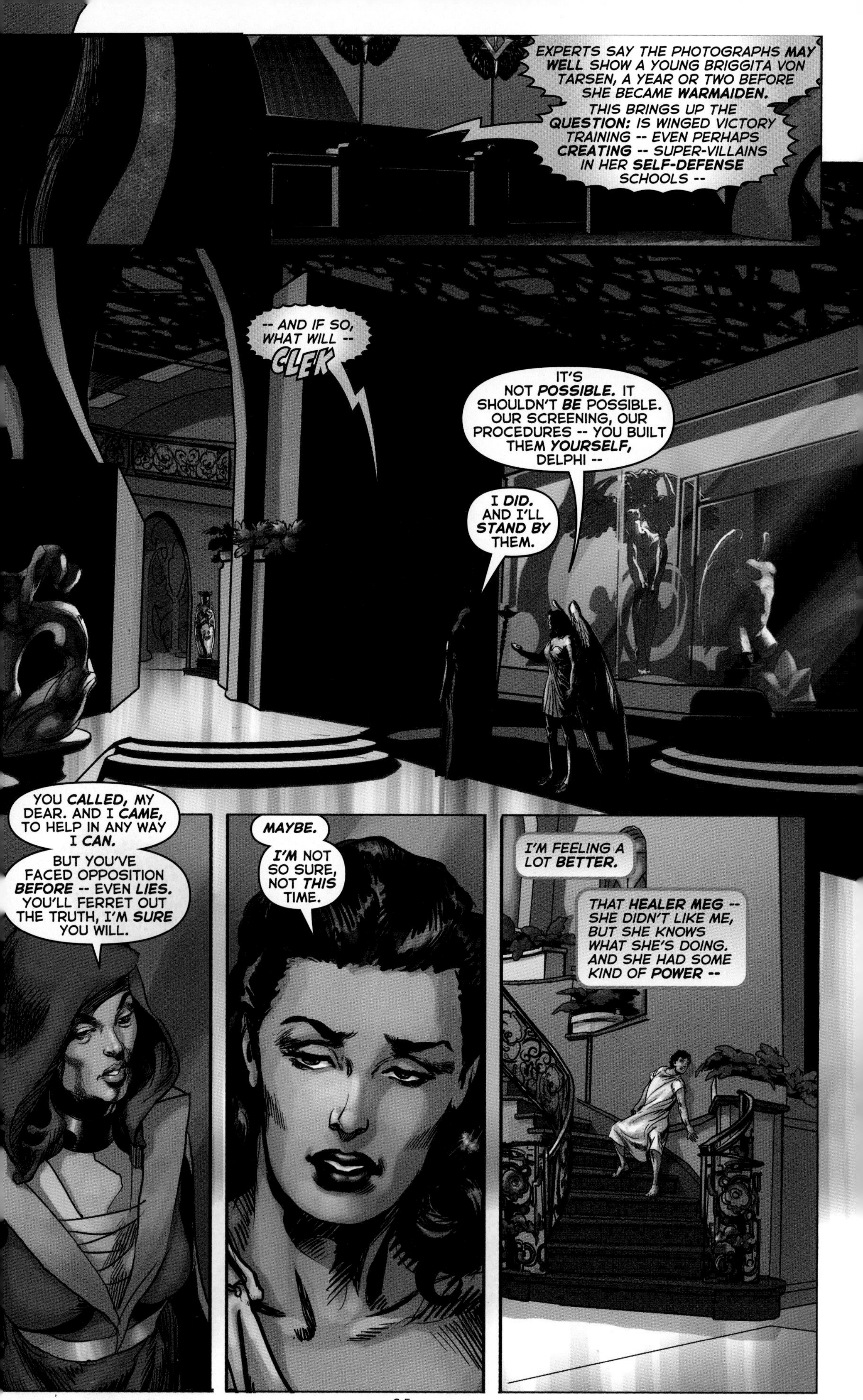
EXPERTS SAY THE PHOTOGRAPHS MAY WELL SHOW A YOUNG BRIGGITA VON TARSEN, A YEAR OR TWO BEFORE SHE BECAME WARMAIDEN.
THIS BRINGS UP THE QUESTION: IS WINGED VICTORY TRAINING -- EVEN PERHAPS CREATING -- SUPER-VILLAINS IN HER SELF-DEFENSE SCHOOLS --
-- AND IF SO, WHAT WILL --
CLEK
IT'S NOT POSSIBLE. IT SHOULDN'T BE POSSIBLE. OUR SCREENING, OUR PROCEDURES -- YOU BUILT THEM YOURSELF, DELPHI --
I DID. AND I'LL STAND BY THEM.
YOU CALLED, MY DEAR. AND I CAME, TO HELP IN ANY WAY I CAN.
BUT YOU'VE FACED OPPOSITION BEFORE -- EVEN LIES. YOU'LL FERRET OUT THE TRUTH, I'M SURE YOU WILL.
MAYBE.
I'M NOT SO SURE, NOT THIS TIME.
I'M FEELING A LOT BETTER.
THAT HEALER MEG -- SHE DIDN'T LIKE ME, BUT SHE KNOWS WHAT SHE'S DOING. AND SHE HAD SOME KIND OF POWER --

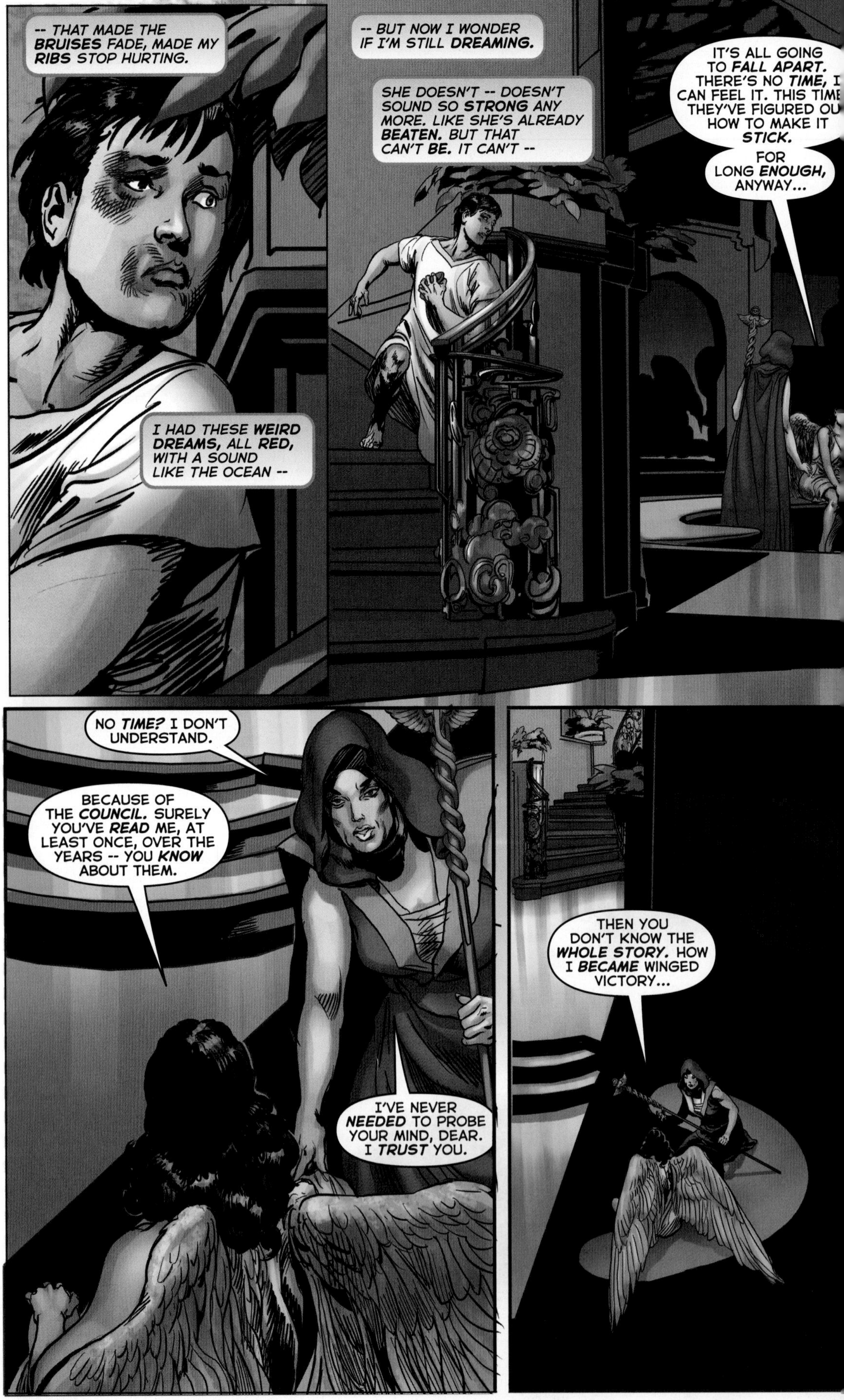
-- THAT MADE THE BRUISES FADE, MADE MY RIBS STOP HURTING.
I HAD THESE WEIRD DREAMS, ALL RED, WITH A SOUND LIKE THE OCEAN --
-- BUT NOW I WONDER IF I'M STILL DREAMING.
SHE DOESN'T -- DOESN'T SOUND SO STRONG ANY MORE. LIKE SHE'S ALREADY BEATEN. BUT THAT CAN'T BE. IT CAN'T --
IT'S ALL GOING TO FALL APART. THERE'S NO TIME, I CAN FEEL IT. THIS TIME THEY'VE FIGURED OU HOW TO MAKE IT STICK.
FOR LONG ENOUGH, ANYWAY...
NO TIME? I DON'T UNDERSTAND.
BECAUSE OF THE COUNCIL. SURELY YOU'VE READ ME, AT LEAST ONCE, OVER THE YEARS -- YOU KNOW ABOUT THEM.
I'VE NEVER NEEDED TO PROBE YOUR MIND, DEAR. I TRUST YOU.
THEN YOU DON'T KNOW THE WHOLE STORY. HOW I BECAME WINGED VICTORY...

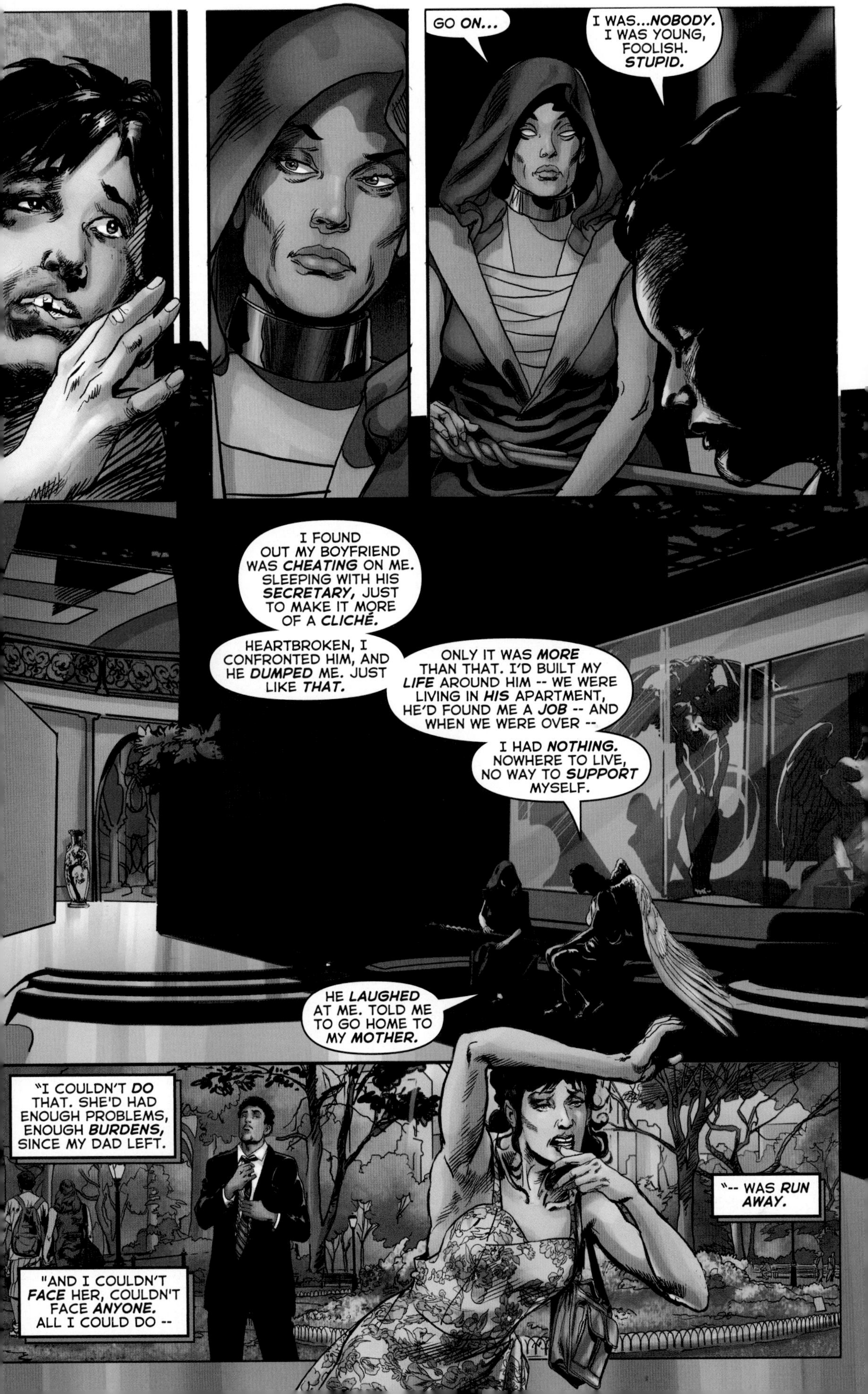
GO ON...
I WAS...NOBODY. I WAS YOUNG, FOOLISH. STUPID.
I FOUND OUT MY BOYFRIEND WAS CHEATING ON ME. SLEEPING WITH HIS SECRETARY, JUST TO MAKE IT MORE OF A CLICHÉ.
HEARTBROKEN, I CONFRONTED HIM, AND HE DUMPED ME. JUST LIKE THAT.
ONLY IT WAS MORE THAN THAT. I'D BUILT MY LIFE AROUND HIM -- WE WERE LIVING IN HIS APARTMENT, HE'D FOUND ME A JOB -- AND WHEN WE WERE OVER --
I HAD NOTHING. NOWHERE TO LIVE, NO WAY TO SUPPORT MYSELF.
HE LAUGHED AT ME. TOLD ME TO GO HOME TO MY MOTHER.
"I COULDN'T DO THAT. SHE'D HAD ENOUGH PROBLEMS, ENOUGH BURDENS, SINCE MY DAD LEFT.
"AND I COULDN'T FACE HER, COULDN'T FACE ANYONE. ALL I COULD DO --
"-- WAS RUN AWAY.

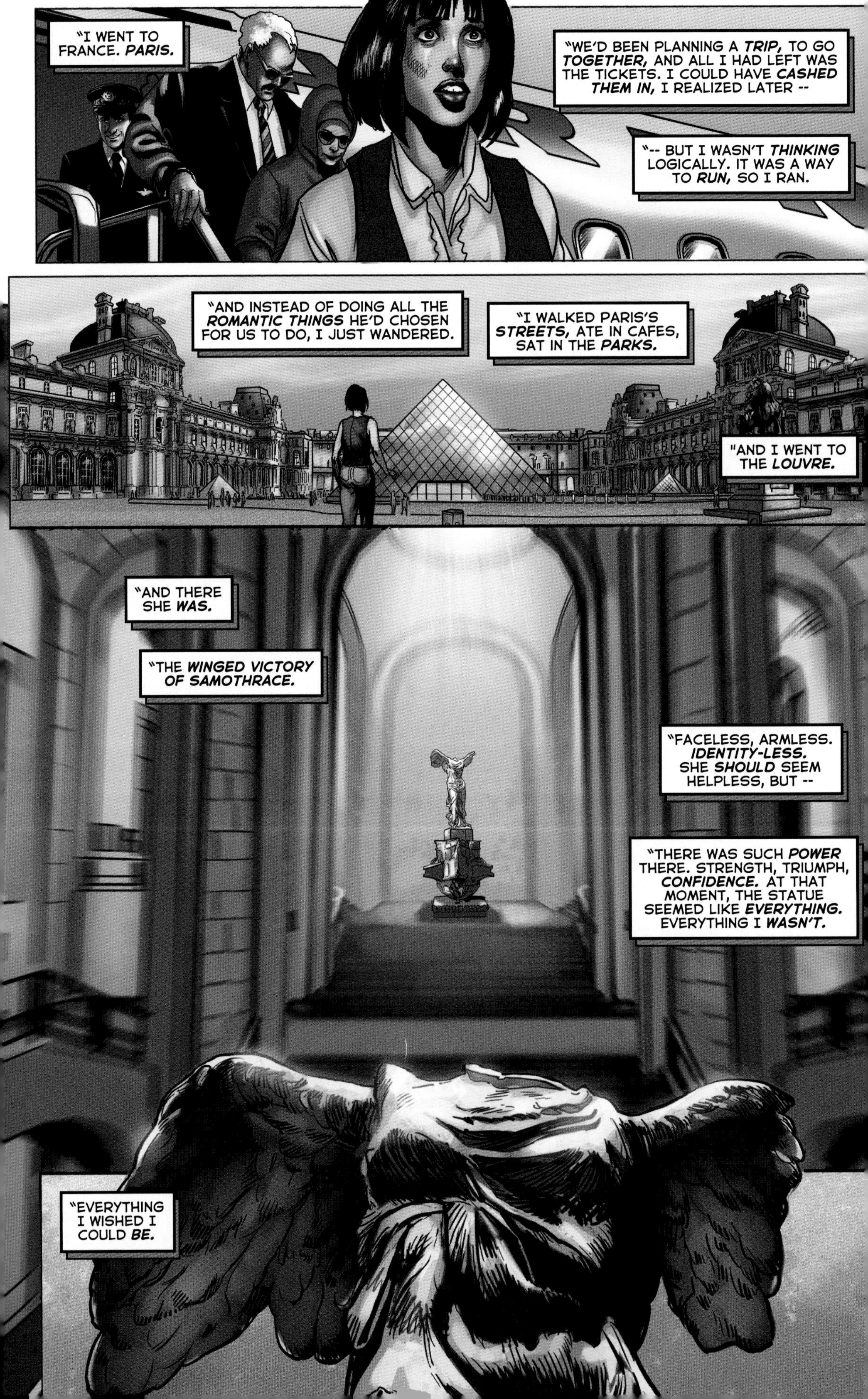
"I WENT TO FRANCE. PARIS.
"WE'D BEEN PLANNING A TRIP, TO GO TOGETHER, AND ALL I HAD LEFT WAS THE TICKETS. I COULD HAVE CASHED THEM IN, I REALIZED LATER --
"-- BUT I WASN'T THINKING LOGICALLY. IT WAS A WAY TO RUN, SO I RAN.
"AND INSTEAD OF DOING ALL THE ROMANTIC THINGS HE'D CHOSEN FOR US TO DO, I JUST WANDERED.
"I WALKED PARIS'S STREETS, ATE IN CAFES, SAT IN THE PARKS.
"AND I WENT TO THE LOUVRE.
"AND THERE SHE WAS.
"THE WINGED VICTORY OF SAMOTHRACE.
"FACELESS, ARMLESS. IDENTITY-LESS. SHE SHOULD SEEM HELPLESS, BUT --
"THERE WAS SUCH POWER THERE. STRENGTH, TRIUMPH, CONFIDENCE. AT THAT MOMENT, THE STATUE SEEMED LIKE EVERYTHING. EVERYTHING I WASN'T.
"EVERYTHING I WISHED I COULD BE.

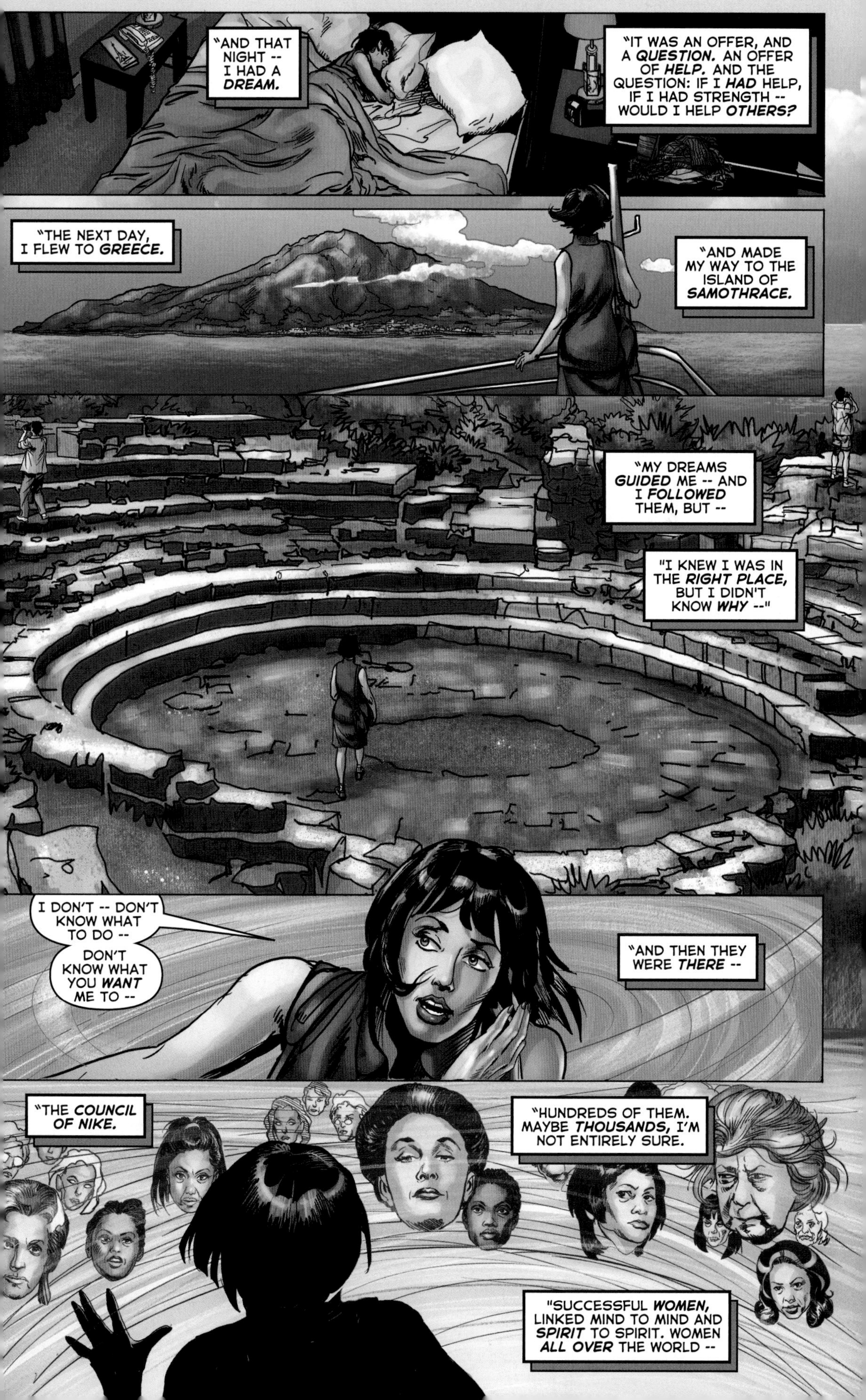
"AND THAT NIGHT -- I HAD A DREAM.
"IT WAS AN OFFER, AND A QUESTION. AN OFFER OF HELP. AND THE QUESTION: IF I HAD HELP, IF I HAD STRENGTH -- WOULD I HELP OTHERS?
"THE NEXT DAY, I FLEW TO GREECE.
"AND MADE MY WAY TO THE ISLAND OF SAMOTHRACE.
"MY DREAMS GUIDED ME -- AND I FOLLOWED THEM, BUT --
"I KNEW I WAS IN THE RIGHT PLACE, BUT I DIDN'T KNOW WHY --"
I DON'T -- DON'T KNOW WHAT TO DO --
DON'T KNOW WHAT YOU WANT ME TO --
"AND THEN THEY WERE THERE --
"THE COUNCIL OF NIKE.
"HUNDREDS OF THEM. MAYBE THOUSANDS, I'M NOT ENTIRELY SURE.
"SUCCESSFUL WOMEN, LINKED MIND TO MIND AND SPIRIT TO SPIRIT. WOMEN ALL OVER THE WORLD --

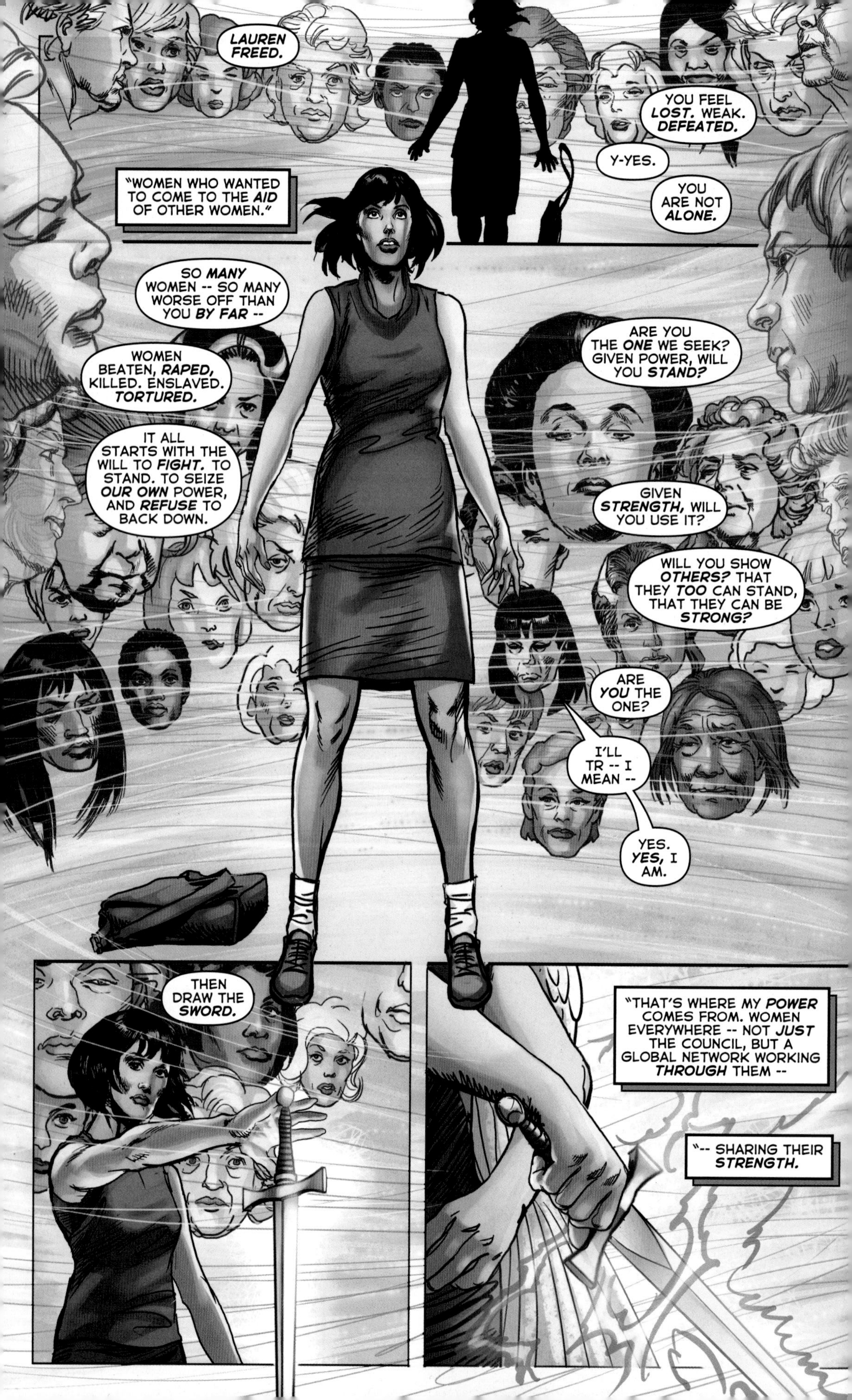

LAUREN FREED.
YOU FEEL LOST. WEAK. DEFEATED.
Y-YES.
YOU ARE NOT ALONE.
"WOMEN WHO WANTED TO COME TO THE AID OF OTHER WOMEN."
SO MANY WOMEN -- SO MANY WORSE OFF THAN YOU BY FAR --
WOMEN BEATEN, RAPED, KILLED. ENSLAVED. TORTURED.
IT ALL STARTS WITH THE WILL TO FIGHT. TO STAND. TO SEIZE OUR OWN POWER, AND REFUSE TO BACK DOWN.
ARE YOU THE ONE WE SEEK? GIVEN POWER, WILL YOU STAND?
GIVEN STRENGTH, WILL YOU USE IT?
WILL YOU SHOW OTHERS? THAT THEY TOO CAN STAND, THAT THEY CAN BE STRONG?
ARE YOU THE ONE?
I'LL TR -- I MEAN --
YES. YES, I AM.
THEN DRAW THE SWORD.
"THAT'S WHERE MY POWER COMES FROM. WOMEN EVERYWHERE -- NOT JUST THE COUNCIL, BUT A GLOBAL NETWORK WORKING THROUGH THEM --
"-- SHARING THEIR STRENGTH.

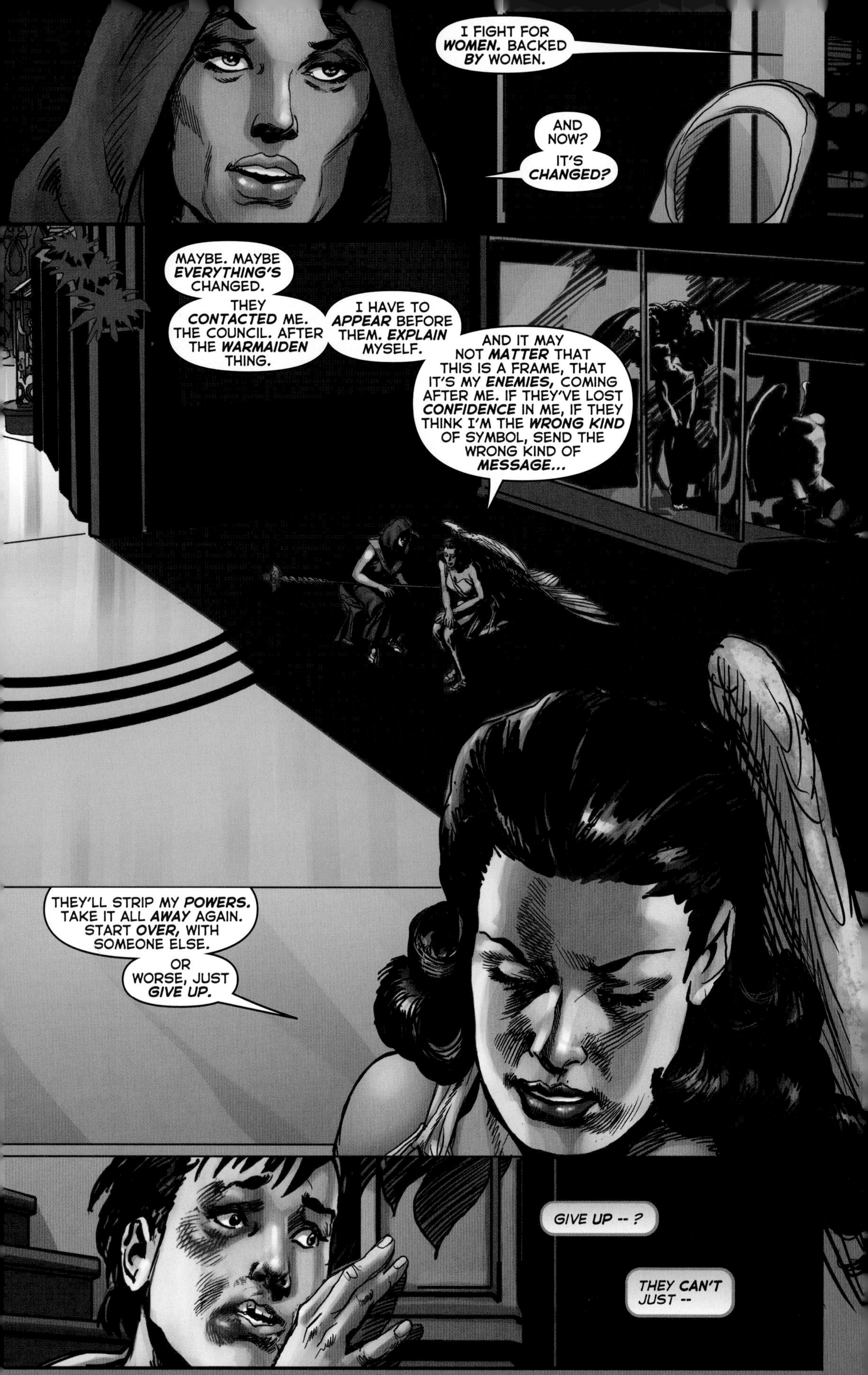
I FIGHT FOR WOMEN. BACKED BY WOMEN.
AND NOW?
IT'S CHANGED?
MAYBE. MAYBE EVERYTHING'S CHANGED.
THEY CONTACTED ME. THE COUNCIL. AFTER THE WARMAIDEN THING.
I HAVE TO APPEAR BEFORE THEM. EXPLAIN MYSELF.
AND IT MAY NOT MATTER THAT THIS IS A FRAME, THAT IT'S MY ENEMIES, COMING AFTER ME. IF THEY'VE LOST CONFIDENCE IN ME, IF THEY THINK I'M THE WRONG KIND OF SYMBOL, SEND THE WRONG KIND OF MESSAGE...
THEY'LL STRIP MY POWERS. TAKE IT ALL AWAY AGAIN. START OVER, WITH SOMEONE ELSE.
OR WORSE, JUST GIVE UP.
GIVE UP -- ?
THEY CAN'T JUST --

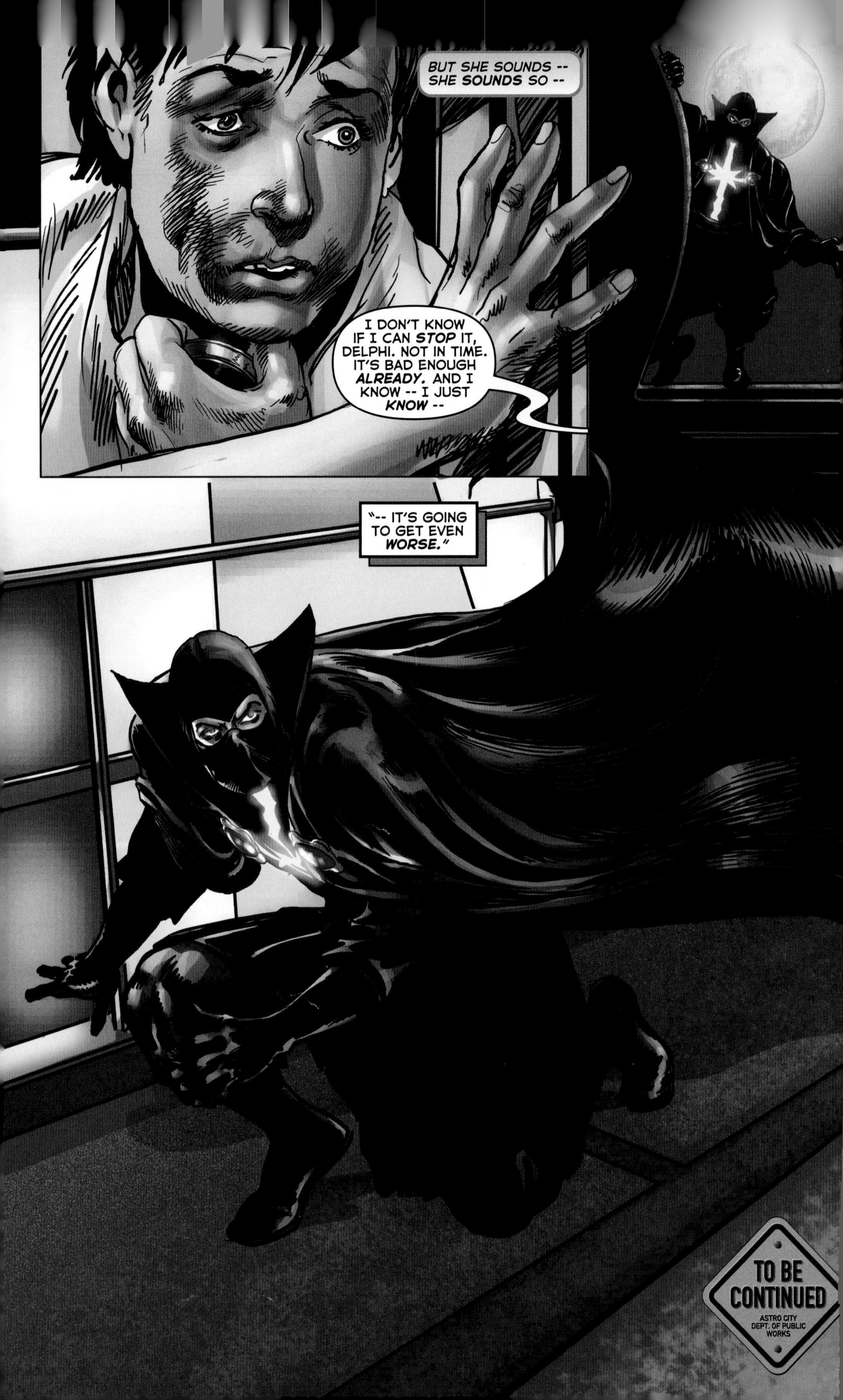
BUT SHE SOUNDS -- SHE SOUNDS SO --
I DON'T KNOW IF I CAN STOP IT, DELPHI. NOT IN TIME. IT'S BAD ENOUGH ALREADY. AND I KNOW -- I JUST KNOW --
"-- IT'S GOING TO GET EVEN WORSE."
TO BE CONTINUED
ASTRO CITY DEPT. OF PUBLIC WORKS

TWO

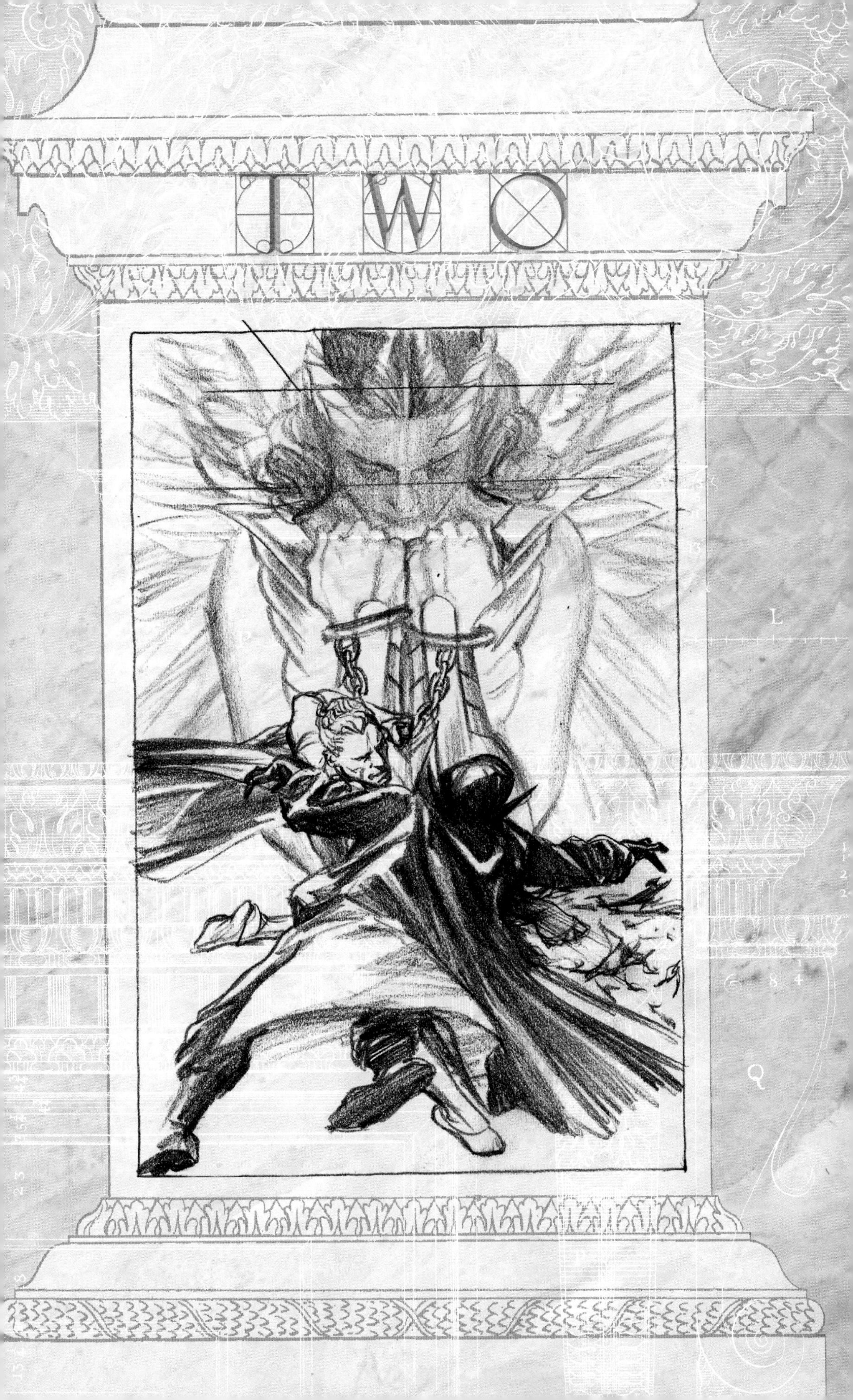

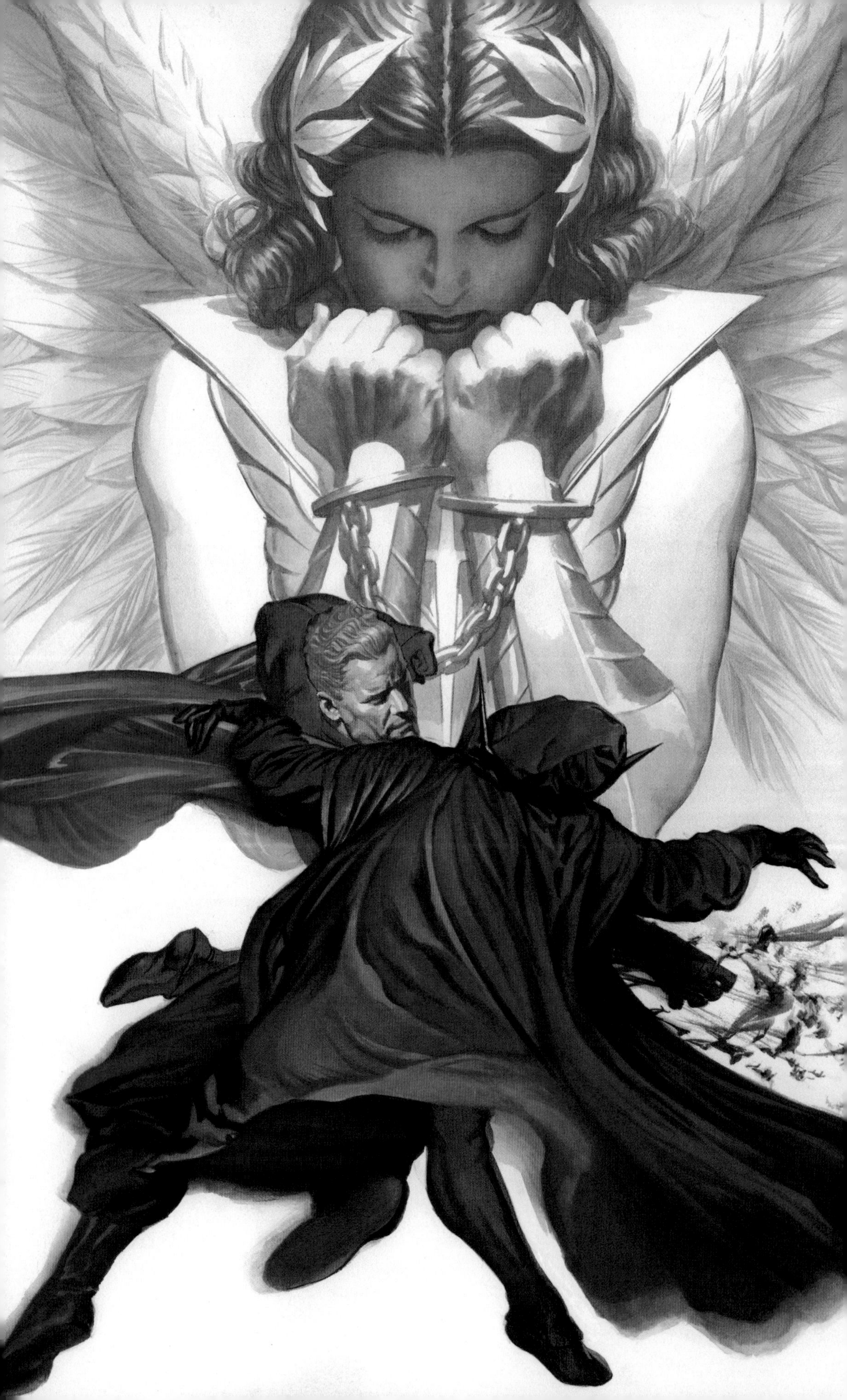

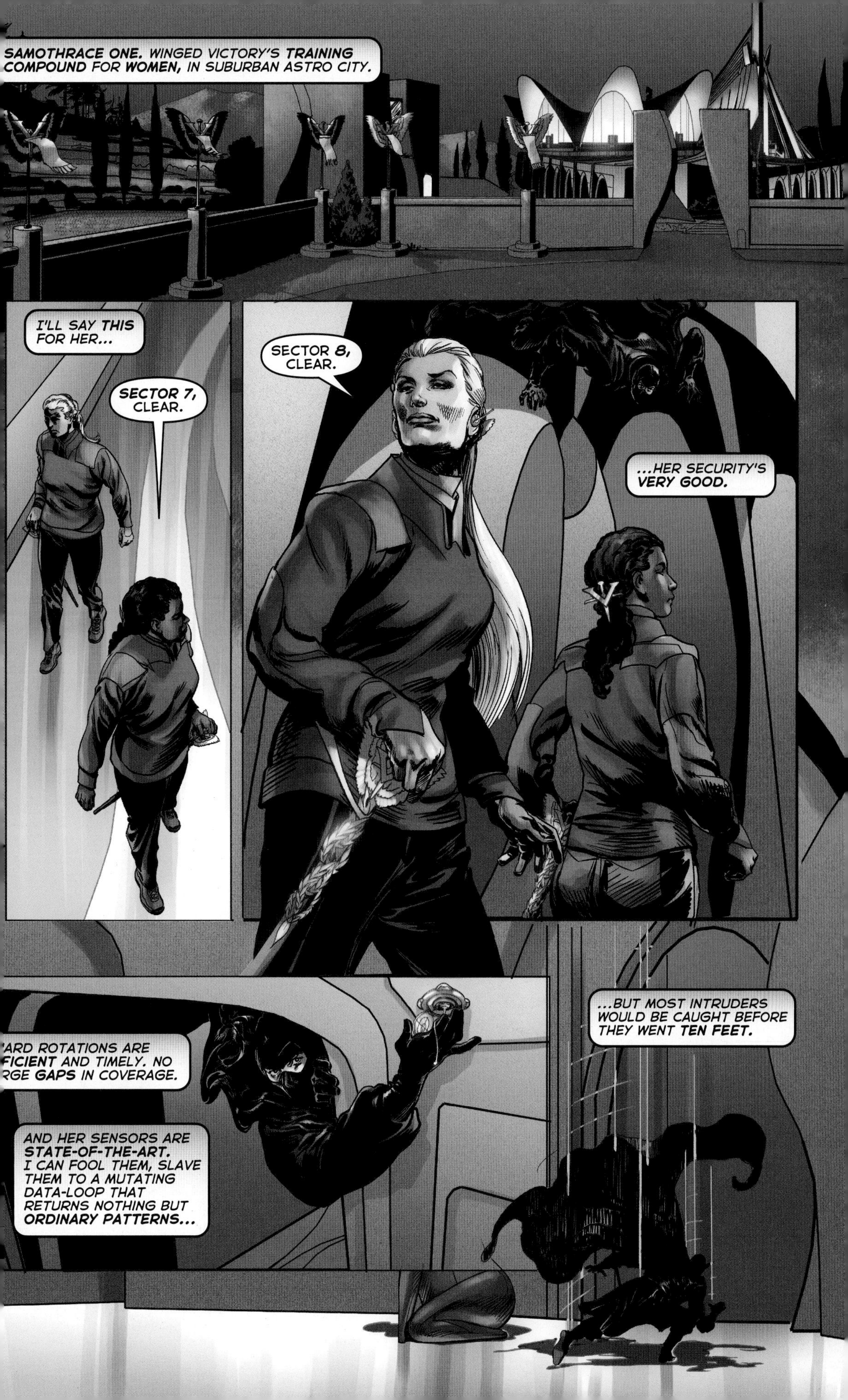
SAMOTHRACE ONE. WINGED VICTORY'S TRAINING COMPOUND FOR WOMEN, IN SUBURBAN ASTRO CITY.
I'LL SAY THIS FOR HER...
SECTOR 7, CLEAR.
SECTOR 8, CLEAR.
...HER SECURITY'S VERY GOOD.
ARD ROTATIONS ARE FICIENT AND TIMELY. NO RGE GAPS IN COVERAGE.
AND HER SENSORS ARE STATE-OF-THE-ART. I CAN FOOL THEM, SLAVE THEM TO A MUTATING DATA-LOOP THAT RETURNS NOTHING BUT ORDINARY PATTERNS...
...BUT MOST INTRUDERS WOULD BE CAUGHT BEFORE THEY WENT TEN FEET.

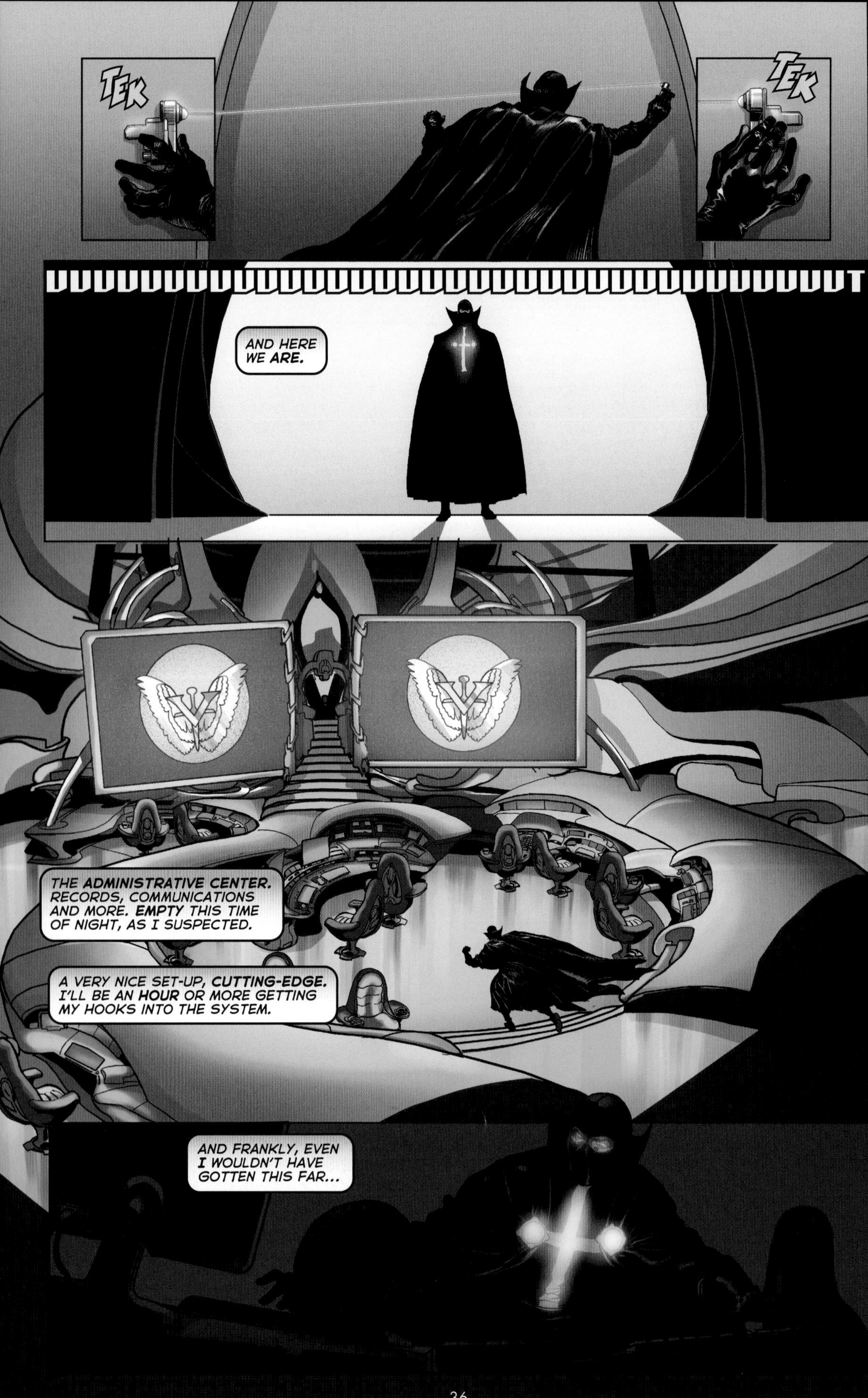
TEK
TEK
VVVVVVVVVVVVVVVVVVVVVVVVVVVVVVVVVVVVVVVVT
AND HERE WE ARE.
THE ADMINISTRATIVE CENTER. RECORDS, COMMUNICATIONS AND MORE. EMPTY THIS TIME OF NIGHT, AS I SUSPECTED.
A VERY NICE SET-UP, CUTTING-EDGE. I'LL BE AN HOUR OR MORE GETTING MY HOOKS INTO THE SYSTEM.
AND FRANKLY, EVEN I WOULDN'T HAVE GOTTEN THIS FAR...

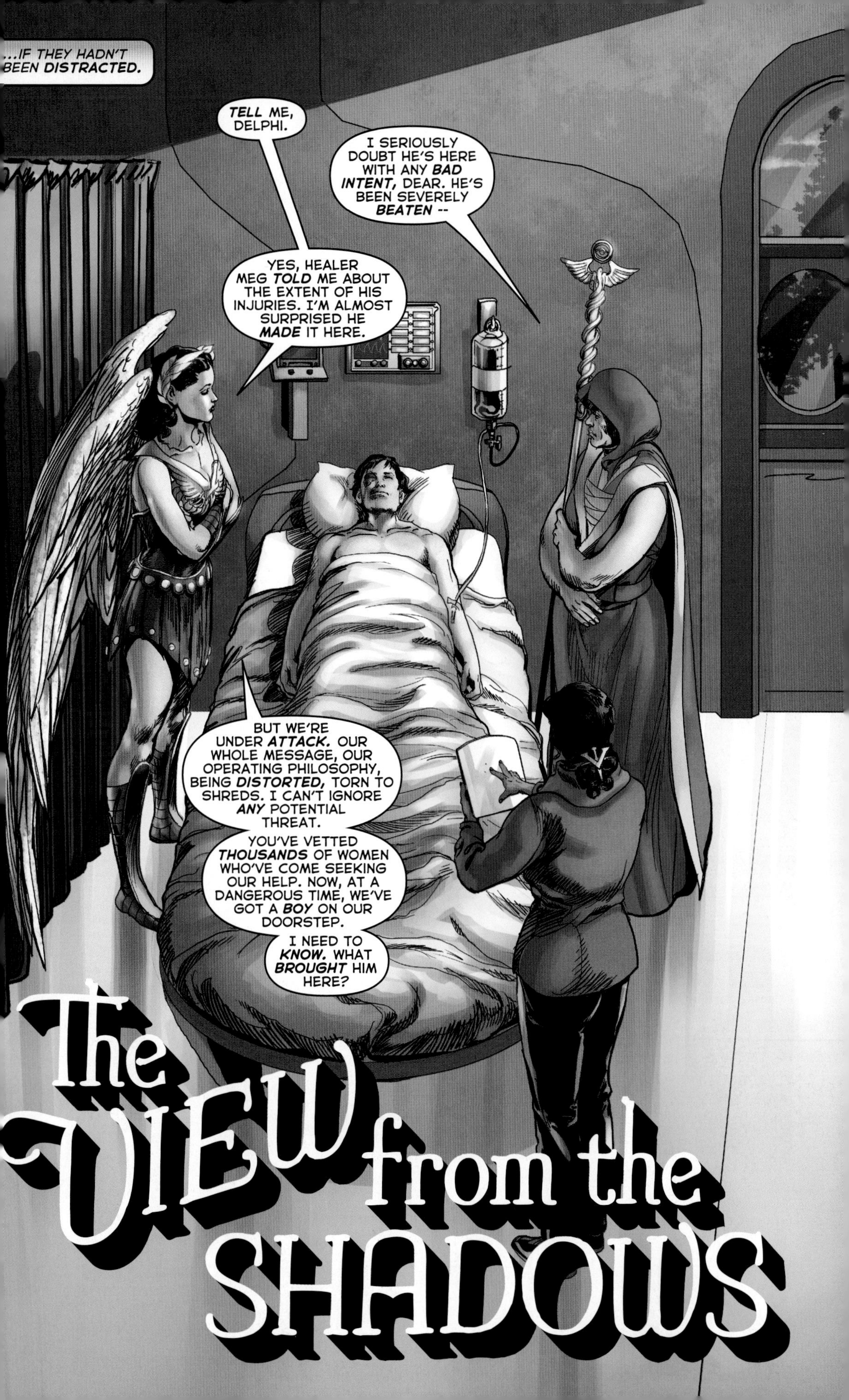
...IF THEY HADN'T BEEN DISTRACTED.
TELL ME, DELPHI.
I SERIOUSLY DOUBT HE'S HERE WITH ANY BAD INTENT, DEAR. HE'S BEEN SEVERELY BEATEN --
YES, HEALER MEG TOLD ME ABOUT THE EXTENT OF HIS INJURIES. I'M ALMOST SURPRISED HE MADE IT HERE.
BUT WE'RE UNDER ATTACK. OUR WHOLE MESSAGE, OUR OPERATING PHILOSOPHY, BEING DISTORTED, TORN TO SHREDS. I CAN'T IGNORE ANY POTENTIAL THREAT.
YOU'VE VETTED THOUSANDS OF WOMEN WHO'VE COME SEEKING OUR HELP. NOW, AT A DANGEROUS TIME, WE'VE GOT A BOY ON OUR DOORSTEP.
I NEED TO KNOW. WHAT BROUGHT HIM HERE?
The VIEW from the SHADOWS

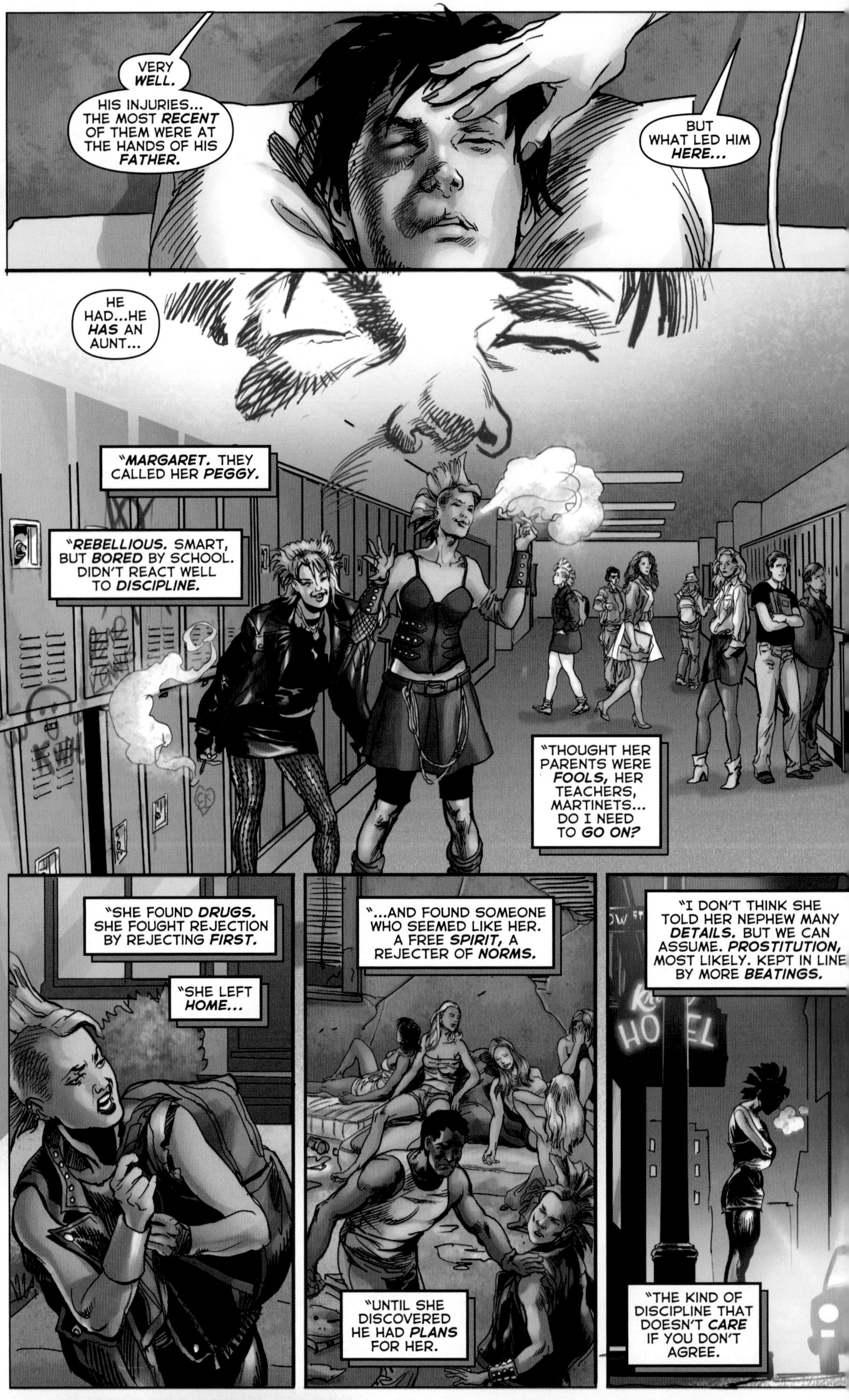
VERY WELL.
HIS INJURIES... THE MOST RECENT OF THEM WERE AT THE HANDS OF HIS FATHER.
BUT WHAT LED HIM HERE...
HE HAD...HE HAS AN AUNT...
"MARGARET. THEY CALLED HER PEGGY.
"REBELLIOUS. SMART, BUT BORED BY SCHOOL. DIDN'T REACT WELL TO DISCIPLINE.
"THOUGHT HER PARENTS WERE FOOLS, HER TEACHERS, MARTINETS... DO I NEED TO GO ON?
"SHE FOUND DRUGS. SHE FOUGHT REJECTION BY REJECTING FIRST.
"SHE LEFT HOME...
"...AND FOUND SOMEONE WHO SEEMED LIKE HER. A FREE SPIRIT, A REJECTER OF NORMS.
"UNTIL SHE DISCOVERED HE HAD PLANS FOR HER.
"I DON'T THINK SHE TOLD HER NEPHEW MANY DETAILS. BUT WE CAN ASSUME. PROSTITUTION, MOST LIKELY. KEPT IN LINE BY MORE BEATINGS.
"THE KIND OF DISCIPLINE THAT DOESN'T CARE IF YOU DON'T AGREE.

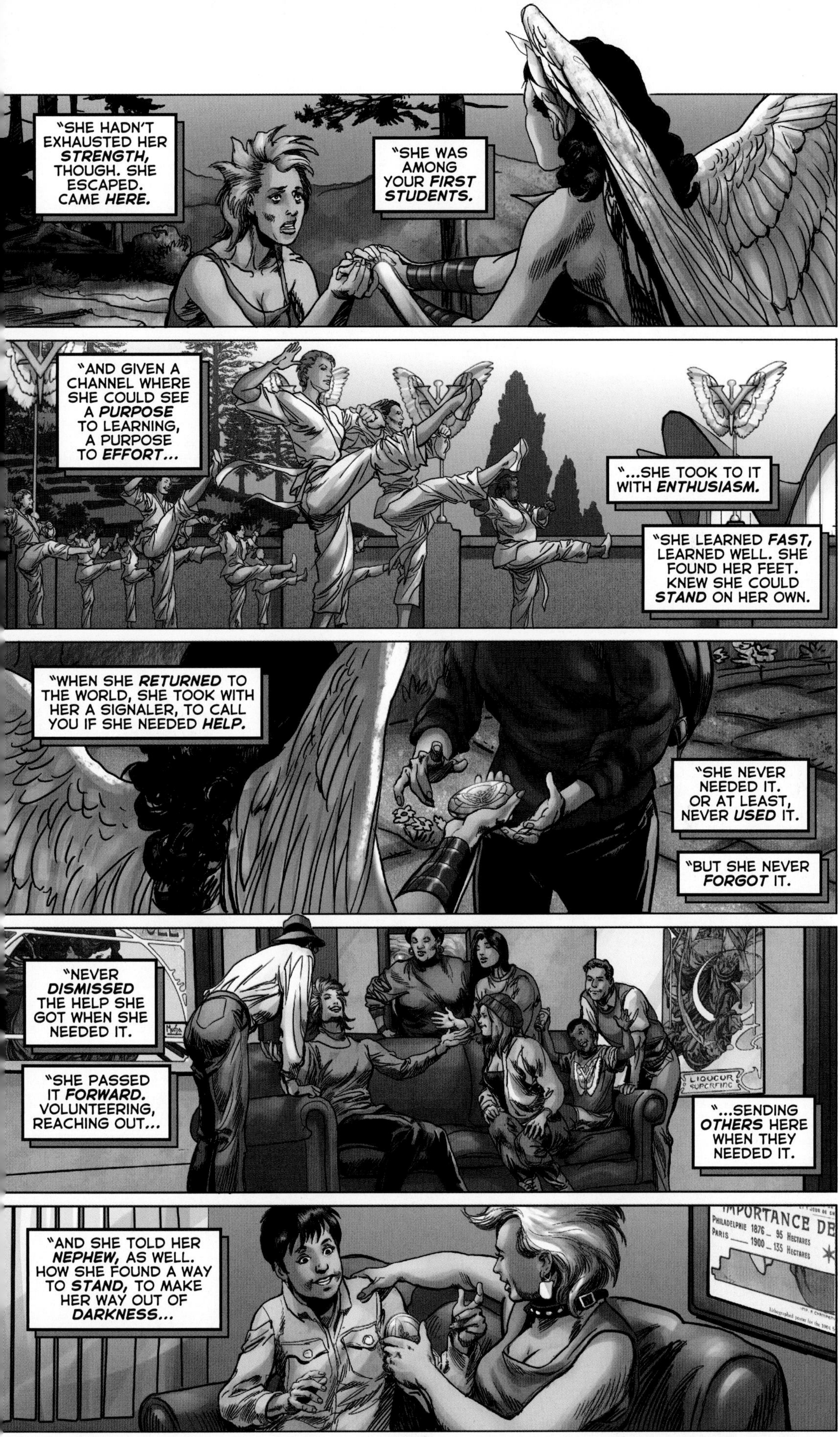
"SHE HADN'T EXHAUSTED HER ***STRENGTH,*** THOUGH. SHE ESCAPED. CAME ***HERE.***
"SHE WAS AMONG YOUR ***FIRST STUDENTS.***
"AND GIVEN A CHANNEL WHERE SHE COULD SEE A ***PURPOSE*** TO LEARNING, A PURPOSE TO ***EFFORT...***
"...SHE TOOK TO IT WITH ***ENTHUSIASM.***
"SHE LEARNED ***FAST,*** LEARNED WELL. SHE FOUND HER FEET. KNEW SHE COULD ***STAND*** ON HER OWN.
"WHEN SHE ***RETURNED*** TO THE WORLD, SHE TOOK WITH HER A SIGNALER, TO CALL YOU IF SHE NEEDED ***HELP.***
"SHE NEVER NEEDED IT. OR AT LEAST, NEVER ***USED*** IT.
"BUT SHE NEVER ***FORGOT*** IT.
"NEVER ***DISMISSED*** THE HELP SHE GOT WHEN SHE NEEDED IT.
"SHE PASSED IT ***FORWARD.*** VOLUNTEERING, REACHING OUT...
"...SENDING ***OTHERS*** HERE WHEN THEY NEEDED IT.
"AND SHE TOLD HER ***NEPHEW,*** AS WELL. HOW SHE FOUND A WAY TO ***STAND,*** TO MAKE HER WAY OUT OF ***DARKNESS...***

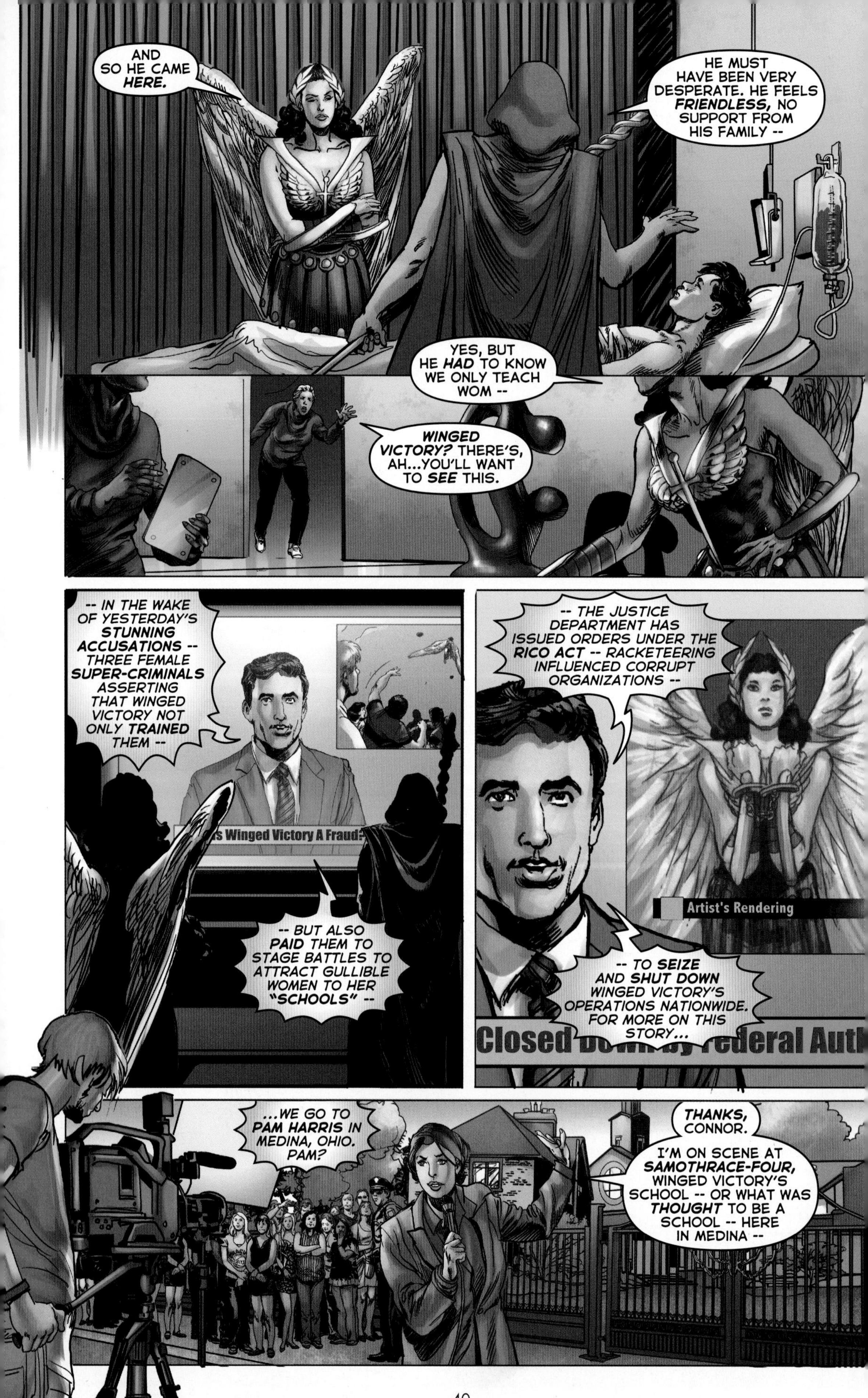
AND SO HE CAME HERE.
HE MUST HAVE BEEN VERY DESPERATE. HE FEELS FRIENDLESS, NO SUPPORT FROM HIS FAMILY --
YES, BUT HE HAD TO KNOW WE ONLY TEACH WOM --
WINGED VICTORY? THERE'S, AH...YOU'LL WANT TO SEE THIS.
-- IN THE WAKE OF YESTERDAY'S STUNNING ACCUSATIONS -- THREE FEMALE SUPER-CRIMINALS ASSERTING THAT WINGED VICTORY NOT ONLY TRAINED THEM --
Is Winged Victory A Fraud?
-- BUT ALSO PAID THEM TO STAGE BATTLES TO ATTRACT GULLIBLE WOMEN TO HER "SCHOOLS" --
-- THE JUSTICE DEPARTMENT HAS ISSUED ORDERS UNDER THE RICO ACT -- RACKETEERING INFLUENCED CORRUPT ORGANIZATIONS --
Artist's Rendering
-- TO SEIZE AND SHUT DOWN WINGED VICTORY'S OPERATIONS NATIONWIDE. FOR MORE ON THIS STORY...
Closed Down by Federal Auth
...WE GO TO PAM HARRIS IN MEDINA, OHIO. PAM?
THANKS, CONNOR.
I'M ON SCENE AT SAMOTHRACE-FOUR, WINGED VICTORY'S SCHOOL -- OR WHAT WAS THOUGHT TO BE A SCHOOL -- HERE IN MEDINA --

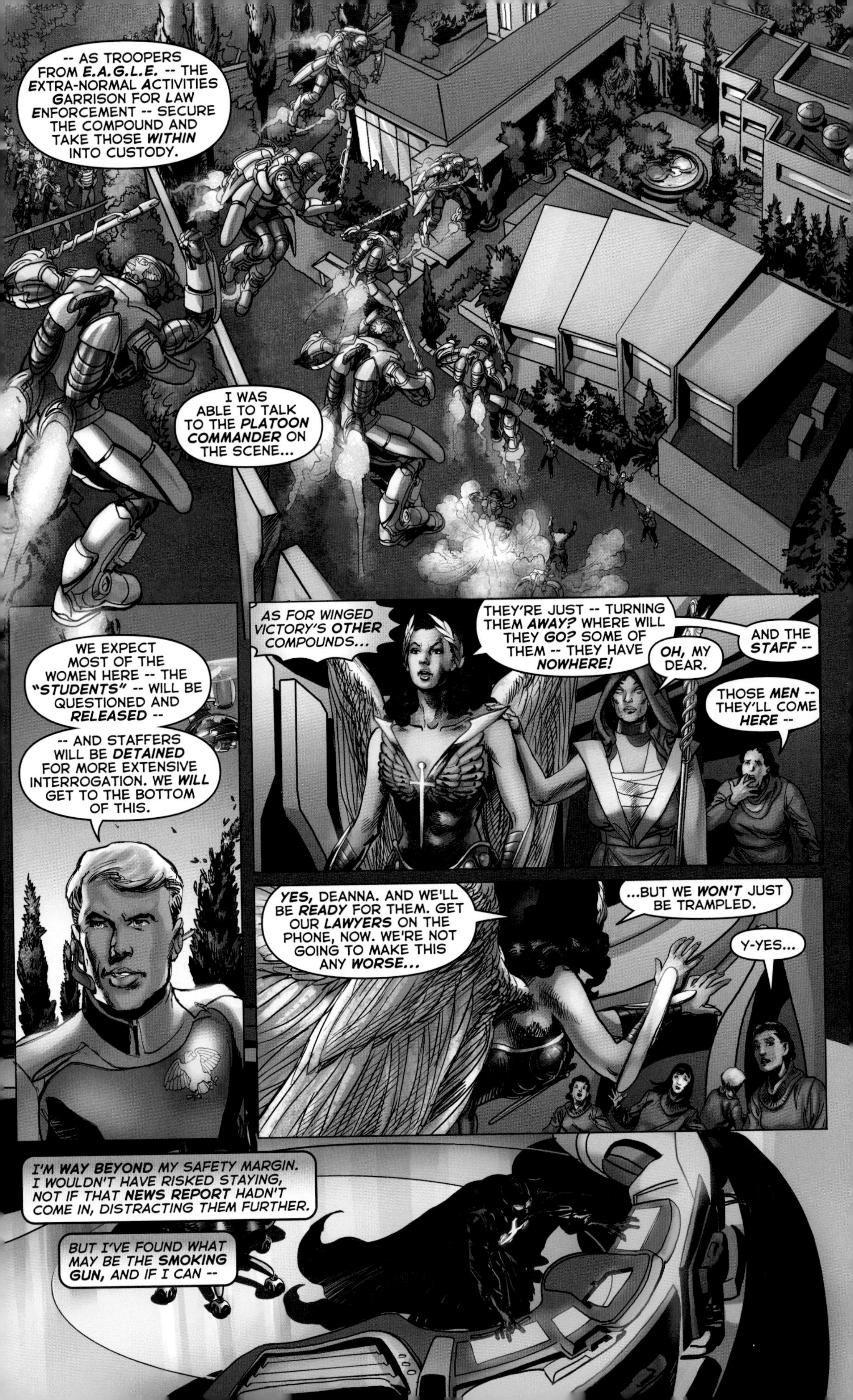
-- AS TROOPERS FROM E.A.G.L.E. -- THE EXTRA-NORMAL ACTIVITIES GARRISON FOR LAW ENFORCEMENT -- SECURE THE COMPOUND AND TAKE THOSE WITHIN INTO CUSTODY.
I WAS ABLE TO TALK TO THE PLATOON COMMANDER ON THE SCENE...
WE EXPECT MOST OF THE WOMEN HERE -- THE "STUDENTS" -- WILL BE QUESTIONED AND RELEASED --
-- AND STAFFERS WILL BE DETAINED FOR MORE EXTENSIVE INTERROGATION. WE WILL GET TO THE BOTTOM OF THIS.
AS FOR WINGED VICTORY'S OTHER COMPOUNDS...
THEY'RE JUST -- TURNING THEM AWAY? WHERE WILL THEY GO? SOME OF THEM -- THEY HAVE NOWHERE!
OH, MY DEAR.
AND THE STAFF --
THOSE MEN -- THEY'LL COME HERE --
YES, DEANNA. AND WE'LL BE READY FOR THEM. GET OUR LAWYERS ON THE PHONE, NOW. WE'RE NOT GOING TO MAKE THIS ANY WORSE...
...BUT WE WON'T JUST BE TRAMPLED.
Y-YES...
I'M WAY BEYOND MY SAFETY MARGIN. I WOULDN'T HAVE RISKED STAYING, NOT IF THAT NEWS REPORT HADN'T COME IN, DISTRACTING THEM FURTHER.
BUT I'VE FOUND WHAT MAY BE THE SMOKING GUN, AND IF I CAN --

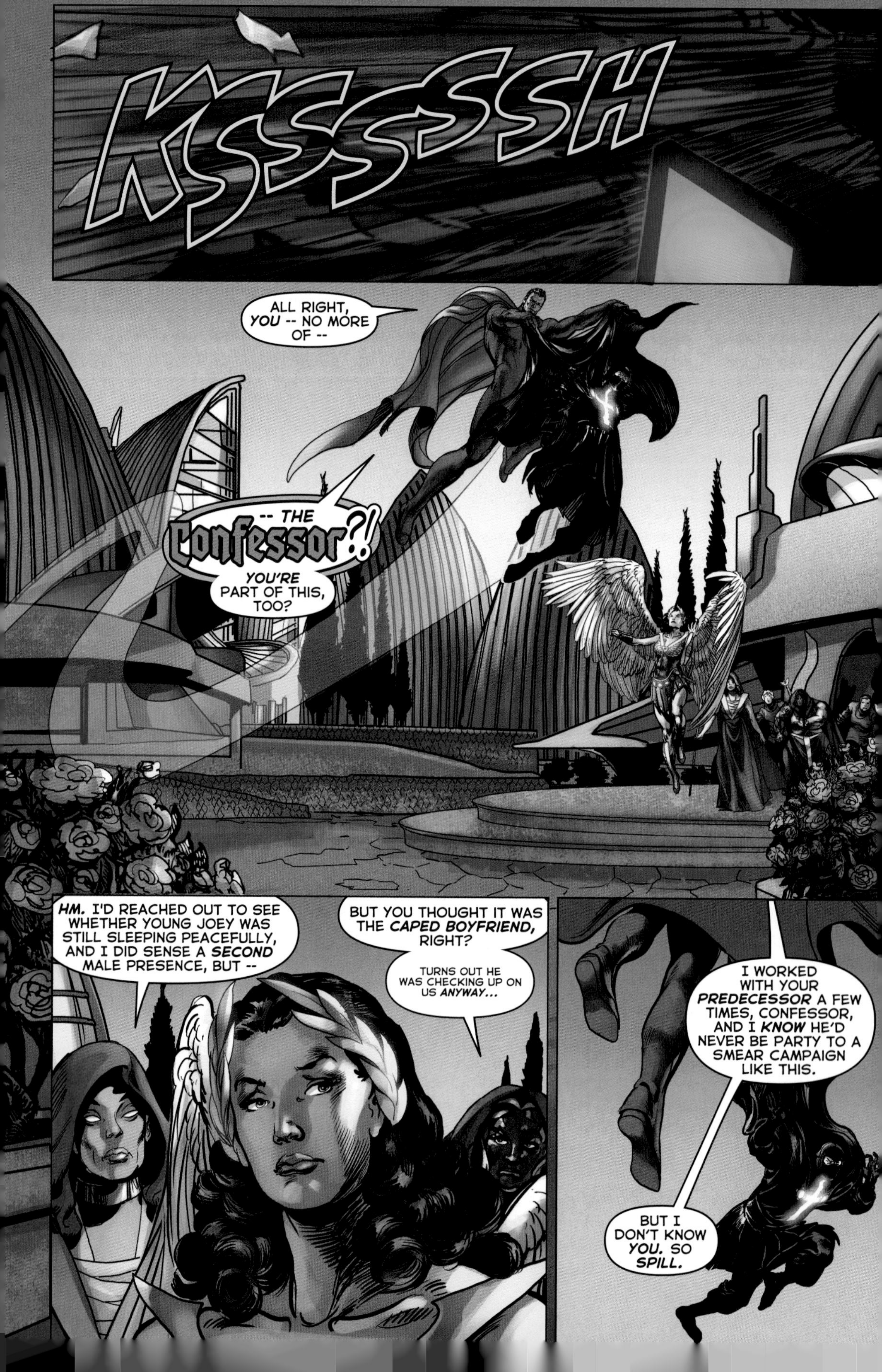
KSSSSSH
ALL RIGHT, YOU -- NO MORE OF --
-- THE Confessor?!
YOU'RE PART OF THIS, TOO?
HM. I'D REACHED OUT TO SEE WHETHER YOUNG JOEY WAS STILL SLEEPING PEACEFULLY, AND I DID SENSE A SECOND MALE PRESENCE, BUT --
BUT YOU THOUGHT IT WAS THE CAPED BOYFRIEND, RIGHT?
TURNS OUT HE WAS CHECKING UP ON US ANYWAY...
I WORKED WITH YOUR PREDECESSOR A FEW TIMES, CONFESSOR, AND I KNOW HE'D NEVER BE PARTY TO A SMEAR CAMPAIGN LIKE THIS.
BUT I DON'T KNOW YOU. SO SPILL.

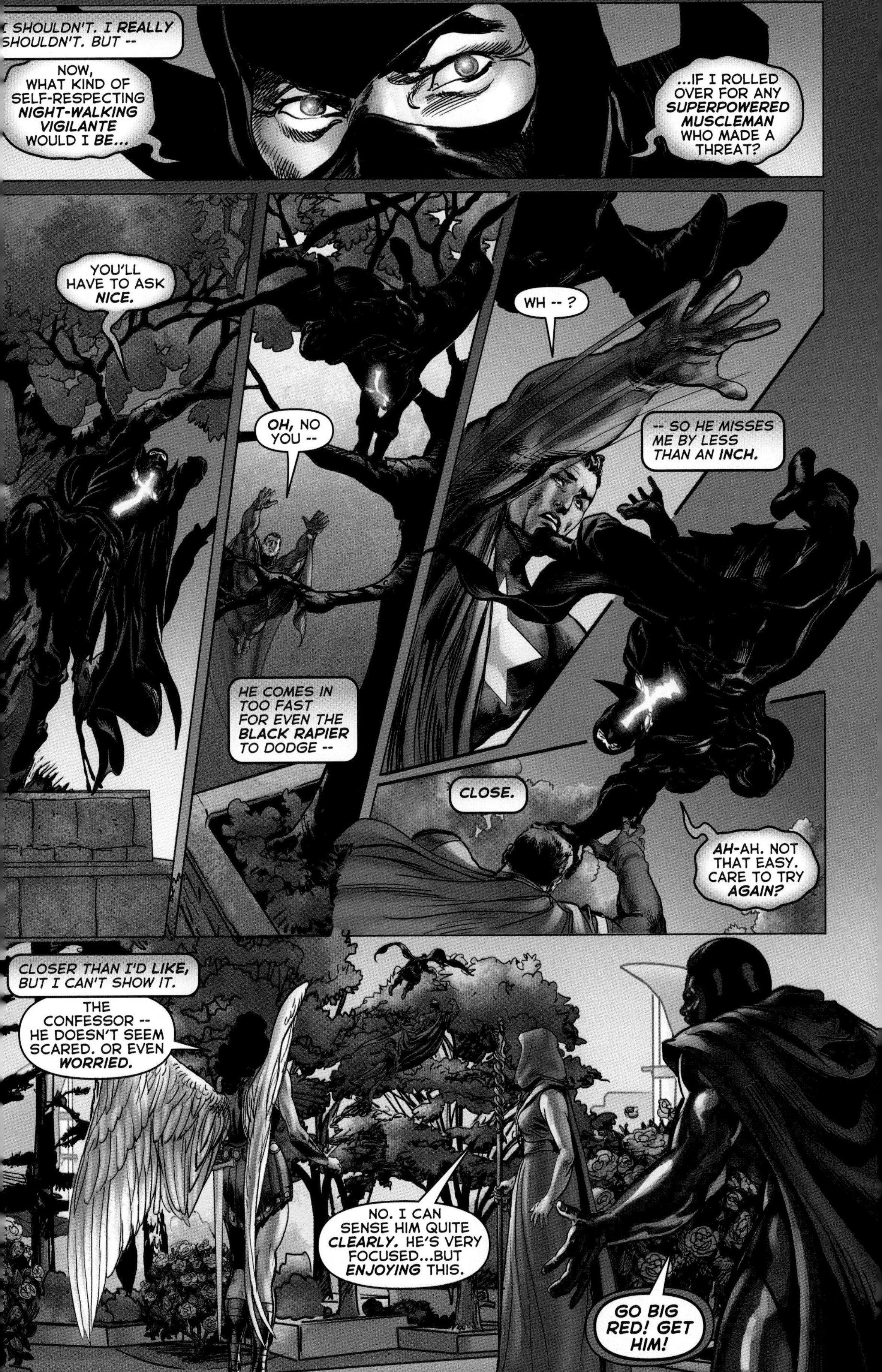
I SHOULDN'T. I REALLY SHOULDN'T. BUT --
NOW, WHAT KIND OF SELF-RESPECTING NIGHT-WALKING VIGILANTE WOULD I BE...
...IF I ROLLED OVER FOR ANY SUPERPOWERED MUSCLEMAN WHO MADE A THREAT?
YOU'LL HAVE TO ASK NICE.
OH, NO YOU --
WH -- ?
-- SO HE MISSES ME BY LESS THAN AN INCH.
HE COMES IN TOO FAST FOR EVEN THE BLACK RAPIER TO DODGE --
CLOSE.
AH-AH. NOT THAT EASY. CARE TO TRY AGAIN?
CLOSER THAN I'D LIKE, BUT I CAN'T SHOW IT.
THE CONFESSOR -- HE DOESN'T SEEM SCARED. OR EVEN WORRIED.
NO. I CAN SENSE HIM QUITE CLEARLY. HE'S VERY FOCUSED...BUT ENJOYING THIS.
GO BIG RED! GET HIM!

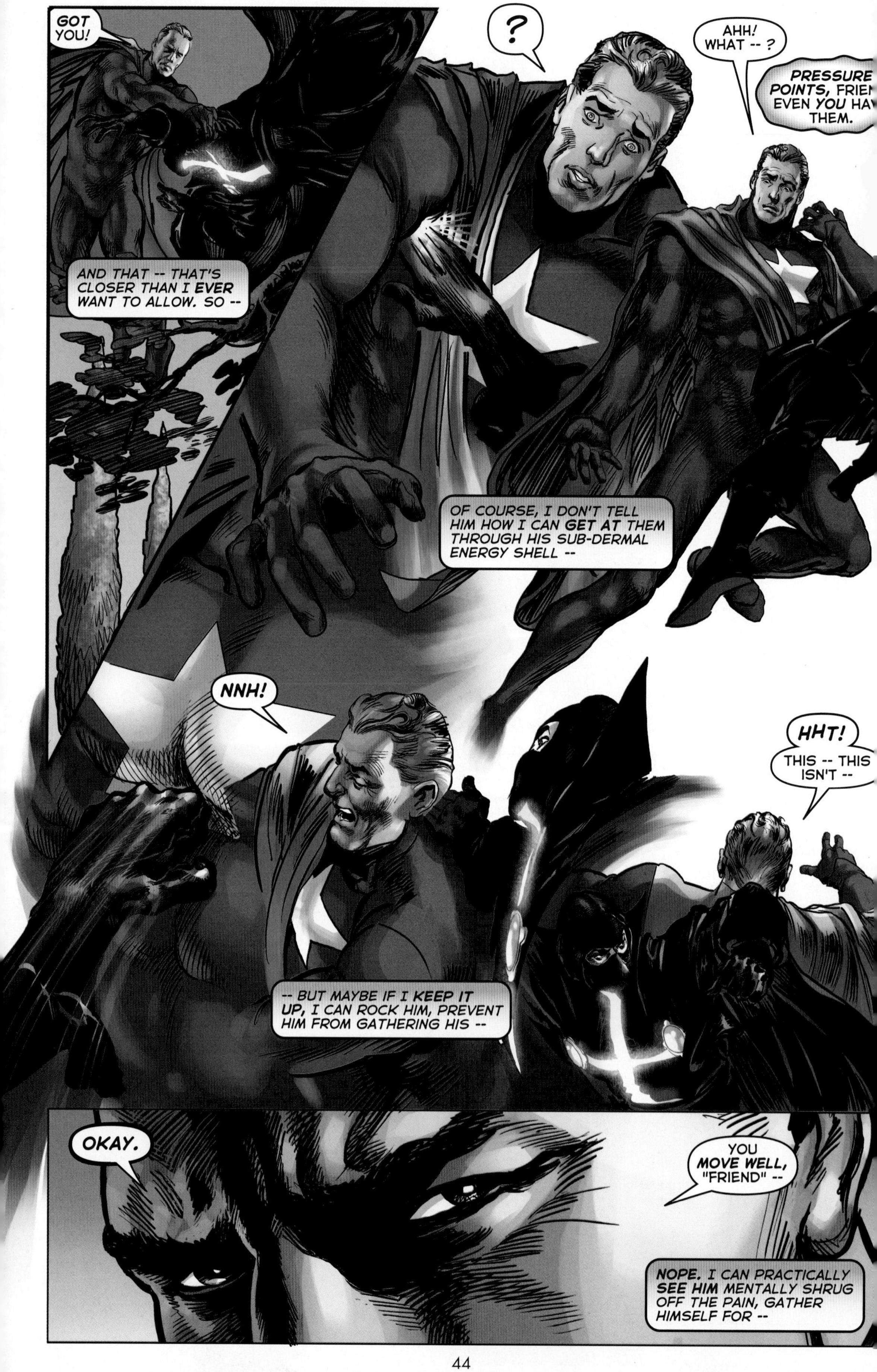
GOT YOU!
?
AHH! WHAT -- ?
PRESSURE POINTS, FRIEN
EVEN YOU HA
THEM.
AND THAT -- THAT'S CLOSER THAN I EVER WANT TO ALLOW. SO --
OF COURSE, I DON'T TELL HIM HOW I CAN GET AT THEM THROUGH HIS SUB-DERMAL ENERGY SHELL --
NNH!
HHT!
THIS -- THIS ISN'T --
-- BUT MAYBE IF I KEEP IT UP, I CAN ROCK HIM, PREVENT HIM FROM GATHERING HIS --
OKAY.
YOU MOVE WELL, "FRIEND" --
NOPE. I CAN PRACTICALLY SEE HIM MENTALLY SHRUG OFF THE PAIN, GATHER HIMSELF FOR --

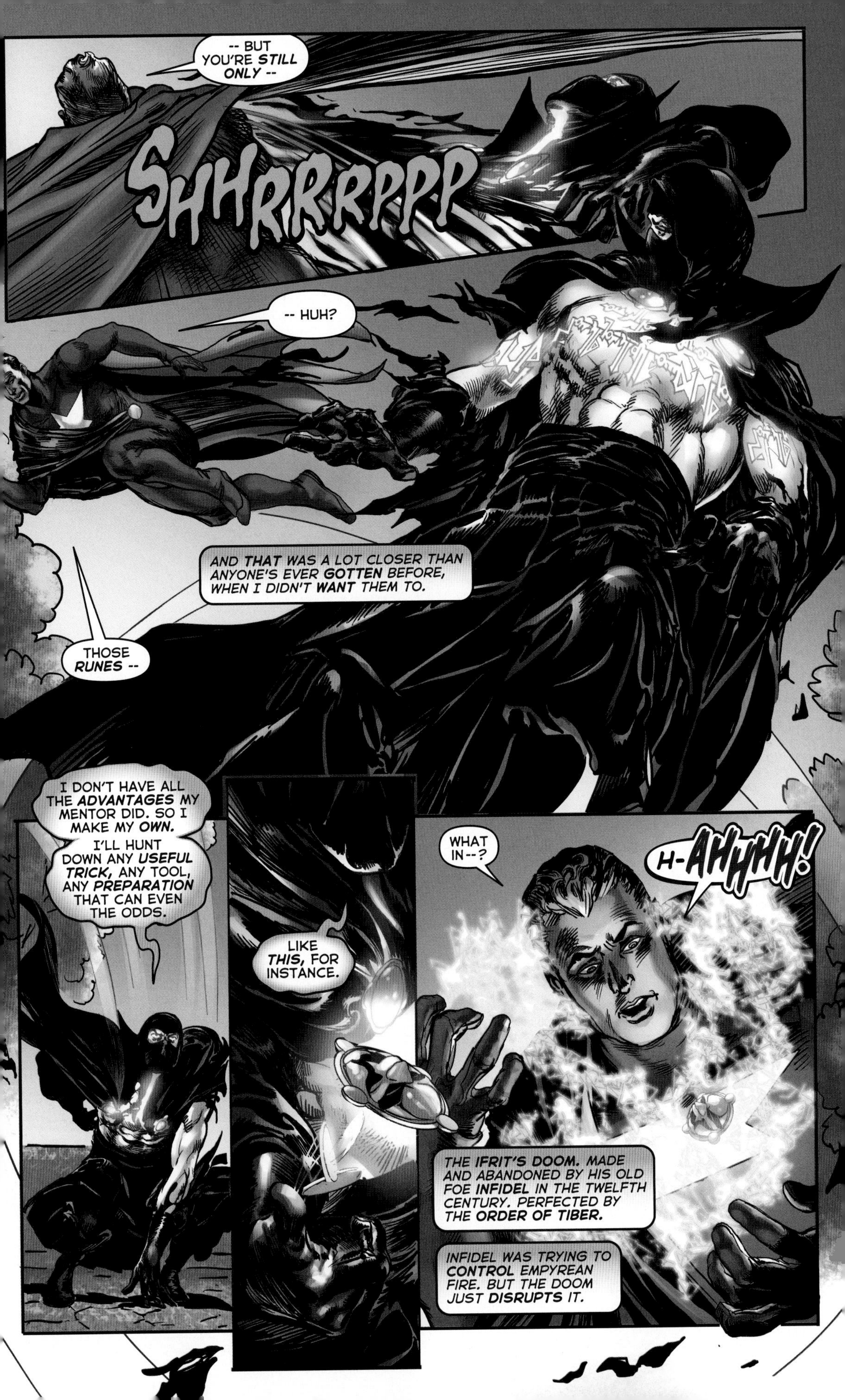

-- BUT YOU'RE STILL ONLY --
SHHRRRPPP
-- HUH?
AND THAT WAS A LOT CLOSER THAN ANYONE'S EVER GOTTEN BEFORE, WHEN I DIDN'T WANT THEM TO.
THOSE RUNES --
I DON'T HAVE ALL THE ADVANTAGES MY MENTOR DID. SO I MAKE MY OWN.
I'LL HUNT DOWN ANY USEFUL TRICK, ANY TOOL, ANY PREPARATION THAT CAN EVEN THE ODDS.
LIKE THIS, FOR INSTANCE.
WHAT IN--?
H-AHHHH!
THE IFRIT'S DOOM. MADE AND ABANDONED BY HIS OLD FOE INFIDEL IN THE TWELFTH CENTURY. PERFECTED BY THE ORDER OF TIBER.
INFIDEL WAS TRYING TO CONTROL EMPYREAN FIRE. BUT THE DOOM JUST DISRUPTS IT.

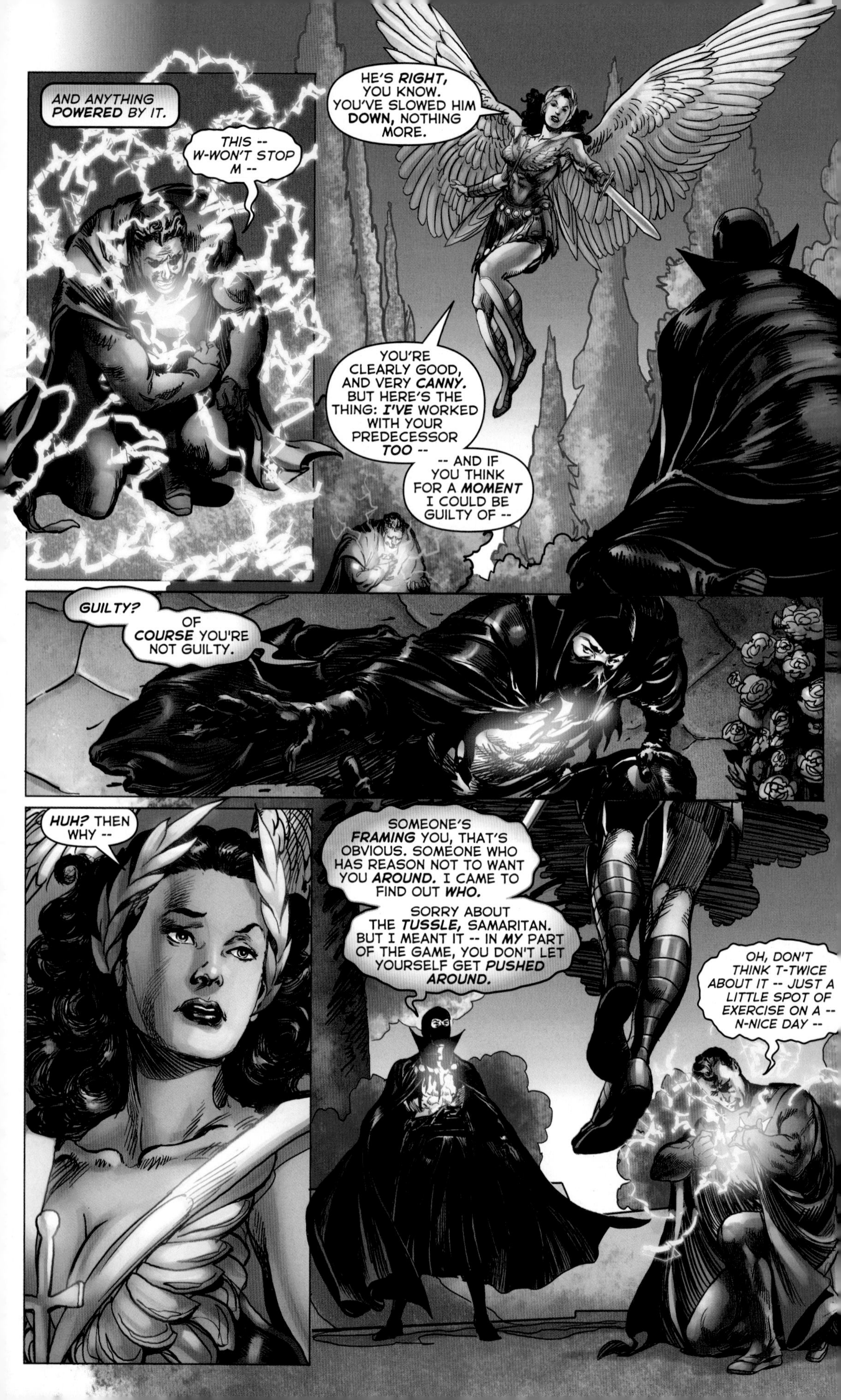
AND ANYTHING POWERED BY IT.
THIS -- W-WON'T STOP M --
HE'S RIGHT, YOU KNOW. YOU'VE SLOWED HIM DOWN, NOTHING MORE.
YOU'RE CLEARLY GOOD, AND VERY CANNY. BUT HERE'S THE THING: I'VE WORKED WITH YOUR PREDECESSOR TOO --
-- AND IF YOU THINK FOR A MOMENT I COULD BE GUILTY OF --
GUILTY?
OF COURSE YOU'RE NOT GUILTY.
HUH? THEN WHY --
SOMEONE'S FRAMING YOU, THAT'S OBVIOUS. SOMEONE WHO HAS REASON NOT TO WANT YOU AROUND. I CAME TO FIND OUT WHO.
SORRY ABOUT THE TUSSLE, SAMARITAN. BUT I MEANT IT -- IN MY PART OF THE GAME, YOU DON'T LET YOURSELF GET PUSHED AROUND.
OH, DON'T THINK T-TWICE ABOUT IT -- JUST A LITTLE SPOT OF EXERCISE ON A -- N-NICE DAY --

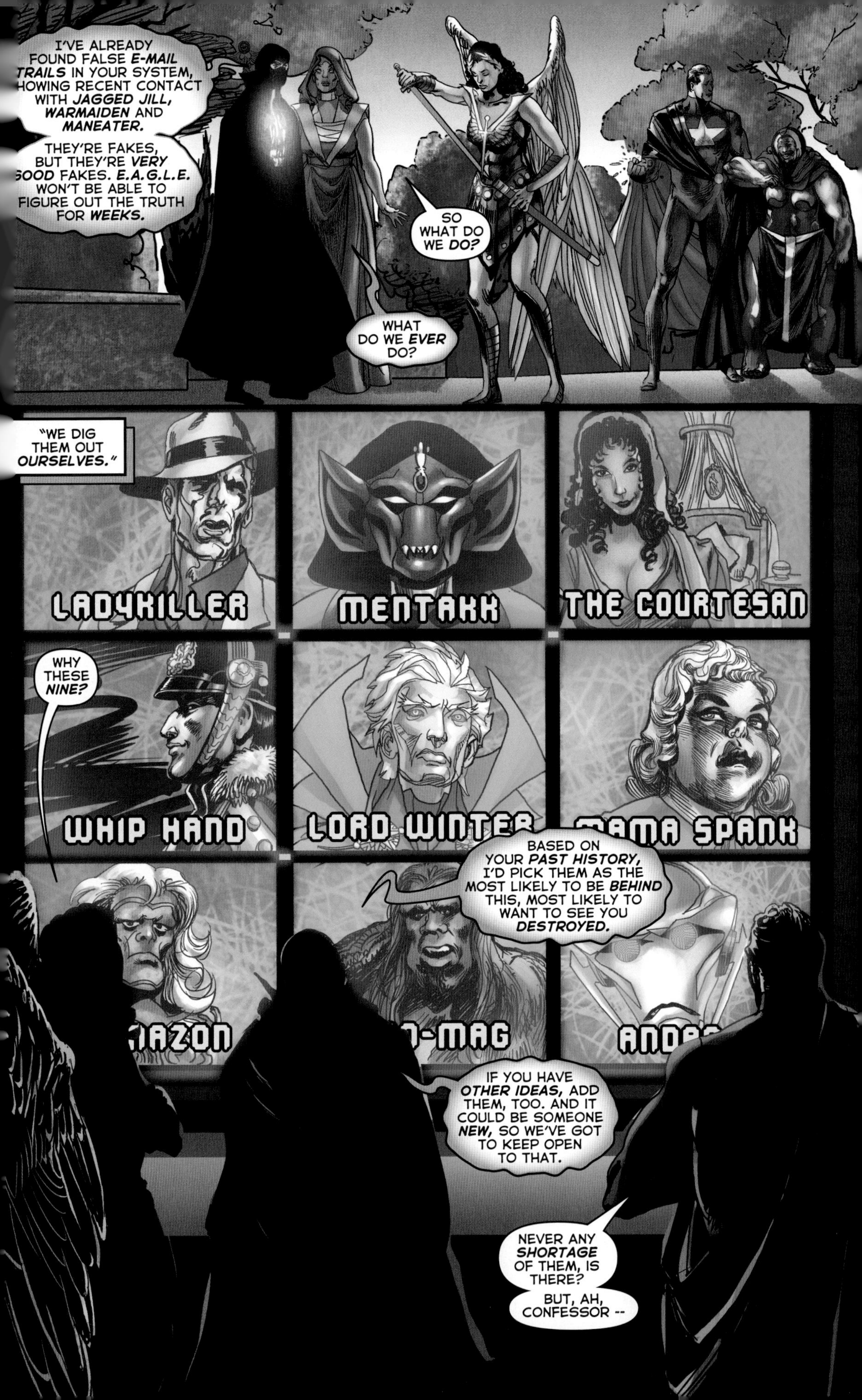

I'VE ALREADY FOUND FALSE E-MAIL TRAILS IN YOUR SYSTEM, SHOWING RECENT CONTACT WITH JAGGED JILL, WARMAIDEN AND MANEATER.
THEY'RE FAKES, BUT THEY'RE VERY GOOD FAKES. E.A.G.L.E. WON'T BE ABLE TO FIGURE OUT THE TRUTH FOR WEEKS.
SO WHAT DO WE DO?
WHAT DO WE EVER DO?
"WE DIG THEM OUT OURSELVES."
LADYKILLER
MENTAKK
THE COURTESAN
WHY THESE NINE?
WHIP HAND
LORD WINTER
MAMA SPANK
BASED ON YOUR PAST HISTORY, I'D PICK THEM AS THE MOST LIKELY TO BE BEHIND THIS, MOST LIKELY TO WANT TO SEE YOU DESTROYED.
IF YOU HAVE OTHER IDEAS, ADD THEM, TOO. AND IT COULD BE SOMEONE NEW, SO WE'VE GOT TO KEEP OPEN TO THAT.
NEVER ANY SHORTAGE OF THEM, IS THERE?
BUT, AH, CONFESSOR --

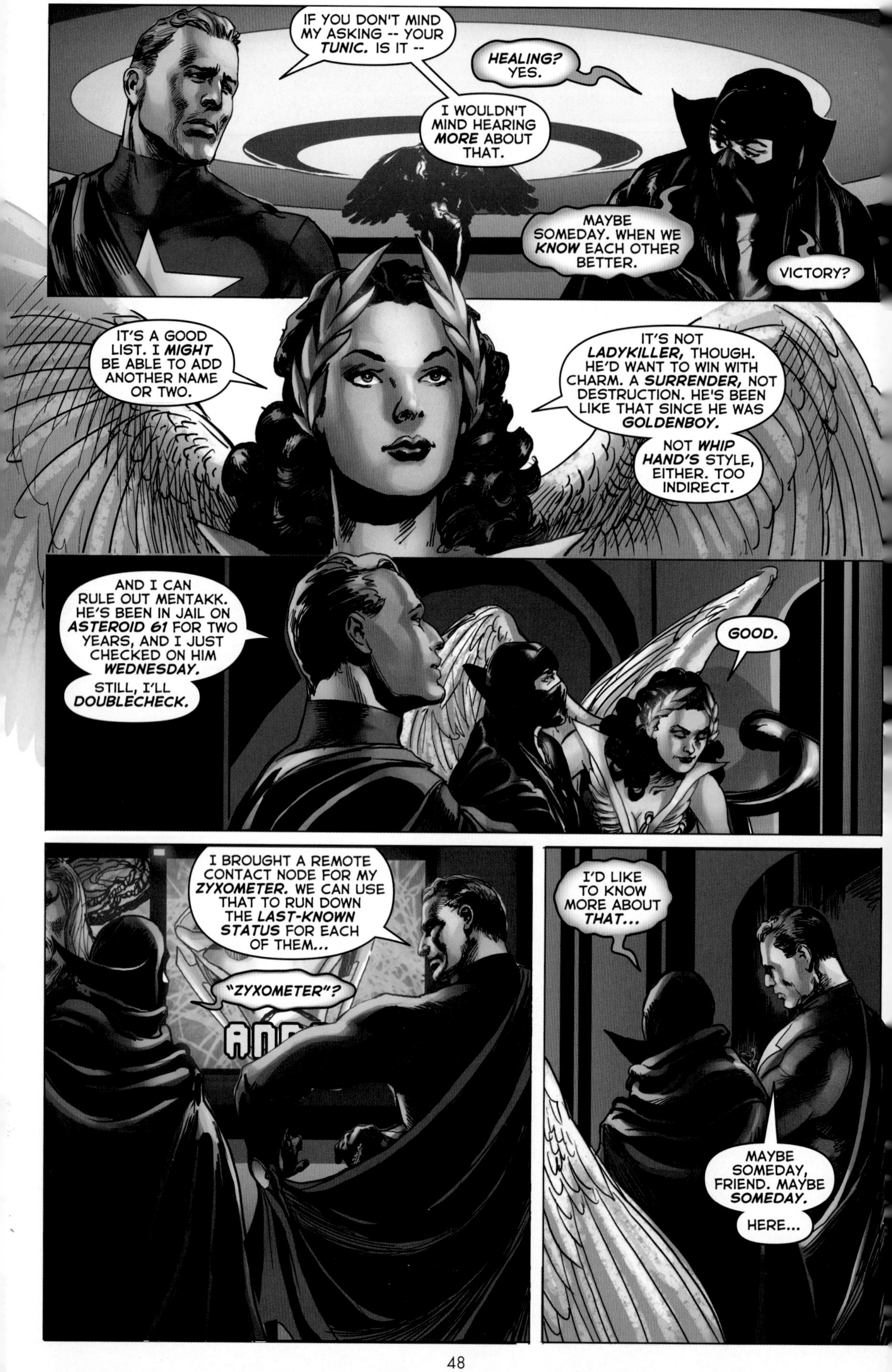

IF YOU DON'T MIND MY ASKING -- YOUR *TUNIC.* IS IT --
HEALING? YES.
I WOULDN'T MIND HEARING *MORE* ABOUT THAT.
MAYBE SOMEDAY. WHEN WE *KNOW* EACH OTHER BETTER.
VICTORY?
IT'S A GOOD LIST. I *MIGHT* BE ABLE TO ADD ANOTHER NAME OR TWO.
IT'S NOT *LADYKILLER,* THOUGH. HE'D WANT TO WIN WITH CHARM. A *SURRENDER,* NOT DESTRUCTION. HE'S BEEN LIKE THAT SINCE HE WAS *GOLDENBOY.*
NOT *WHIP HAND'S* STYLE, EITHER. TOO INDIRECT.
AND I CAN RULE OUT MENTAKK. HE'S BEEN IN JAIL ON *ASTEROID 61* FOR TWO YEARS, AND I JUST CHECKED ON HIM *WEDNESDAY.*
STILL, I'LL *DOUBLECHECK.*
GOOD.
I BROUGHT A REMOTE CONTACT NODE FOR MY *ZYXOMETER.* WE CAN USE THAT TO RUN DOWN THE *LAST-KNOWN STATUS* FOR EACH OF THEM...
"ZYXOMETER"?
I'D LIKE TO KNOW MORE ABOUT *THAT...*
MAYBE SOMEDAY, FRIEND. MAYBE *SOMEDAY.*
HERE...

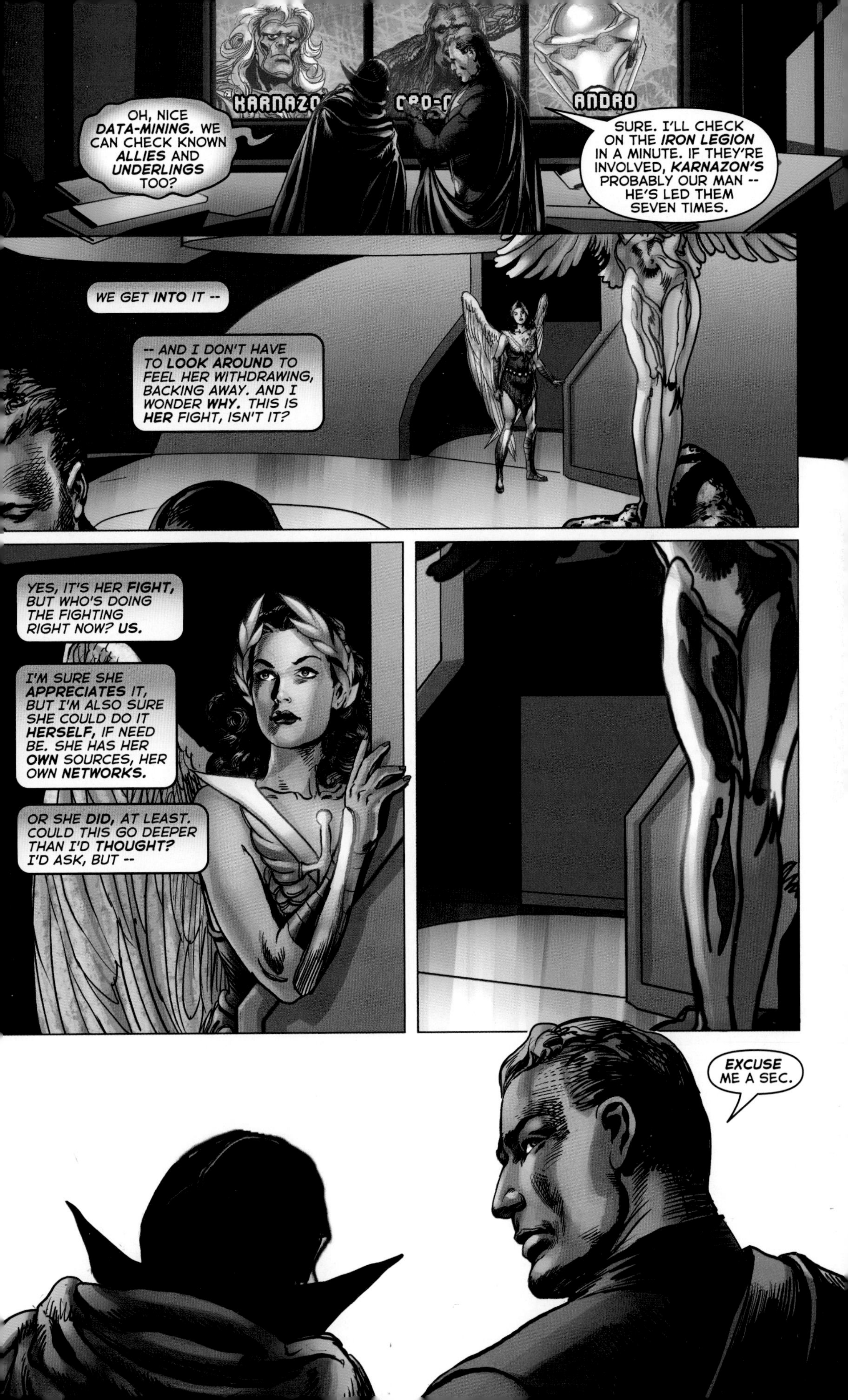
KARNAZON
ANDRO
OH, NICE DATA-MINING. WE CAN CHECK KNOWN ALLIES AND UNDERLINGS TOO?
SURE. I'LL CHECK ON THE IRON LEGION IN A MINUTE. IF THEY'RE INVOLVED, KARNAZON'S PROBABLY OUR MAN -- HE'S LED THEM SEVEN TIMES.
WE GET INTO IT --
-- AND I DON'T HAVE TO LOOK AROUND TO FEEL HER WITHDRAWING, BACKING AWAY. AND I WONDER WHY. THIS IS HER FIGHT, ISN'T IT?
YES, IT'S HER FIGHT, BUT WHO'S DOING THE FIGHTING RIGHT NOW? US.
I'M SURE SHE APPRECIATES IT, BUT I'M ALSO SURE SHE COULD DO IT HERSELF, IF NEED BE. SHE HAS HER OWN SOURCES, HER OWN NETWORKS.
OR SHE DID, AT LEAST. COULD THIS GO DEEPER THAN I'D THOUGHT? I'D ASK, BUT --
EXCUSE ME A SEC.

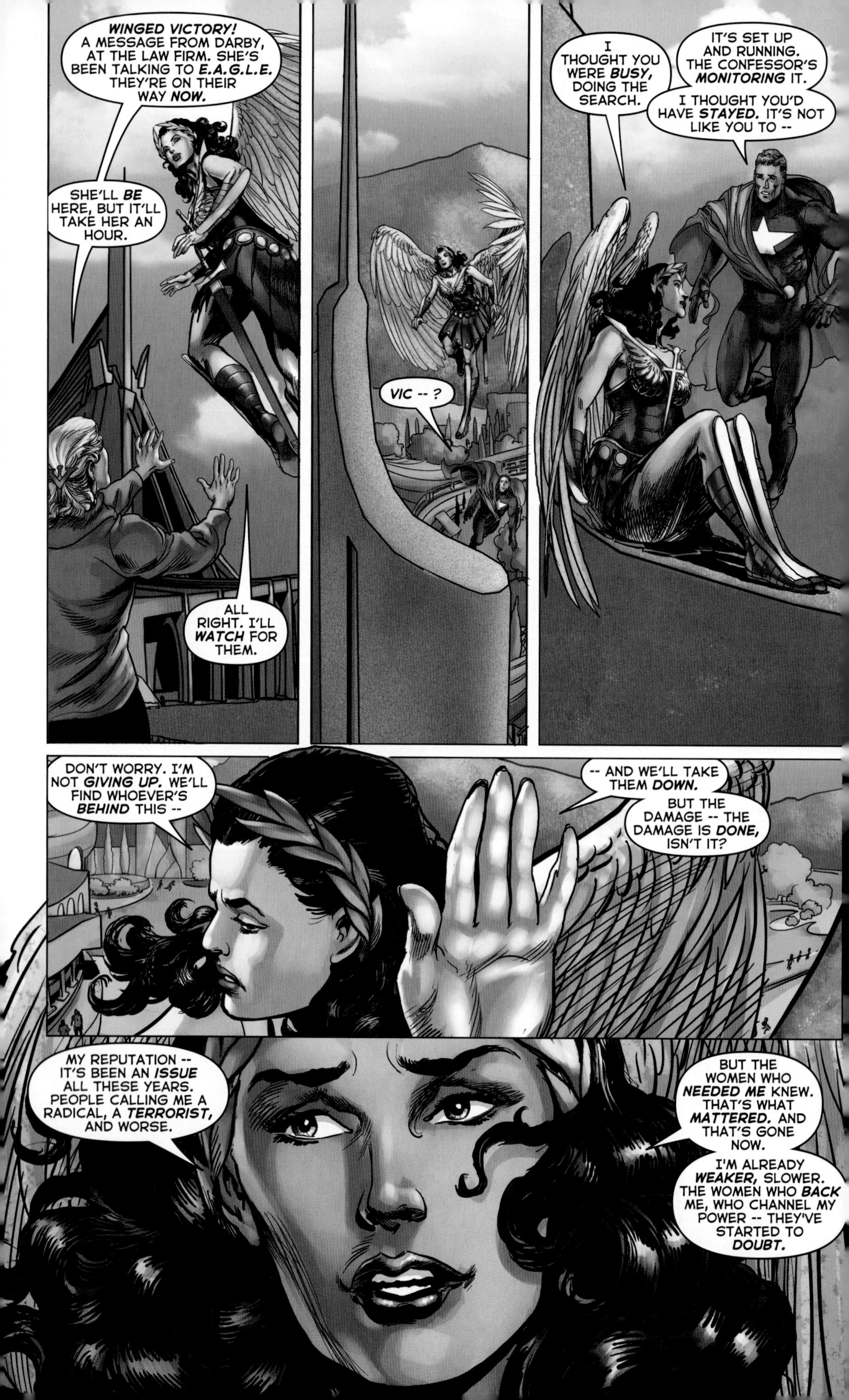
WINGED VICTORY! A MESSAGE FROM DARBY, AT THE LAW FIRM. SHE'S BEEN TALKING TO E.A.G.L.E. THEY'RE ON THEIR WAY NOW.
SHE'LL BE HERE, BUT IT'LL TAKE HER AN HOUR.
ALL RIGHT. I'LL WATCH FOR THEM.
VIC -- ?
I THOUGHT YOU WERE BUSY, DOING THE SEARCH.
IT'S SET UP AND RUNNING. THE CONFESSOR'S MONITORING IT.
I THOUGHT YOU'D HAVE STAYED. IT'S NOT LIKE YOU TO --
DON'T WORRY. I'M NOT GIVING UP. WE'LL FIND WHOEVER'S BEHIND THIS --
-- AND WE'LL TAKE THEM DOWN.
BUT THE DAMAGE -- THE DAMAGE IS DONE, ISN'T IT?
MY REPUTATION -- IT'S BEEN AN ISSUE ALL THESE YEARS. PEOPLE CALLING ME A RADICAL, A TERRORIST, AND WORSE.
BUT THE WOMEN WHO NEEDED ME KNEW. THAT'S WHAT MATTERED. AND THAT'S GONE NOW.
I'M ALREADY WEAKER, SLOWER. THE WOMEN WHO BACK ME, WHO CHANNEL MY POWER -- THEY'VE STARTED TO DOUBT.

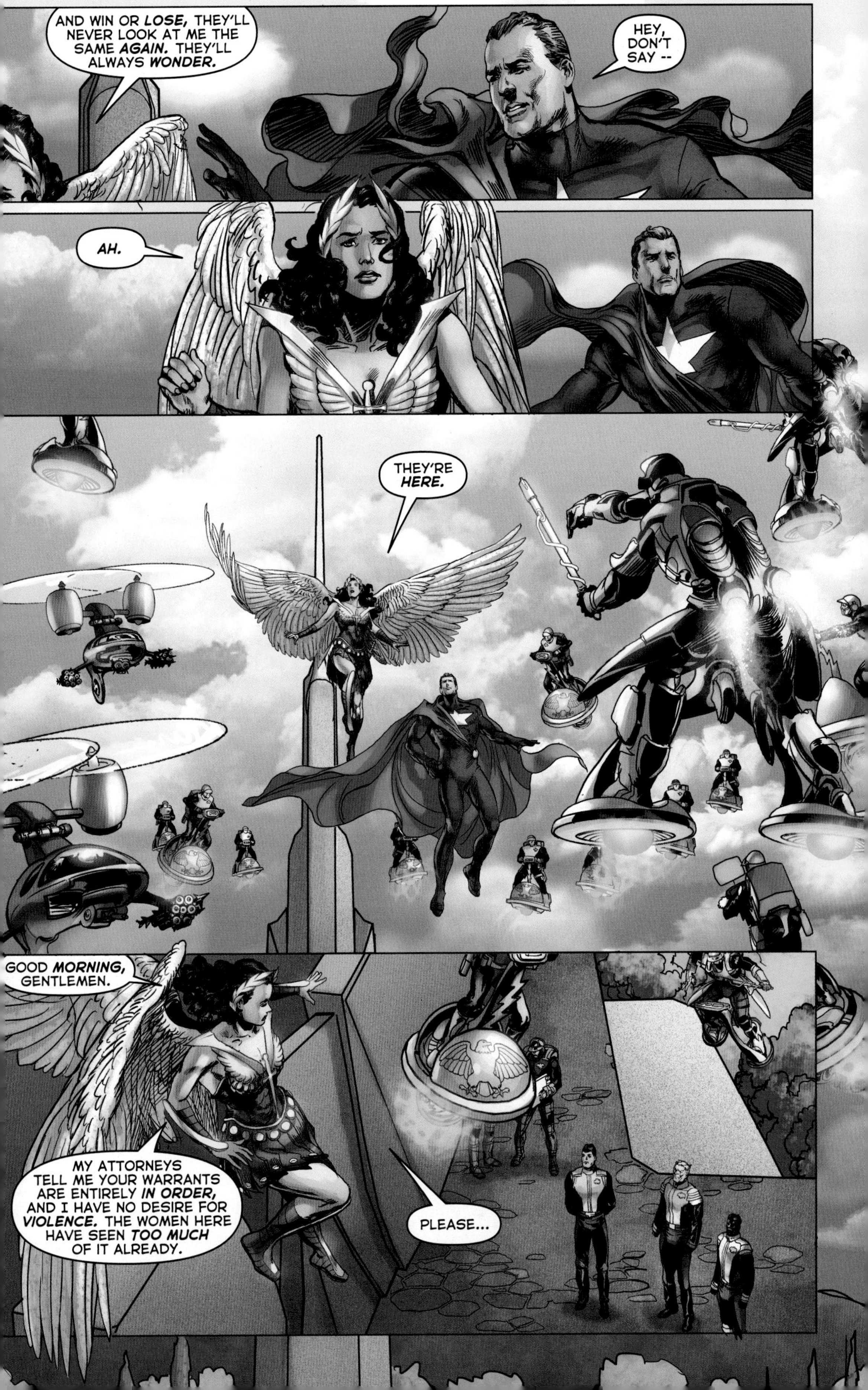
AND WIN OR LOSE, THEY'LL NEVER LOOK AT ME THE SAME AGAIN. THEY'LL ALWAYS WONDER.
HEY, DON'T SAY --
AH.
THEY'RE HERE.
GOOD MORNING, GENTLEMEN.
MY ATTORNEYS TELL ME YOUR WARRANTS ARE ENTIRELY IN ORDER, AND I HAVE NO DESIRE FOR VIOLENCE. THE WOMEN HERE HAVE SEEN TOO MUCH OF IT ALREADY.
PLEASE...

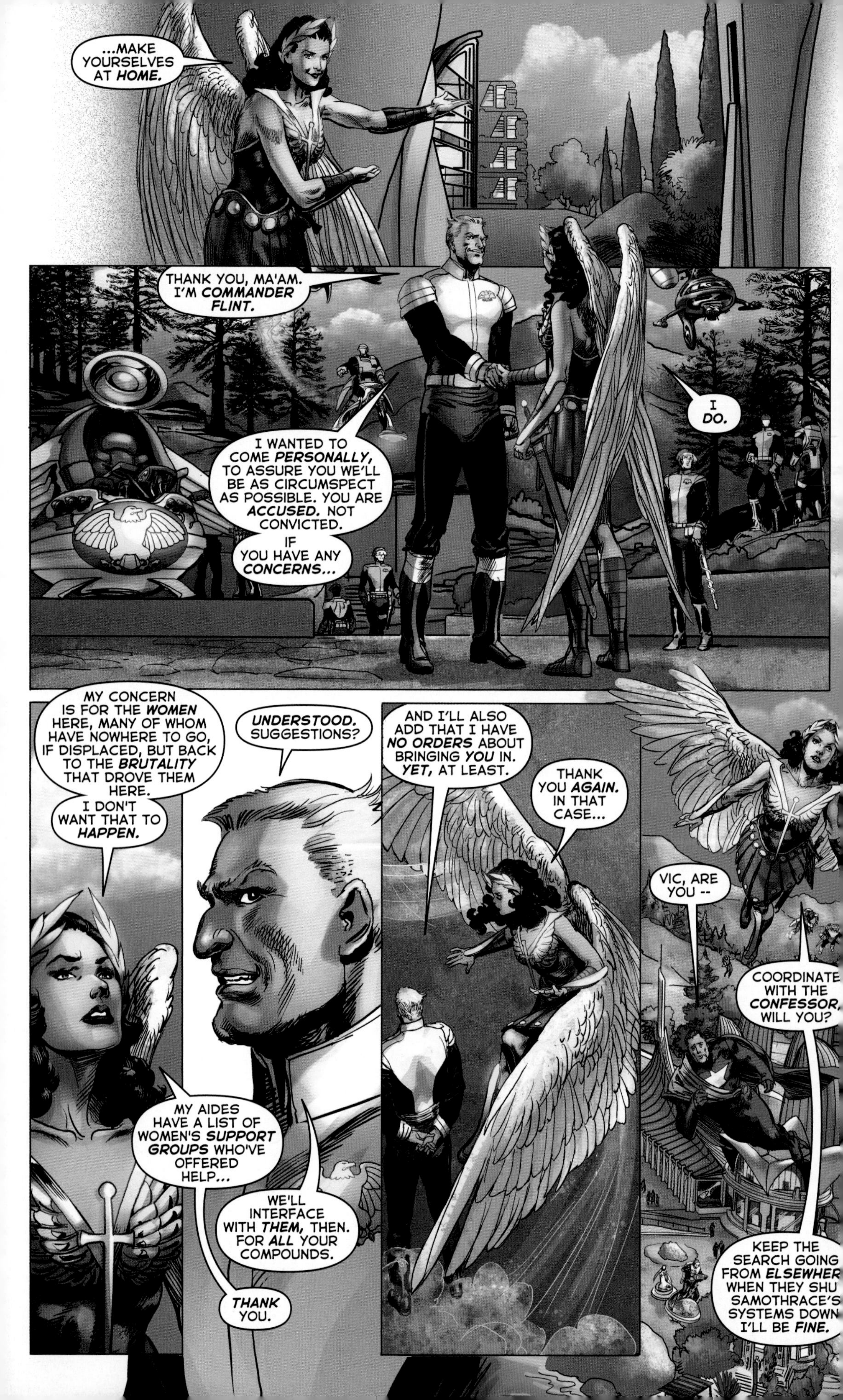
...MAKE YOURSELVES AT HOME.
THANK YOU, MA'AM. I'M COMMANDER FLINT.
I WANTED TO COME PERSONALLY, TO ASSURE YOU WE'LL BE AS CIRCUMSPECT AS POSSIBLE. YOU ARE ACCUSED. NOT CONVICTED.
IF YOU HAVE ANY CONCERNS...
I DO.
MY CONCERN IS FOR THE WOMEN HERE, MANY OF WHOM HAVE NOWHERE TO GO, IF DISPLACED, BUT BACK TO THE BRUTALITY THAT DROVE THEM HERE.
I DON'T WANT THAT TO HAPPEN.
UNDERSTOOD. SUGGESTIONS?
MY AIDES HAVE A LIST OF WOMEN'S SUPPORT GROUPS WHO'VE OFFERED HELP...
WE'LL INTERFACE WITH THEM, THEN. FOR ALL YOUR COMPOUNDS.
THANK YOU.
AND I'LL ALSO ADD THAT I HAVE NO ORDERS ABOUT BRINGING YOU IN. YET, AT LEAST.
THANK YOU AGAIN. IN THAT CASE...
VIC, ARE YOU --
COORDINATE WITH THE CONFESSOR, WILL YOU?
KEEP THE SEARCH GOING FROM ELSEWHER WHEN THEY SHU SAMOTHRACE'S SYSTEMS DOWN I'LL BE FINE.

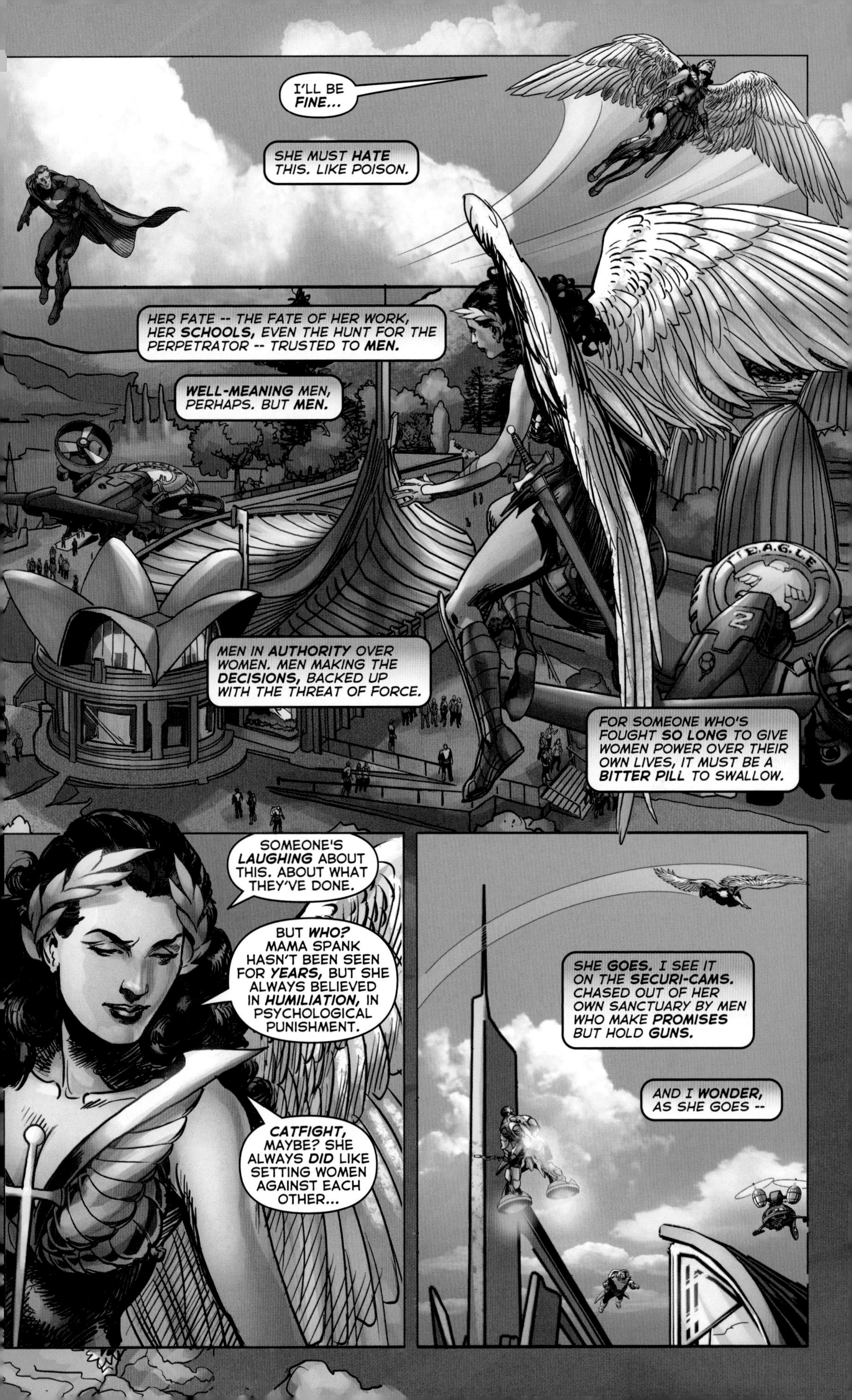
I'LL BE FINE...
SHE MUST HATE THIS. LIKE POISON.
HER FATE -- THE FATE OF HER WORK, HER SCHOOLS, EVEN THE HUNT FOR THE PERPETRATOR -- TRUSTED TO MEN.
WELL-MEANING MEN, PERHAPS. BUT MEN.
MEN IN AUTHORITY OVER WOMEN. MEN MAKING THE DECISIONS, BACKED UP WITH THE THREAT OF FORCE.
E.A.G.L.E
2
FOR SOMEONE WHO'S FOUGHT SO LONG TO GIVE WOMEN POWER OVER THEIR OWN LIVES, IT MUST BE A BITTER PILL TO SWALLOW.
SOMEONE'S LAUGHING ABOUT THIS. ABOUT WHAT THEY'VE DONE.
BUT WHO? MAMA SPANK HASN'T BEEN SEEN FOR YEARS, BUT SHE ALWAYS BELIEVED IN HUMILIATION, IN PSYCHOLOGICAL PUNISHMENT.
CATFIGHT, MAYBE? SHE ALWAYS DID LIKE SETTING WOMEN AGAINST EACH OTHER...
SHE GOES. I SEE IT ON THE SECURI-CAMS. CHASED OUT OF HER OWN SANCTUARY BY MEN WHO MAKE PROMISES BUT HOLD GUNS.
AND I WONDER, AS SHE GOES --

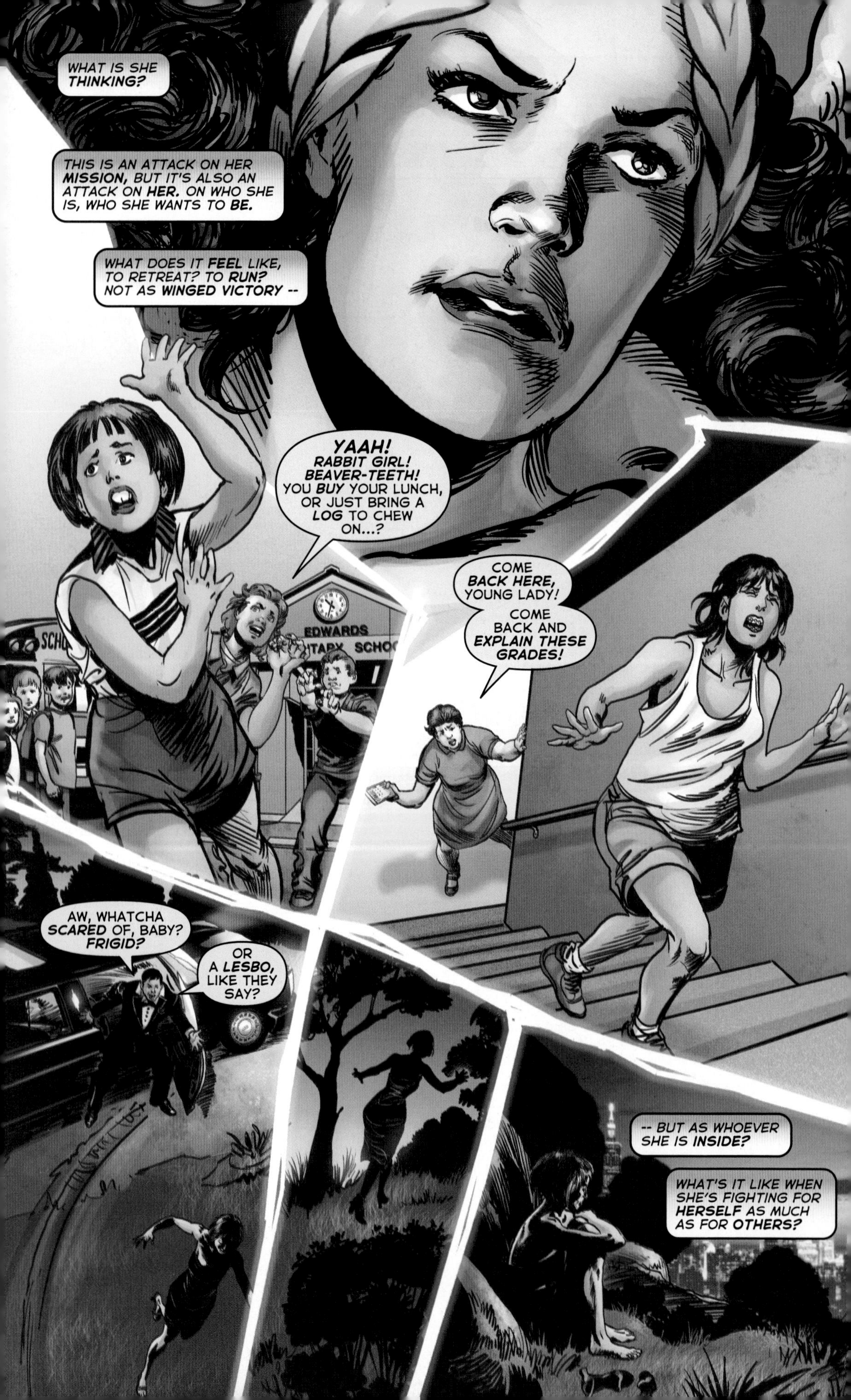
WHAT IS SHE THINKING?
THIS IS AN ATTACK ON HER MISSION, BUT IT'S ALSO AN ATTACK ON HER. ON WHO SHE IS, WHO SHE WANTS TO BE.
WHAT DOES IT FEEL LIKE, TO RETREAT? TO RUN? NOT AS WINGED VICTORY --
YAAH! RABBIT GIRL! BEAVER-TEETH! YOU BUY YOUR LUNCH, OR JUST BRING A LOG TO CHEW ON...?
EDWARDS
COME BACK HERE, YOUNG LADY!
COME BACK AND EXPLAIN THESE GRADES!
AW, WHATCHA SCARED OF, BABY? FRIGID?
OR A LESBO, LIKE THEY SAY?
-- BUT AS WHOEVER SHE IS INSIDE?
WHAT'S IT LIKE WHEN SHE'S FIGHTING FOR HERSELF AS MUCH AS FOR OTHERS?

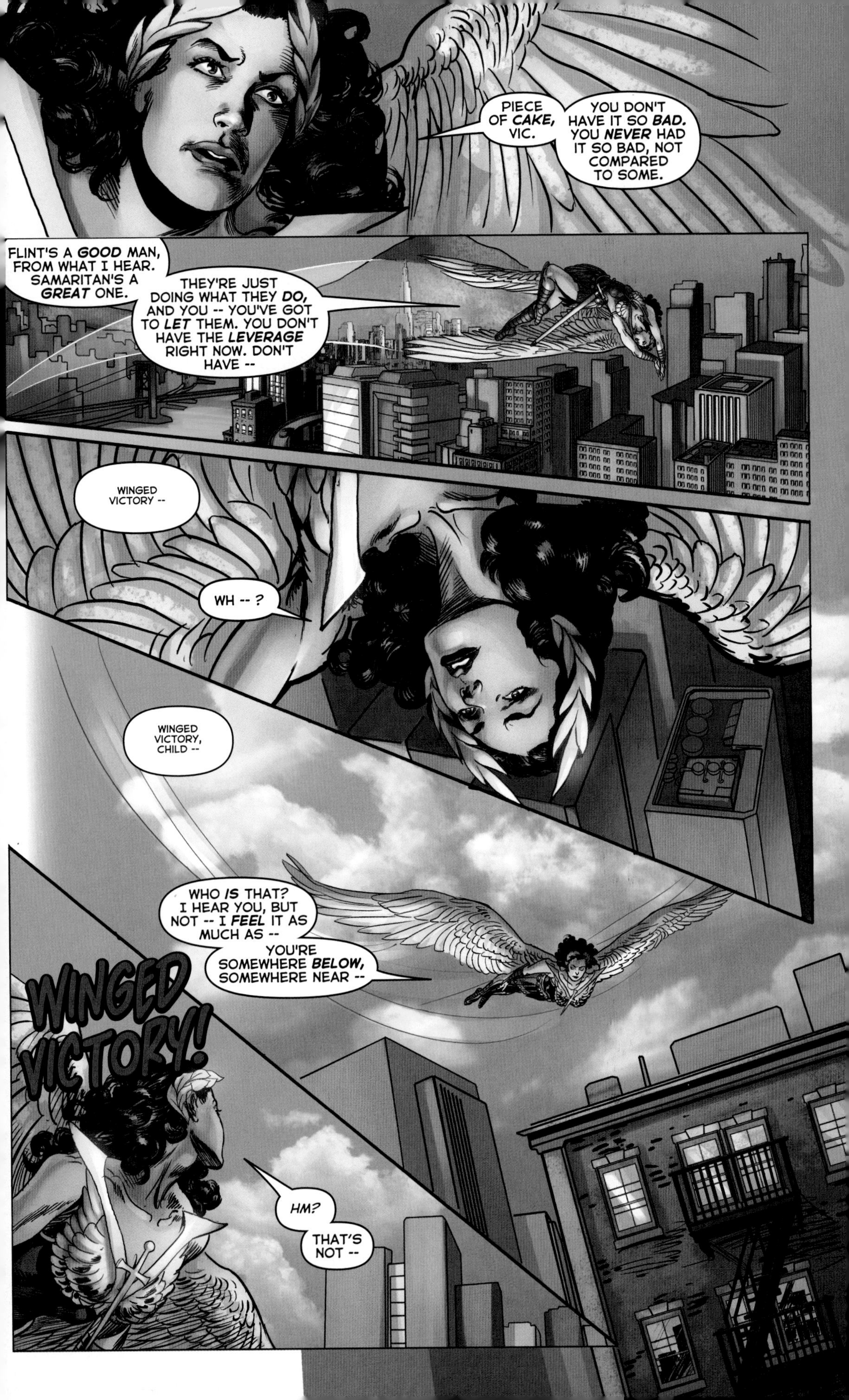
PIECE OF CAKE, VIC.
YOU DON'T HAVE IT SO BAD. YOU NEVER HAD IT SO BAD, NOT COMPARED TO SOME.
FLINT'S A GOOD MAN, FROM WHAT I HEAR. SAMARITAN'S A GREAT ONE.
THEY'RE JUST DOING WHAT THEY DO, AND YOU -- YOU'VE GOT TO LET THEM. YOU DON'T HAVE THE LEVERAGE RIGHT NOW. DON'T HAVE --
WINGED VICTORY --
WH -- ?
WINGED VICTORY, CHILD --
WHO IS THAT? I HEAR YOU, BUT NOT -- I FEEL IT AS MUCH AS --
YOU'RE SOMEWHERE BELOW, SOMEWHERE NEAR --
WINGED VICTORY!
HM?
THAT'S NOT --

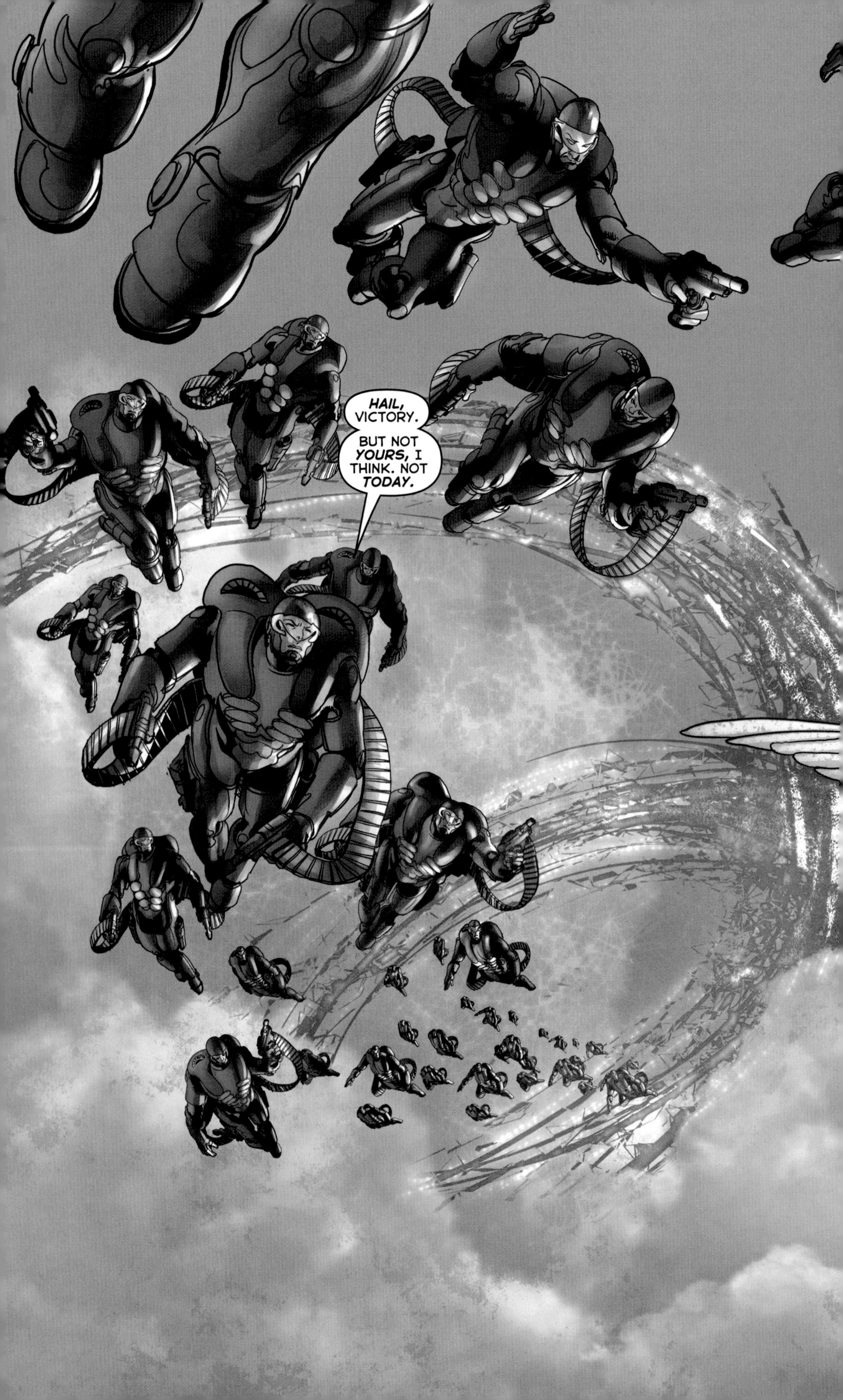
HAIL, VICTORY.
BUT NOT YOURS, I THINK. NOT TODAY.

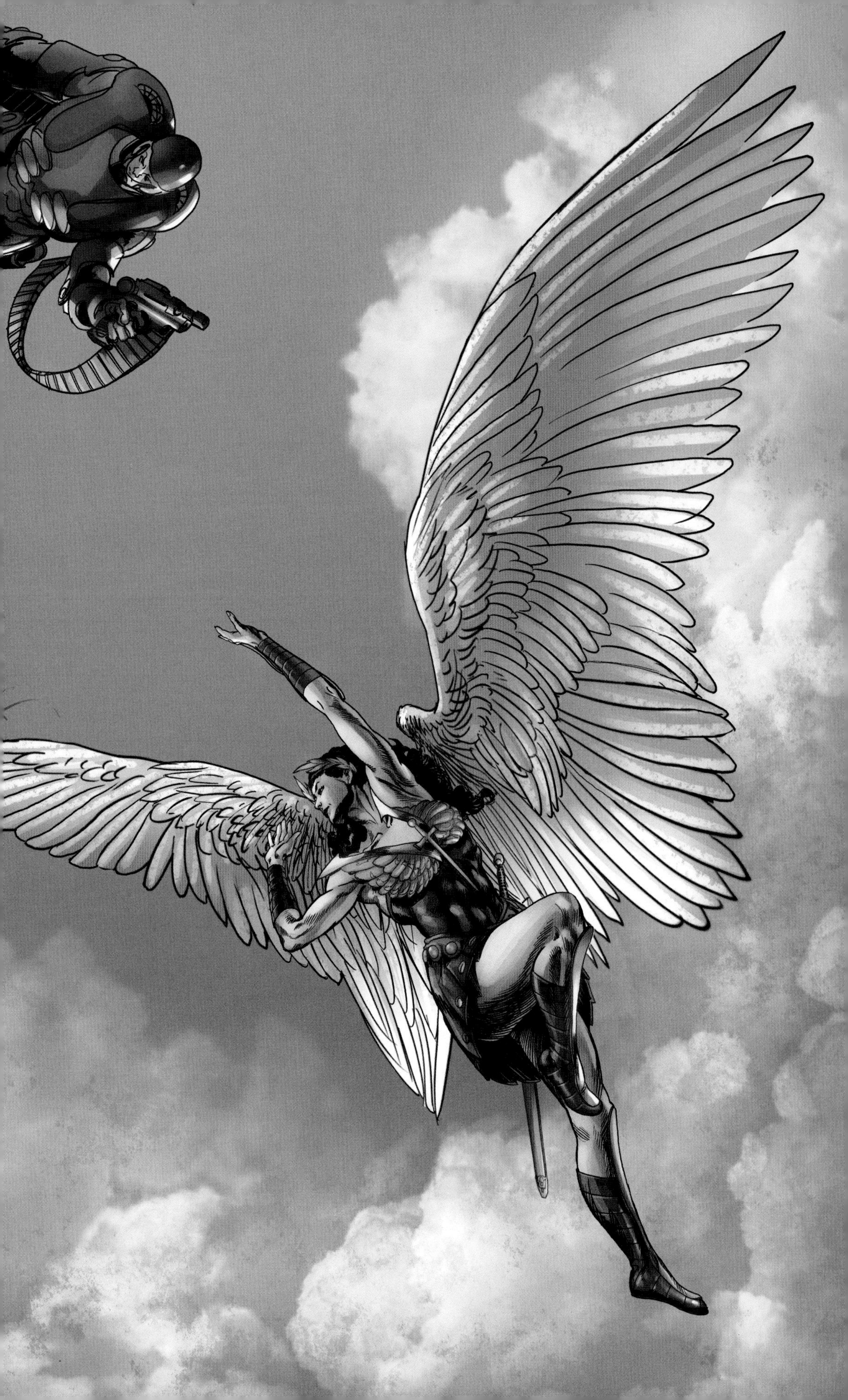

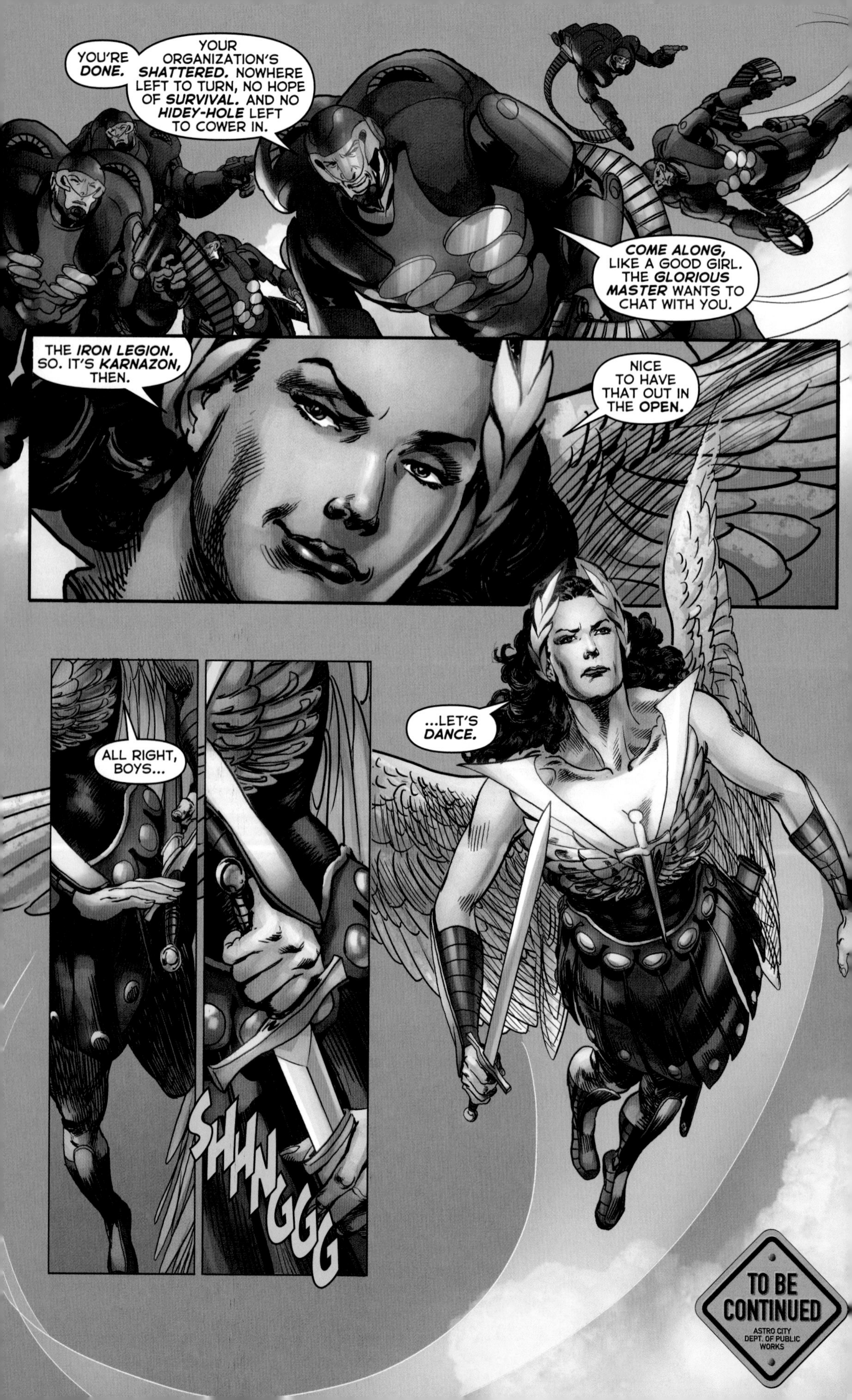
YOU'RE DONE.
YOUR ORGANIZATION'S SHATTERED. NOWHERE LEFT TO TURN, NO HOPE OF SURVIVAL. AND NO HIDEY-HOLE LEFT TO COWER IN.
COME ALONG, LIKE A GOOD GIRL. THE GLORIOUS MASTER WANTS TO CHAT WITH YOU.
THE IRON LEGION. SO. IT'S KARNAZON, THEN.
NICE TO HAVE THAT OUT IN THE OPEN.
ALL RIGHT, BOYS...
SHHNGGG
...LET'S DANCE.
TO BE CONTINUED
ASTRO CITY DEPT. OF PUBLIC WORKS

THREE

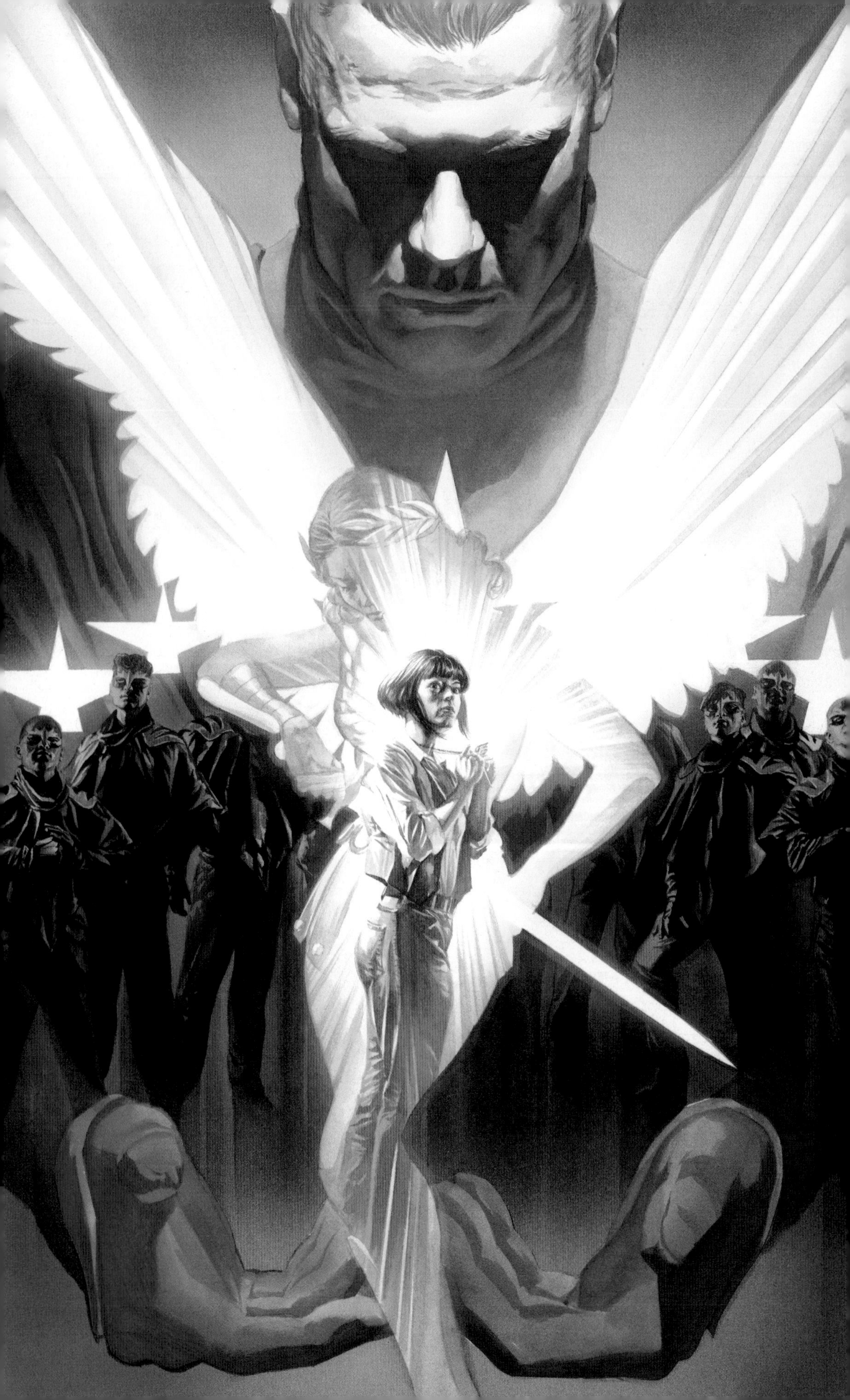

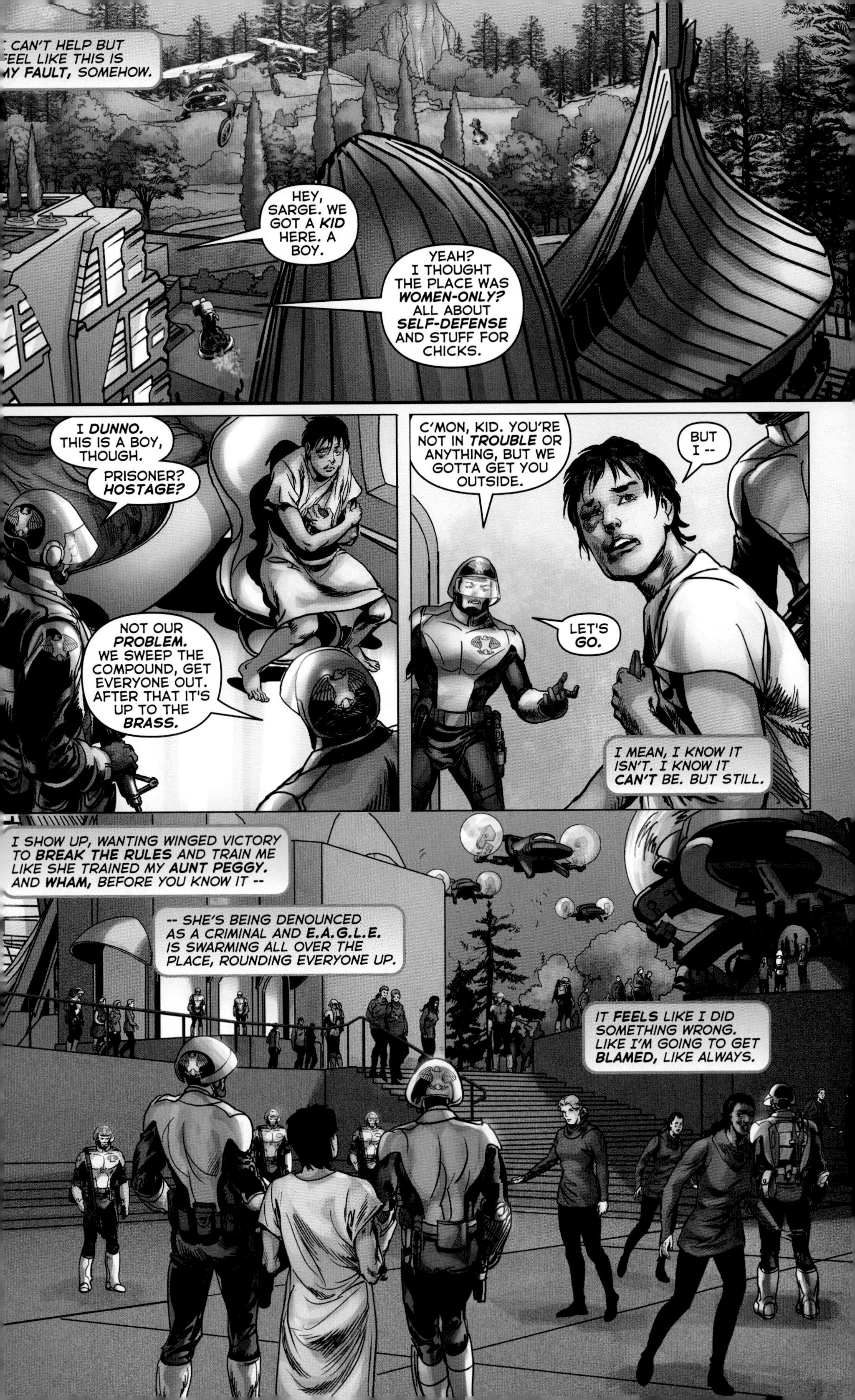
I CAN'T HELP BUT FEEL LIKE THIS IS MY FAULT, SOMEHOW.
HEY, SARGE. WE GOT A KID HERE. A BOY.
YEAH? I THOUGHT THE PLACE WAS WOMEN-ONLY? ALL ABOUT SELF-DEFENSE AND STUFF FOR CHICKS.
I DUNNO. THIS IS A BOY, THOUGH.
PRISONER? HOSTAGE?
NOT OUR PROBLEM. WE SWEEP THE COMPOUND, GET EVERYONE OUT. AFTER THAT IT'S UP TO THE BRASS.
C'MON, KID. YOU'RE NOT IN TROUBLE OR ANYTHING, BUT WE GOTTA GET YOU OUTSIDE.
BUT I --
LET'S GO.
I MEAN, I KNOW IT ISN'T. I KNOW IT CAN'T BE. BUT STILL.
I SHOW UP, WANTING WINGED VICTORY TO BREAK THE RULES AND TRAIN ME LIKE SHE TRAINED MY AUNT PEGGY. AND WHAM, BEFORE YOU KNOW IT --
-- SHE'S BEING DENOUNCED AS A CRIMINAL AND E.A.G.L.E. IS SWARMING ALL OVER THE PLACE, ROUNDING EVERYONE UP.
IT FEELS LIKE I DID SOMETHING WRONG. LIKE I'M GOING TO GET BLAMED, LIKE ALWAYS.

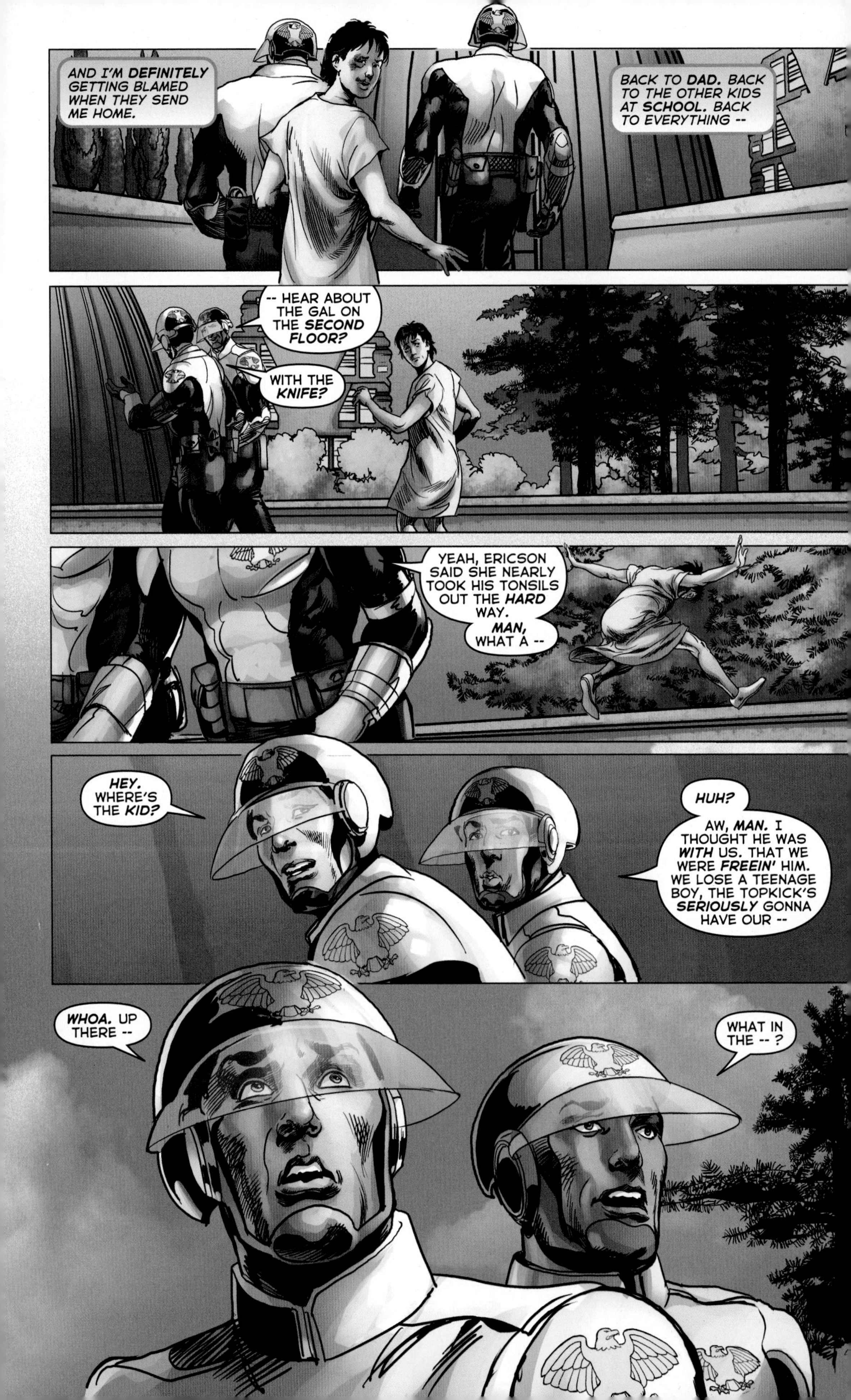
AND I'M DEFINITELY GETTING BLAMED WHEN THEY SEND ME HOME.
BACK TO DAD. BACK TO THE OTHER KIDS AT SCHOOL. BACK TO EVERYTHING --
-- HEAR ABOUT THE GAL ON THE SECOND FLOOR?
WITH THE KNIFE?
YEAH, ERICSON SAID SHE NEARLY TOOK HIS TONSILS OUT THE HARD WAY. MAN, WHAT A --
HEY. WHERE'S THE KID?
HUH?
AW, MAN. I THOUGHT HE WAS WITH US. THAT WE WERE FREEIN' HIM. WE LOSE A TEENAGE BOY, THE TOPKICK'S SERIOUSLY GONNA HAVE OUR --
WHOA. UP THERE --
WHAT IN THE -- ?

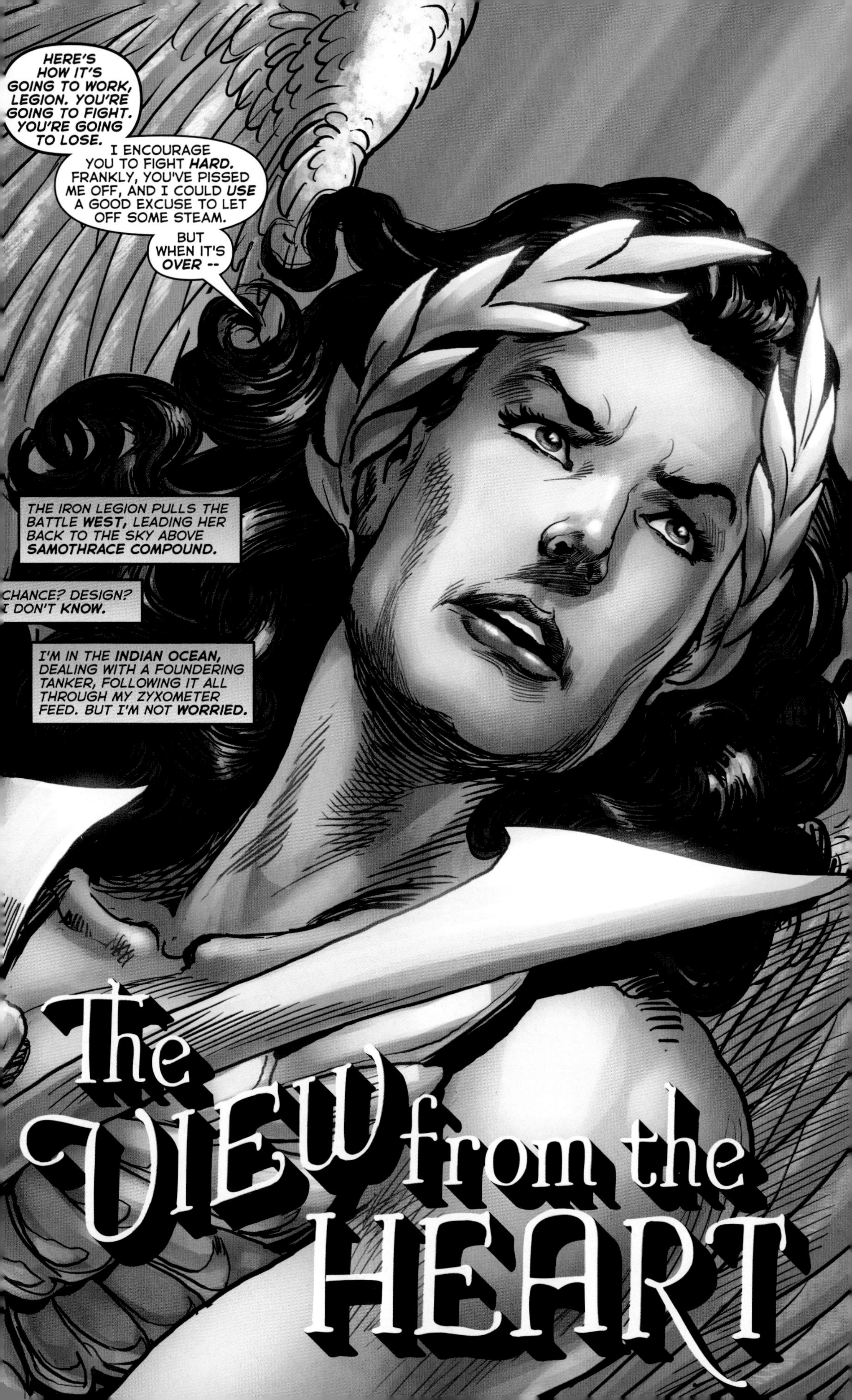

HERE'S HOW IT'S GOING TO WORK, LEGION. YOU'RE GOING TO FIGHT. YOU'RE GOING TO LOSE.
I ENCOURAGE YOU TO FIGHT HARD. FRANKLY, YOU'VE PISSED ME OFF, AND I COULD USE A GOOD EXCUSE TO LET OFF SOME STEAM.
BUT WHEN IT'S OVER --
THE IRON LEGION PULLS THE BATTLE WEST, LEADING HER BACK TO THE SKY ABOVE SAMOTHRACE COMPOUND.
CHANCE? DESIGN? I DON'T KNOW.
I'M IN THE INDIAN OCEAN, DEALING WITH A FOUNDERING TANKER, FOLLOWING IT ALL THROUGH MY ZYXOMETER FEED. BUT I'M NOT WORRIED.
The VIEW from the HEART

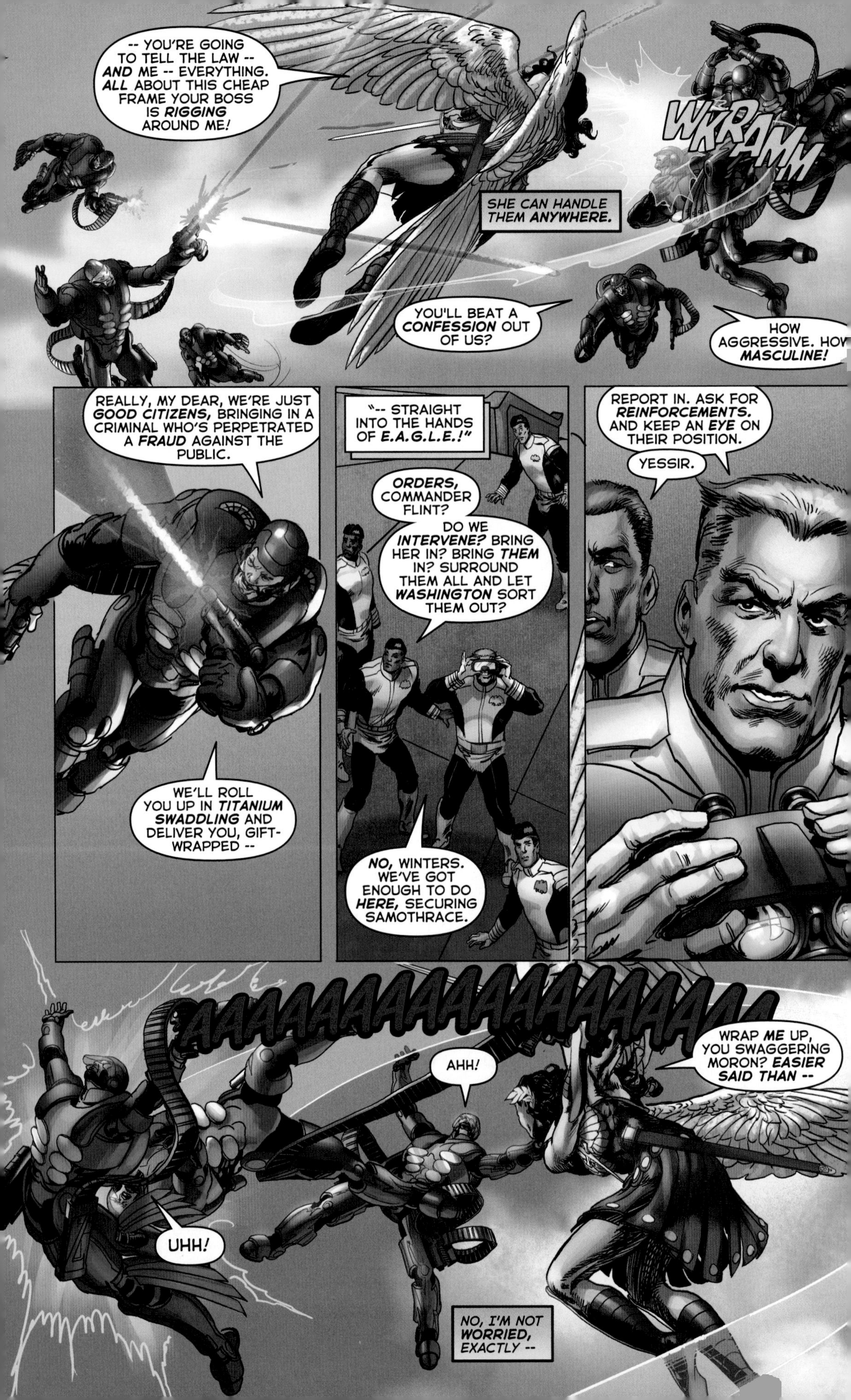
-- YOU'RE GOING TO TELL THE LAW -- AND ME -- EVERYTHING. ALL ABOUT THIS CHEAP FRAME YOUR BOSS IS RIGGING AROUND ME!
WKRAMM
SHE CAN HANDLE THEM ANYWHERE.
YOU'LL BEAT A CONFESSION OUT OF US?
HOW AGGRESSIVE. HOW MASCULINE!
REALLY, MY DEAR, WE'RE JUST GOOD CITIZENS, BRINGING IN A CRIMINAL WHO'S PERPETRATED A FRAUD AGAINST THE PUBLIC.
WE'LL ROLL YOU UP IN TITANIUM SWADDLING AND DELIVER YOU, GIFT-WRAPPED --
"-- STRAIGHT INTO THE HANDS OF E.A.G.L.E.!"
ORDERS, COMMANDER FLINT?
DO WE INTERVENE? BRING HER IN? BRING THEM IN? SURROUND THEM ALL AND LET WASHINGTON SORT THEM OUT?
NO, WINTERS. WE'VE GOT ENOUGH TO DO HERE, SECURING SAMOTHRACE.
REPORT IN. ASK FOR REINFORCEMENTS. AND KEEP AN EYE ON THEIR POSITION.
YESSIR.
AAAAAAAAAAAAAAAAAAA
AHH!
WRAP ME UP, YOU SWAGGERING MORON? EASIER SAID THAN --
UHH!
NO, I'M NOT WORRIED, EXACTLY --

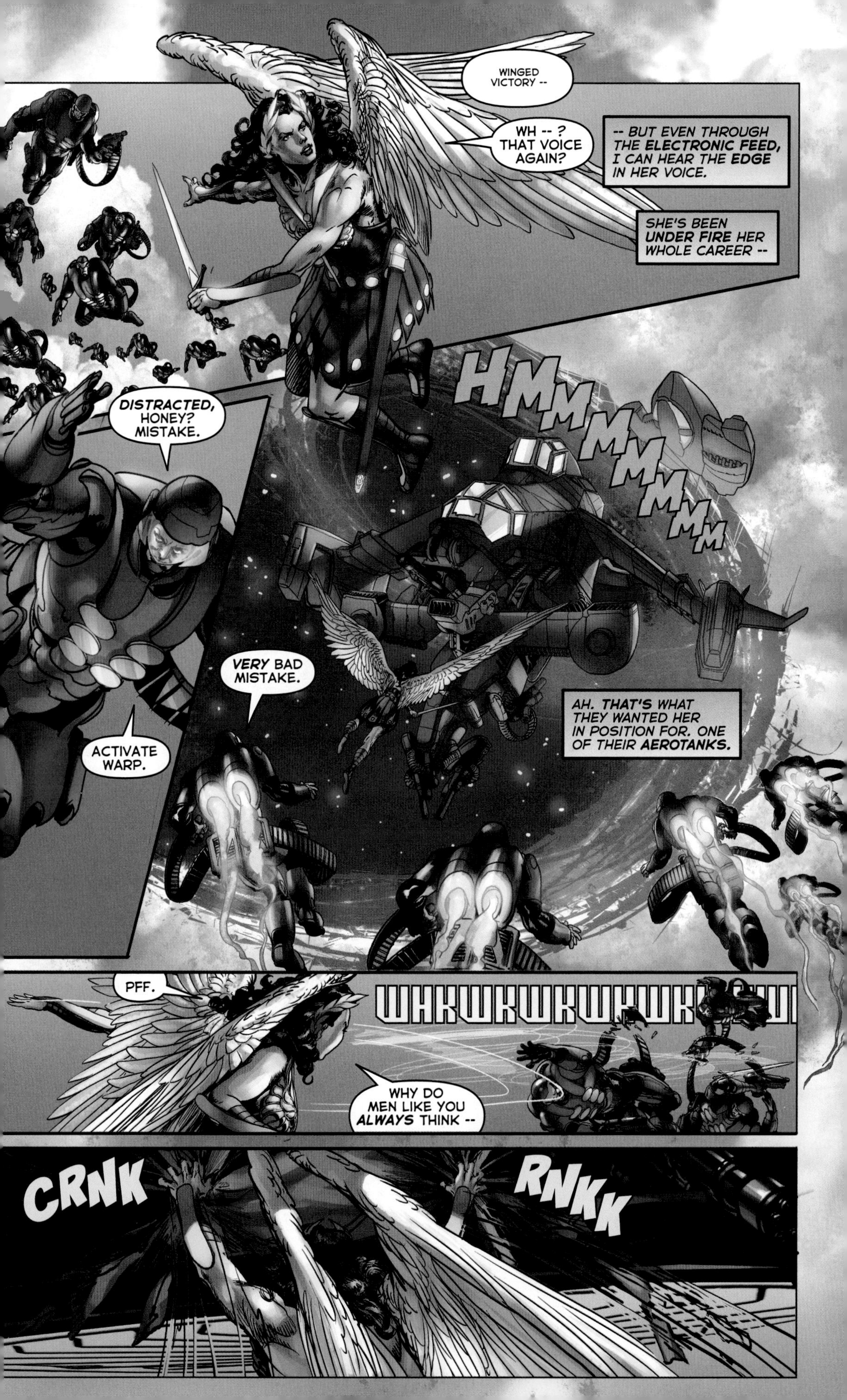
WINGED VICTORY --
WH -- ? THAT VOICE AGAIN?
-- BUT EVEN THROUGH THE ELECTRONIC FEED, I CAN HEAR THE EDGE IN HER VOICE.
SHE'S BEEN UNDER FIRE HER WHOLE CAREER --
DISTRACTED, HONEY? MISTAKE.
HMMMMMMMMMMM
VERY BAD MISTAKE.
ACTIVATE WARP.
AH. THAT'S WHAT THEY WANTED HER IN POSITION FOR. ONE OF THEIR AEROTANKS.
PFF.
WHKWKWKWKWK
WHY DO MEN LIKE YOU ALWAYS THINK --
CRNK
RNKK

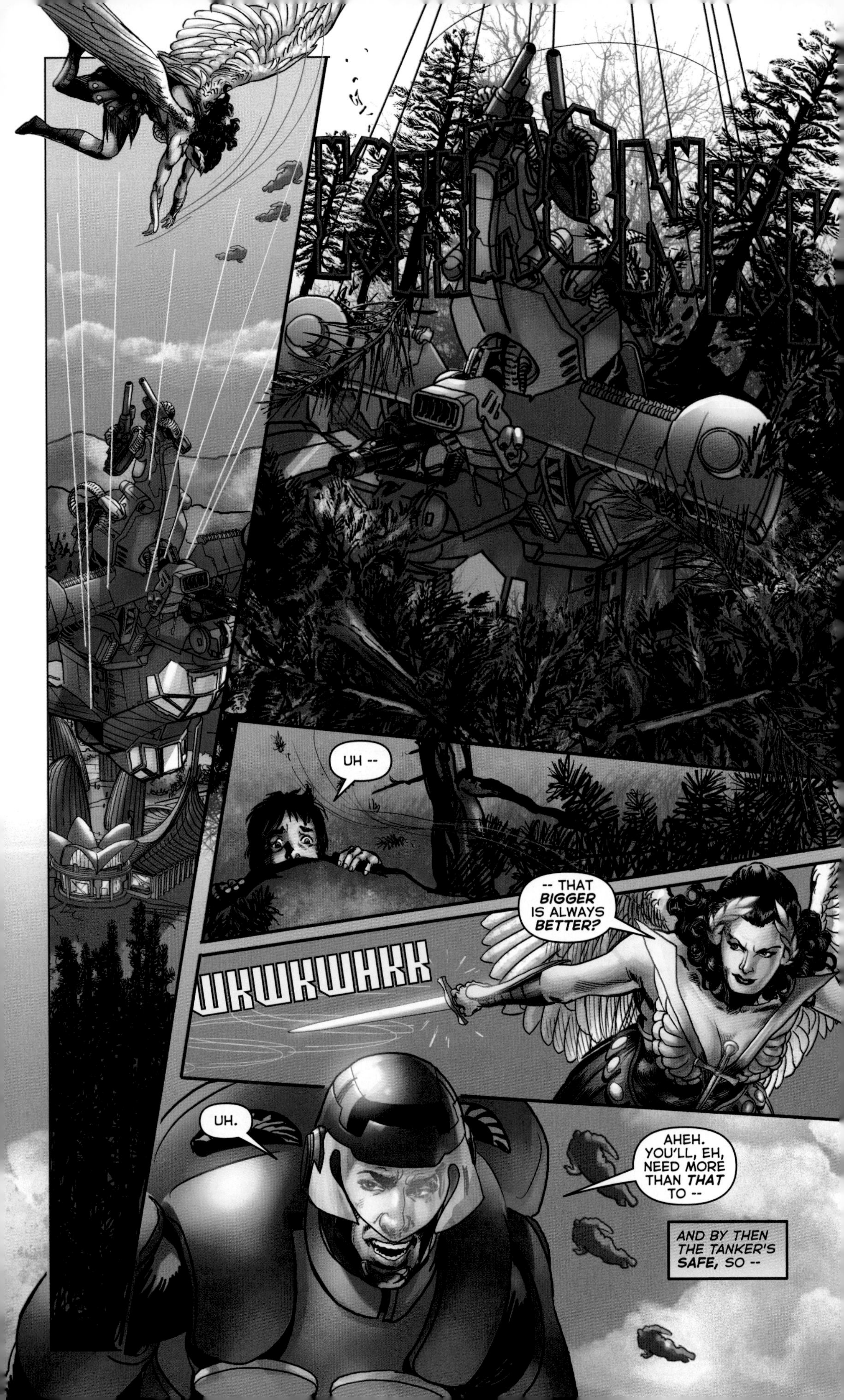
KKRUNK
UH --
-- THAT BIGGER IS ALWAYS BETTER?
WKWKWAKK
UH.
AHEH. YOU'LL, EH, NEED MORE THAN THAT TO --
AND BY THEN THE TANKER'S SAFE, SO --

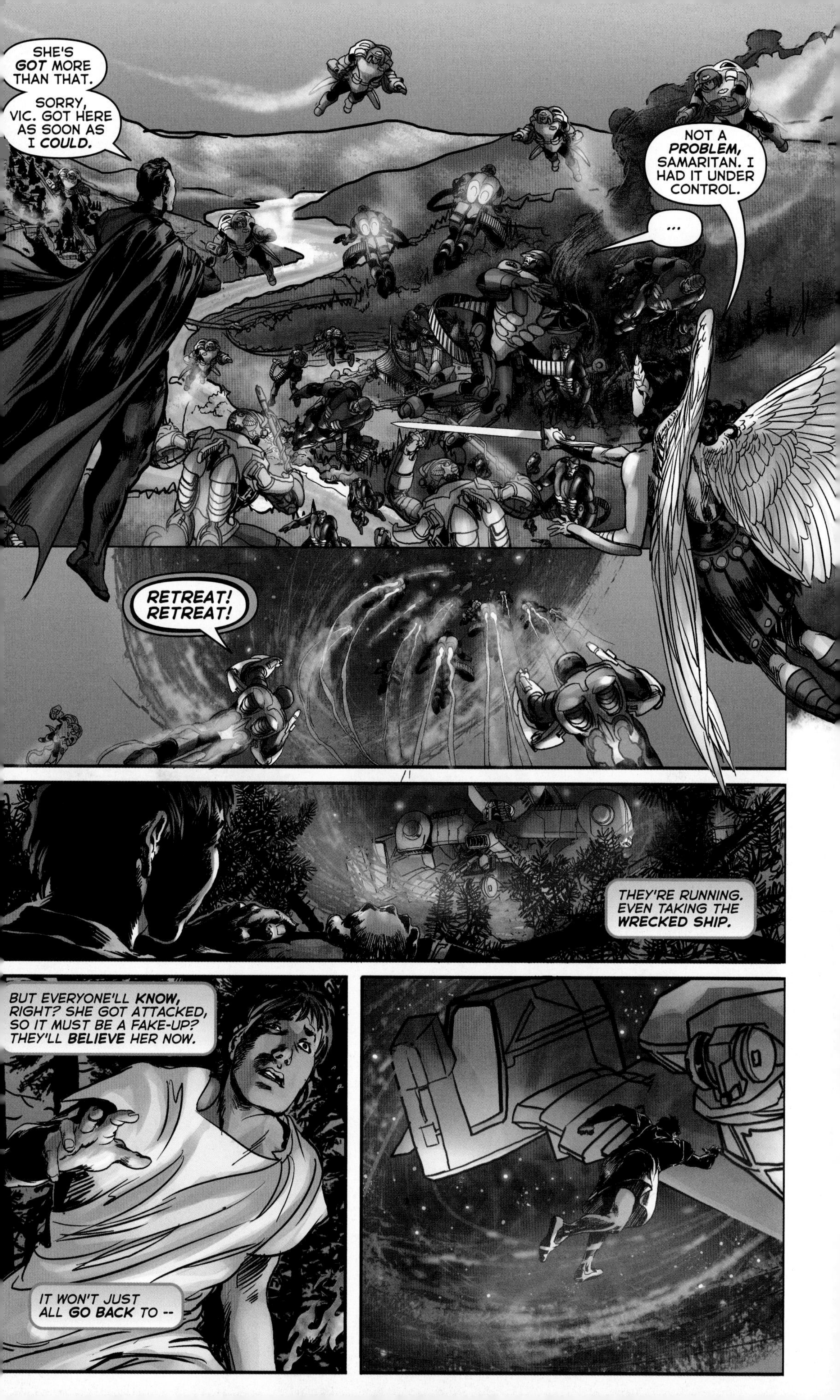
SHE'S GOT MORE THAN THAT.
SORRY, VIC. GOT HERE AS SOON AS I COULD.
NOT A PROBLEM, SAMARITAN. I HAD IT UNDER CONTROL.
...
RETREAT! RETREAT!
THEY'RE RUNNING. EVEN TAKING THE WRECKED SHIP.
BUT EVERYONE'LL KNOW, RIGHT? SHE GOT ATTACKED, SO IT MUST BE A FAKE-UP? THEY'LL BELIEVE HER NOW.
IT WON'T JUST ALL GO BACK TO --

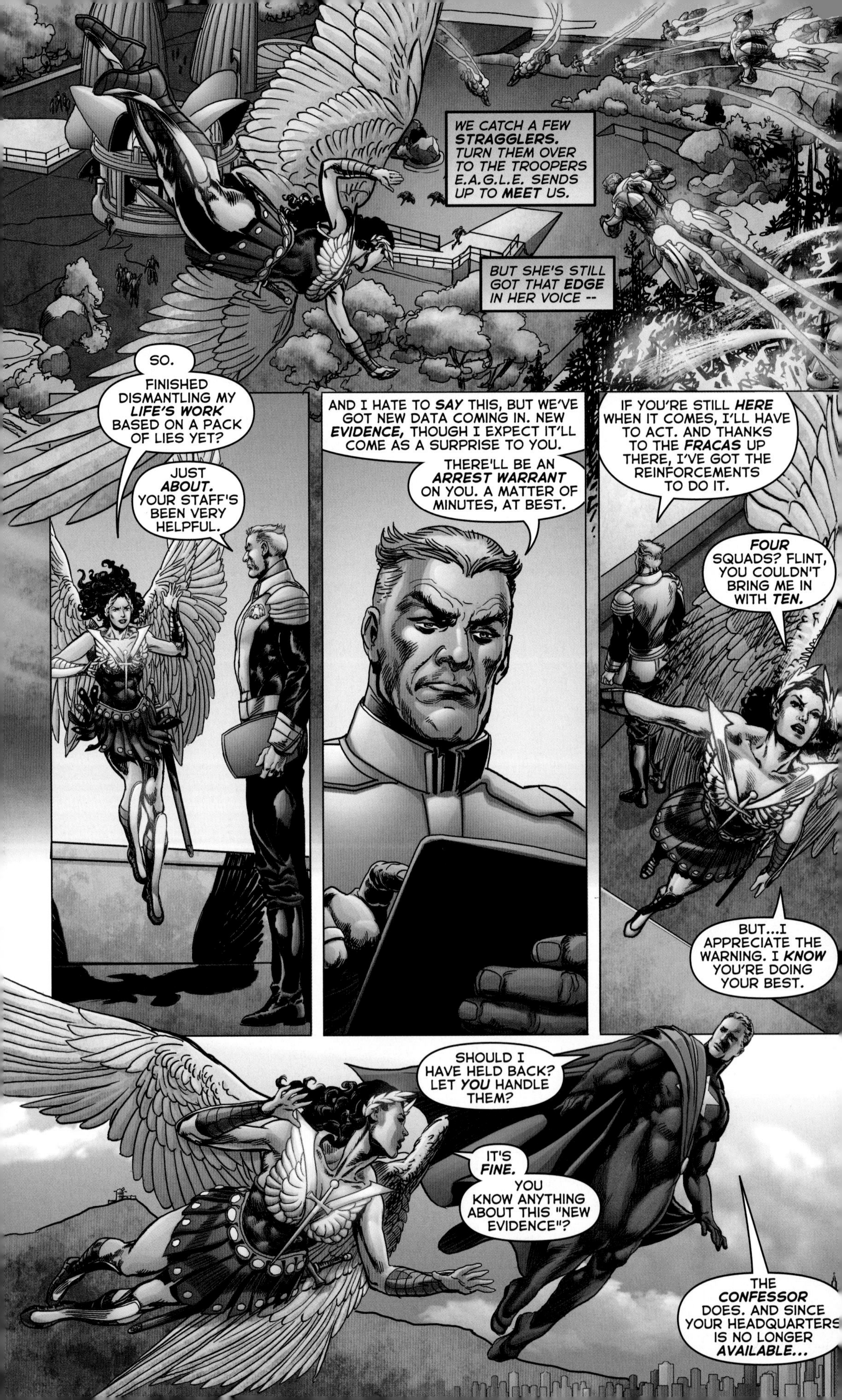

WE CATCH A FEW STRAGGLERS. TURN THEM OVER TO THE TROOPERS E.A.G.L.E. SENDS UP TO MEET US.
BUT SHE'S STILL GOT THAT EDGE IN HER VOICE --
SO.
FINISHED DISMANTLING MY LIFE'S WORK BASED ON A PACK OF LIES YET?
JUST ABOUT. YOUR STAFF'S BEEN VERY HELPFUL.
AND I HATE TO SAY THIS, BUT WE'VE GOT NEW DATA COMING IN. NEW EVIDENCE, THOUGH I EXPECT IT'LL COME AS A SURPRISE TO YOU.
THERE'LL BE AN ARREST WARRANT ON YOU. A MATTER OF MINUTES, AT BEST.
IF YOU'RE STILL HERE WHEN IT COMES, I'LL HAVE TO ACT. AND THANKS TO THE FRACAS UP THERE, I'VE GOT THE REINFORCEMENTS TO DO IT.
FOUR SQUADS? FLINT, YOU COULDN'T BRING ME IN WITH TEN.
BUT...I APPRECIATE THE WARNING. I KNOW YOU'RE DOING YOUR BEST.
SHOULD I HAVE HELD BACK? LET YOU HANDLE THEM?
IT'S FINE.
YOU KNOW ANYTHING ABOUT THIS "NEW EVIDENCE"?
THE CONFESSOR DOES. AND SINCE YOUR HEADQUARTERS IS NO LONGER AVAILABLE...

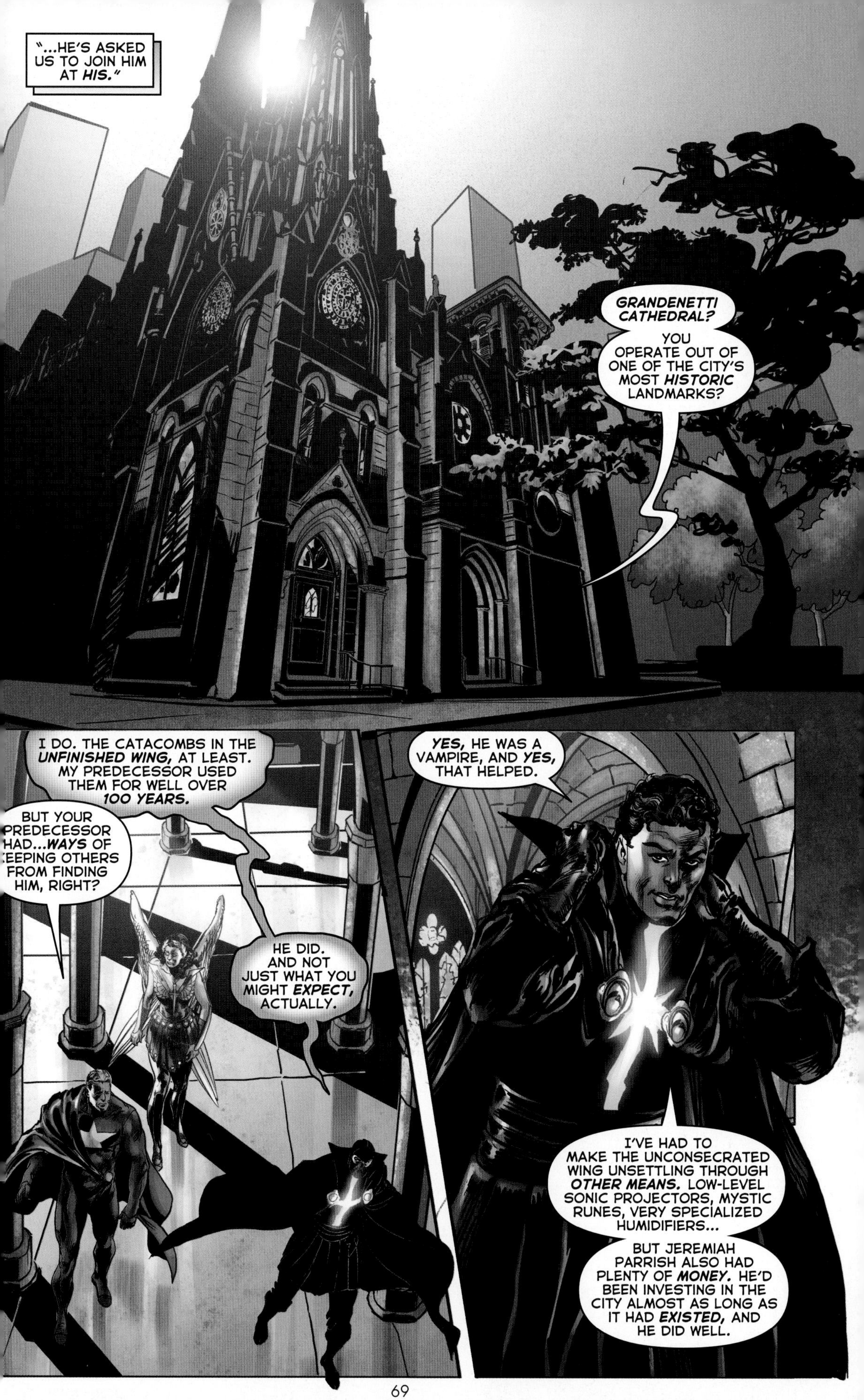
"...HE'S ASKED US TO JOIN HIM AT HIS."
GRANDENETTI CATHEDRAL?
YOU OPERATE OUT OF ONE OF THE CITY'S MOST HISTORIC LANDMARKS?
I DO. THE CATACOMBS IN THE UNFINISHED WING, AT LEAST. MY PREDECESSOR USED THEM FOR WELL OVER 100 YEARS.
BUT YOUR PREDECESSOR HAD...WAYS OF KEEPING OTHERS FROM FINDING HIM, RIGHT?
HE DID. AND NOT JUST WHAT YOU MIGHT EXPECT, ACTUALLY.
YES, HE WAS A VAMPIRE, AND YES, THAT HELPED.
I'VE HAD TO MAKE THE UNCONSECRATED WING UNSETTLING THROUGH OTHER MEANS. LOW-LEVEL SONIC PROJECTORS, MYSTIC RUNES, VERY SPECIALIZED HUMIDIFIERS...
BUT JEREMIAH PARRISH ALSO HAD PLENTY OF MONEY. HE'D BEEN INVESTING IN THE CITY ALMOST AS LONG AS IT HAD EXISTED, AND HE DID WELL.

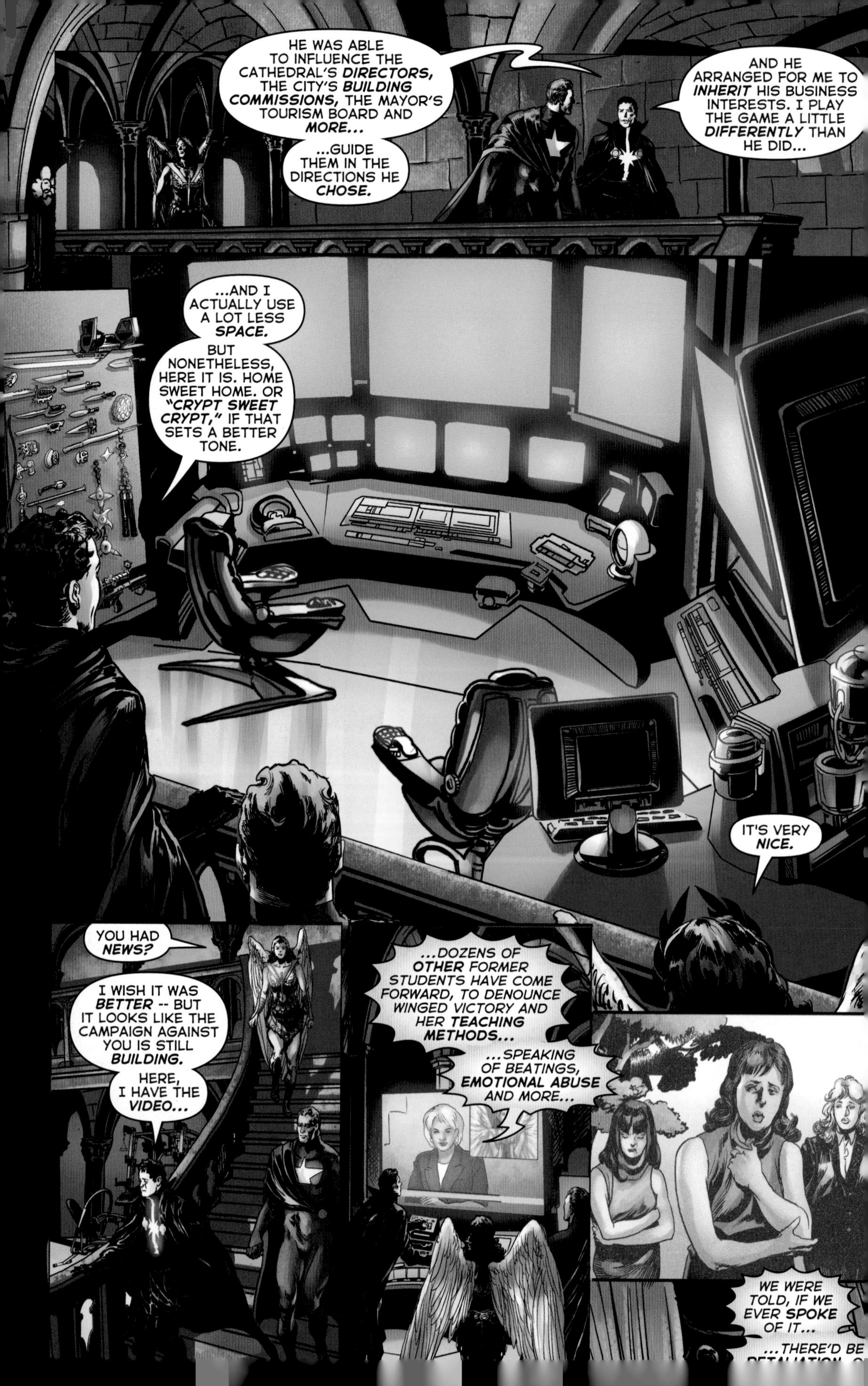
HE WAS ABLE TO INFLUENCE THE CATHEDRAL'S DIRECTORS, THE CITY'S BUILDING COMMISSIONS, THE MAYOR'S TOURISM BOARD AND MORE...
...GUIDE THEM IN THE DIRECTIONS HE CHOSE.
AND HE ARRANGED FOR ME TO INHERIT HIS BUSINESS INTERESTS. I PLAY THE GAME A LITTLE DIFFERENTLY THAN HE DID...
...AND I ACTUALLY USE A LOT LESS SPACE.
BUT NONETHELESS, HERE IT IS. HOME SWEET HOME. OR "CRYPT SWEET CRYPT," IF THAT SETS A BETTER TONE.
IT'S VERY NICE.
YOU HAD NEWS?
I WISH IT WAS BETTER -- BUT IT LOOKS LIKE THE CAMPAIGN AGAINST YOU IS STILL BUILDING.
HERE, I HAVE THE VIDEO...
...DOZENS OF OTHER FORMER STUDENTS HAVE COME FORWARD, TO DENOUNCE WINGED VICTORY AND HER TEACHING METHODS...
...SPEAKING OF BEATINGS, EMOTIONAL ABUSE AND MORE...
WE WERE TOLD, IF WE EVER SPOKE OF IT...
...THERE'D BE

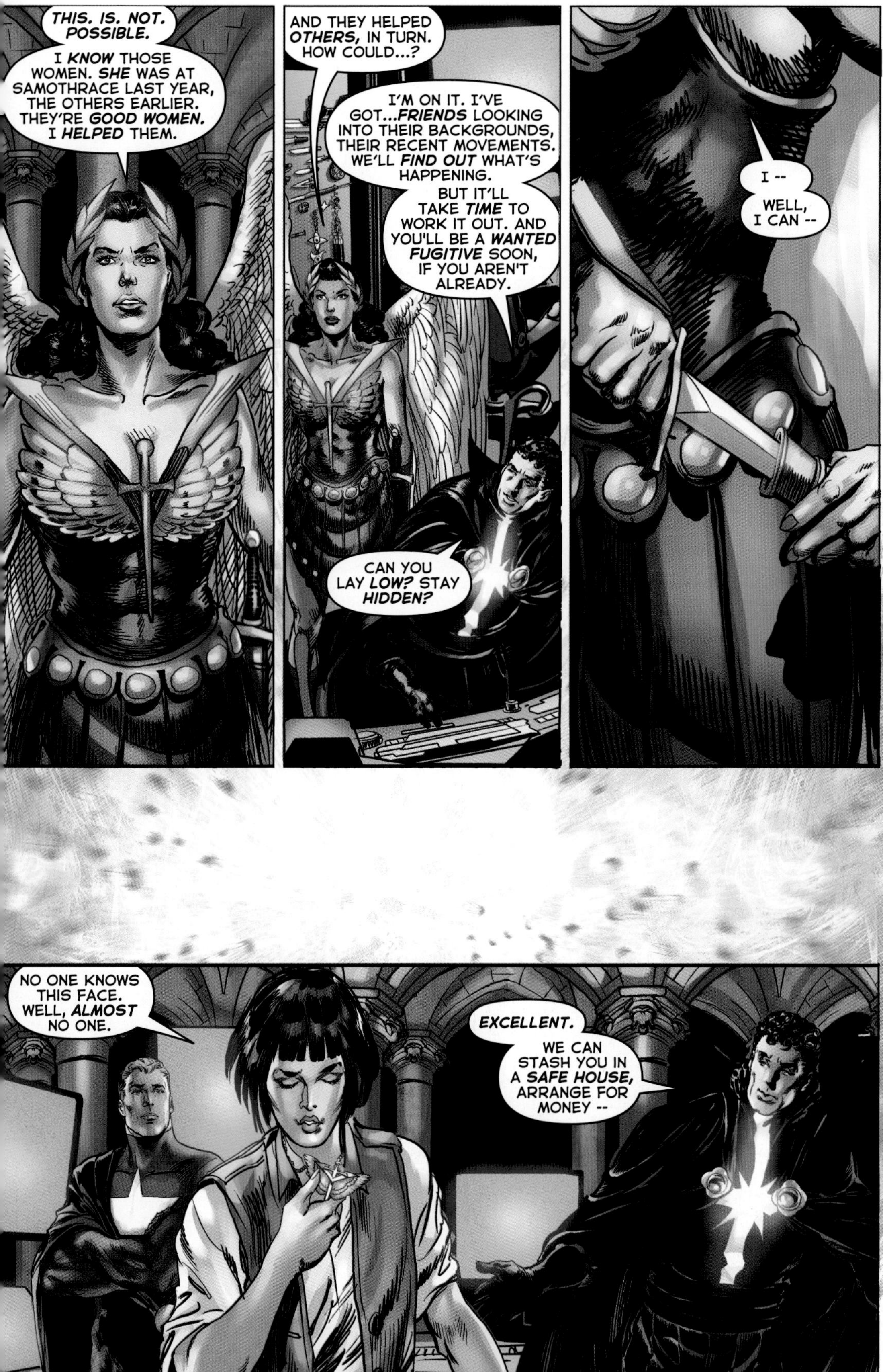
THIS. IS. NOT. POSSIBLE.
I KNOW THOSE WOMEN. SHE WAS AT SAMOTHRACE LAST YEAR, THE OTHERS EARLIER. THEY'RE GOOD WOMEN. I HELPED THEM.
AND THEY HELPED OTHERS, IN TURN. HOW COULD...?
I'M ON IT. I'VE GOT...FRIENDS LOOKING INTO THEIR BACKGROUNDS, THEIR RECENT MOVEMENTS. WE'LL FIND OUT WHAT'S HAPPENING.
BUT IT'LL TAKE TIME TO WORK IT OUT. AND YOU'LL BE A WANTED FUGITIVE SOON, IF YOU AREN'T ALREADY.
CAN YOU LAY LOW? STAY HIDDEN?
I --
WELL, I CAN --
NO ONE KNOWS THIS FACE. WELL, ALMOST NO ONE.
EXCELLENT.
WE CAN STASH YOU IN A SAFE HOUSE, ARRANGE FOR MONEY --

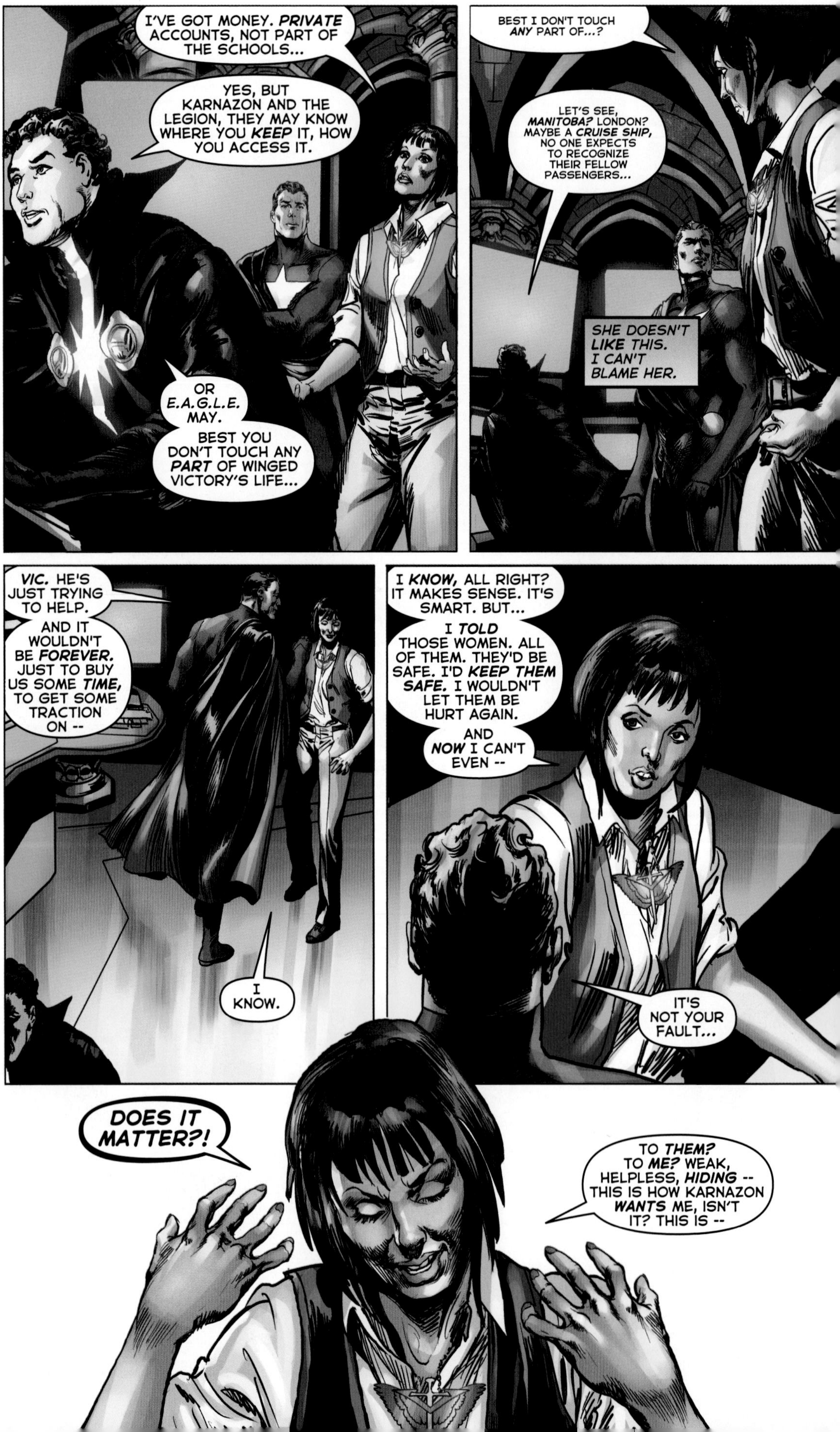
I'VE GOT MONEY. PRIVATE ACCOUNTS, NOT PART OF THE SCHOOLS...
YES, BUT KARNAZON AND THE LEGION, THEY MAY KNOW WHERE YOU KEEP IT, HOW YOU ACCESS IT.
OR E.A.G.L.E. MAY.
BEST YOU DON'T TOUCH ANY PART OF WINGED VICTORY'S LIFE...
BEST I DON'T TOUCH ANY PART OF...?
LET'S SEE, MANITOBA? LONDON? MAYBE A CRUISE SHIP, NO ONE EXPECTS TO RECOGNIZE THEIR FELLOW PASSENGERS...
SHE DOESN'T LIKE THIS. I CAN'T BLAME HER.
VIC. HE'S JUST TRYING TO HELP.
AND IT WOULDN'T BE FOREVER. JUST TO BUY US SOME TIME, TO GET SOME TRACTION ON --
I KNOW.
I KNOW, ALL RIGHT? IT MAKES SENSE. IT'S SMART. BUT...
I TOLD THOSE WOMEN. ALL OF THEM. THEY'D BE SAFE. I'D KEEP THEM SAFE. I WOULDN'T LET THEM BE HURT AGAIN.
AND NOW I CAN'T EVEN --
IT'S NOT YOUR FAULT...
DOES IT MATTER?!
TO THEM? TO ME? WEAK, HELPLESS, HIDING -- THIS IS HOW KARNAZON WANTS ME, ISN'T IT? THIS IS --

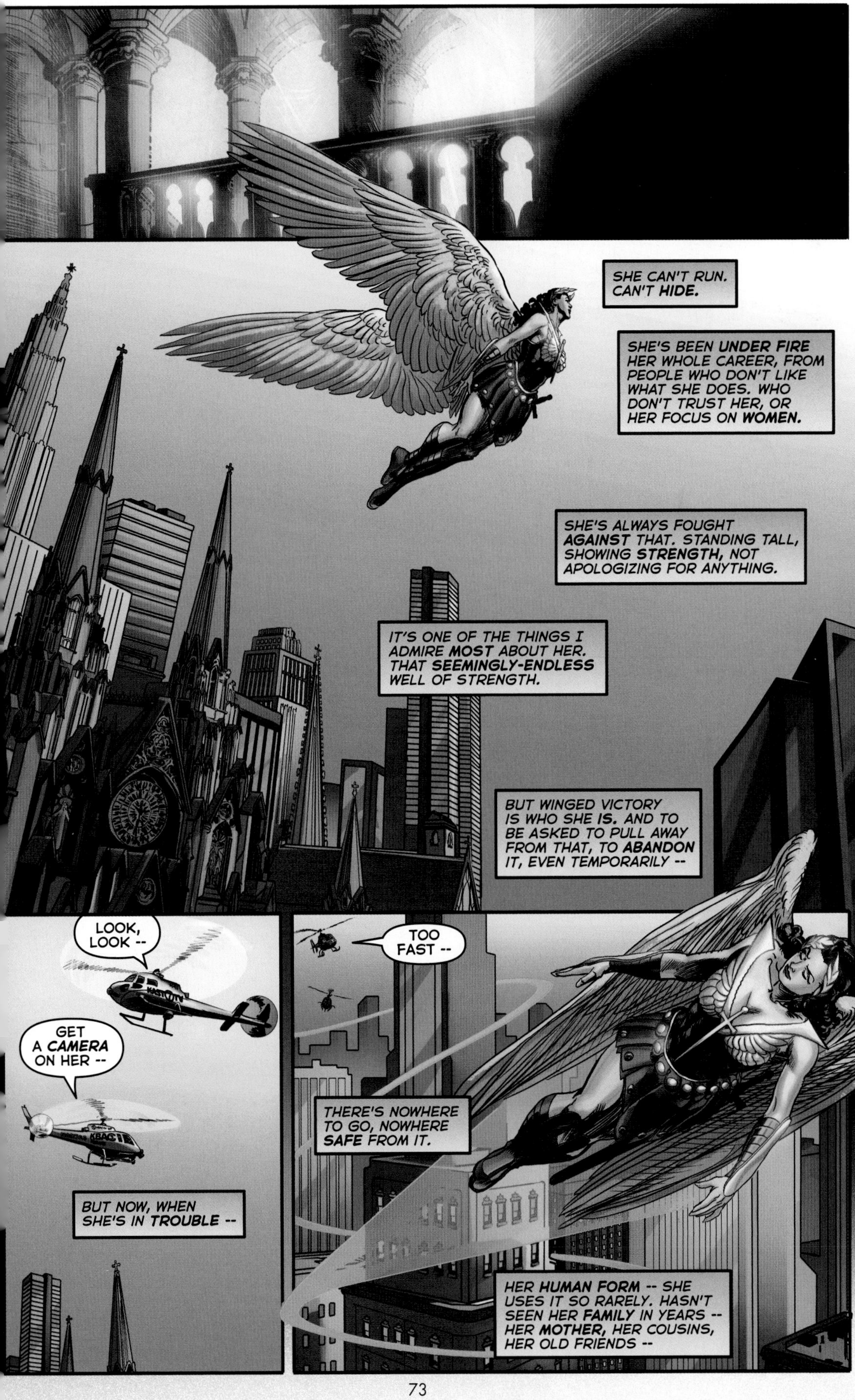
SHE CAN'T RUN. CAN'T HIDE.
SHE'S BEEN UNDER FIRE HER WHOLE CAREER, FROM PEOPLE WHO DON'T LIKE WHAT SHE DOES. WHO DON'T TRUST HER, OR HER FOCUS ON WOMEN.
SHE'S ALWAYS FOUGHT AGAINST THAT. STANDING TALL, SHOWING STRENGTH, NOT APOLOGIZING FOR ANYTHING.
IT'S ONE OF THE THINGS I ADMIRE MOST ABOUT HER. THAT SEEMINGLY-ENDLESS WELL OF STRENGTH.
BUT WINGED VICTORY IS WHO SHE IS. AND TO BE ASKED TO PULL AWAY FROM THAT, TO ABANDON IT, EVEN TEMPORARILY --
LOOK, LOOK --
GET A CAMERA ON HER --
BUT NOW, WHEN SHE'S IN TROUBLE --
TOO FAST --
THERE'S NOWHERE TO GO, NOWHERE SAFE FROM IT.
HER HUMAN FORM -- SHE USES IT SO RARELY. HASN'T SEEN HER FAMILY IN YEARS -- HER MOTHER, HER COUSINS, HER OLD FRIENDS --

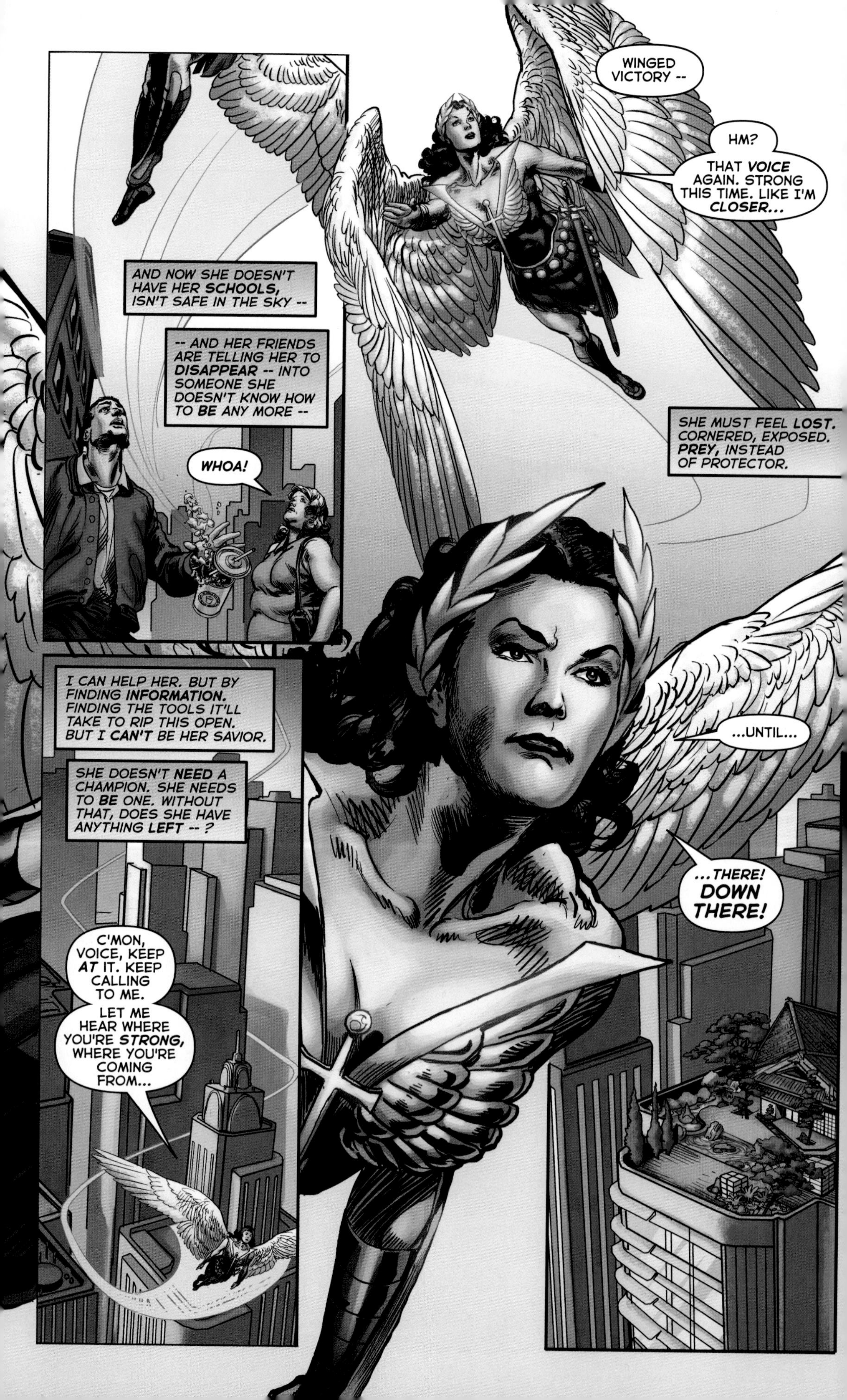
AND NOW SHE DOESN'T HAVE HER SCHOOLS, ISN'T SAFE IN THE SKY --
-- AND HER FRIENDS ARE TELLING HER TO DISAPPEAR -- INTO SOMEONE SHE DOESN'T KNOW HOW TO BE ANY MORE --
WHOA!
WINGED VICTORY --
HM?
THAT VOICE AGAIN. STRONG THIS TIME. LIKE I'M CLOSER...
SHE MUST FEEL LOST. CORNERED, EXPOSED. PREY, INSTEAD OF PROTECTOR.
I CAN HELP HER. BUT BY FINDING INFORMATION. FINDING THE TOOLS IT'LL TAKE TO RIP THIS OPEN. BUT I CAN'T BE HER SAVIOR.
SHE DOESN'T NEED A CHAMPION. SHE NEEDS TO BE ONE. WITHOUT THAT, DOES SHE HAVE ANYTHING LEFT -- ?
C'MON, VOICE, KEEP AT IT. KEEP CALLING TO ME.
LET ME HEAR WHERE YOU'RE STRONG, WHERE YOU'RE COMING FROM...
...UNTIL...
...THERE! DOWN THERE!

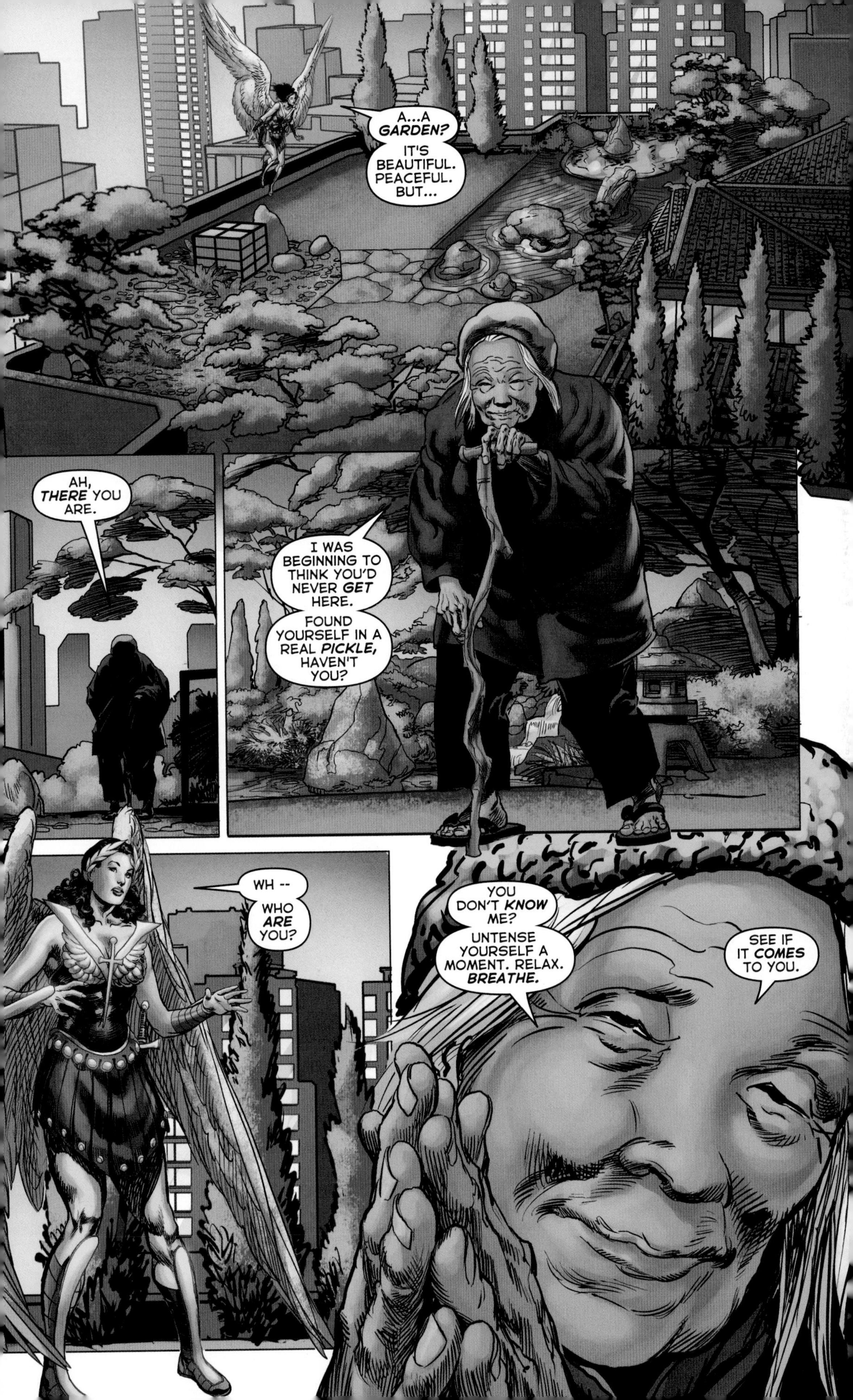
A...A *GARDEN?*
IT'S BEAUTIFUL. PEACEFUL. BUT...
AH, *THERE* YOU ARE.
I WAS BEGINNING TO THINK YOU'D NEVER *GET* HERE.
FOUND YOURSELF IN A REAL *PICKLE,* HAVEN'T YOU?
WH --
WHO *ARE* YOU?
YOU DON'T *KNOW* ME?
UNTENSE YOURSELF A MOMENT. RELAX. *BREATHE.*
SEE IF IT *COMES* TO YOU.

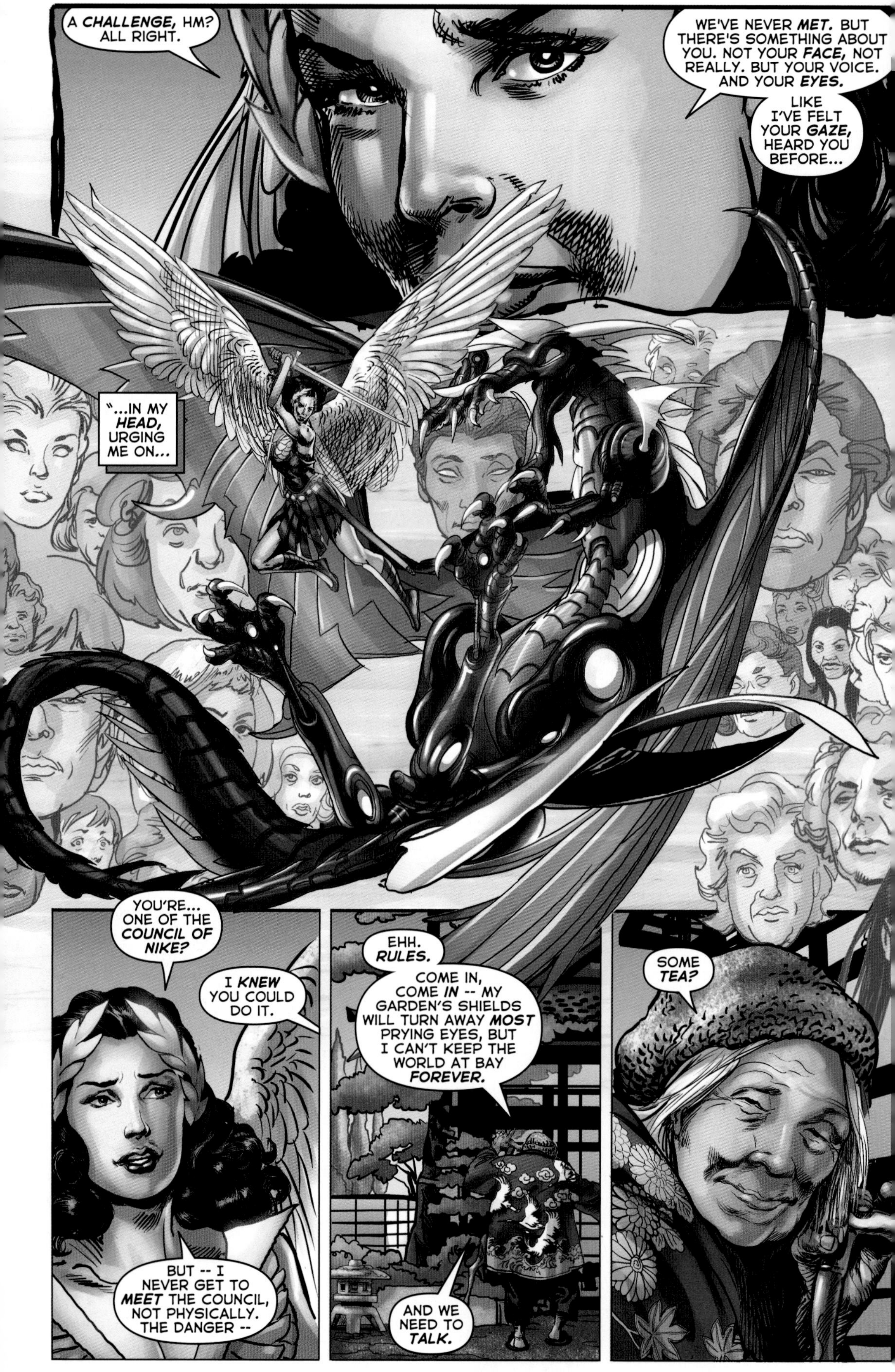

A CHALLENGE, HM? ALL RIGHT.
WE'VE NEVER MET. BUT THERE'S SOMETHING ABOUT YOU. NOT YOUR FACE, NOT REALLY. BUT YOUR VOICE. AND YOUR EYES.
LIKE I'VE FELT YOUR GAZE, HEARD YOU BEFORE...
"...IN MY HEAD, URGING ME ON...
YOU'RE... ONE OF THE COUNCIL OF NIKE?
I KNEW YOU COULD DO IT.
BUT -- I NEVER GET TO MEET THE COUNCIL, NOT PHYSICALLY. THE DANGER --
EHH. RULES.
COME IN, COME IN -- MY GARDEN'S SHIELDS WILL TURN AWAY MOST PRYING EYES, BUT I CAN'T KEEP THE WORLD AT BAY FOREVER.
AND WE NEED TO TALK.
SOME TEA?

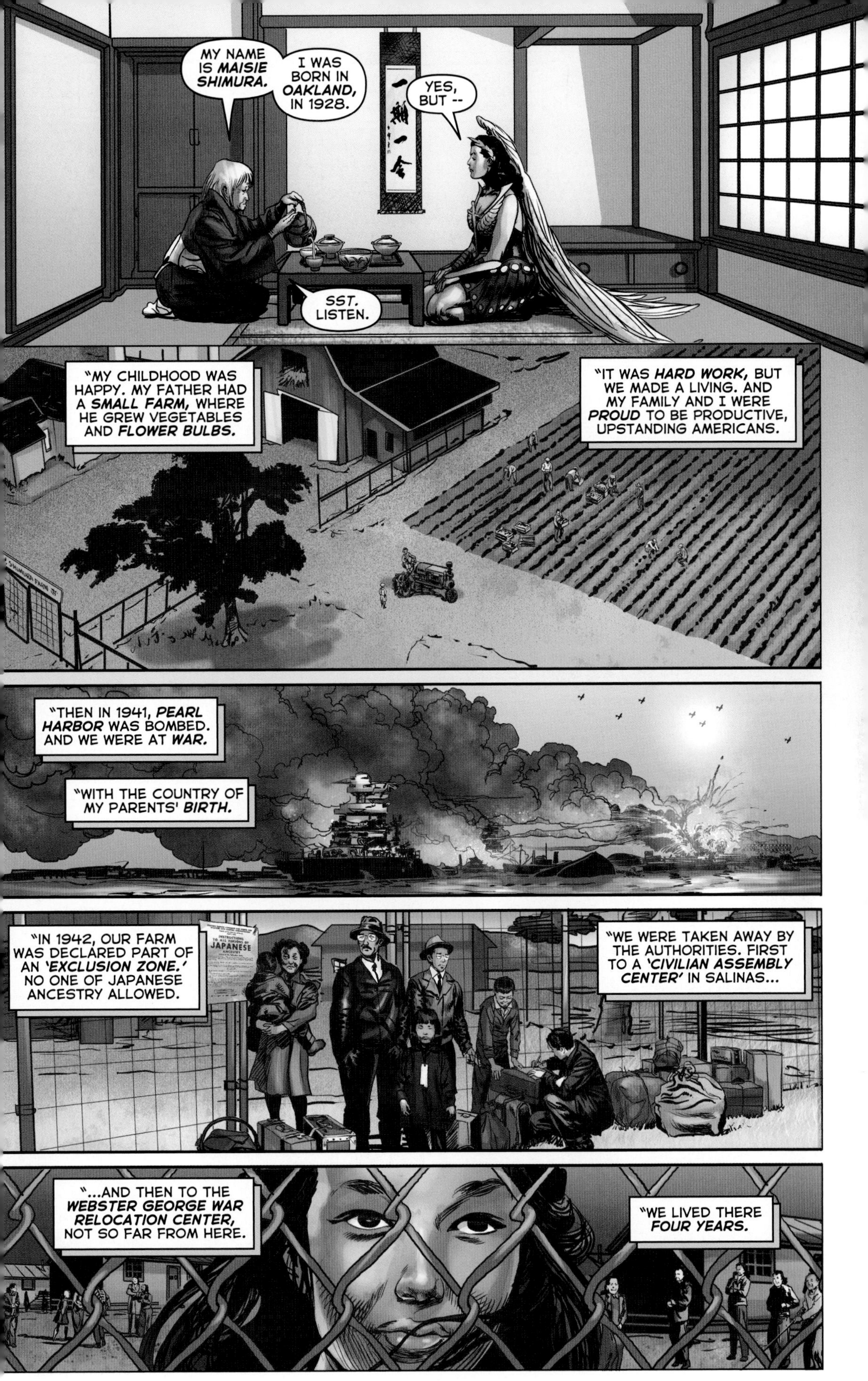
MY NAME IS MAISIE SHIMURA.
I WAS BORN IN OAKLAND, IN 1928.
YES, BUT --
SST. LISTEN.
"MY CHILDHOOD WAS HAPPY. MY FATHER HAD A SMALL FARM, WHERE HE GREW VEGETABLES AND FLOWER BULBS.
"IT WAS HARD WORK, BUT WE MADE A LIVING. AND MY FAMILY AND I WERE PROUD TO BE PRODUCTIVE, UPSTANDING AMERICANS.
"THEN IN 1941, PEARL HARBOR WAS BOMBED. AND WE WERE AT WAR.
"WITH THE COUNTRY OF MY PARENTS' BIRTH.
"IN 1942, OUR FARM WAS DECLARED PART OF AN 'EXCLUSION ZONE.' NO ONE OF JAPANESE ANCESTRY ALLOWED.
INSTRUCTIONS TO ALL PERSONS OF JAPANESE ANCESTRY
"WE WERE TAKEN AWAY BY THE AUTHORITIES. FIRST TO A 'CIVILIAN ASSEMBLY CENTER' IN SALINAS...
"...AND THEN TO THE WEBSTER GEORGE WAR RELOCATION CENTER, NOT SO FAR FROM HERE.
"WE LIVED THERE FOUR YEARS.

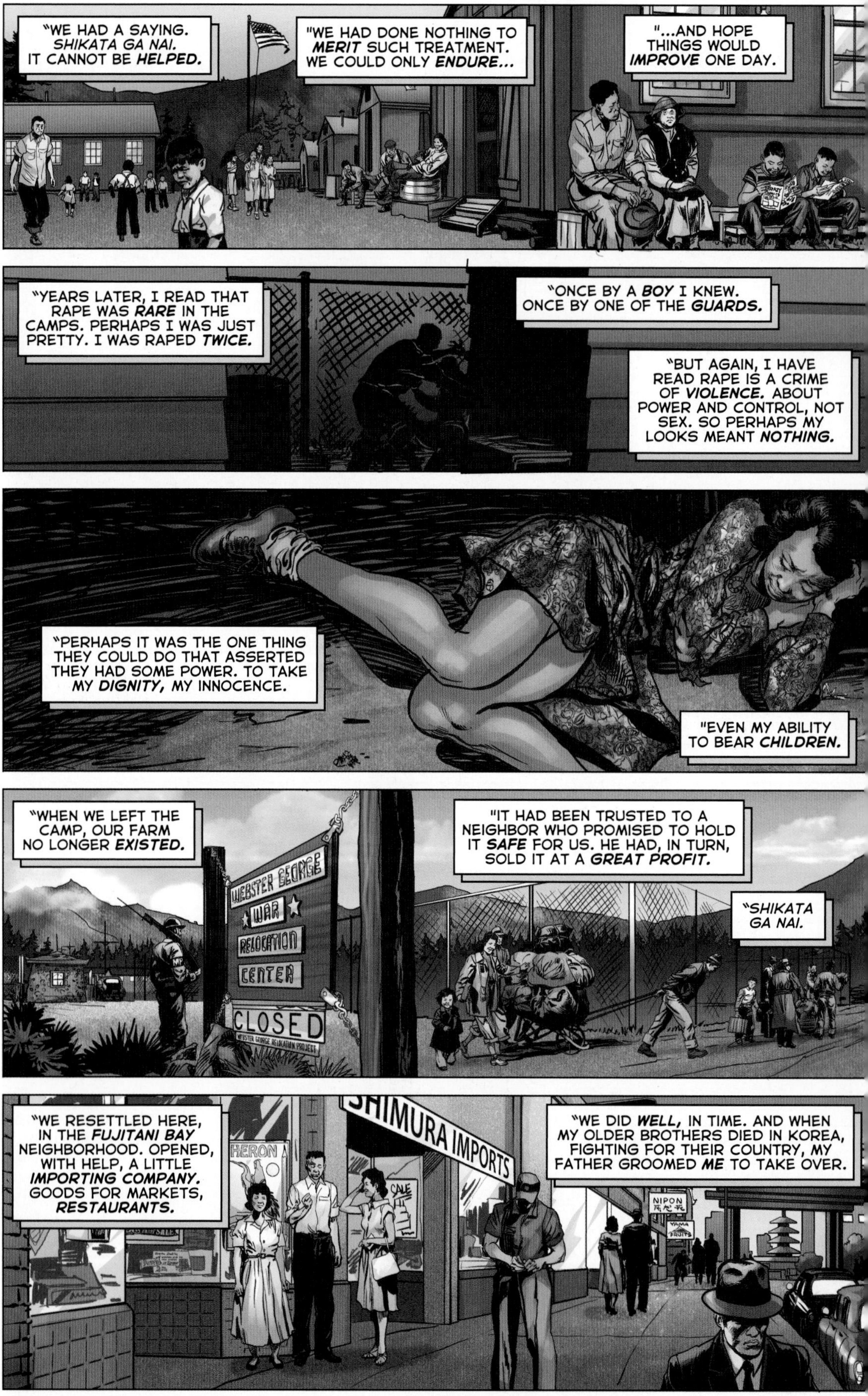
"WE HAD A SAYING. SHIKATA GA NAI. IT CANNOT BE HELPED.
"WE HAD DONE NOTHING TO MERIT SUCH TREATMENT. WE COULD ONLY ENDURE...
"...AND HOPE THINGS WOULD IMPROVE ONE DAY.
"YEARS LATER, I READ THAT RAPE WAS RARE IN THE CAMPS. PERHAPS I WAS JUST PRETTY. I WAS RAPED TWICE.
"ONCE BY A BOY I KNEW. ONCE BY ONE OF THE GUARDS.
"BUT AGAIN, I HAVE READ RAPE IS A CRIME OF VIOLENCE. ABOUT POWER AND CONTROL, NOT SEX. SO PERHAPS MY LOOKS MEANT NOTHING.
"PERHAPS IT WAS THE ONE THING THEY COULD DO THAT ASSERTED THEY HAD SOME POWER. TO TAKE MY DIGNITY, MY INNOCENCE.
"EVEN MY ABILITY TO BEAR CHILDREN.
"WHEN WE LEFT THE CAMP, OUR FARM NO LONGER EXISTED.
"IT HAD BEEN TRUSTED TO A NEIGHBOR WHO PROMISED TO HOLD IT SAFE FOR US. HE HAD, IN TURN, SOLD IT AT A GREAT PROFIT.
WEBSTER GEORGE
WAR
RELOCATION
CENTER
CLOSED
"SHIKATA GA NAI.
"WE RESETTLED HERE, IN THE FUJITANI BAY NEIGHBORHOOD. OPENED, WITH HELP, A LITTLE IMPORTING COMPANY. GOODS FOR MARKETS, RESTAURANTS.
SHIMURA IMPORTS
HERON
"WE DID WELL, IN TIME. AND WHEN MY OLDER BROTHERS DIED IN KOREA, FIGHTING FOR THEIR COUNTRY, MY FATHER GROOMED ME TO TAKE OVER.
NIPON
YAMA FRUITS

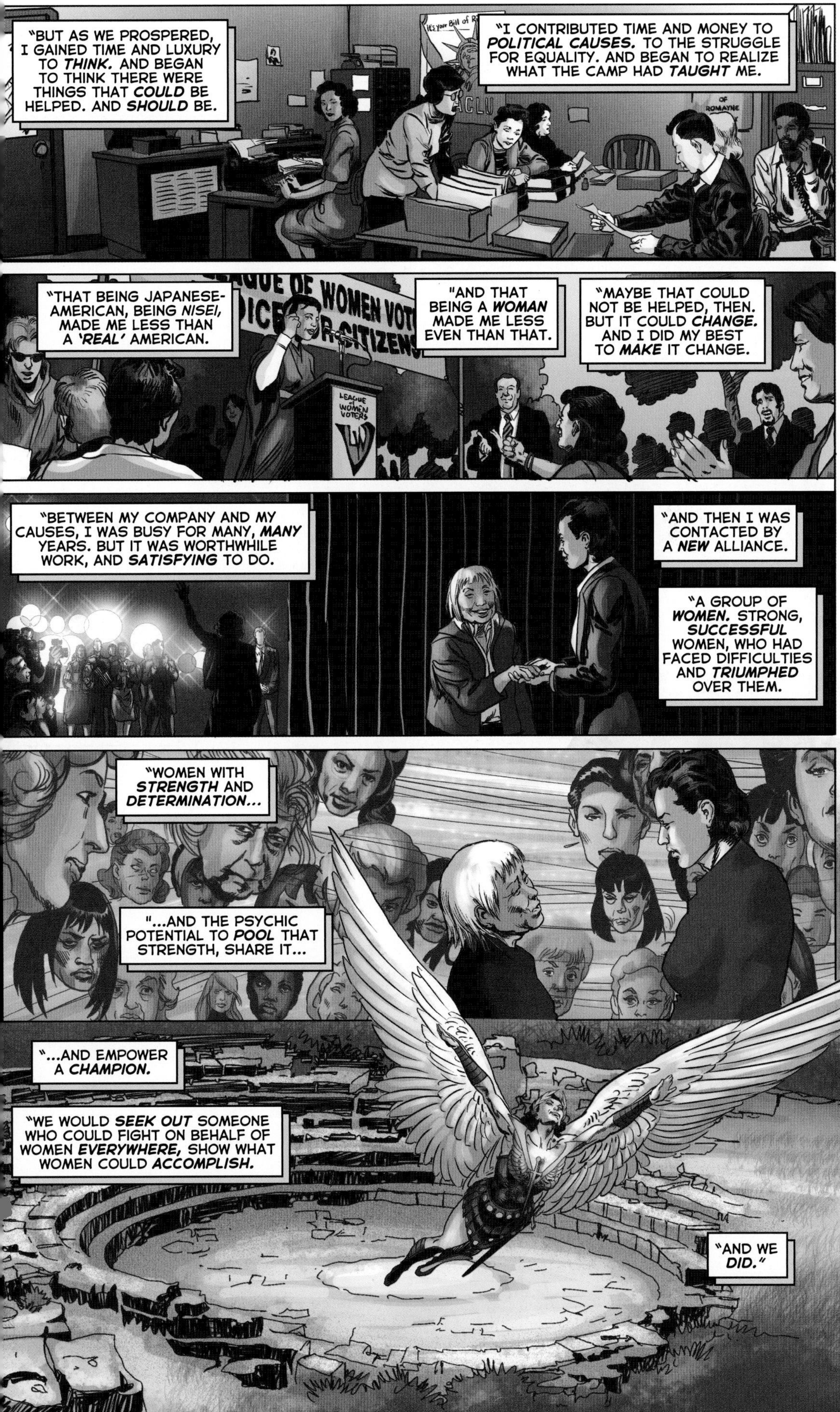
"BUT AS WE PROSPERED, I GAINED TIME AND LUXURY TO THINK. AND BEGAN TO THINK THERE WERE THINGS THAT COULD BE HELPED. AND SHOULD BE.
"I CONTRIBUTED TIME AND MONEY TO POLITICAL CAUSES. TO THE STRUGGLE FOR EQUALITY. AND BEGAN TO REALIZE WHAT THE CAMP HAD TAUGHT ME.
It's your Bill of R
ACLU
"THAT BEING JAPANESE-AMERICAN, BEING NISEI, MADE ME LESS THAN A 'REAL' AMERICAN.
LEAGUE OF WOMEN VOTERS
"AND THAT BEING A WOMAN MADE ME LESS EVEN THAN THAT.
"MAYBE THAT COULD NOT BE HELPED, THEN. BUT IT COULD CHANGE. AND I DID MY BEST TO MAKE IT CHANGE.
"BETWEEN MY COMPANY AND MY CAUSES, I WAS BUSY FOR MANY, MANY YEARS. BUT IT WAS WORTHWHILE WORK, AND SATISFYING TO DO.
"AND THEN I WAS CONTACTED BY A NEW ALLIANCE.
"A GROUP OF WOMEN. STRONG, SUCCESSFUL WOMEN, WHO HAD FACED DIFFICULTIES AND TRIUMPHED OVER THEM.
"WOMEN WITH STRENGTH AND DETERMINATION...
"...AND THE PSYCHIC POTENTIAL TO POOL THAT STRENGTH, SHARE IT...
"...AND EMPOWER A CHAMPION.
"WE WOULD SEEK OUT SOMEONE WHO COULD FIGHT ON BEHALF OF WOMEN EVERYWHERE, SHOW WHAT WOMEN COULD ACCOMPLISH.
"AND WE DID."

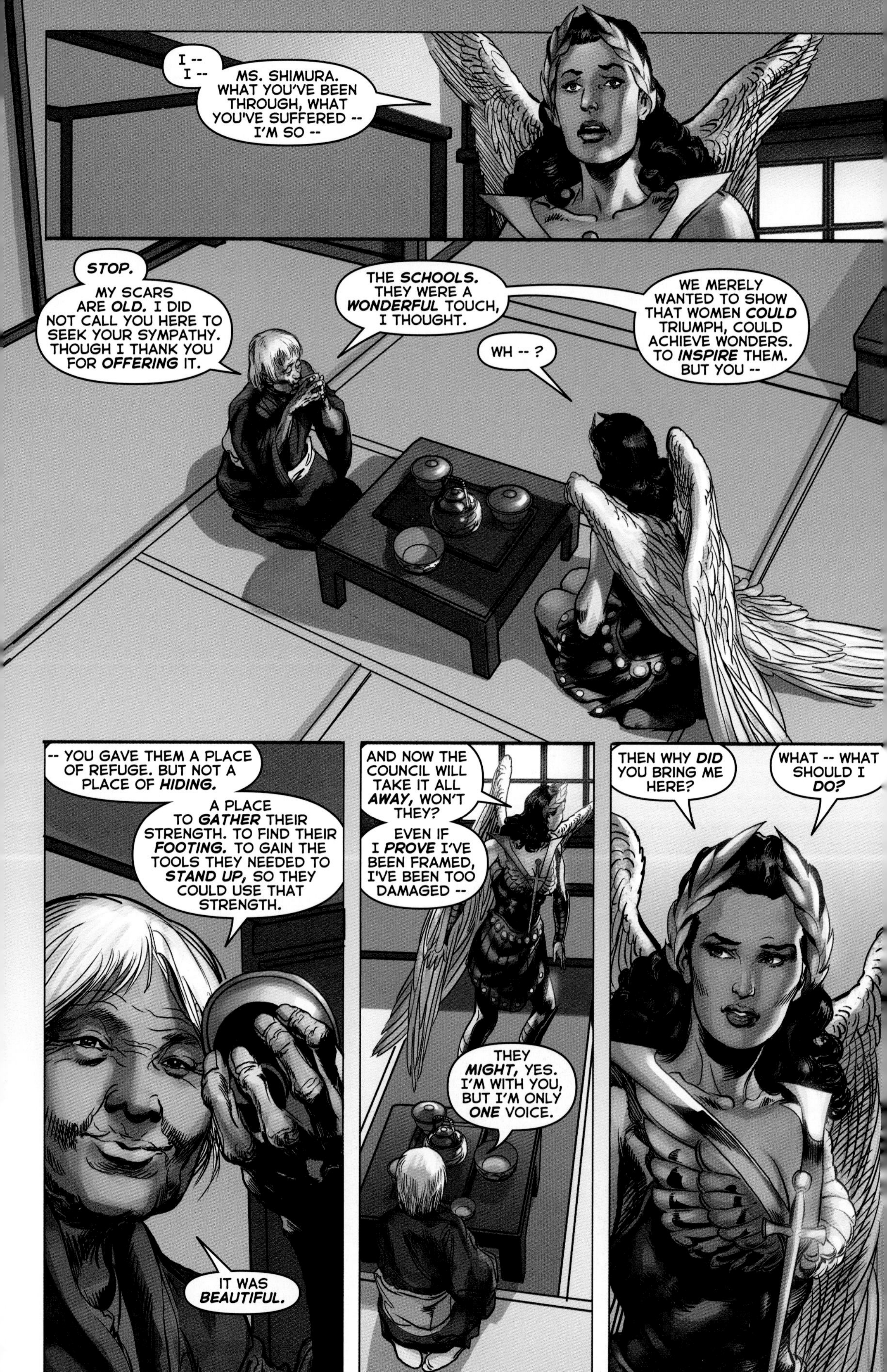
I -- I --
MS. SHIMURA. WHAT YOU'VE BEEN THROUGH, WHAT YOU'VE SUFFERED -- I'M SO --
STOP.
MY SCARS ARE OLD. I DID NOT CALL YOU HERE TO SEEK YOUR SYMPATHY. THOUGH I THANK YOU FOR OFFERING IT.
THE SCHOOLS. THEY WERE A WONDERFUL TOUCH, I THOUGHT.
WH -- ?
WE MERELY WANTED TO SHOW THAT WOMEN COULD TRIUMPH, COULD ACHIEVE WONDERS. TO INSPIRE THEM. BUT YOU --
-- YOU GAVE THEM A PLACE OF REFUGE. BUT NOT A PLACE OF HIDING.
A PLACE TO GATHER THEIR STRENGTH. TO FIND THEIR FOOTING. TO GAIN THE TOOLS THEY NEEDED TO STAND UP, SO THEY COULD USE THAT STRENGTH.
IT WAS BEAUTIFUL.
AND NOW THE COUNCIL WILL TAKE IT ALL AWAY, WON'T THEY?
EVEN IF I PROVE I'VE BEEN FRAMED, I'VE BEEN TOO DAMAGED --
THEY MIGHT, YES. I'M WITH YOU, BUT I'M ONLY ONE VOICE.
THEN WHY DID YOU BRING ME HERE?
WHAT -- WHAT SHOULD I DO?

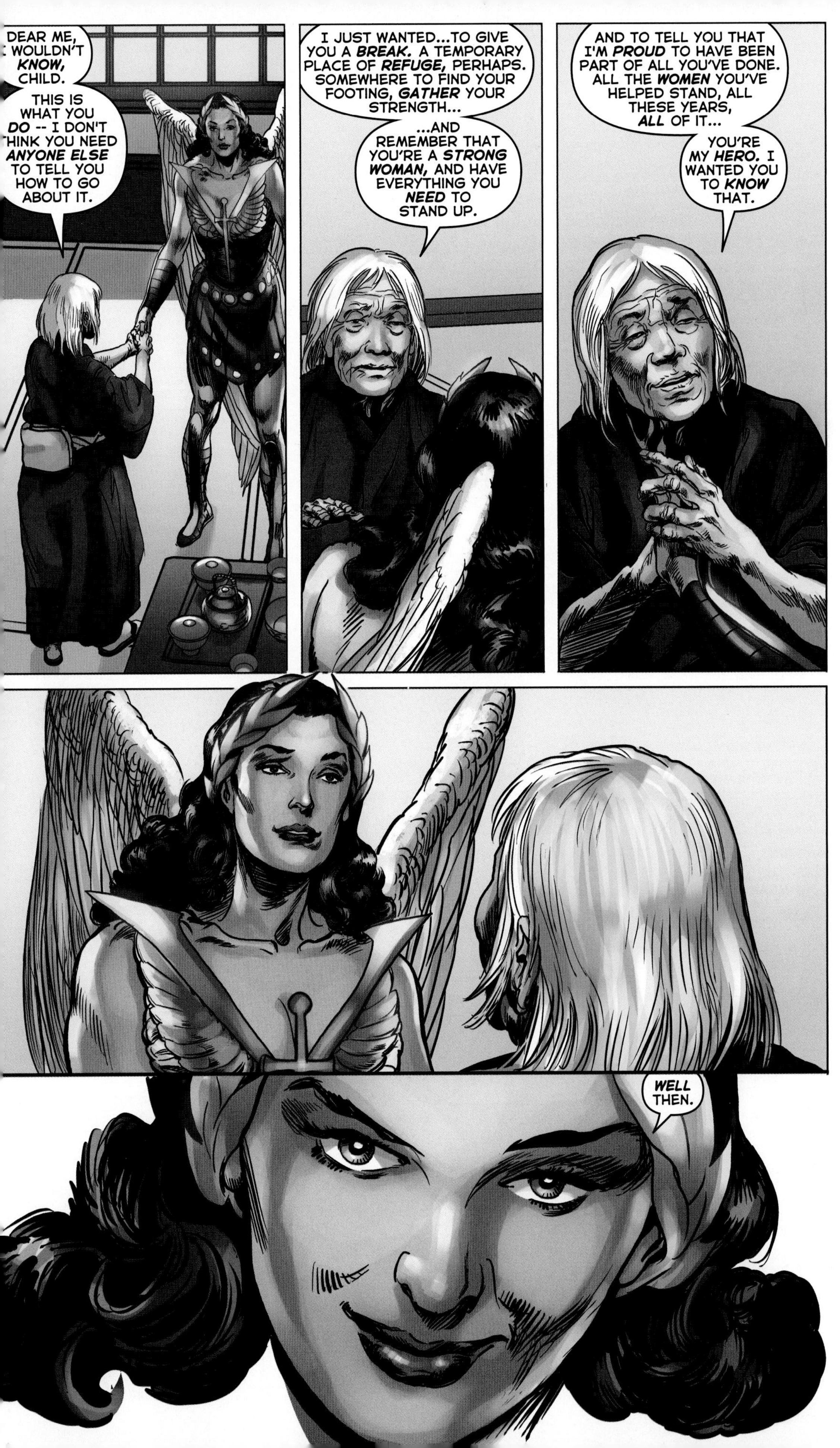
DEAR ME, I WOULDN'T KNOW, CHILD.
THIS IS WHAT YOU DO -- I DON'T THINK YOU NEED ANYONE ELSE TO TELL YOU HOW TO GO ABOUT IT.
I JUST WANTED...TO GIVE YOU A BREAK. A TEMPORARY PLACE OF REFUGE, PERHAPS. SOMEWHERE TO FIND YOUR FOOTING, GATHER YOUR STRENGTH...
...AND REMEMBER THAT YOU'RE A STRONG WOMAN, AND HAVE EVERYTHING YOU NEED TO STAND UP.
AND TO TELL YOU THAT I'M PROUD TO HAVE BEEN PART OF ALL YOU'VE DONE. ALL THE WOMEN YOU'VE HELPED STAND, ALL THESE YEARS, ALL OF IT...
YOU'RE MY HERO. I WANTED YOU TO KNOW THAT.
WELL THEN.

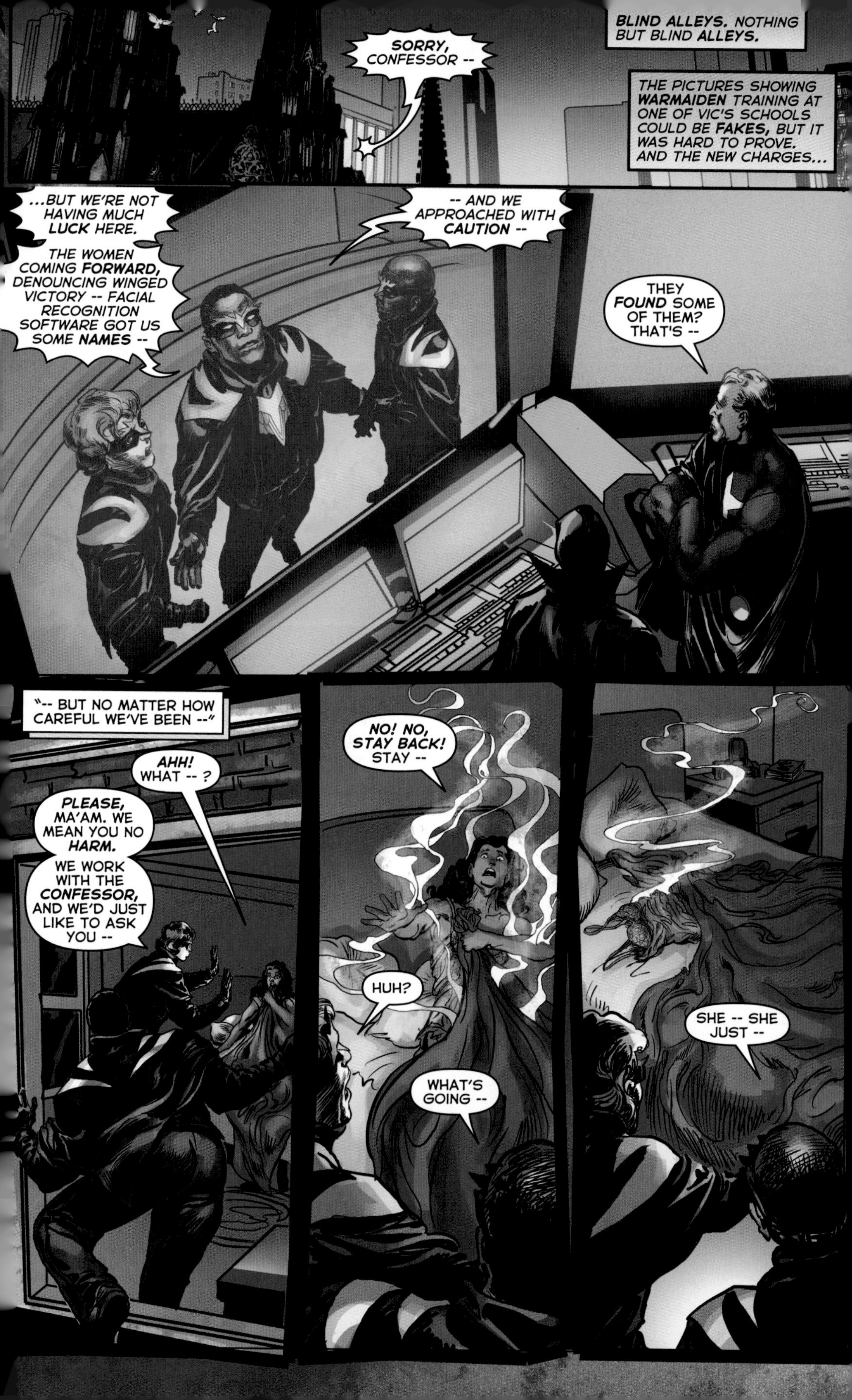

SORRY, CONFESSOR --
BLIND ALLEYS. NOTHING BUT BLIND ALLEYS.
THE PICTURES SHOWING WARMAIDEN TRAINING AT ONE OF VIC'S SCHOOLS COULD BE FAKES, BUT IT WAS HARD TO PROVE. AND THE NEW CHARGES...
...BUT WE'RE NOT HAVING MUCH LUCK HERE.
THE WOMEN COMING FORWARD, DENOUNCING WINGED VICTORY -- FACIAL RECOGNITION SOFTWARE GOT US SOME NAMES --
-- AND WE APPROACHED WITH CAUTION --
THEY FOUND SOME OF THEM? THAT'S --
"-- BUT NO MATTER HOW CAREFUL WE'VE BEEN --"
AHH! WHAT -- ?
PLEASE, MA'AM. WE MEAN YOU NO HARM.
WE WORK WITH THE CONFESSOR, AND WE'D JUST LIKE TO ASK YOU --
NO! NO, STAY BACK! STAY --
HUH?
WHAT'S GOING --
SHE -- SHE JUST --

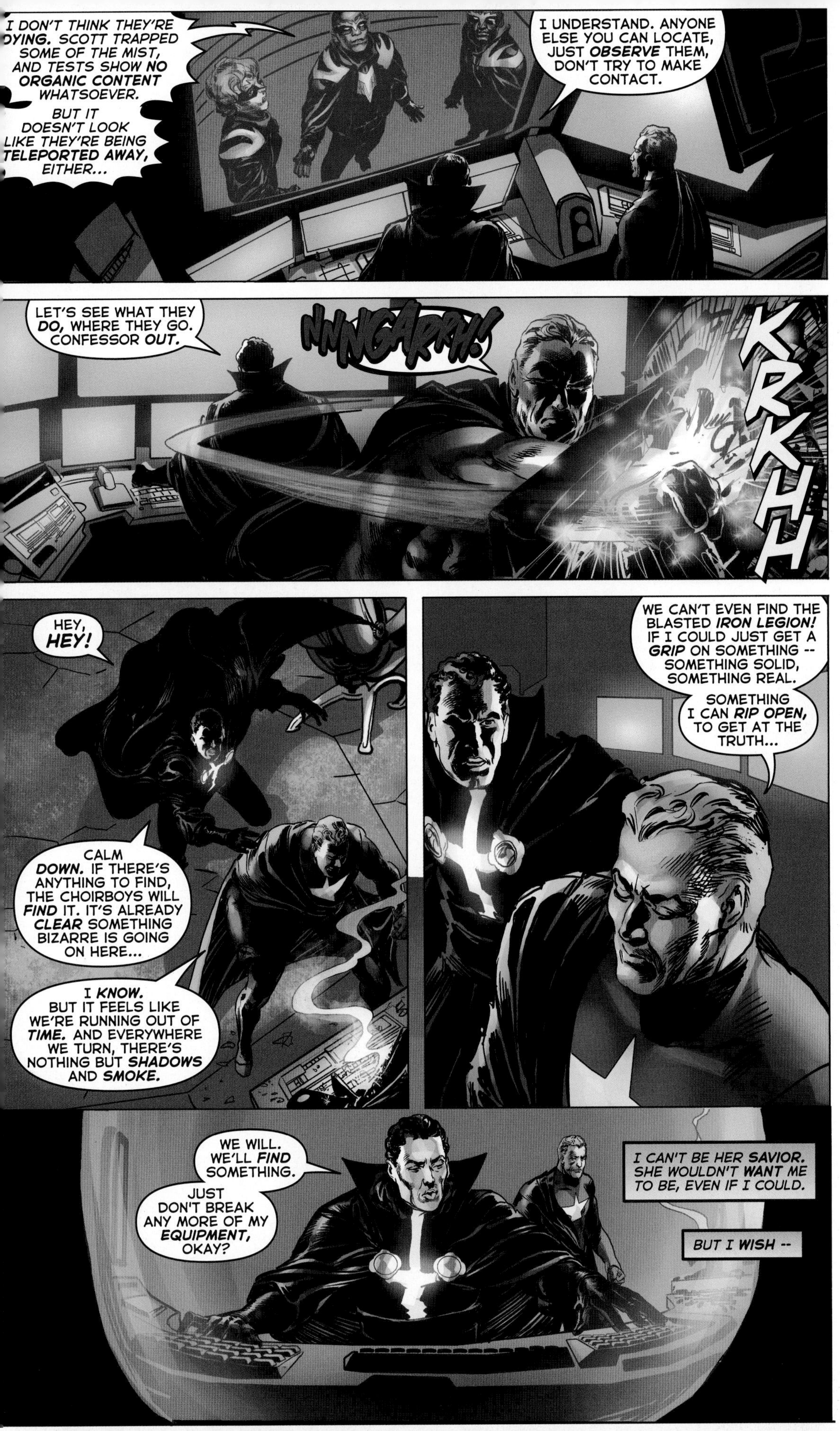
I DON'T THINK THEY'RE DYING. SCOTT TRAPPED SOME OF THE MIST, AND TESTS SHOW NO ORGANIC CONTENT WHATSOEVER.
BUT IT DOESN'T LOOK LIKE THEY'RE BEING TELEPORTED AWAY, EITHER...
I UNDERSTAND. ANYONE ELSE YOU CAN LOCATE, JUST OBSERVE THEM, DON'T TRY TO MAKE CONTACT.
LET'S SEE WHAT THEY DO, WHERE THEY GO. CONFESSOR OUT.
NNNGARRH!
KRKHH
HEY, HEY!
CALM DOWN. IF THERE'S ANYTHING TO FIND, THE CHOIRBOYS WILL FIND IT. IT'S ALREADY CLEAR SOMETHING BIZARRE IS GOING ON HERE...
I KNOW. BUT IT FEELS LIKE WE'RE RUNNING OUT OF TIME. AND EVERYWHERE WE TURN, THERE'S NOTHING BUT SHADOWS AND SMOKE.
WE CAN'T EVEN FIND THE BLASTED IRON LEGION! IF I COULD JUST GET A GRIP ON SOMETHING -- SOMETHING SOLID, SOMETHING REAL.
SOMETHING I CAN RIP OPEN, TO GET AT THE TRUTH...
WE WILL. WE'LL FIND SOMETHING.
JUST DON'T BREAK ANY MORE OF MY EQUIPMENT, OKAY?
I CAN'T BE HER SAVIOR. SHE WOULDN'T WANT ME TO BE, EVEN IF I COULD.
BUT I WISH --

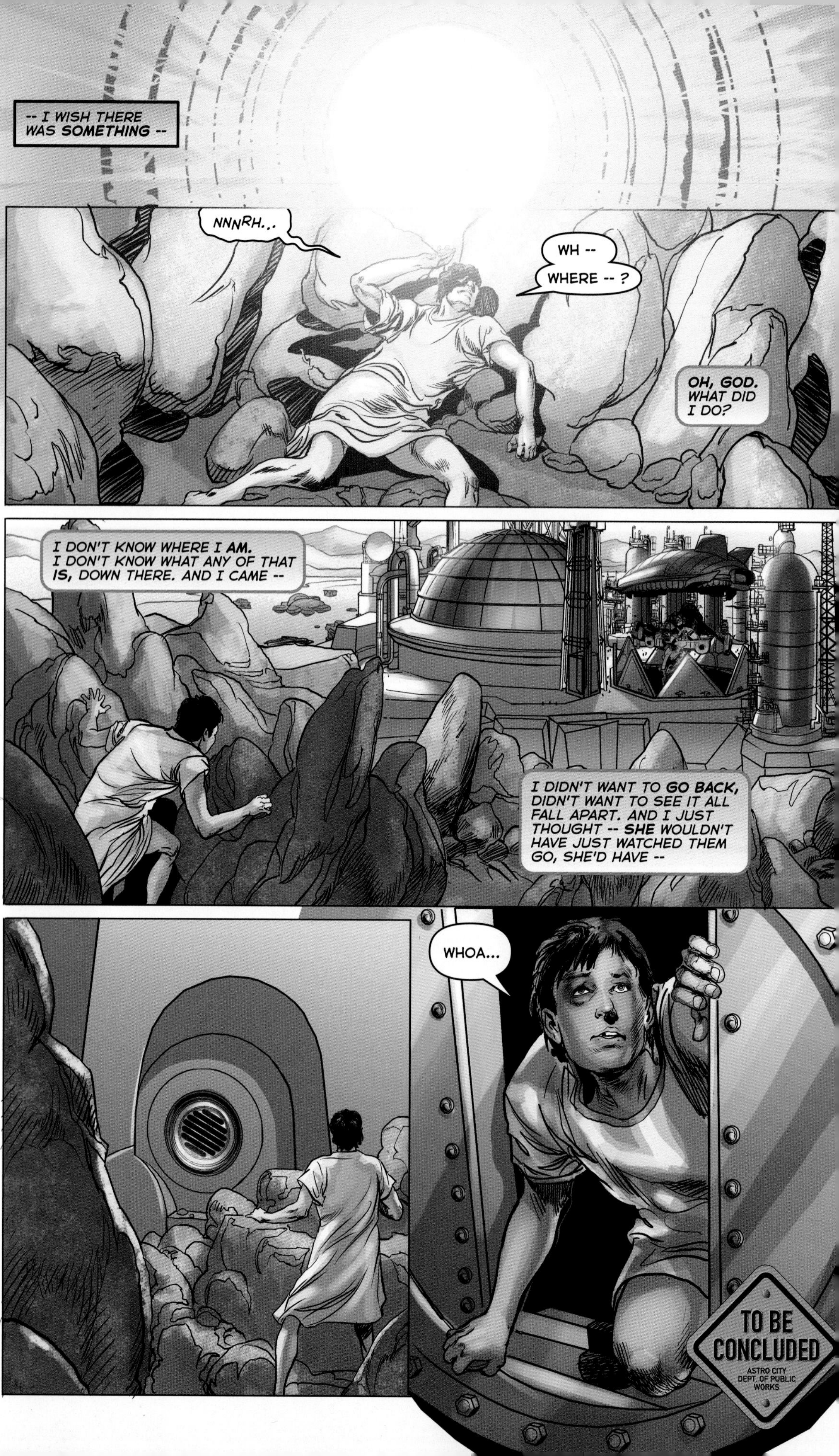
-- I WISH THERE WAS SOMETHING --
NNNRH...
WH --
WHERE -- ?
OH, GOD. WHAT DID I DO?
I DON'T KNOW WHERE I AM. I DON'T KNOW WHAT ANY OF THAT IS, DOWN THERE. AND I CAME --
I DIDN'T WANT TO GO BACK, DIDN'T WANT TO SEE IT ALL FALL APART. AND I JUST THOUGHT -- SHE WOULDN'T HAVE JUST WATCHED THEM GO, SHE'D HAVE --
WHOA...
TO BE CONCLUDED
ASTRO CITY DEPT. OF PUBLIC WORKS

FOUR

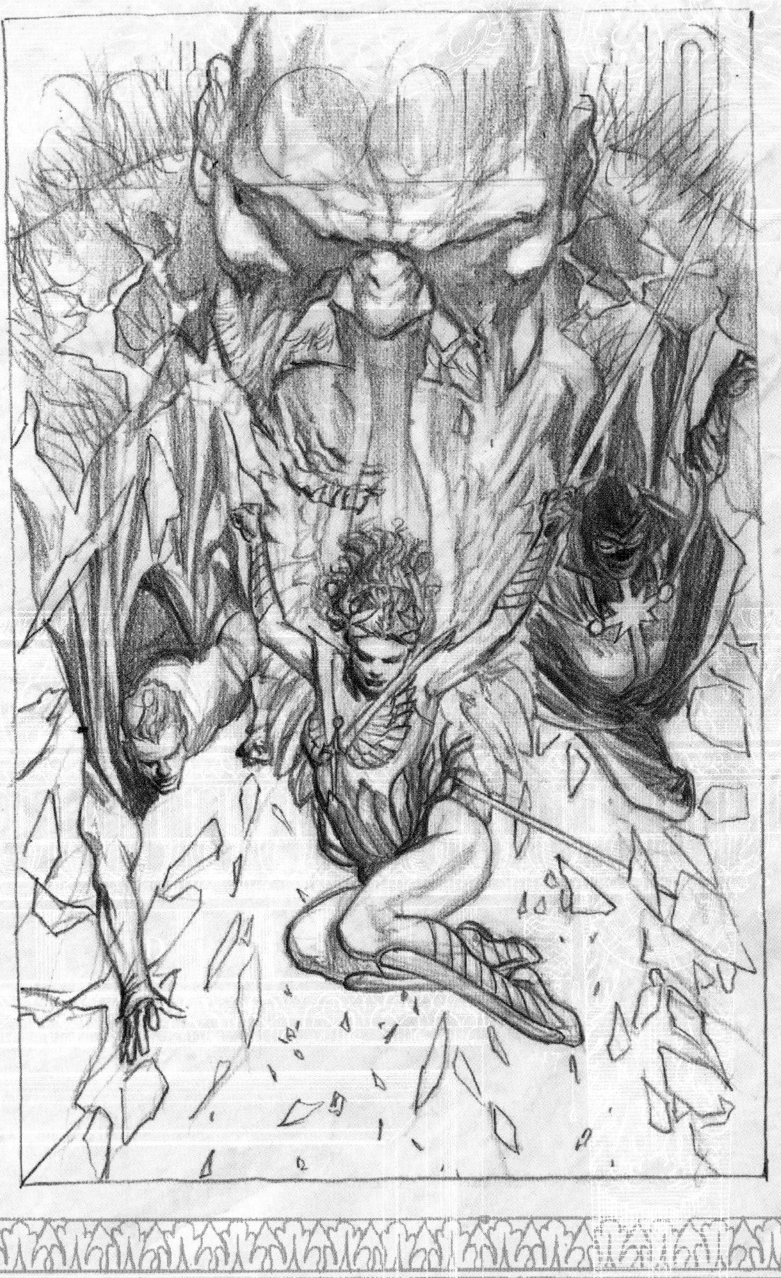

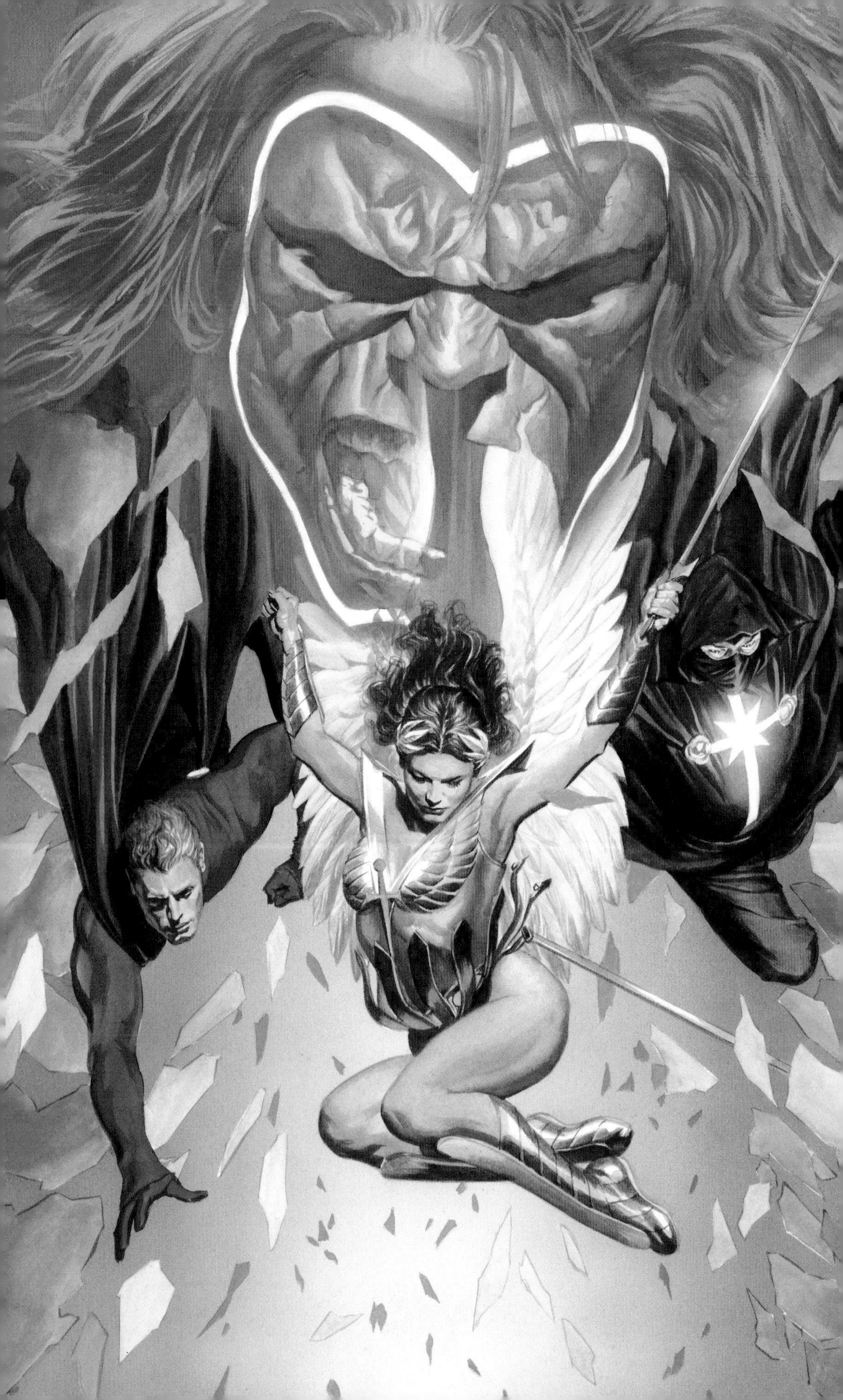

KRSSSHHHHH
I'VE BEEN DOING THINGS WRONG, I THINK. OR I LOST SIGHT OF SOMETHING.
I DIDN'T MEAN TO, IT JUST KIND OF CREPT UP ON ME. BUT I'M GETTING AHEAD OF THINGS.
THE DAY DIDN'T START LIKE THIS --
VICTORY

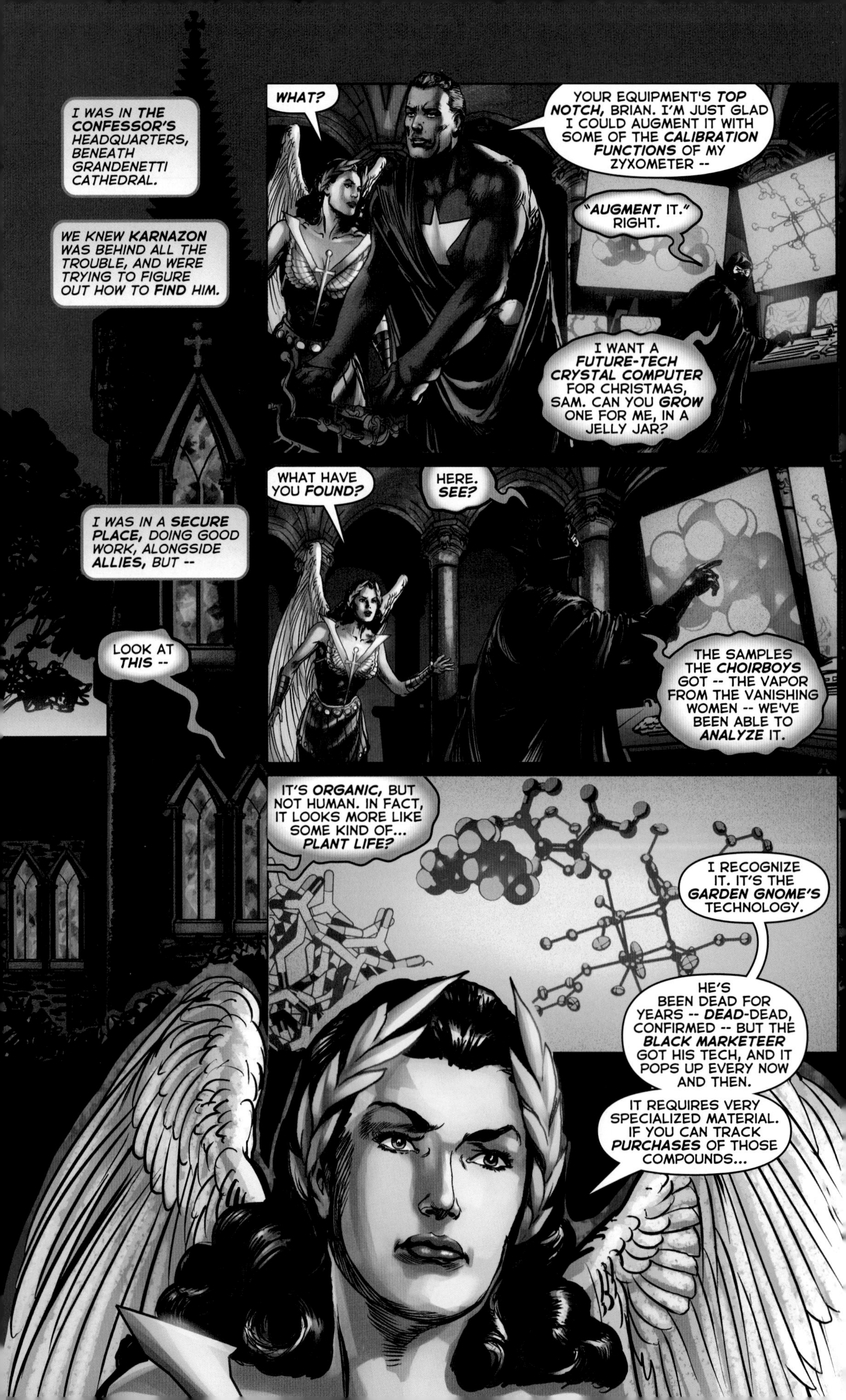
I WAS IN THE CONFESSOR'S HEADQUARTERS, BENEATH GRANDENETTI CATHEDRAL.
WE KNEW KARNAZON WAS BEHIND ALL THE TROUBLE, AND WERE TRYING TO FIGURE OUT HOW TO FIND HIM.
WHAT?
YOUR EQUIPMENT'S TOP NOTCH, BRIAN. I'M JUST GLAD I COULD AUGMENT IT WITH SOME OF THE CALIBRATION FUNCTIONS OF MY ZYXOMETER --
"AUGMENT IT." RIGHT.
I WANT A FUTURE-TECH CRYSTAL COMPUTER FOR CHRISTMAS, SAM. CAN YOU GROW ONE FOR ME, IN A JELLY JAR?
I WAS IN A SECURE PLACE, DOING GOOD WORK, ALONGSIDE ALLIES, BUT --
WHAT HAVE YOU FOUND?
HERE. SEE?
LOOK AT THIS --
THE SAMPLES THE CHOIRBOYS GOT -- THE VAPOR FROM THE VANISHING WOMEN -- WE'VE BEEN ABLE TO ANALYZE IT.
IT'S ORGANIC, BUT NOT HUMAN. IN FACT, IT LOOKS MORE LIKE SOME KIND OF... PLANT LIFE?
I RECOGNIZE IT. IT'S THE GARDEN GNOME'S TECHNOLOGY.
HE'S BEEN DEAD FOR YEARS -- DEAD-DEAD, CONFIRMED -- BUT THE BLACK MARKETEER GOT HIS TECH, AND IT POPS UP EVERY NOW AND THEN.
IT REQUIRES VERY SPECIALIZED MATERIAL. IF YOU CAN TRACK PURCHASES OF THOSE COMPOUNDS...

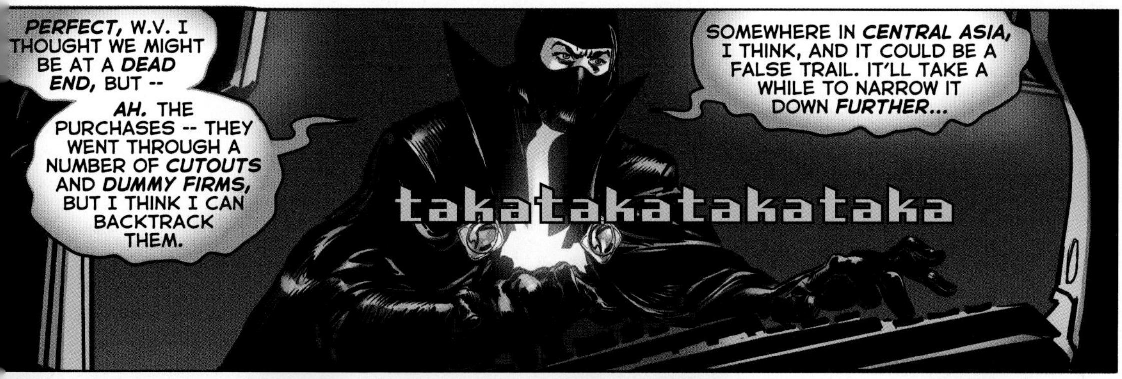
PERFECT, W.V. I THOUGHT WE MIGHT BE AT A DEAD END, BUT --
AH. THE PURCHASES -- THEY WENT THROUGH A NUMBER OF CUTOUTS AND DUMMY FIRMS, BUT I THINK I CAN BACKTRACK THEM.
takatakatakatakataka
SOMEWHERE IN CENTRAL ASIA, I THINK, AND IT COULD BE A FALSE TRAIL. IT'LL TAKE A WHILE TO NARROW IT DOWN FURTHER...

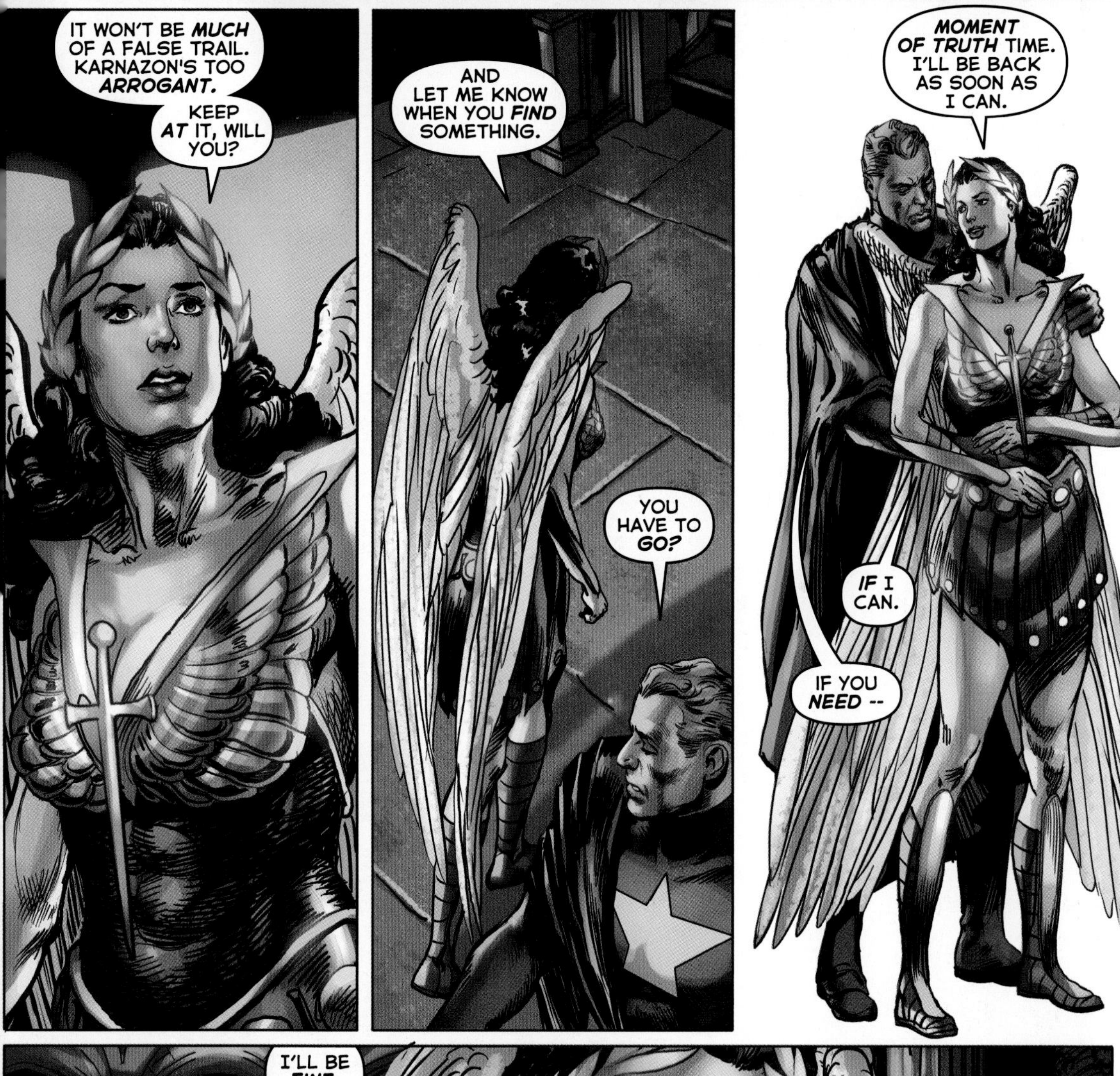
IT WON'T BE MUCH OF A FALSE TRAIL. KARNAZON'S TOO ARROGANT.
KEEP AT IT, WILL YOU?
AND LET ME KNOW WHEN YOU FIND SOMETHING.
YOU HAVE TO GO?
MOMENT OF TRUTH TIME. I'LL BE BACK AS SOON AS I CAN.
IF I CAN.
IF YOU NEED --

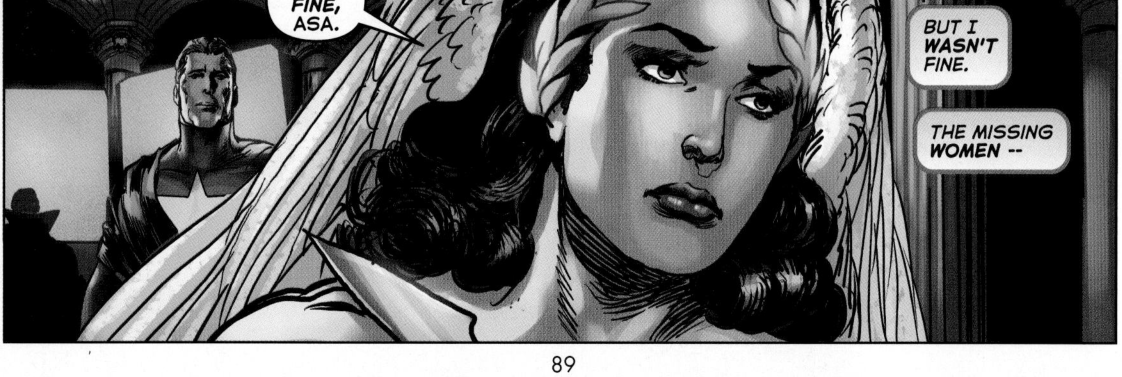
I'LL BE FINE, ASA.
BUT I WASN'T FINE.
THE MISSING WOMEN --

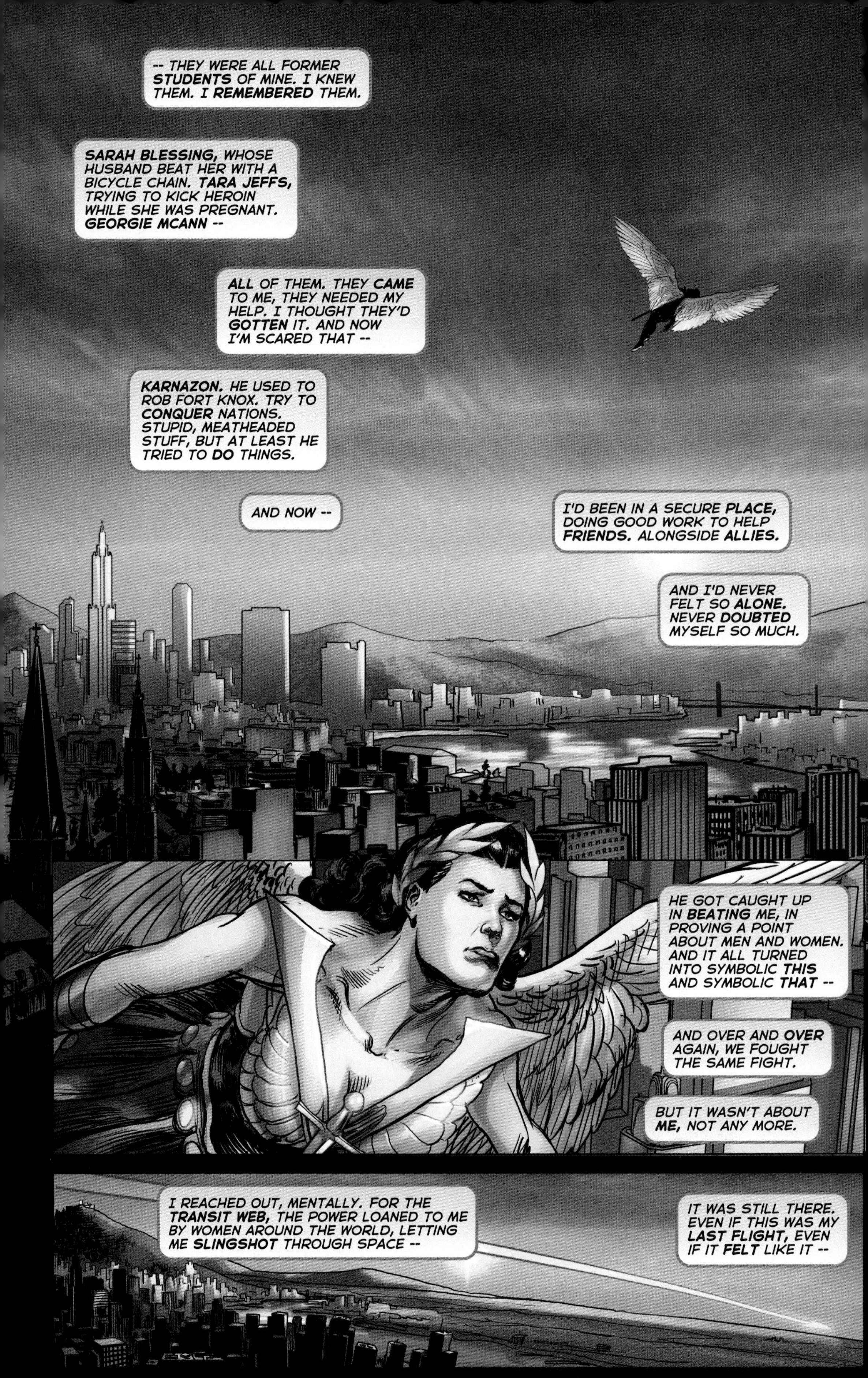
-- THEY WERE ALL FORMER STUDENTS OF MINE. I KNEW THEM. I REMEMBERED THEM.
SARAH BLESSING, WHOSE HUSBAND BEAT HER WITH A BICYCLE CHAIN. TARA JEFFS, TRYING TO KICK HEROIN WHILE SHE WAS PREGNANT. GEORGIE MCANN --
ALL OF THEM. THEY CAME TO ME, THEY NEEDED MY HELP. I THOUGHT THEY'D GOTTEN IT. AND NOW I'M SCARED THAT --
KARNAZON. HE USED TO ROB FORT KNOX. TRY TO CONQUER NATIONS. STUPID, MEATHEADED STUFF, BUT AT LEAST HE TRIED TO DO THINGS.
AND NOW --
I'D BEEN IN A SECURE PLACE, DOING GOOD WORK TO HELP FRIENDS. ALONGSIDE ALLIES.
AND I'D NEVER FELT SO ALONE. NEVER DOUBTED MYSELF SO MUCH.
HE GOT CAUGHT UP IN BEATING ME, IN PROVING A POINT ABOUT MEN AND WOMEN. AND IT ALL TURNED INTO SYMBOLIC THIS AND SYMBOLIC THAT --
AND OVER AND OVER AGAIN, WE FOUGHT THE SAME FIGHT.
BUT IT WASN'T ABOUT ME, NOT ANY MORE.
I REACHED OUT, MENTALLY. FOR THE TRANSIT WEB, THE POWER LOANED TO ME BY WOMEN AROUND THE WORLD, LETTING ME SLINGSHOT THROUGH SPACE --
IT WAS STILL THERE. EVEN IF THIS WAS MY LAST FLIGHT, EVEN IF IT FELT LIKE IT --

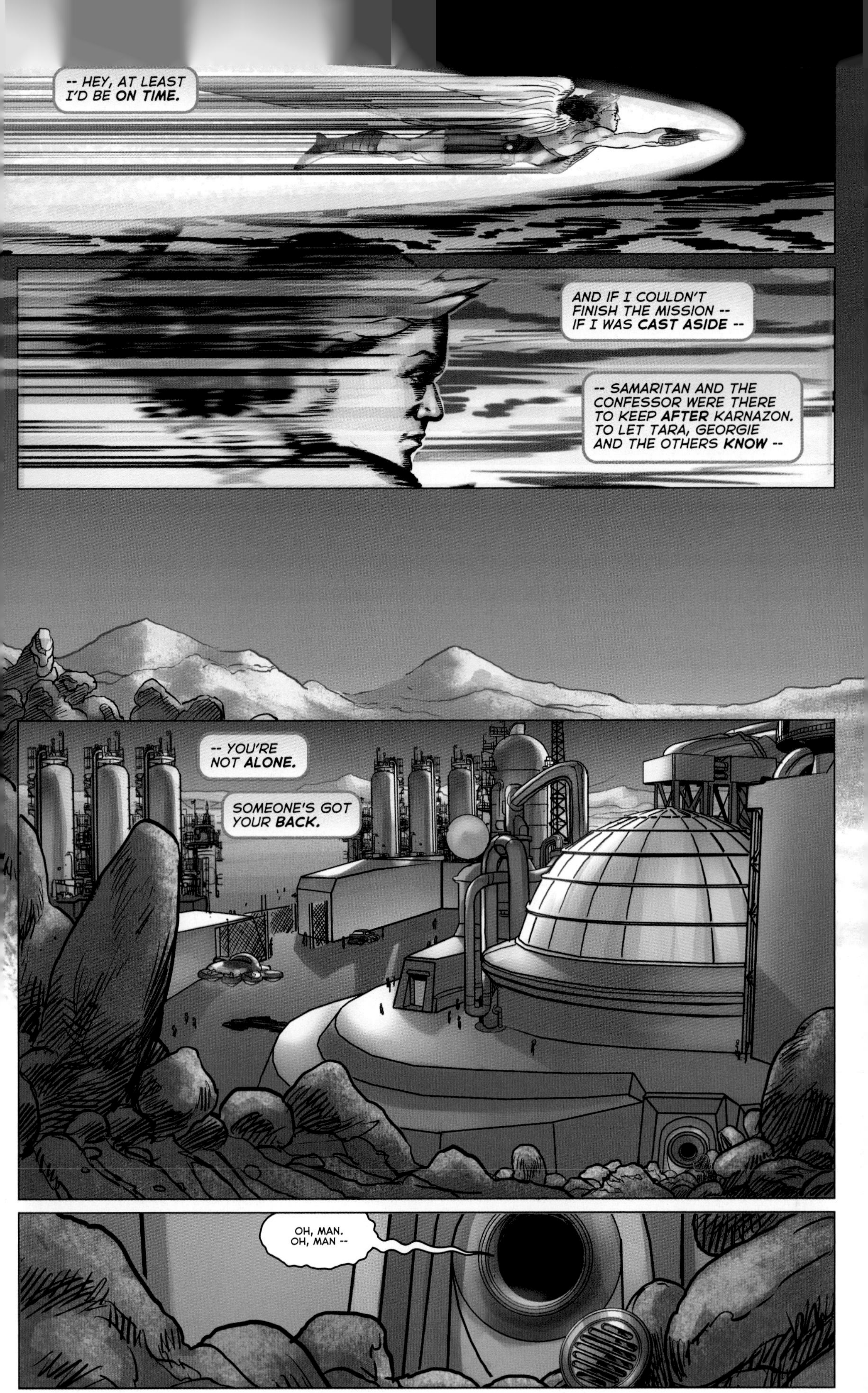
-- HEY, AT LEAST I'D BE ON TIME.
AND IF I COULDN'T FINISH THE MISSION -- IF I WAS CAST ASIDE --
-- SAMARITAN AND THE CONFESSOR WERE THERE TO KEEP AFTER KARNAZON. TO LET TARA, GEORGIE AND THE OTHERS KNOW --
-- YOU'RE NOT ALONE.
SOMEONE'S GOT YOUR BACK.
OH, MAN. OH, MAN --

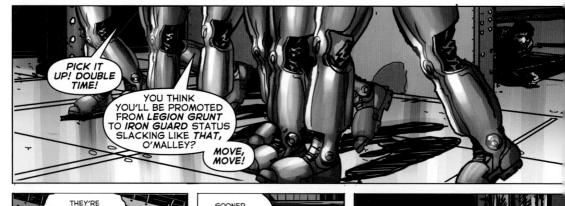

PICK IT UP! DOUBLE TIME!

YOU THINK YOU'LL BE PROMOTED FROM *LEGION GRUNT* TO *IRON GUARD* STATUS SLACKING LIKE *THAT*, O'MALLEY?

MOVE, MOVE!

THEY'RE ALL OVER.

THEY'RE ALL OVER, AND I CAN'T KEEP --

SOONER OR LATER THEY'LL --

HUH?

WHOA.

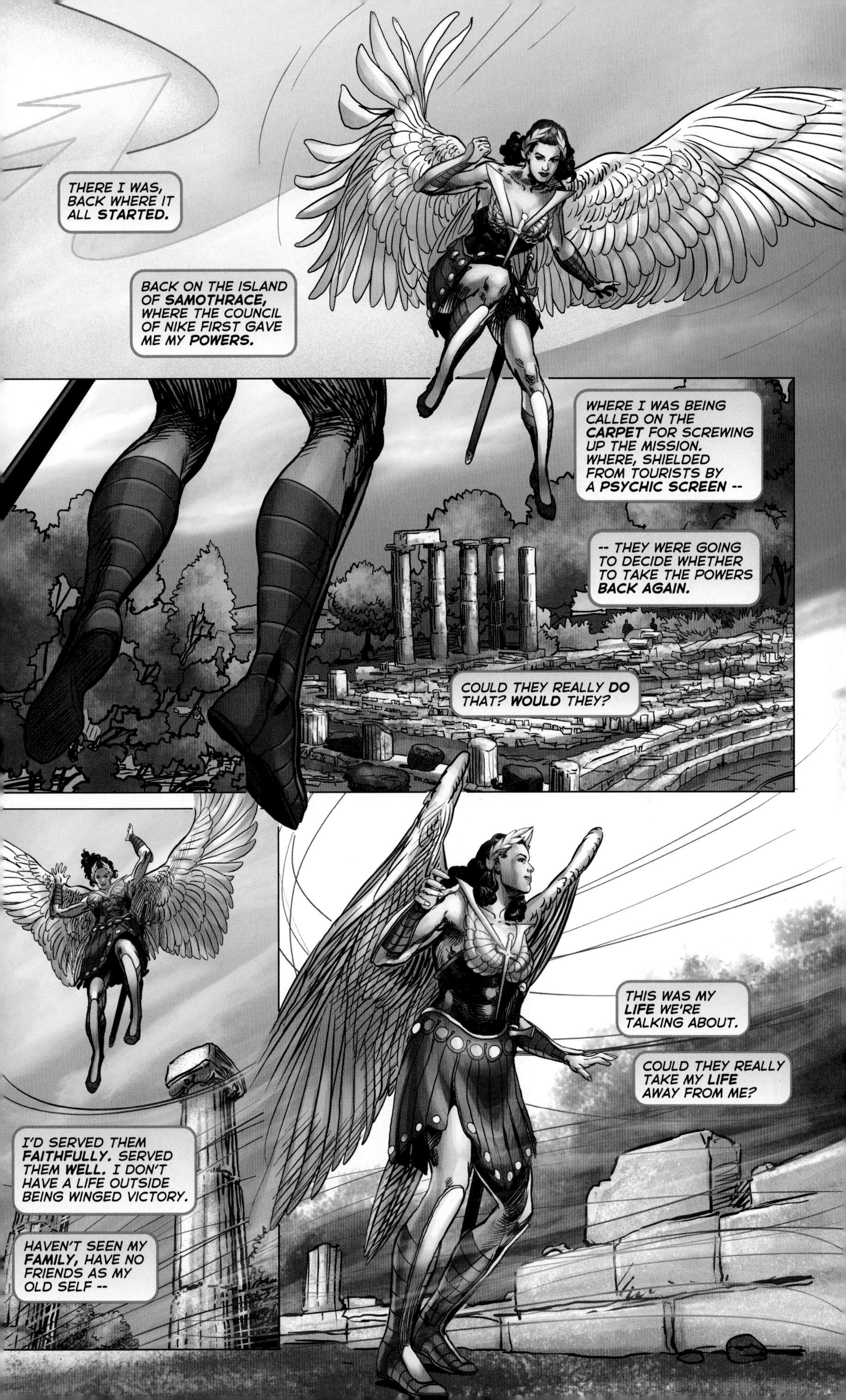
THERE I WAS, BACK WHERE IT ALL STARTED.
BACK ON THE ISLAND OF SAMOTHRACE, WHERE THE COUNCIL OF NIKE FIRST GAVE ME MY POWERS.
WHERE I WAS BEING CALLED ON THE CARPET FOR SCREWING UP THE MISSION. WHERE, SHIELDED FROM TOURISTS BY A PSYCHIC SCREEN --
-- THEY WERE GOING TO DECIDE WHETHER TO TAKE THE POWERS BACK AGAIN.
COULD THEY REALLY DO THAT? WOULD THEY?
THIS WAS MY LIFE WE'RE TALKING ABOUT.
COULD THEY REALLY TAKE MY LIFE AWAY FROM ME?
I'D SERVED THEM FAITHFULLY. SERVED THEM WELL. I DON'T HAVE A LIFE OUTSIDE BEING WINGED VICTORY.
HAVEN'T SEEN MY FAMILY, HAVE NO FRIENDS AS MY OLD SELF --

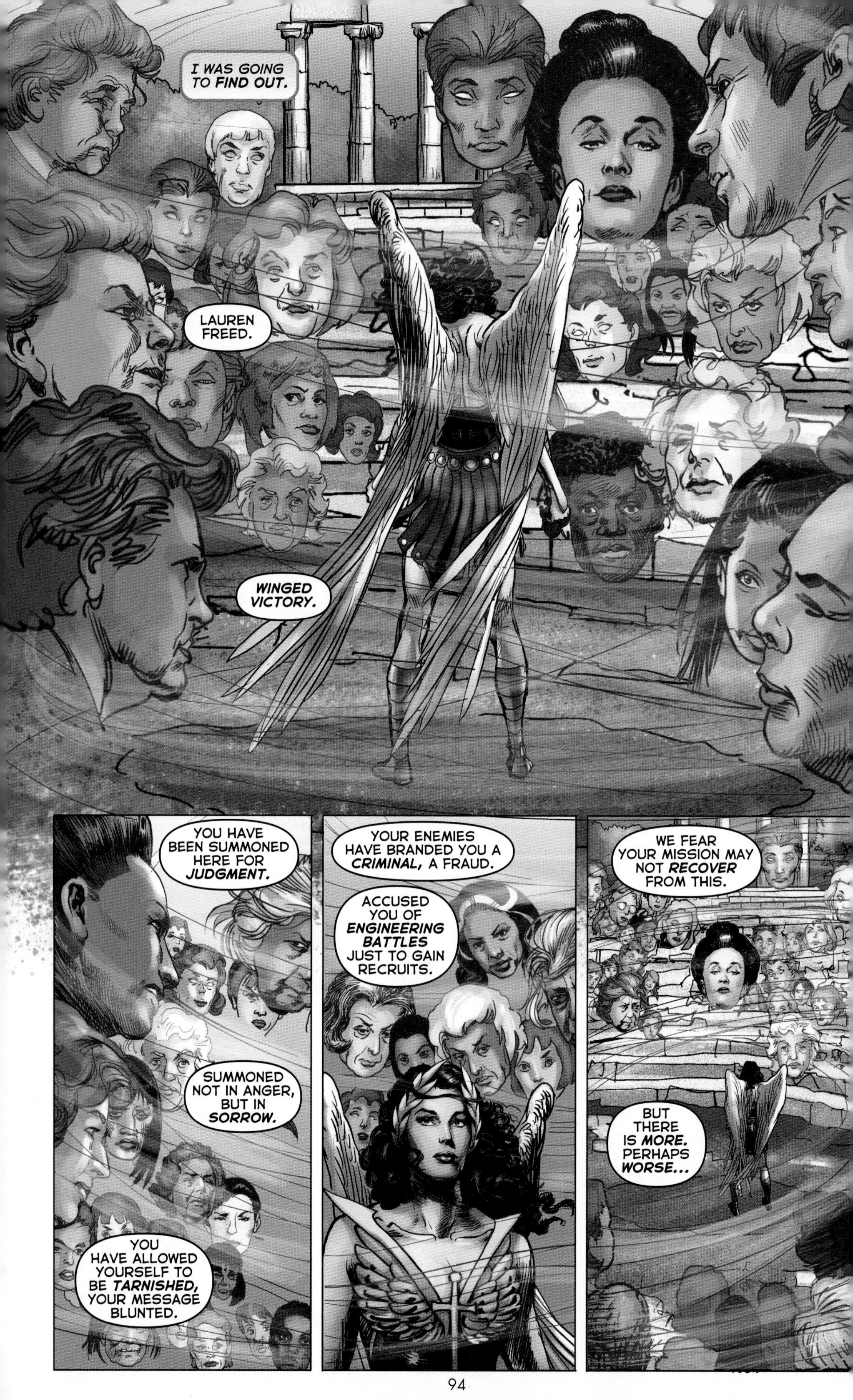
I WAS GOING TO FIND OUT.
LAUREN FREED.
WINGED VICTORY.
YOU HAVE BEEN SUMMONED HERE FOR JUDGMENT.
SUMMONED NOT IN ANGER, BUT IN SORROW.
YOU HAVE ALLOWED YOURSELF TO BE TARNISHED, YOUR MESSAGE BLUNTED.
YOUR ENEMIES HAVE BRANDED YOU A CRIMINAL, A FRAUD.
ACCUSED YOU OF ENGINEERING BATTLES JUST TO GAIN RECRUITS.
WE FEAR YOUR MISSION MAY NOT RECOVER FROM THIS.
BUT THERE IS MORE. PERHAPS WORSE...

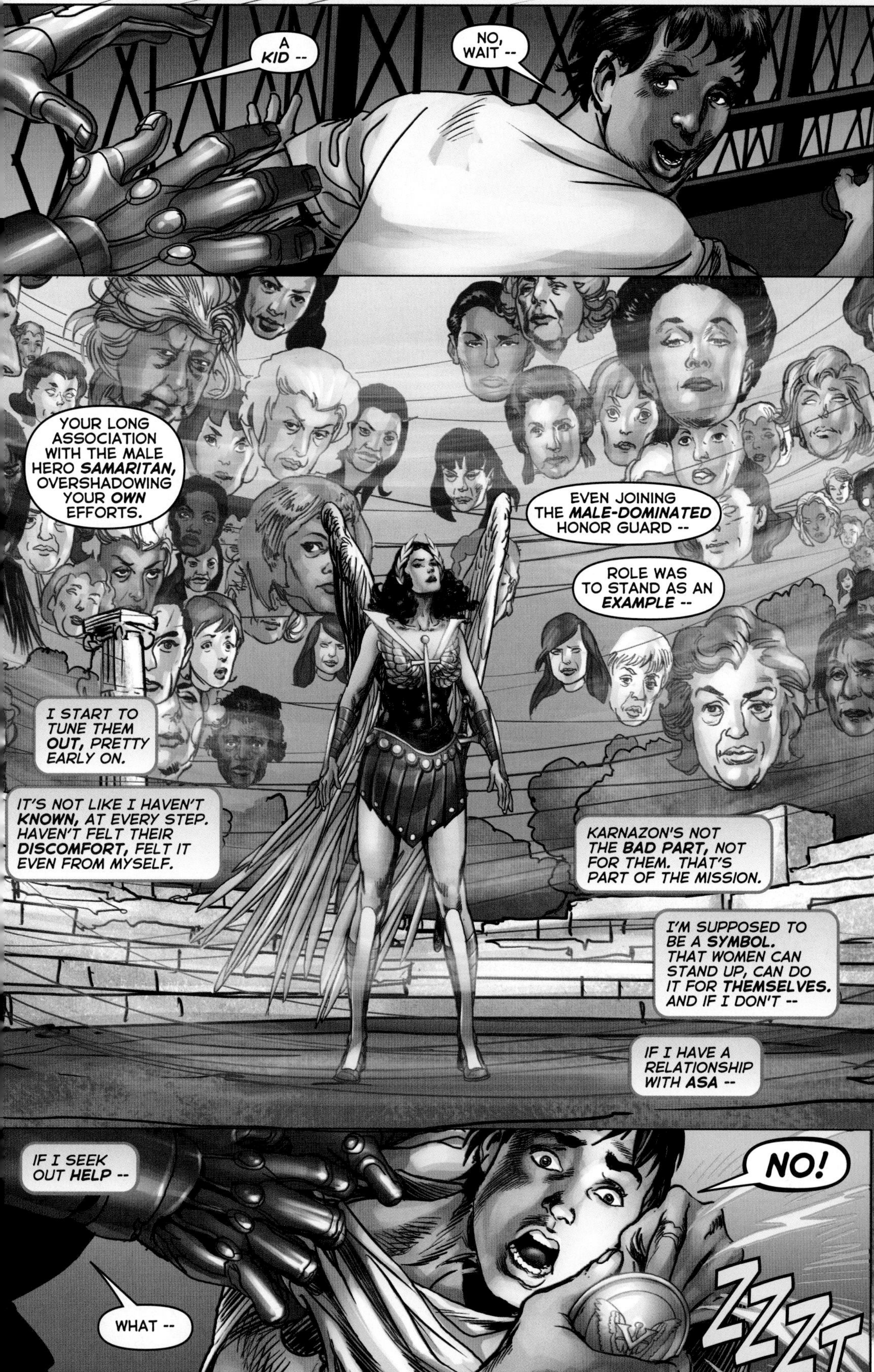
A KID --
NO, WAIT --
YOUR LONG ASSOCIATION WITH THE MALE HERO SAMARITAN, OVERSHADOWING YOUR OWN EFFORTS.
EVEN JOINING THE MALE-DOMINATED HONOR GUARD --
ROLE WAS TO STAND AS AN EXAMPLE --
I START TO TUNE THEM OUT, PRETTY EARLY ON.
IT'S NOT LIKE I HAVEN'T KNOWN, AT EVERY STEP. HAVEN'T FELT THEIR DISCOMFORT, FELT IT EVEN FROM MYSELF.
KARNAZON'S NOT THE BAD PART, NOT FOR THEM. THAT'S PART OF THE MISSION.
I'M SUPPOSED TO BE A SYMBOL. THAT WOMEN CAN STAND UP, CAN DO IT FOR THEMSELVES. AND IF I DON'T --
IF I HAVE A RELATIONSHIP WITH ASA --
IF I SEEK OUT HELP --
NO!
WHAT --
ZZZT

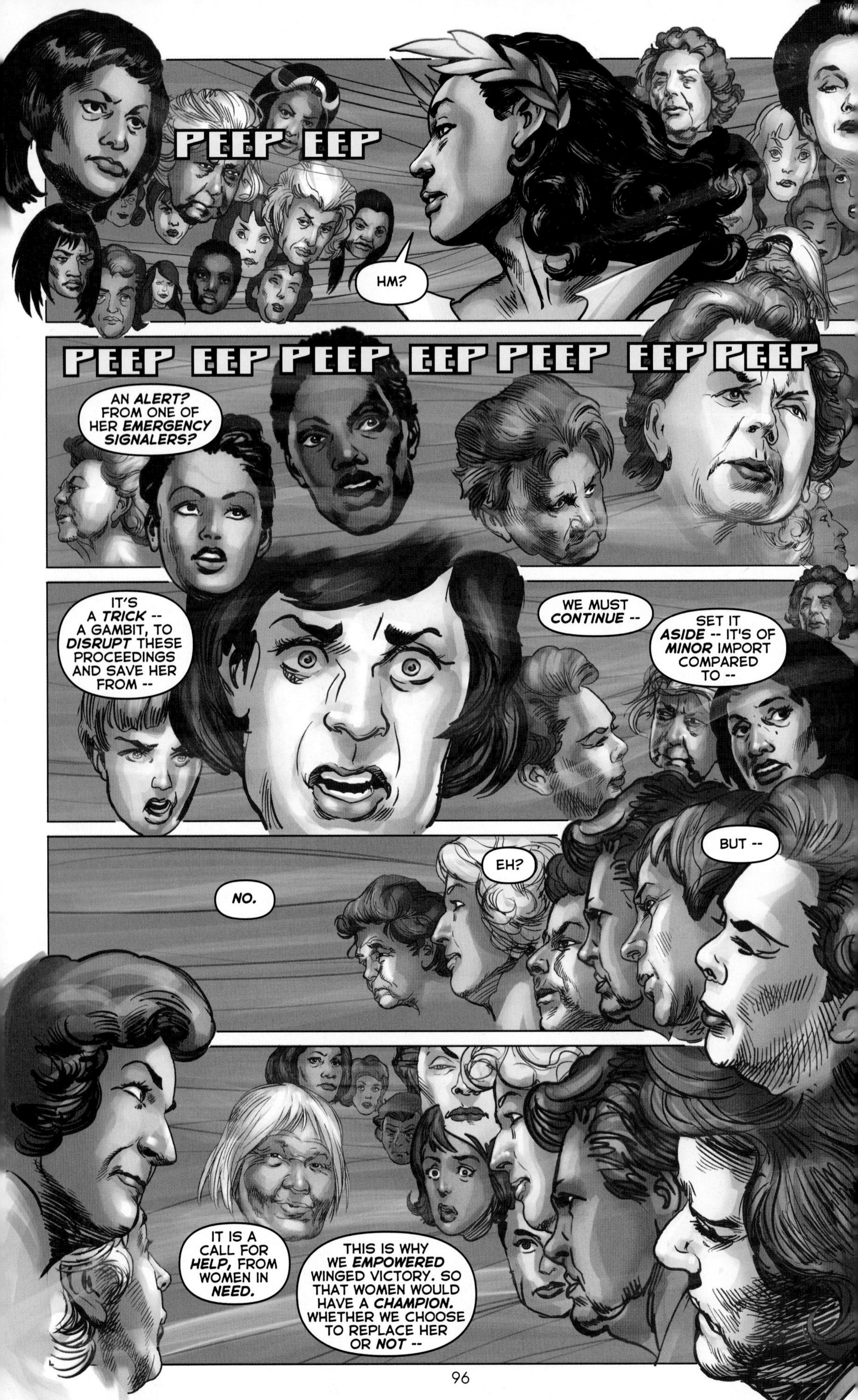
PEEP EEP
HM?
PEEP EEP PEEP EEP PEEP EEP PEEP
AN ALERT? FROM ONE OF HER EMERGENCY SIGNALERS?
IT'S A TRICK -- A GAMBIT, TO DISRUPT THESE PROCEEDINGS AND SAVE HER FROM --
WE MUST CONTINUE --
SET IT ASIDE -- IT'S OF MINOR IMPORT COMPARED TO --
NO.
EH?
BUT --
IT IS A CALL FOR HELP, FROM WOMEN IN NEED.
THIS IS WHY WE EMPOWERED WINGED VICTORY. SO THAT WOMEN WOULD HAVE A CHAMPION. WHETHER WE CHOOSE TO REPLACE HER OR NOT --

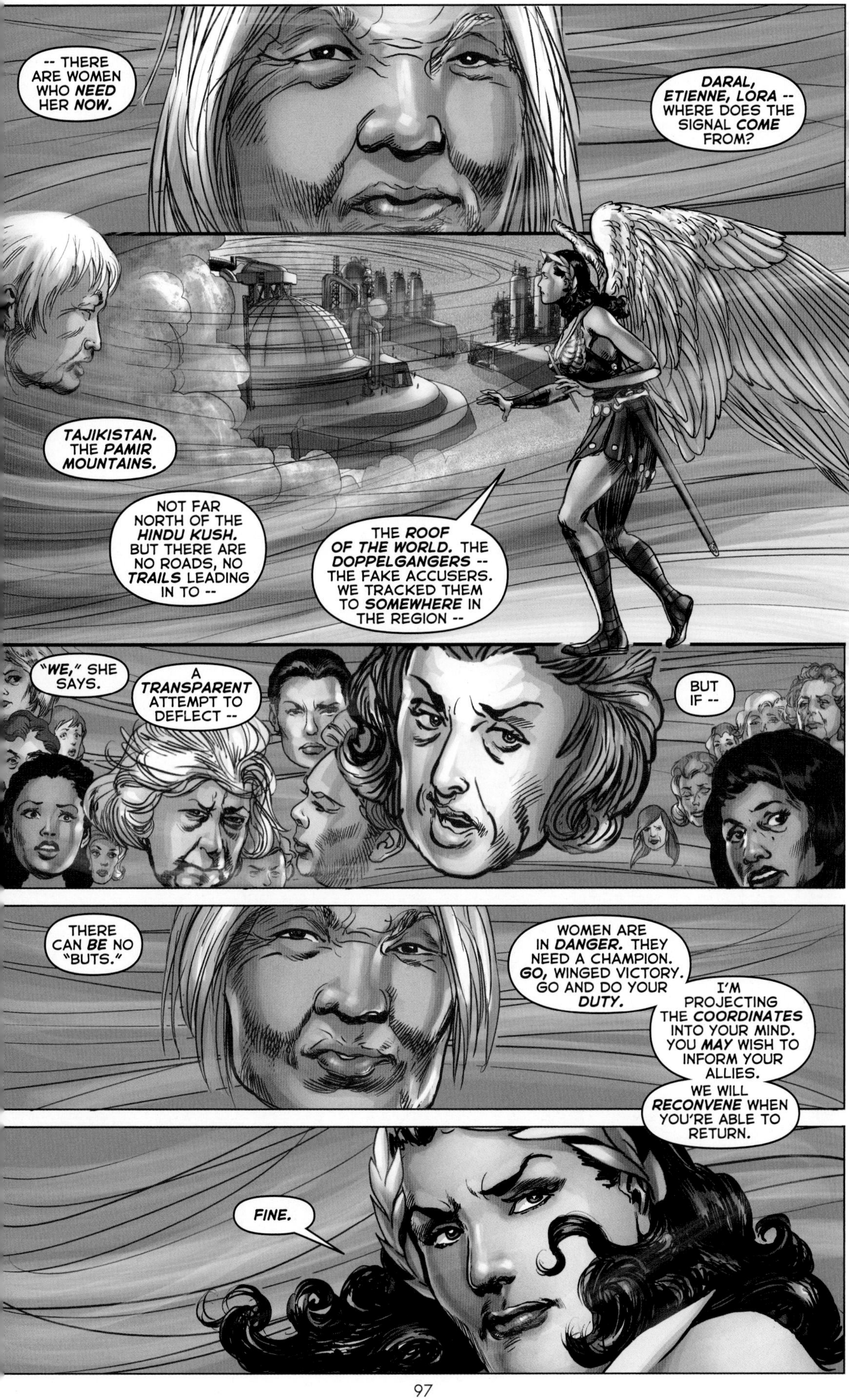
-- THERE ARE WOMEN WHO NEED HER NOW.
DARAL, ETIENNE, LORA -- WHERE DOES THE SIGNAL COME FROM?
TAJIKISTAN. THE PAMIR MOUNTAINS.
NOT FAR NORTH OF THE HINDU KUSH. BUT THERE ARE NO ROADS, NO TRAILS LEADING IN TO --
THE ROOF OF THE WORLD. THE DOPPELGANGERS -- THE FAKE ACCUSERS. WE TRACKED THEM TO SOMEWHERE IN THE REGION --
"WE," SHE SAYS.
A TRANSPARENT ATTEMPT TO DEFLECT --
BUT IF --
THERE CAN BE NO "BUTS."
WOMEN ARE IN DANGER. THEY NEED A CHAMPION. GO, WINGED VICTORY. GO AND DO YOUR DUTY.
I'M PROJECTING THE COORDINATES INTO YOUR MIND. YOU MAY WISH TO INFORM YOUR ALLIES.
WE WILL RECONVENE WHEN YOU'RE ABLE TO RETURN.
FINE.

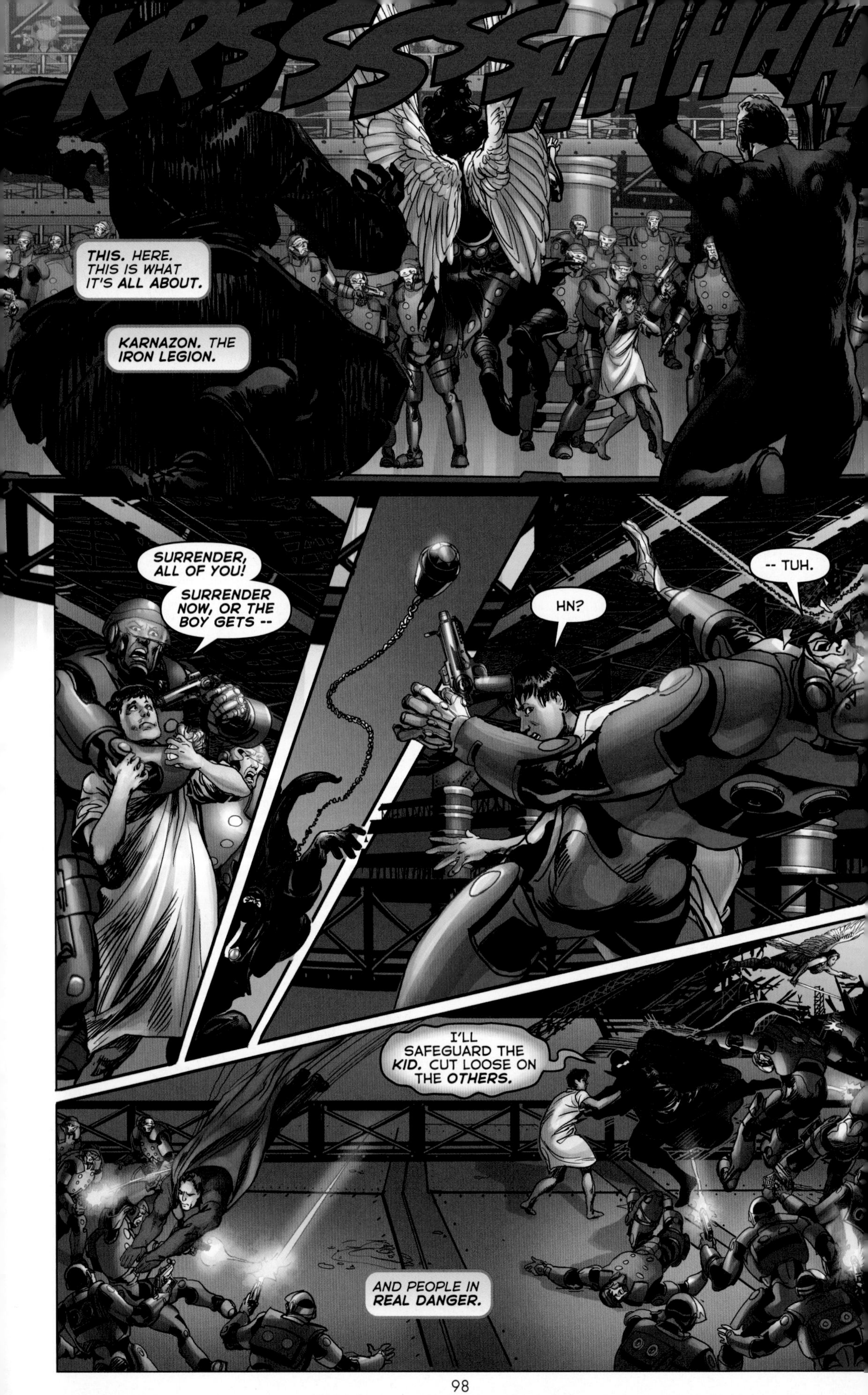
KRSSSSHHHHH
THIS. HERE. THIS IS WHAT IT'S ALL ABOUT.
KARNAZON. THE IRON LEGION.
SURRENDER, ALL OF YOU!
SURRENDER NOW, OR THE BOY GETS --
HN?
-- TUH.
I'LL SAFEGUARD THE KID. CUT LOOSE ON THE OTHERS.
AND PEOPLE IN REAL DANGER.

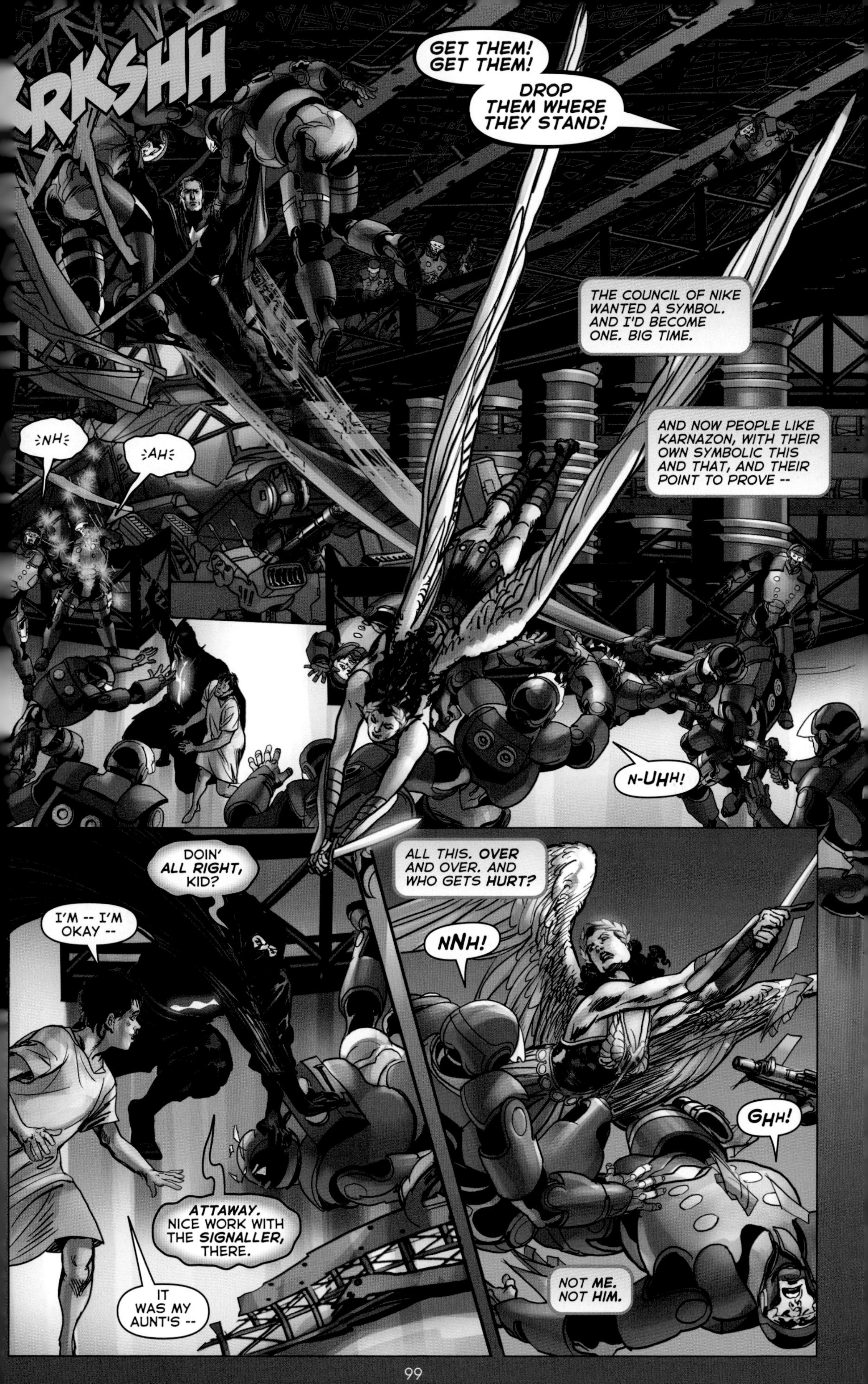
RKSHH
GET THEM! GET THEM!
DROP THEM WHERE THEY STAND!
THE COUNCIL OF NIKE WANTED A SYMBOL. AND I'D BECOME ONE. BIG TIME.
NH
AH
AND NOW PEOPLE LIKE KARNAZON, WITH THEIR OWN SYMBOLIC THIS AND THAT, AND THEIR POINT TO PROVE --
N-UHH!
DOIN' ALL RIGHT, KID?
I'M -- I'M OKAY --
ALL THIS. OVER AND OVER. AND WHO GETS HURT?
NNH!
GHH!
ATTAWAY. NICE WORK WITH THE SIGNALLER, THERE.
IT WAS MY AUNT'S --
NOT ME. NOT HIM.

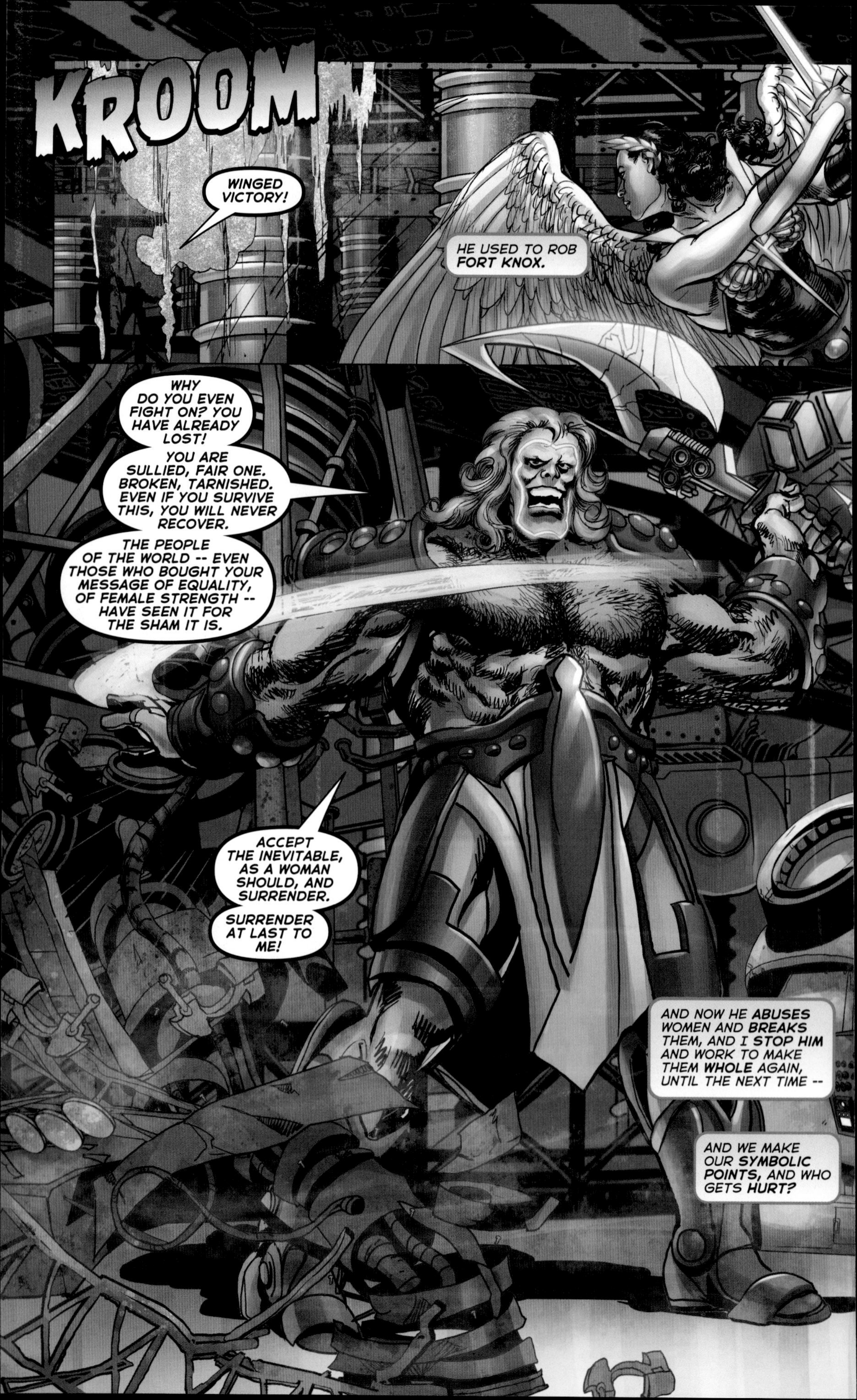
KROOM
WINGED VICTORY!
HE USED TO ROB FORT KNOX.
WHY DO YOU EVEN FIGHT ON? YOU HAVE ALREADY LOST!
YOU ARE SULLIED, FAIR ONE. BROKEN, TARNISHED. EVEN IF YOU SURVIVE THIS, YOU WILL NEVER RECOVER.
THE PEOPLE OF THE WORLD -- EVEN THOSE WHO BOUGHT YOUR MESSAGE OF EQUALITY, OF FEMALE STRENGTH -- HAVE SEEN IT FOR THE SHAM IT IS.
ACCEPT THE INEVITABLE, AS A WOMAN SHOULD, AND SURRENDER.
SURRENDER AT LAST TO ME!
AND NOW HE ABUSES WOMEN AND BREAKS THEM, AND I STOP HIM AND WORK TO MAKE THEM WHOLE AGAIN, UNTIL THE NEXT TIME --
AND WE MAKE OUR SYMBOLIC POINTS, AND WHO GETS HURT?

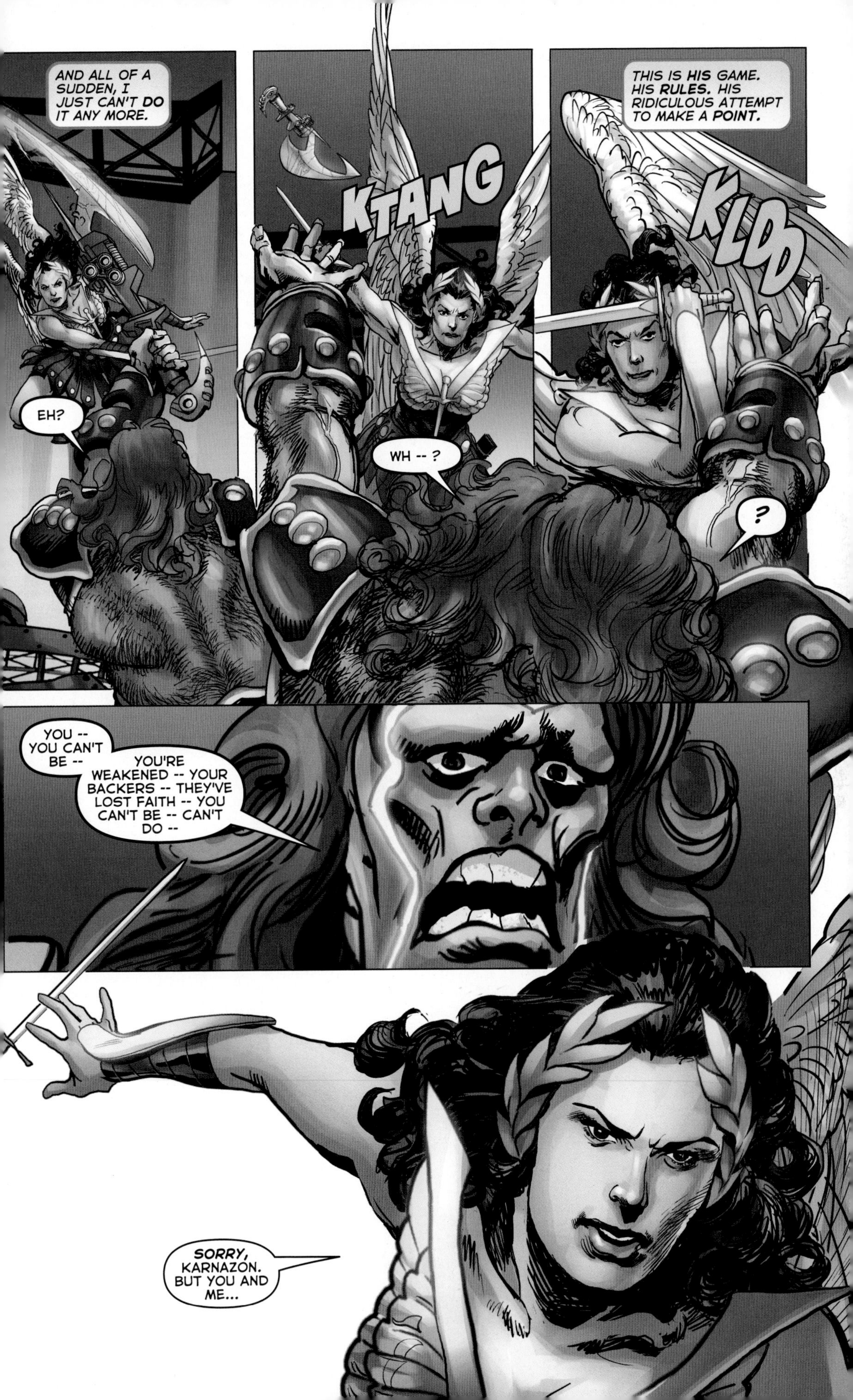
AND ALL OF A SUDDEN, I JUST CAN'T DO IT ANY MORE.
EH?
KTANG
WH -- ?
THIS IS HIS GAME. HIS RULES. HIS RIDICULOUS ATTEMPT TO MAKE A POINT.
KLDD
?
YOU -- YOU CAN'T BE --
YOU'RE WEAKENED -- YOUR BACKERS -- THEY'VE LOST FAITH -- YOU CAN'T BE -- CAN'T DO --
SORRY, KARNAZON. BUT YOU AND ME...

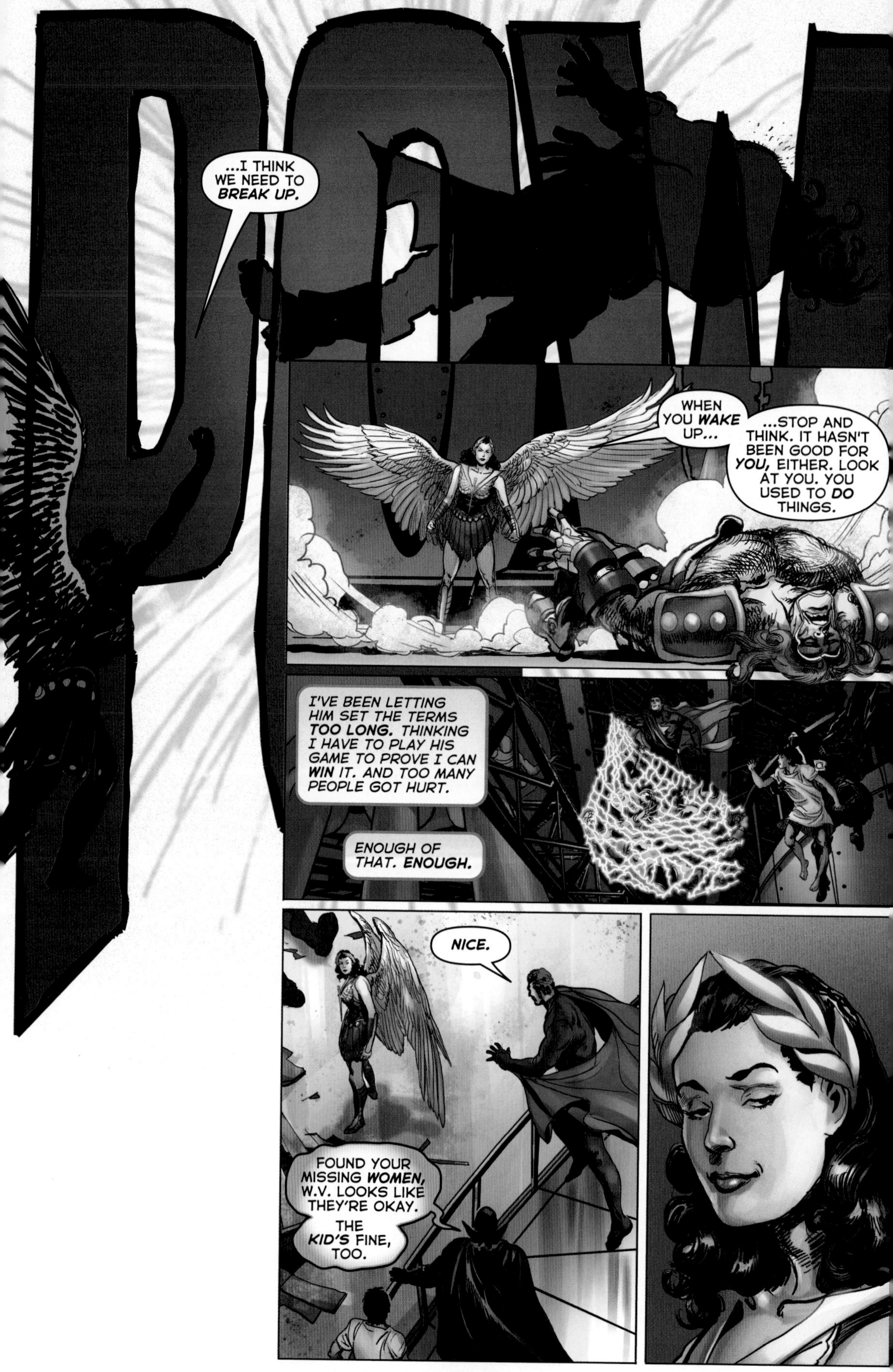

...I THINK WE NEED TO BREAK UP.
WHEN YOU WAKE UP...
...STOP AND THINK. IT HASN'T BEEN GOOD FOR YOU, EITHER. LOOK AT YOU. YOU USED TO DO THINGS.
I'VE BEEN LETTING HIM SET THE TERMS TOO LONG. THINKING I HAVE TO PLAY HIS GAME TO PROVE I CAN WIN IT. AND TOO MANY PEOPLE GOT HURT.
ENOUGH OF THAT. ENOUGH.
NICE.
FOUND YOUR MISSING WOMEN, W.V. LOOKS LIKE THEY'RE OKAY.
THE KID'S FINE, TOO.

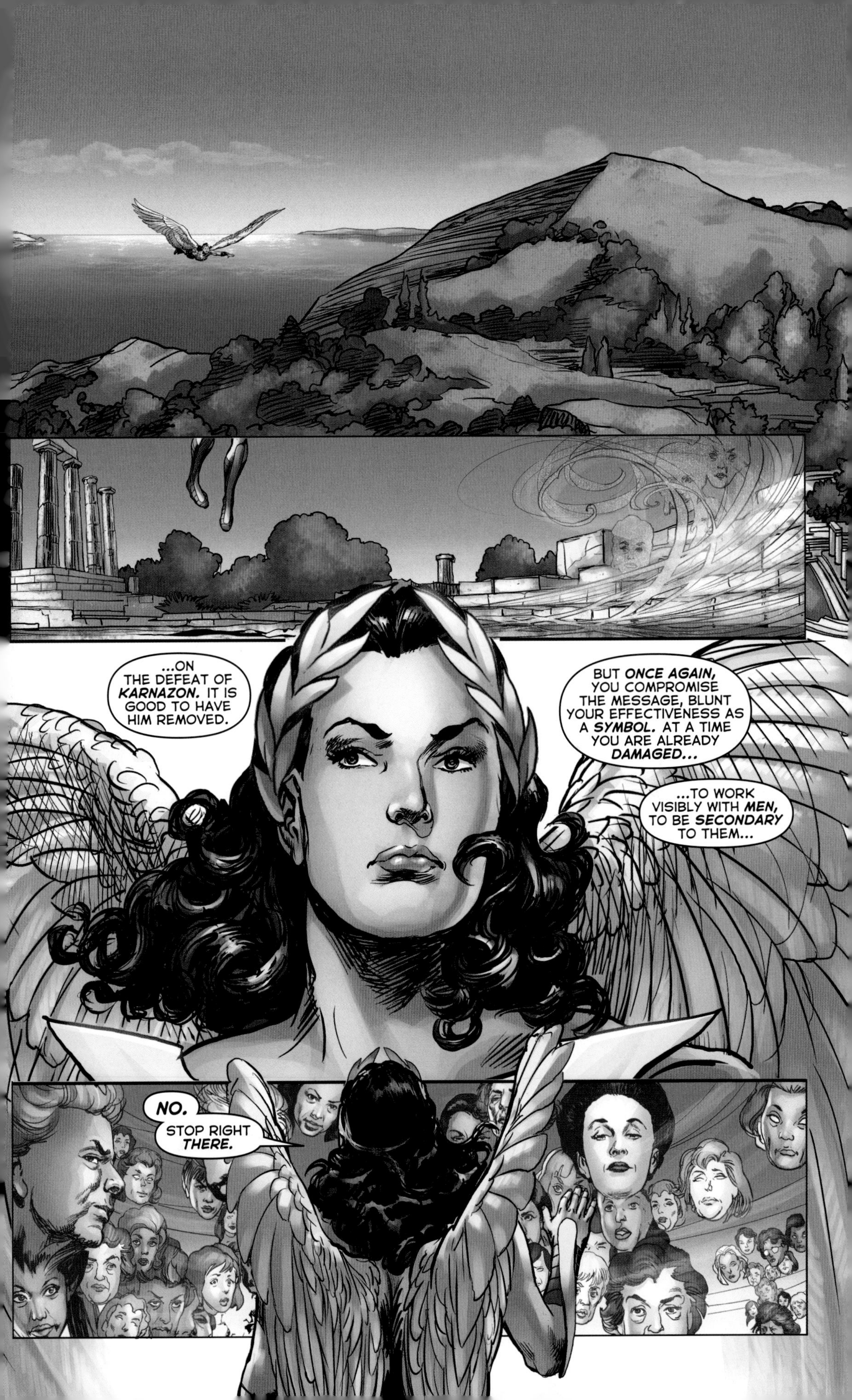
...ON THE DEFEAT OF KARNAZON. IT IS GOOD TO HAVE HIM REMOVED.
BUT ONCE AGAIN, YOU COMPROMISE THE MESSAGE, BLUNT YOUR EFFECTIVENESS AS A SYMBOL. AT A TIME YOU ARE ALREADY DAMAGED...
...TO WORK VISIBLY WITH MEN, TO BE SECONDARY TO THEM...
NO. STOP RIGHT THERE.

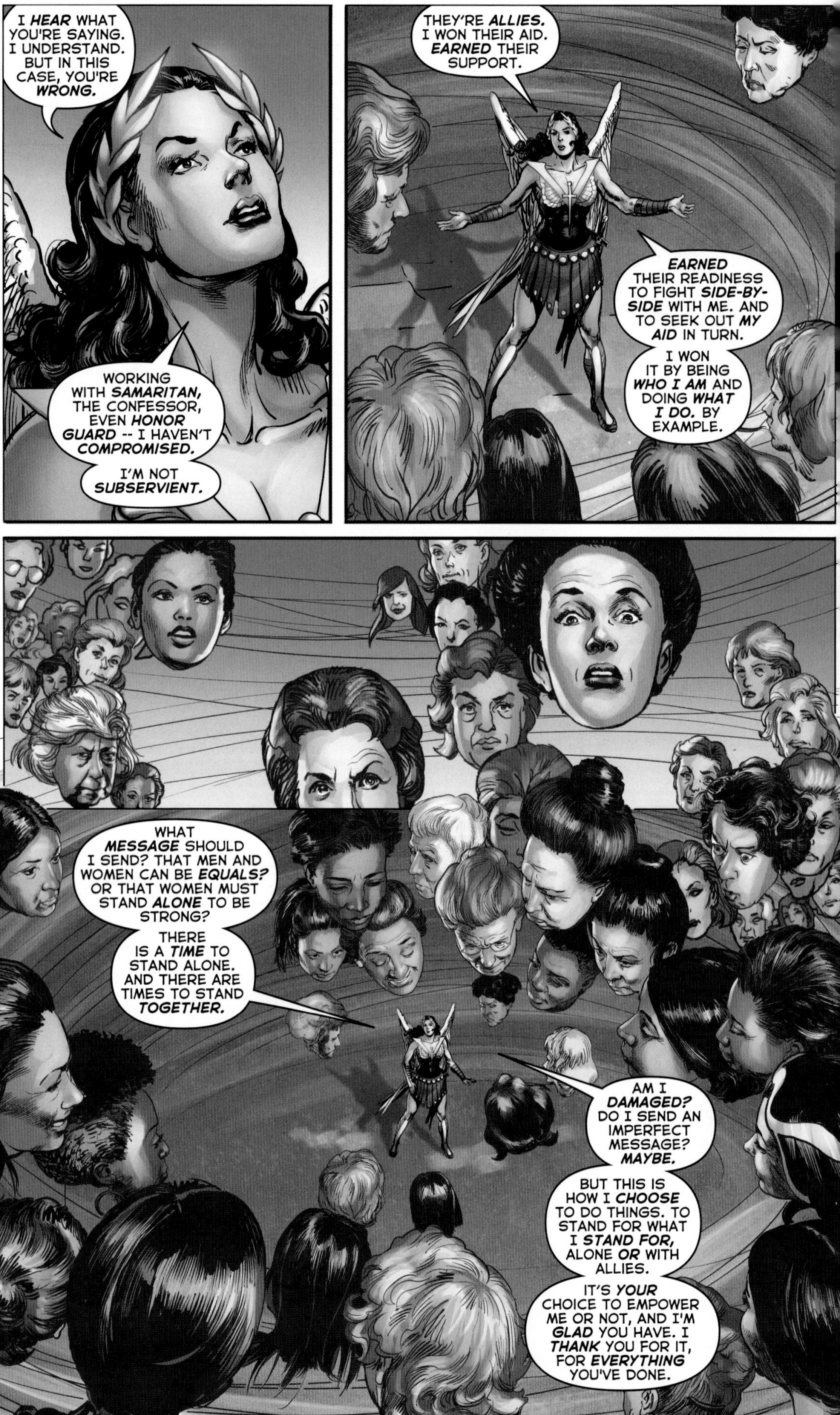
I HEAR WHAT YOU'RE SAYING. I UNDERSTAND. BUT IN THIS CASE, YOU'RE WRONG.
WORKING WITH SAMARITAN, THE CONFESSOR, EVEN HONOR GUARD -- I HAVEN'T COMPROMISED.
I'M NOT SUBSERVIENT.
THEY'RE ALLIES. I WON THEIR AID. EARNED THEIR SUPPORT.
EARNED THEIR READINESS TO FIGHT SIDE-BY-SIDE WITH ME. AND TO SEEK OUT MY AID IN TURN.
I WON IT BY BEING WHO I AM AND DOING WHAT I DO. BY EXAMPLE.
WHAT MESSAGE SHOULD I SEND? THAT MEN AND WOMEN CAN BE EQUALS? OR THAT WOMEN MUST STAND ALONE TO BE STRONG?
THERE IS A TIME TO STAND ALONE. AND THERE ARE TIMES TO STAND TOGETHER.
AM I DAMAGED? DO I SEND AN IMPERFECT MESSAGE? MAYBE.
BUT THIS IS HOW I CHOOSE TO DO THINGS. TO STAND FOR WHAT I STAND FOR, ALONE OR WITH ALLIES.
IT'S YOUR CHOICE TO EMPOWER ME OR NOT, AND I'M GLAD YOU HAVE. I THANK YOU FOR IT, FOR EVERYTHING YOU'VE DONE.

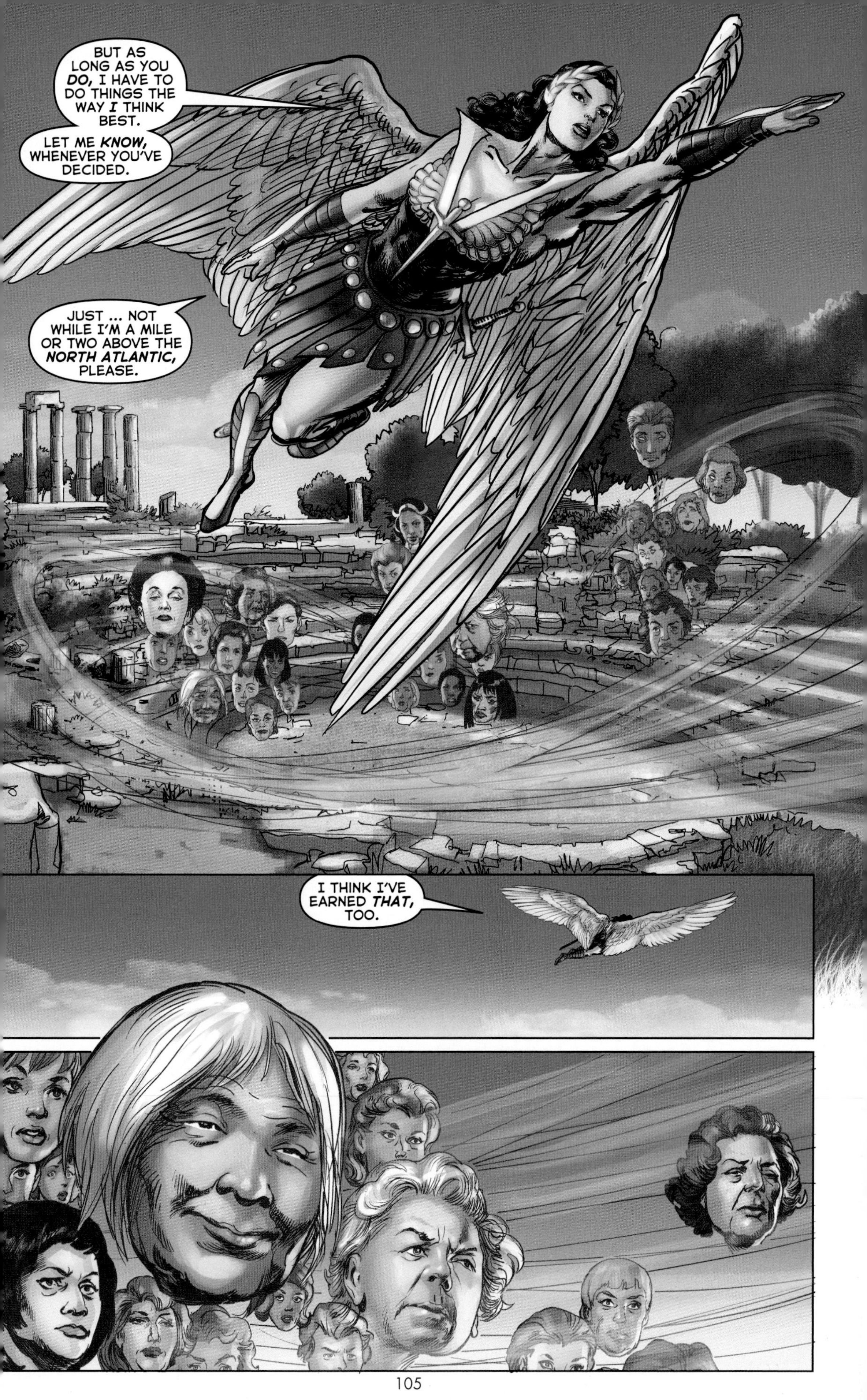
BUT AS LONG AS YOU *DO,* I HAVE TO DO THINGS THE WAY *I* THINK BEST.
LET ME *KNOW,* WHENEVER YOU'VE DECIDED.
JUST ... NOT WHILE I'M A MILE OR TWO ABOVE THE *NORTH ATLANTIC,* PLEASE.
I THINK I'VE EARNED *THAT,* TOO.

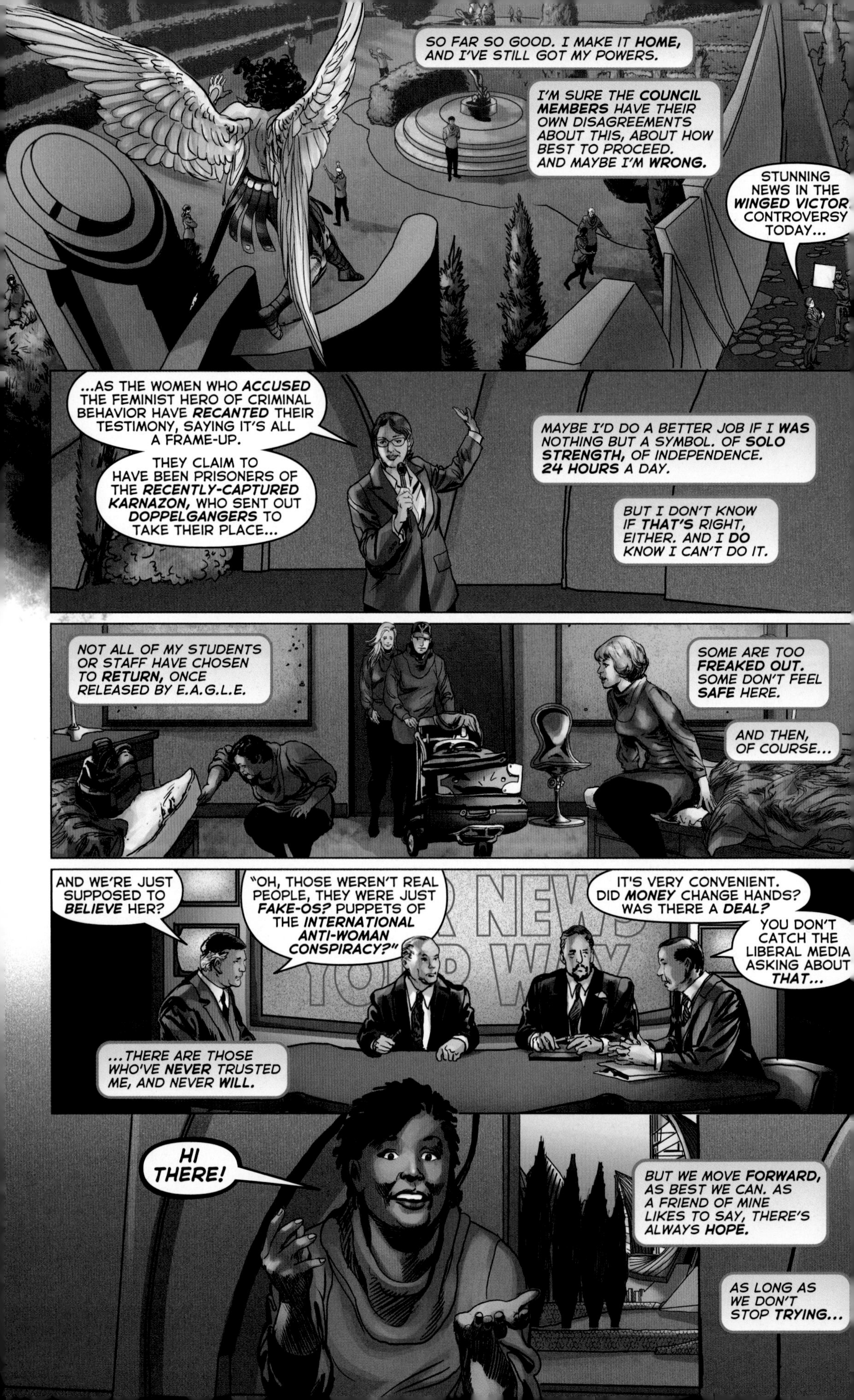
SO FAR SO GOOD. I MAKE IT **HOME,** AND I'VE STILL GOT MY POWERS.
*I'M SURE THE **COUNCIL MEMBERS** HAVE THEIR OWN DISAGREEMENTS ABOUT THIS, ABOUT HOW BEST TO PROCEED. AND MAYBE I'M **WRONG.***
STUNNING NEWS IN THE ***WINGED VICTOR*** CONTROVERSY TODAY...
...AS THE WOMEN WHO ***ACCUSED*** THE FEMINIST HERO OF CRIMINAL BEHAVIOR HAVE ***RECANTED*** THEIR TESTIMONY, SAYING IT'S ALL A FRAME-UP.
THEY CLAIM TO HAVE BEEN PRISONERS OF THE ***RECENTLY-CAPTURED KARNAZON,*** WHO SENT OUT ***DOPPELGANGERS*** TO TAKE THEIR PLACE...
*MAYBE I'D DO A BETTER JOB IF I **WAS** NOTHING BUT A SYMBOL. OF **SOLO STRENGTH,** OF INDEPENDENCE. **24 HOURS** A DAY.*
*BUT I DON'T KNOW IF **THAT'S** RIGHT, EITHER. AND I **DO** KNOW I CAN'T DO IT.*
*NOT ALL OF MY STUDENTS OR STAFF HAVE CHOSEN TO **RETURN,** ONCE RELEASED BY E.A.G.L.E.*
SOME ARE TOO **FREAKED OUT.** SOME DON'T FEEL **SAFE** HERE.
AND THEN, OF COURSE...
AND WE'RE JUST SUPPOSED TO ***BELIEVE*** HER?
"OH, THOSE WEREN'T REAL PEOPLE, THEY WERE JUST ***FAKE-OS?*** PUPPETS OF THE ***INTERNATIONAL ANTI-WOMAN CONSPIRACY?"***
IT'S VERY CONVENIENT. DID ***MONEY*** CHANGE HANDS? WAS THERE A ***DEAL?***
YOU DON'T CATCH THE LIBERAL MEDIA ASKING ABOUT ***THAT...***
*...THERE ARE THOSE WHO'VE **NEVER** TRUSTED ME, AND NEVER **WILL.***
HI THERE!
BUT WE MOVE **FORWARD,** AS BEST WE CAN. AS A FRIEND OF MINE LIKES TO SAY, THERE'S ALWAYS **HOPE.**
AS LONG AS WE DON'T STOP **TRYING...**

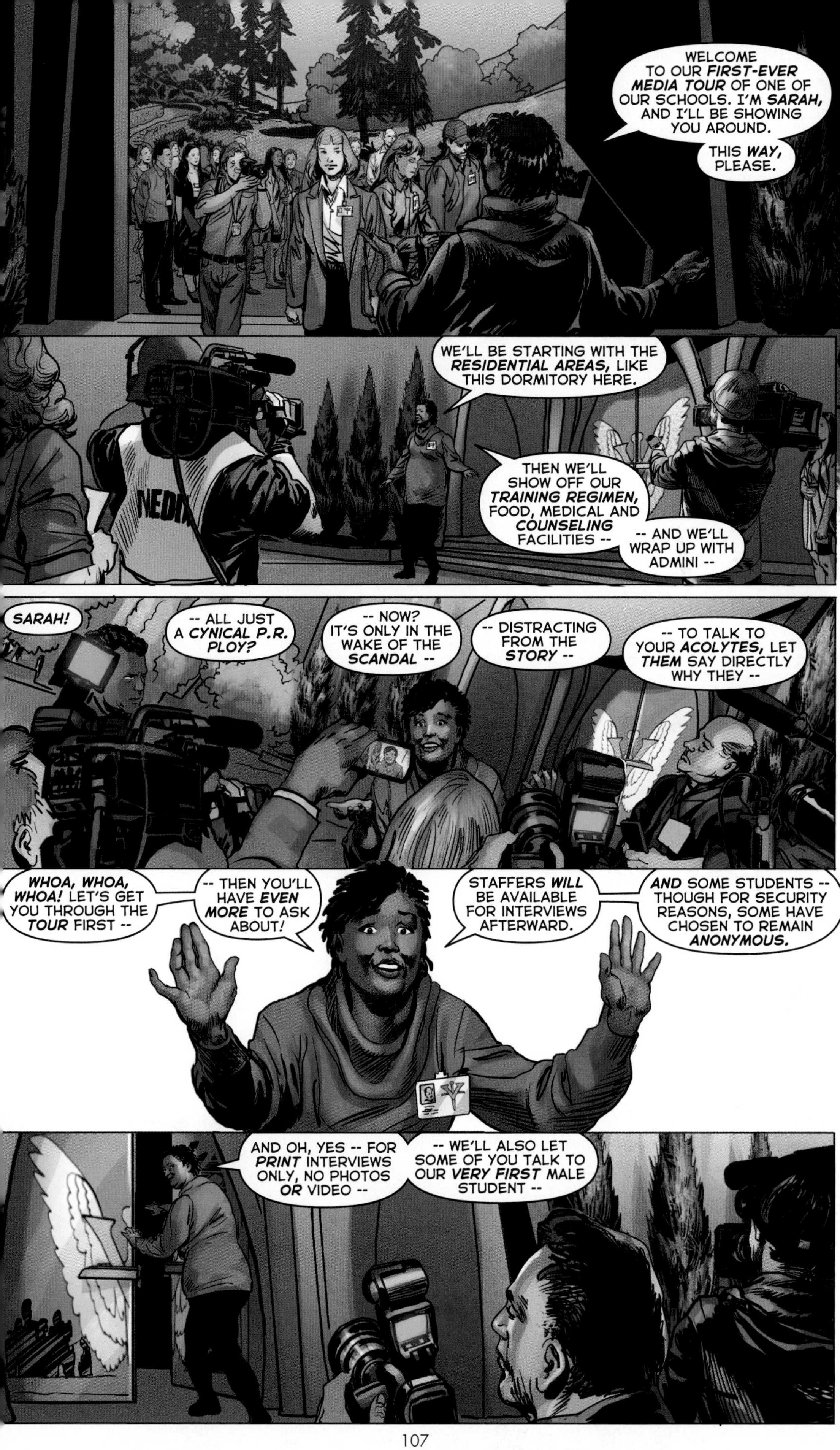
WELCOME TO OUR FIRST-EVER MEDIA TOUR OF ONE OF OUR SCHOOLS. I'M SARAH, AND I'LL BE SHOWING YOU AROUND.
THIS WAY, PLEASE.
WE'LL BE STARTING WITH THE RESIDENTIAL AREAS, LIKE THIS DORMITORY HERE.
THEN WE'LL SHOW OFF OUR TRAINING REGIMEN, FOOD, MEDICAL AND COUNSELING FACILITIES --
-- AND WE'LL WRAP UP WITH ADMINI --
SARAH!
-- ALL JUST A CYNICAL P.R. PLOY?
-- NOW? IT'S ONLY IN THE WAKE OF THE SCANDAL --
-- DISTRACTING FROM THE STORY --
-- TO TALK TO YOUR ACOLYTES, LET THEM SAY DIRECTLY WHY THEY --
WHOA, WHOA, WHOA! LET'S GET YOU THROUGH THE TOUR FIRST --
-- THEN YOU'LL HAVE EVEN MORE TO ASK ABOUT!
STAFFERS WILL BE AVAILABLE FOR INTERVIEWS AFTERWARD.
AND SOME STUDENTS -- THOUGH FOR SECURITY REASONS, SOME HAVE CHOSEN TO REMAIN ANONYMOUS.
AND OH, YES -- FOR PRINT INTERVIEWS ONLY, NO PHOTOS OR VIDEO --
-- WE'LL ALSO LET SOME OF YOU TALK TO OUR VERY FIRST MALE STUDENT --

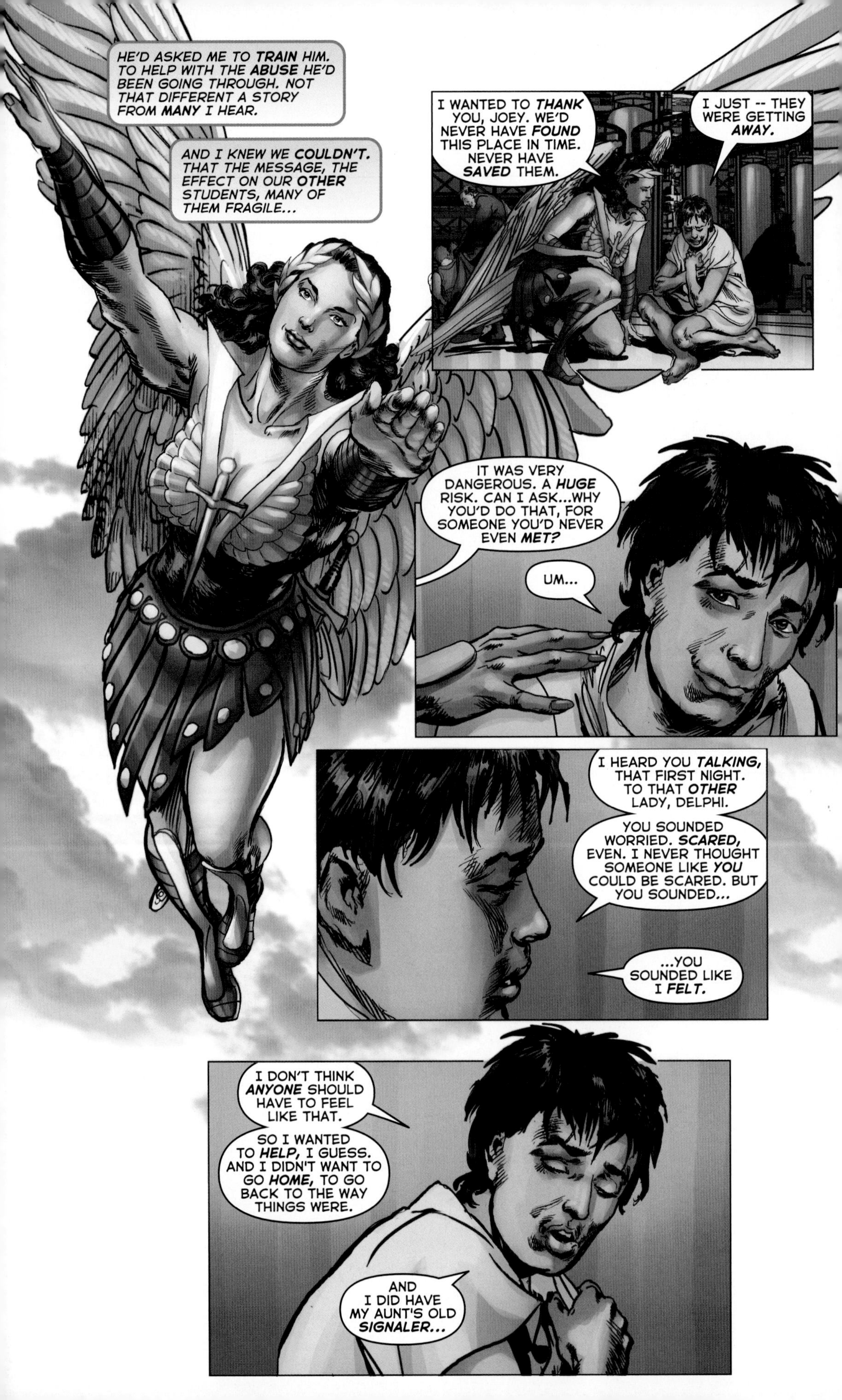
HE'D ASKED ME TO TRAIN HIM. TO HELP WITH THE ABUSE HE'D BEEN GOING THROUGH. NOT THAT DIFFERENT A STORY FROM MANY I HEAR.
AND I KNEW WE COULDN'T. THAT THE MESSAGE, THE EFFECT ON OUR OTHER STUDENTS, MANY OF THEM FRAGILE...
I WANTED TO THANK YOU, JOEY. WE'D NEVER HAVE FOUND THIS PLACE IN TIME. NEVER HAVE SAVED THEM.
I JUST -- THEY WERE GETTING AWAY.
IT WAS VERY DANGEROUS. A HUGE RISK. CAN I ASK...WHY YOU'D DO THAT, FOR SOMEONE YOU'D NEVER EVEN MET?
UM...
I HEARD YOU TALKING, THAT FIRST NIGHT. TO THAT OTHER LADY, DELPHI.
YOU SOUNDED WORRIED. SCARED, EVEN. I NEVER THOUGHT SOMEONE LIKE YOU COULD BE SCARED. BUT YOU SOUNDED...
...YOU SOUNDED LIKE I FELT.
I DON'T THINK ANYONE SHOULD HAVE TO FEEL LIKE THAT.
SO I WANTED TO HELP, I GUESS. AND I DIDN'T WANT TO GO HOME, TO GO BACK TO THE WAY THINGS WERE.
AND I DID HAVE MY AUNT'S OLD SIGNALER...

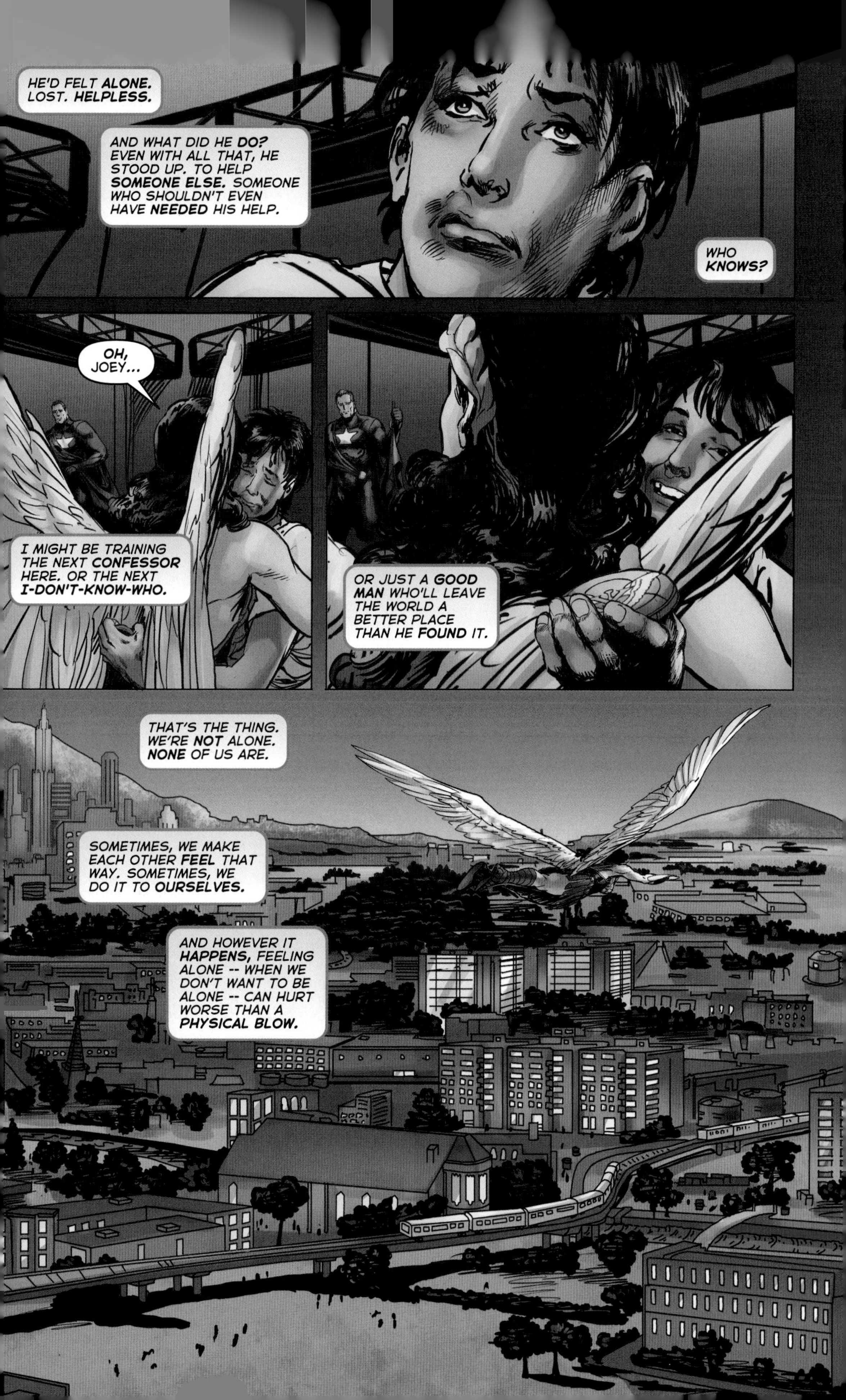

HE'D FELT ALONE. LOST. HELPLESS.
AND WHAT DID HE DO? EVEN WITH ALL THAT, HE STOOD UP. TO HELP SOMEONE ELSE. SOMEONE WHO SHOULDN'T EVEN HAVE NEEDED HIS HELP.
WHO KNOWS?
OH, JOEY...
I MIGHT BE TRAINING THE NEXT CONFESSOR HERE. OR THE NEXT I-DON'T-KNOW-WHO.
OR JUST A GOOD MAN WHO'LL LEAVE THE WORLD A BETTER PLACE THAN HE FOUND IT.
THAT'S THE THING. WE'RE NOT ALONE. NONE OF US ARE.
SOMETIMES, WE MAKE EACH OTHER FEEL THAT WAY. SOMETIMES, WE DO IT TO OURSELVES.
AND HOWEVER IT HAPPENS, FEELING ALONE -- WHEN WE DON'T WANT TO BE ALONE -- CAN HURT WORSE THAN A PHYSICAL BLOW.

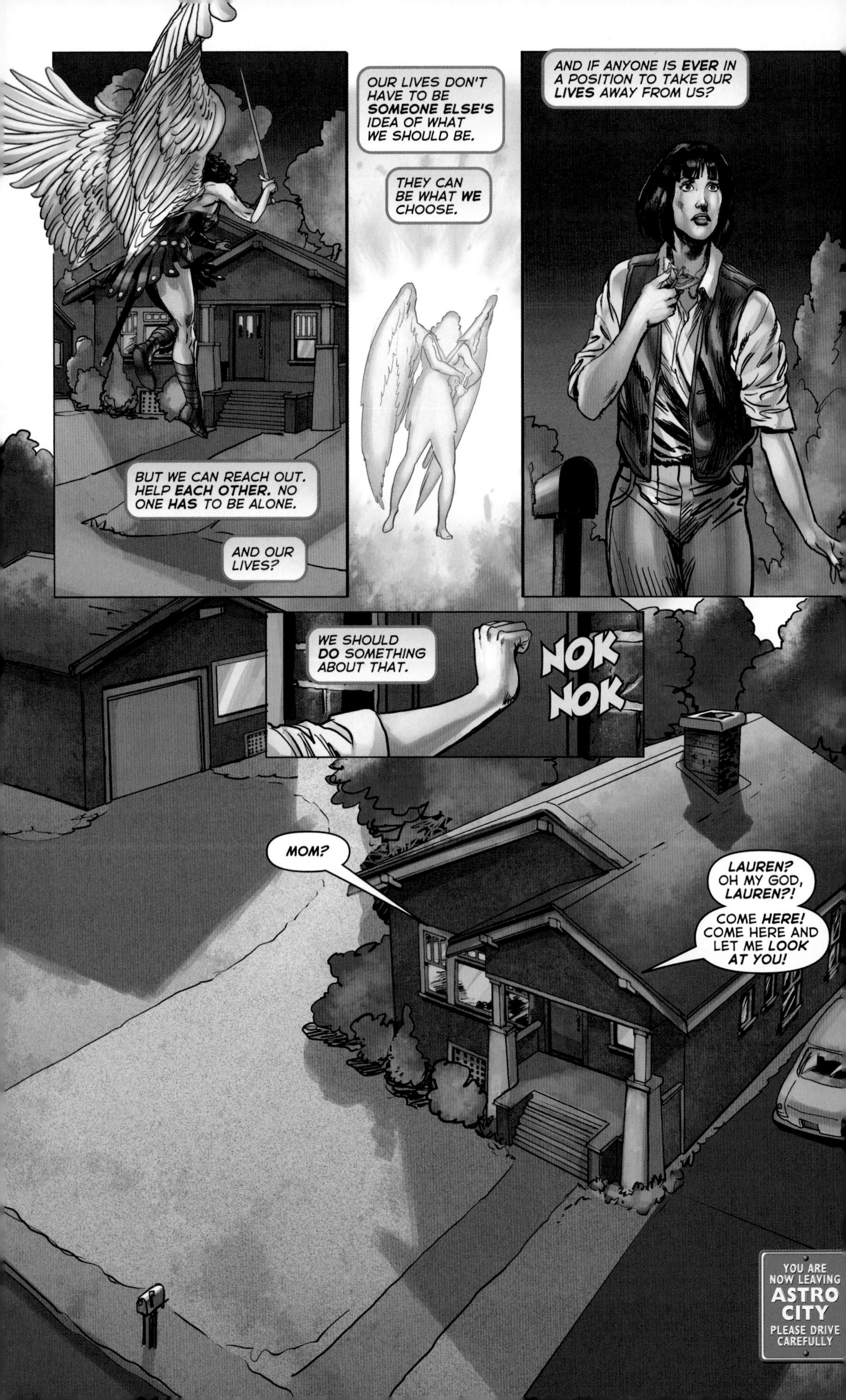
BUT WE CAN REACH OUT. HELP EACH OTHER. NO ONE HAS TO BE ALONE.
AND OUR LIVES?
OUR LIVES DON'T HAVE TO BE SOMEONE ELSE'S IDEA OF WHAT WE SHOULD BE.
THEY CAN BE WHAT WE CHOOSE.
AND IF ANYONE IS EVER IN A POSITION TO TAKE OUR LIVES AWAY FROM US?
WE SHOULD DO SOMETHING ABOUT THAT.
NOK NOK
MOM?
LAUREN? OH MY GOD, LAUREN?!
COME HERE! COME HERE AND LET ME LOOK AT YOU!
YOU ARE NOW LEAVING ASTRO CITY PLEASE DRIVE CAREFULLY

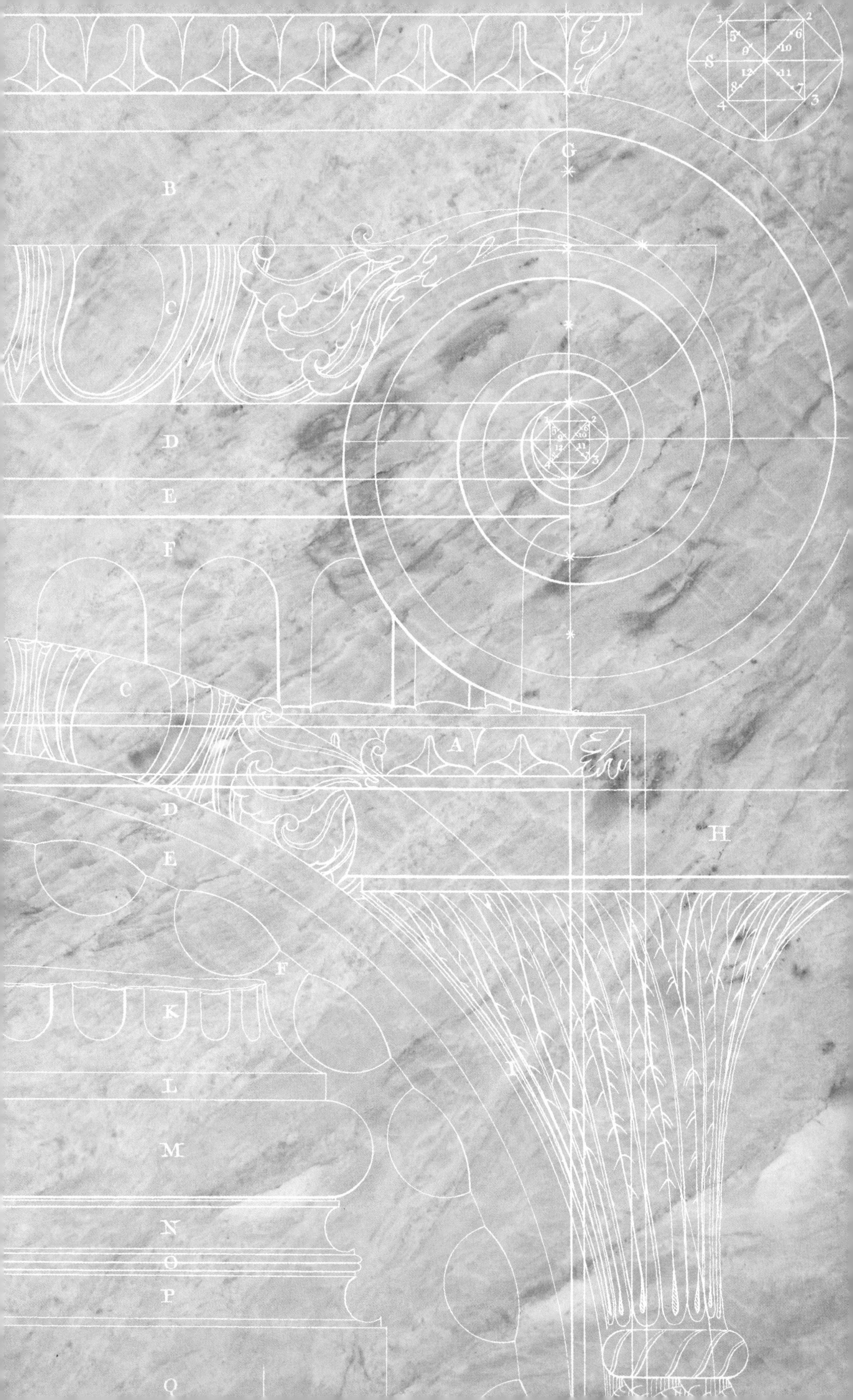

S
G
B
C
D
E
F
C
A
D
E
H
F
K
I
L
M
N
O
P
Q

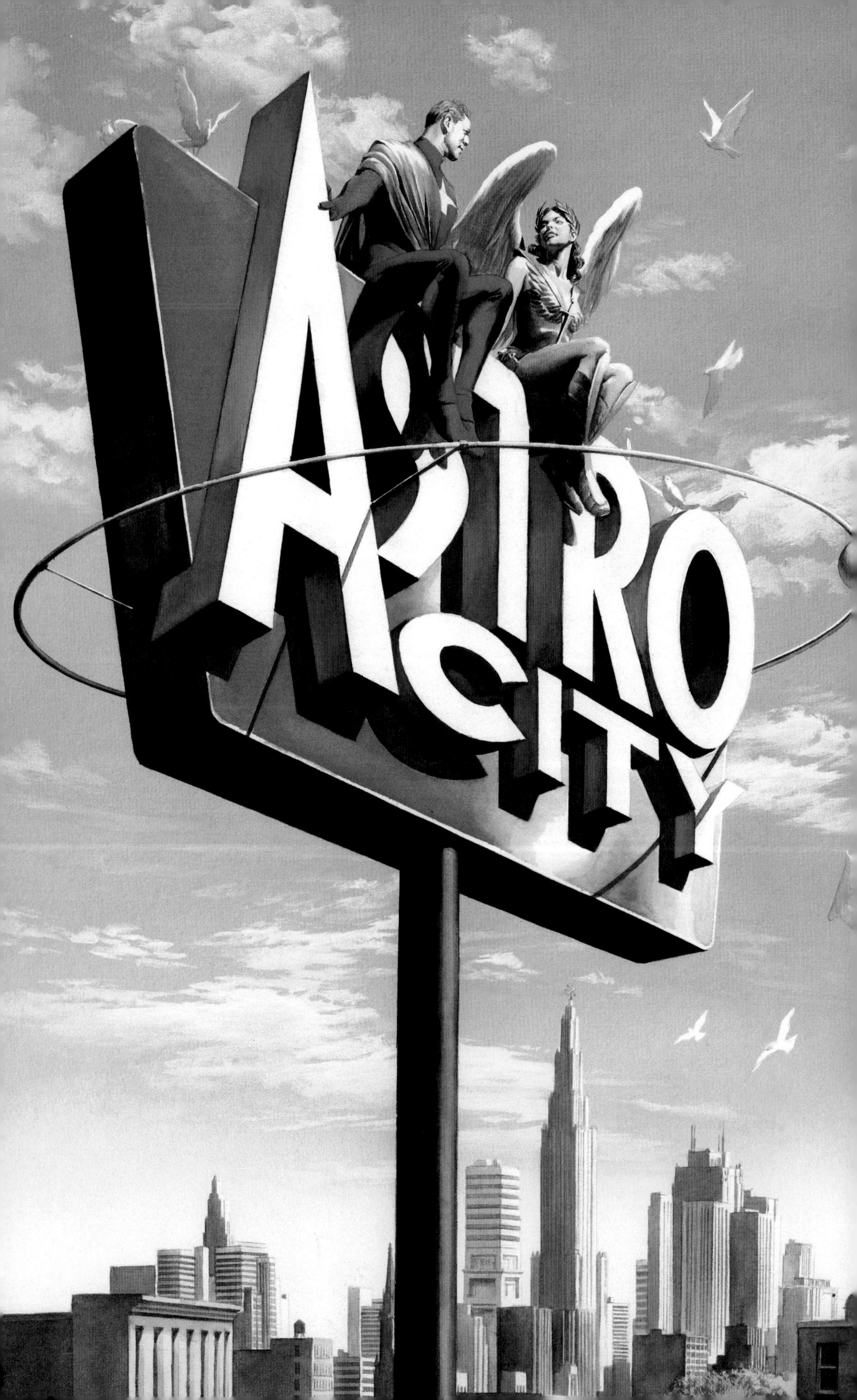
ASTRO
CITY

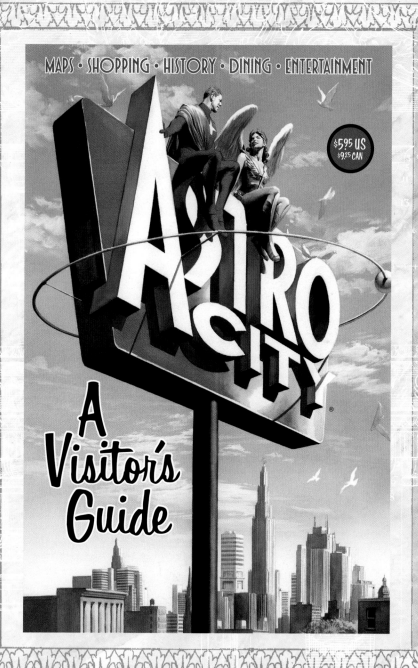

MAPS · SHOPPING · HISTORY · DINING · ENTERTAINMENT

$5.95 US
$9.25 CAN

ASTRO CITY

A Visitor's Guide

A MESSAGE FROM MAYOR GERALD "JERRY" GREENWALD

Gerald Greenwald
Office of the Mayor
City Hall
One Astro Plaza
Astro City

October 13, 2004

Dear Friend:

Welcome! Welcome to Astro City!

As I look out my office window, I see the spires of Grandenetti Cathedral, the AstroBank Tower—commemorating the sacrifice that gave Astro City her name—and above it all, the sheltering bulk of Mount Kirby. I think back to the days when the first pioneers built their homes, farms and that historic mill near the base of Romeyn Falls, and I know they'd be proud of what their tiny settlement has grown into.

Astro City is the perfect home base to explore the natural wonders around us, from breathtaking mountains offering skiing, hiking and more, to rolling farm country full of scenic wonders and agricultural bounties. Or if you're a city person at heart, our museums, theaters, parks and nightclubs are second to none.

And of course, there are the heroes, a virtual galaxy of stars who've graced our home since the dramatic debut of Air Ace—and even earlier, back to the Old West days of Ironhorse and beyond. From Samaritan and the First Family rocketing overhead, to Jack-in-the-Box patrolling the rooftops, there's always something to see. Caution is the watchword, but remember—nowhere on Earth is as well-protected as Astro City.

For my part, I love our five-star restaurants and ethnic enclaves, brimming with gastronomical delights—which sometimes makes my wife say I've been possessed by Gullet the Insatiable Man! But that just spurs me to enjoy our world-class health clubs and countless recreational opportunities.

Whatever your reason for visiting, you're sure to find it here.

Astro City—it's the adventure of your life!

Best,

Jerry

ASTRO CITY
Experience the Adventure!

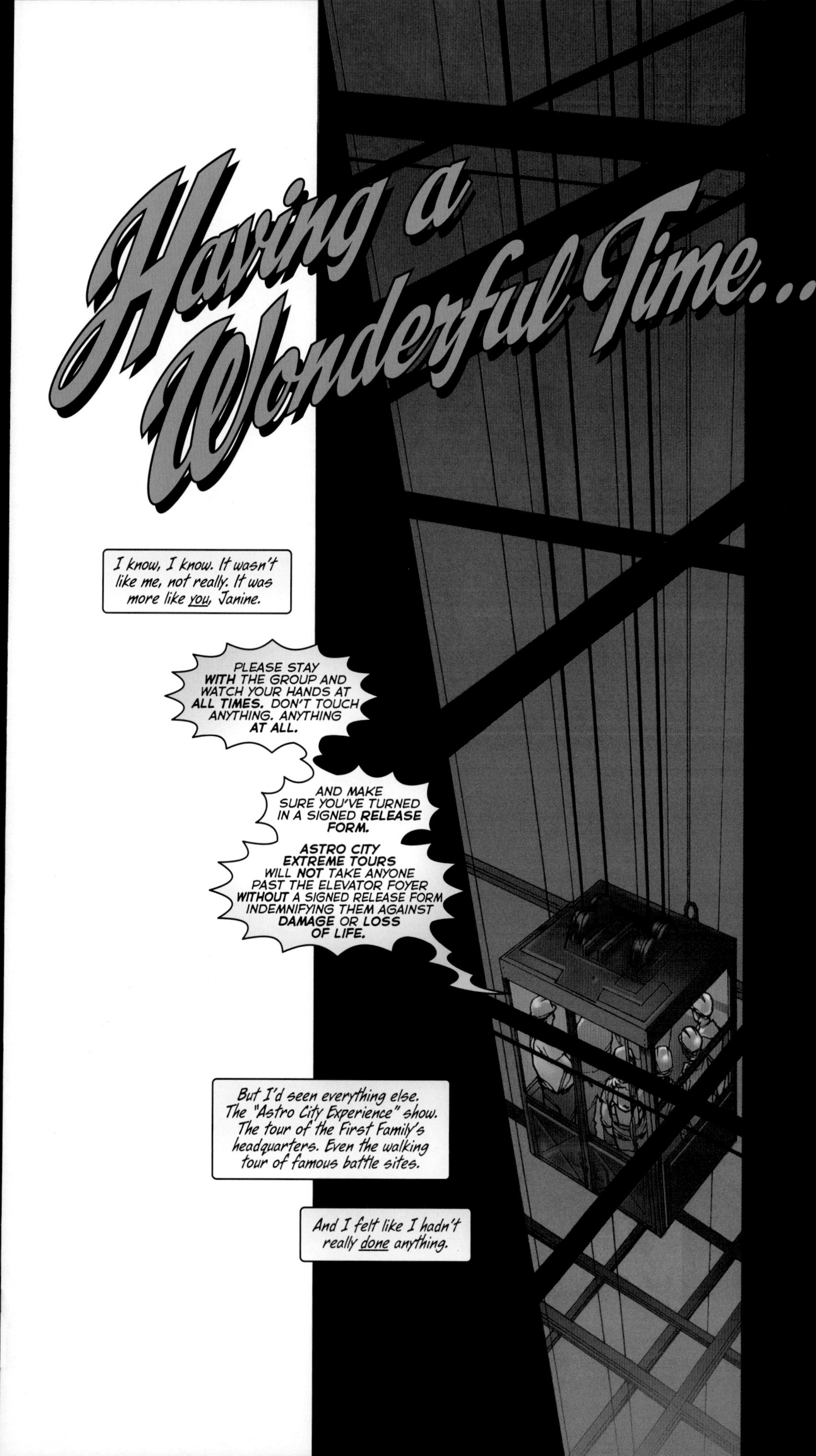
Having a Wonderful Time...
I know, I know. It wasn't like me, not really. It was more like you, Janine.
PLEASE STAY WITH THE GROUP AND WATCH YOUR HANDS AT ALL TIMES. DON'T TOUCH ANYTHING. ANYTHING AT ALL.
AND MAKE SURE YOU'VE TURNED IN A SIGNED RELEASE FORM.
ASTRO CITY EXTREME TOURS WILL NOT TAKE ANYONE PAST THE ELEVATOR FOYER WITHOUT A SIGNED RELEASE FORM INDEMNIFYING THEM AGAINST DAMAGE OR LOSS OF LIFE.
But I'd seen everything else. The "Astro City Experience" show. The tour of the First Family's headquarters. Even the walking tour of famous battle sites.
And I felt like I hadn't really done anything.

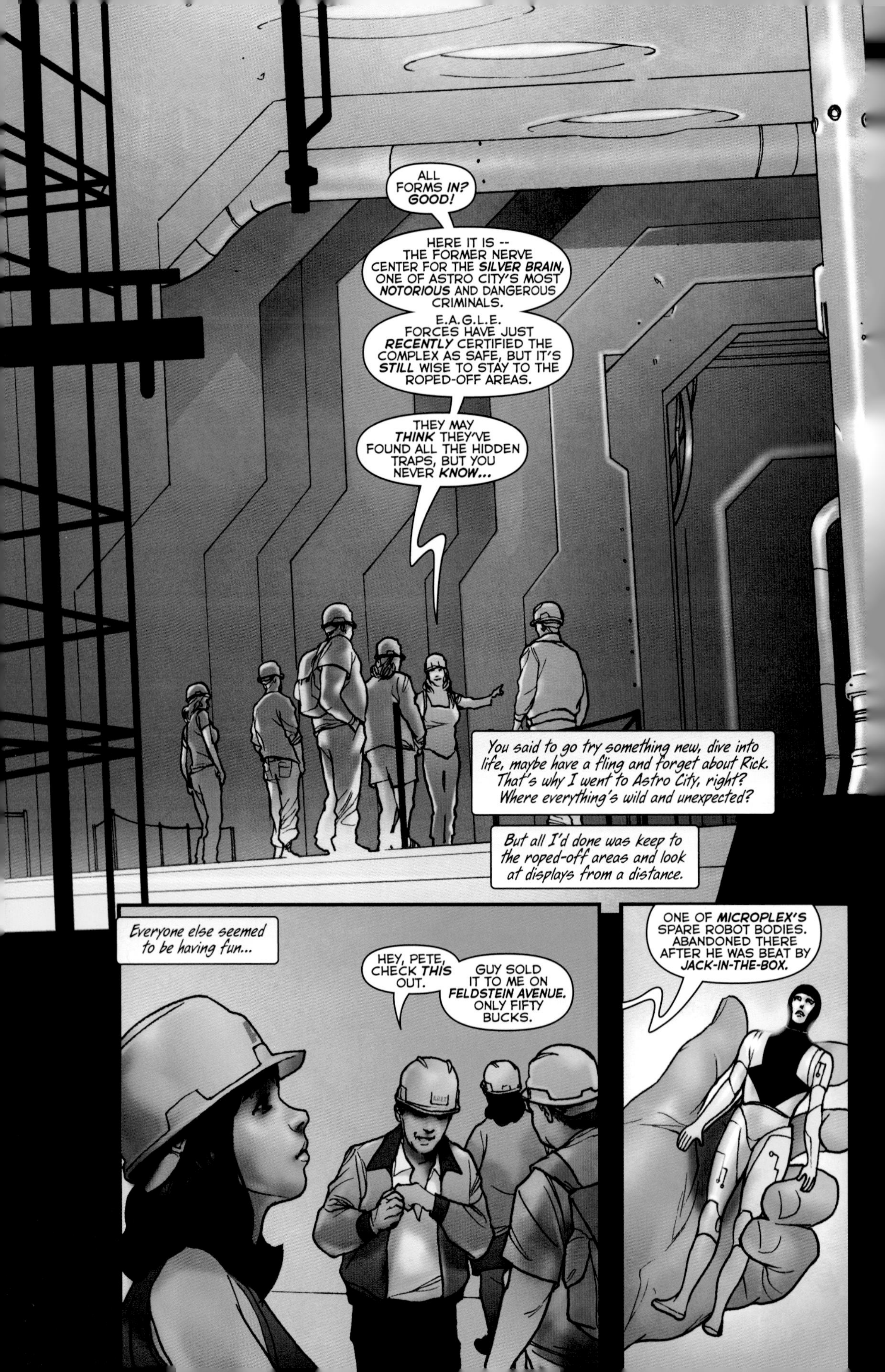
ALL FORMS IN? GOOD!
HERE IT IS -- THE FORMER NERVE CENTER FOR THE SILVER BRAIN, ONE OF ASTRO CITY'S MOST NOTORIOUS AND DANGEROUS CRIMINALS.
E.A.G.L.E. FORCES HAVE JUST RECENTLY CERTIFIED THE COMPLEX AS SAFE, BUT IT'S STILL WISE TO STAY TO THE ROPED-OFF AREAS.
THEY MAY THINK THEY'VE FOUND ALL THE HIDDEN TRAPS, BUT YOU NEVER KNOW...
You said to go try something new, dive into life, maybe have a fling and forget about Rick. That's why I went to Astro City, right? Where everything's wild and unexpected?
But all I'd done was keep to the roped-off areas and look at displays from a distance.
Everyone else seemed to be having fun...
HEY, PETE, CHECK THIS OUT.
GUY SOLD IT TO ME ON FELDSTEIN AVENUE. ONLY FIFTY BUCKS.
ONE OF MICROPLEX'S SPARE ROBOT BODIES. ABANDONED THERE AFTER HE WAS BEAT BY JACK-IN-THE-BOX.

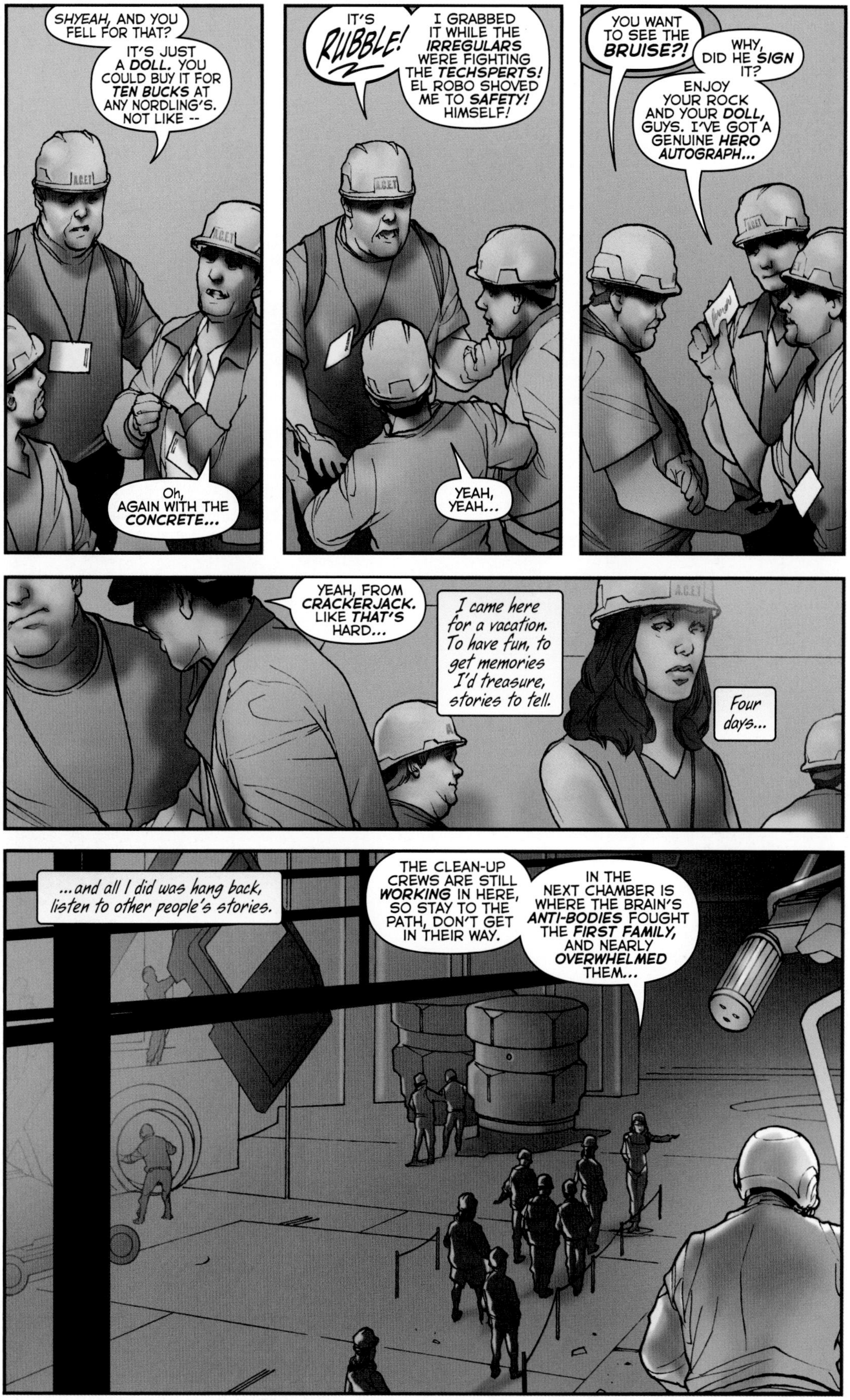
SHYEAH, AND YOU FELL FOR THAT?
IT'S JUST A DOLL. YOU COULD BUY IT FOR TEN BUCKS AT ANY NORDLING'S. NOT LIKE --
Oh, AGAIN WITH THE CONCRETE...
IT'S RUBBLE!
I GRABBED IT WHILE THE IRREGULARS WERE FIGHTING THE TECHSPERTS! EL ROBO SHOVED ME TO SAFETY! HIMSELF!
YEAH, YEAH...
YOU WANT TO SEE THE BRUISE?!
WHY, DID HE SIGN IT?
ENJOY YOUR ROCK AND YOUR DOLL, GUYS. I'VE GOT A GENUINE HERO AUTOGRAPH...
YEAH, FROM CRACKERJACK. LIKE THAT'S HARD...
I came here for a vacation. To have fun, to get memories I'd treasure, stories to tell.
Four days...
...and all I did was hang back, listen to other people's stories.
THE CLEAN-UP CREWS ARE STILL WORKING IN HERE, SO STAY TO THE PATH, DON'T GET IN THEIR WAY.
IN THE NEXT CHAMBER IS WHERE THE BRAIN'S ANTI-BODIES FOUGHT THE FIRST FAMILY, AND NEARLY OVERWHELMED THEM...

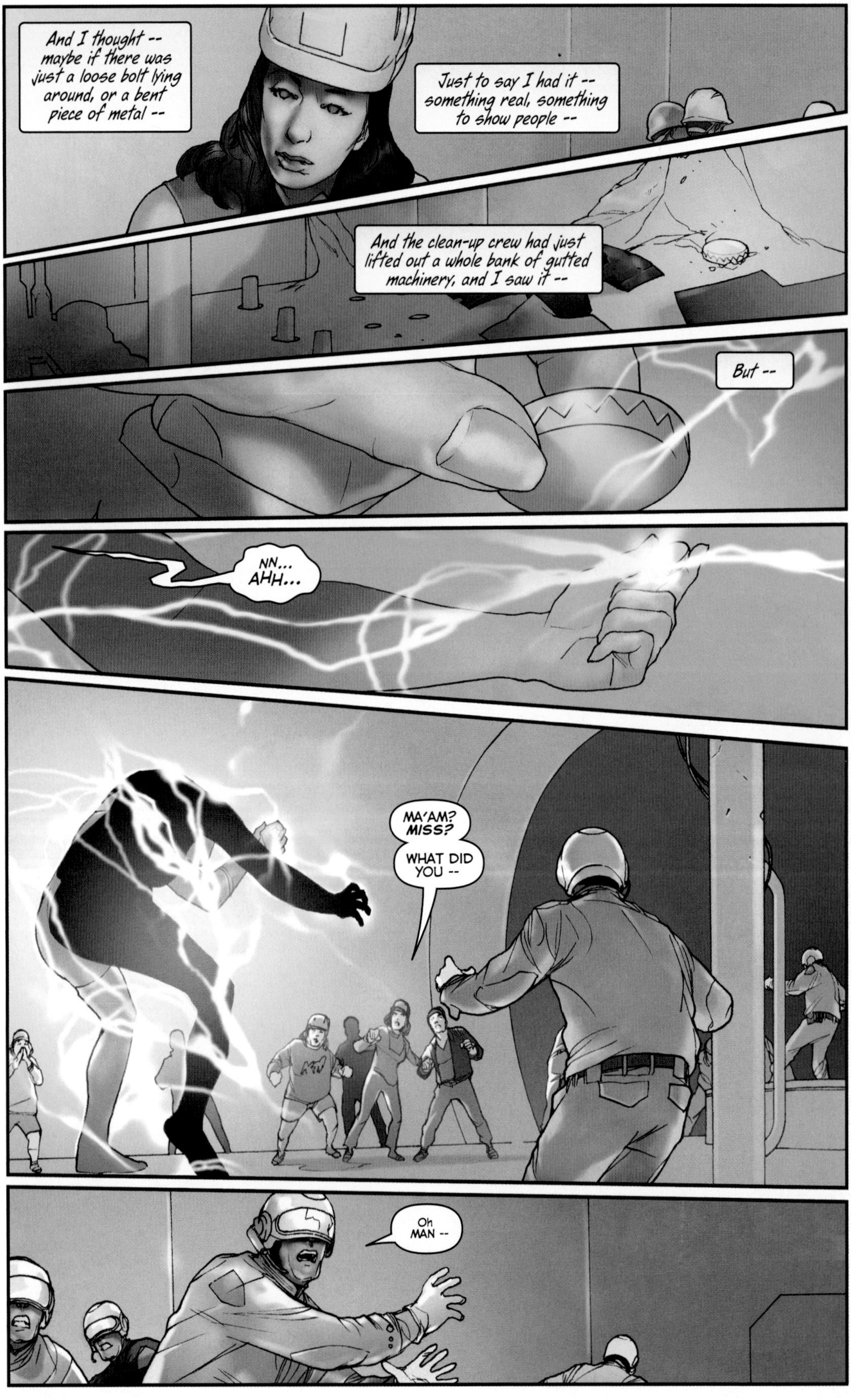
And I thought -- maybe if there was just a loose bolt lying around, or a bent piece of metal --
Just to say I had it -- something real, something to show people --
And the clean-up crew had just lifted out a whole bank of gutted machinery, and I saw it --
But --
NN... AHH...
MA'AM? MISS?
WHAT DID YOU --
Oh MAN --

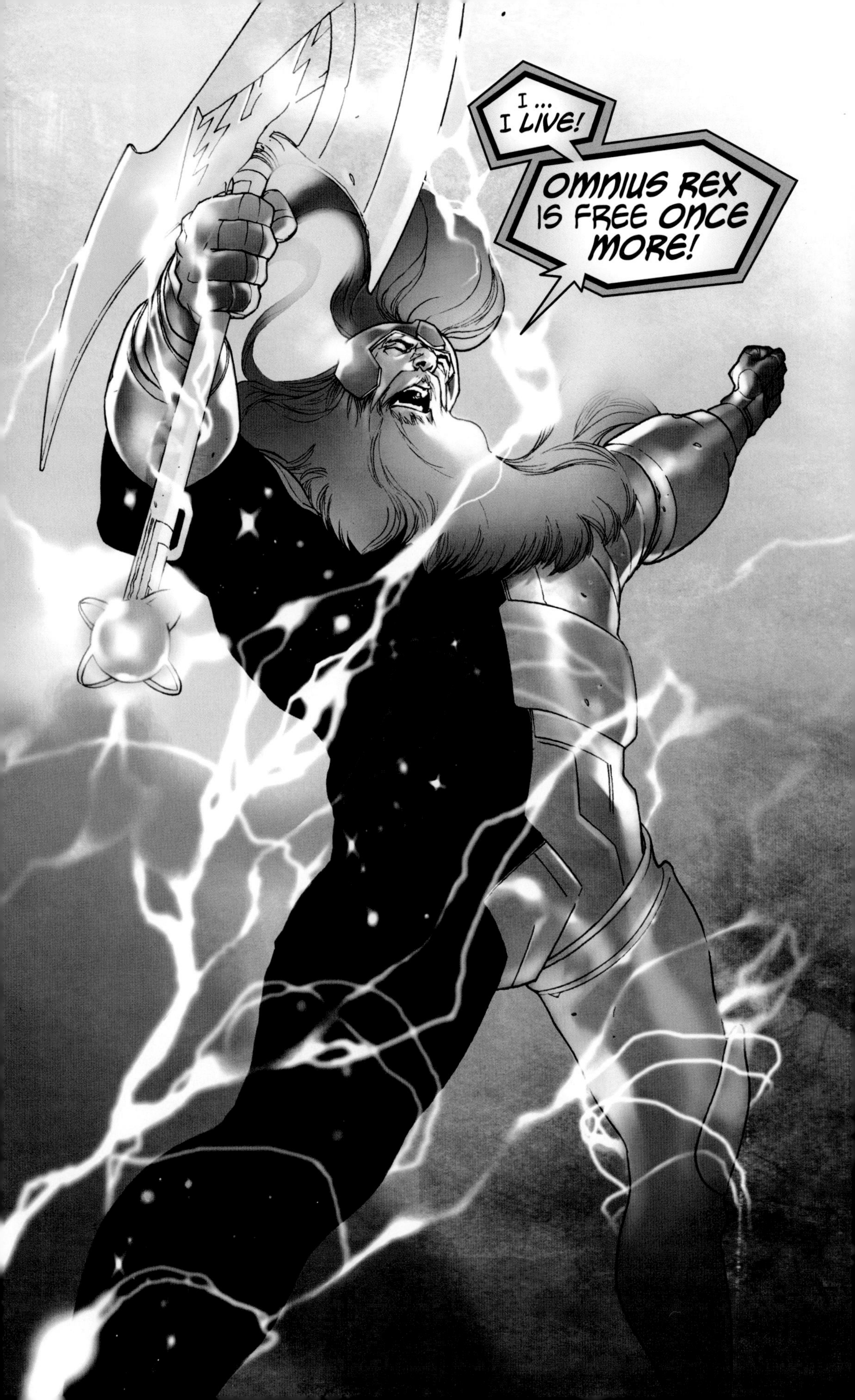
I...
I LIVE!
OMNIUS REX
IS FREE ONCE
MORE!

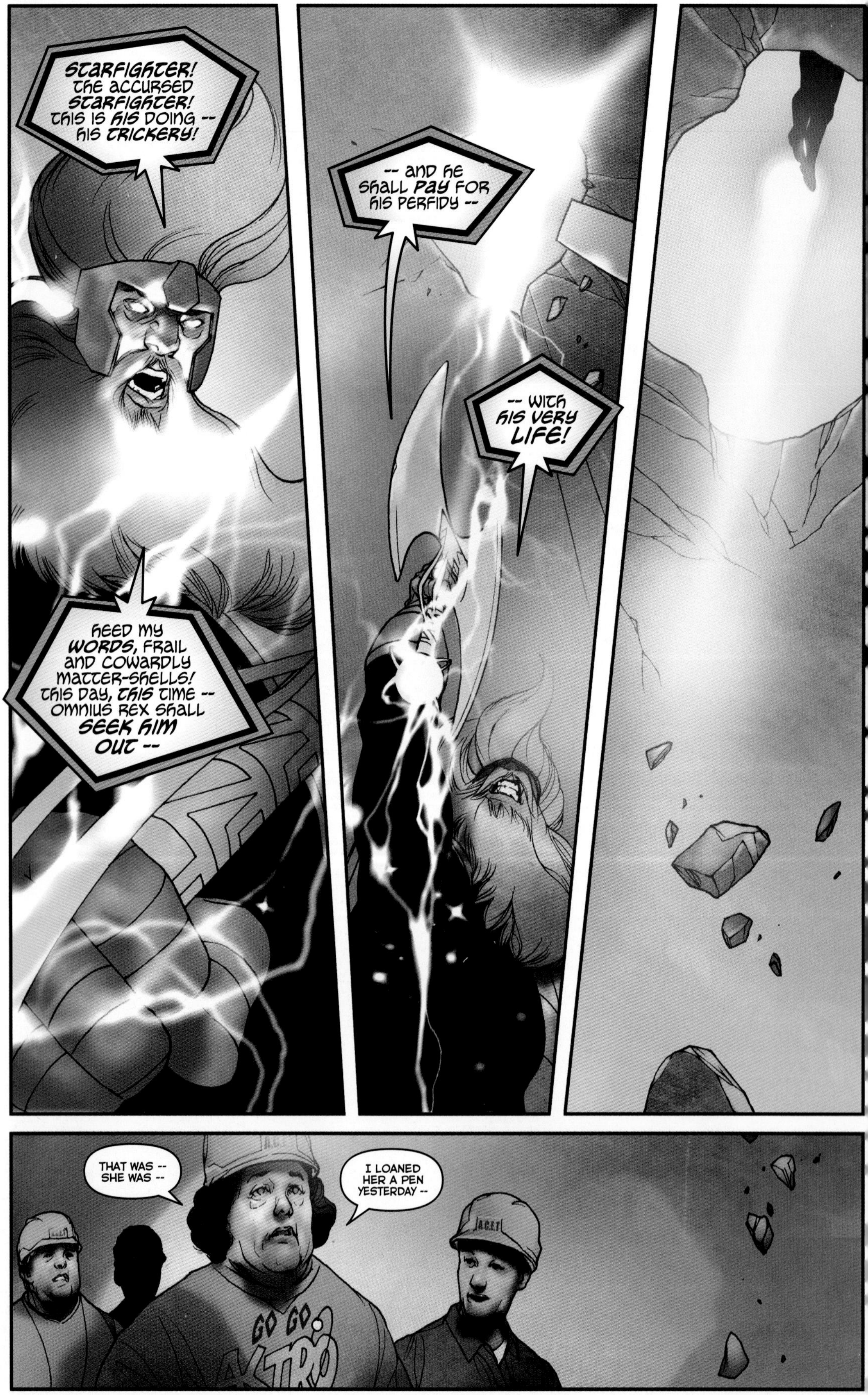
STARFIGHTER! THE ACCURSED STARFIGHTER! THIS IS HIS DOING -- HIS TRICKERY!
HEED MY WORDS, FRAIL AND COWARDLY MATTER-SHELLS! THIS DAY, THIS TIME -- OMNIUS REX SHALL SEEK HIM OUT --
-- AND HE SHALL PAY FOR HIS PERFIDY --
-- WITH HIS VERY LIFE!
THAT WAS -- SHE WAS --
I LOANED HER A PEN YESTERDAY --
GO GO

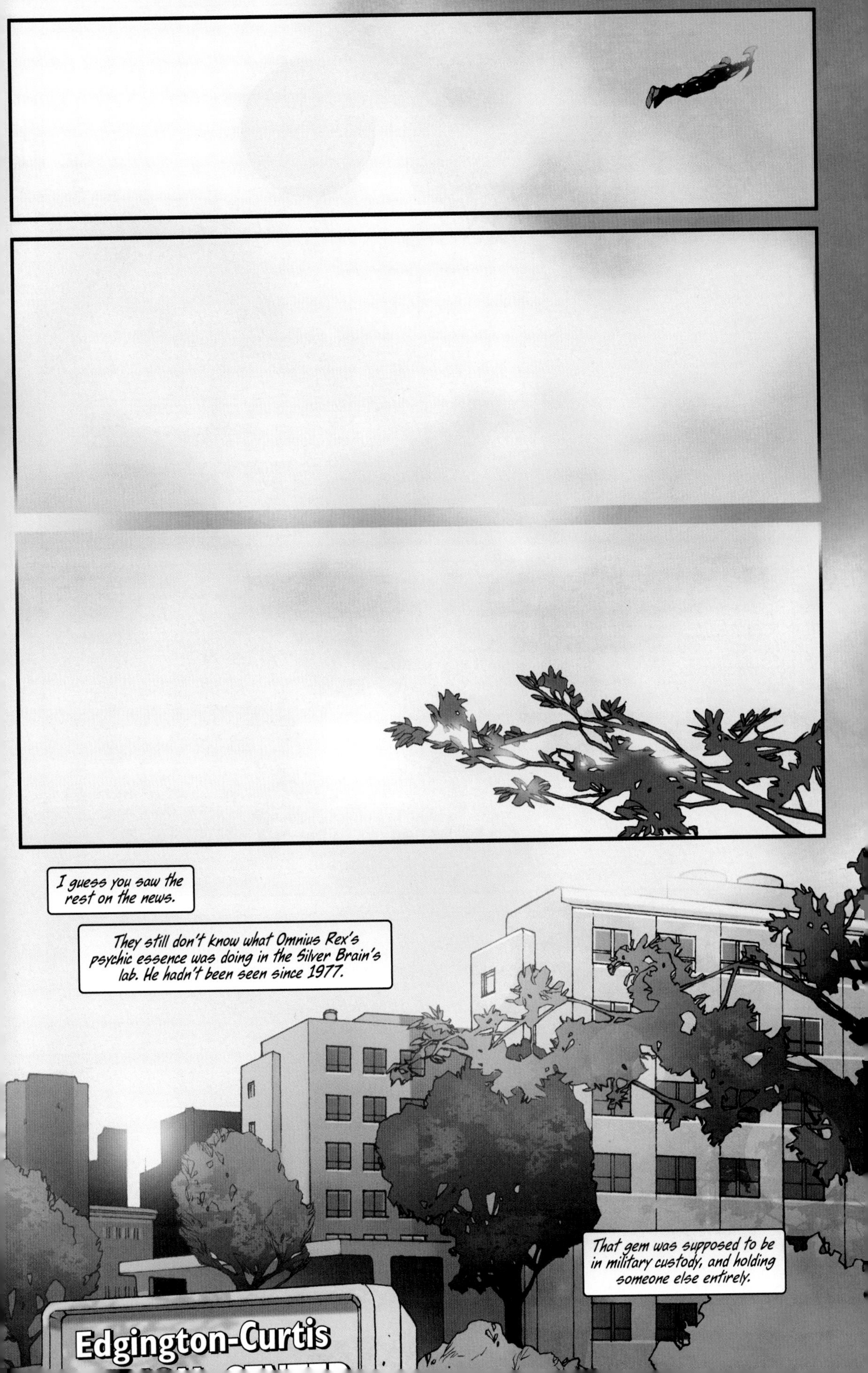

I guess you saw the rest on the news.
They still don't know what Omnius Rex's psychic essence was doing in the Silver Brain's lab. He hadn't been seen since 1977.
That gem was supposed to be in military custody, and holding someone else entirely.
Edgington-Curtis

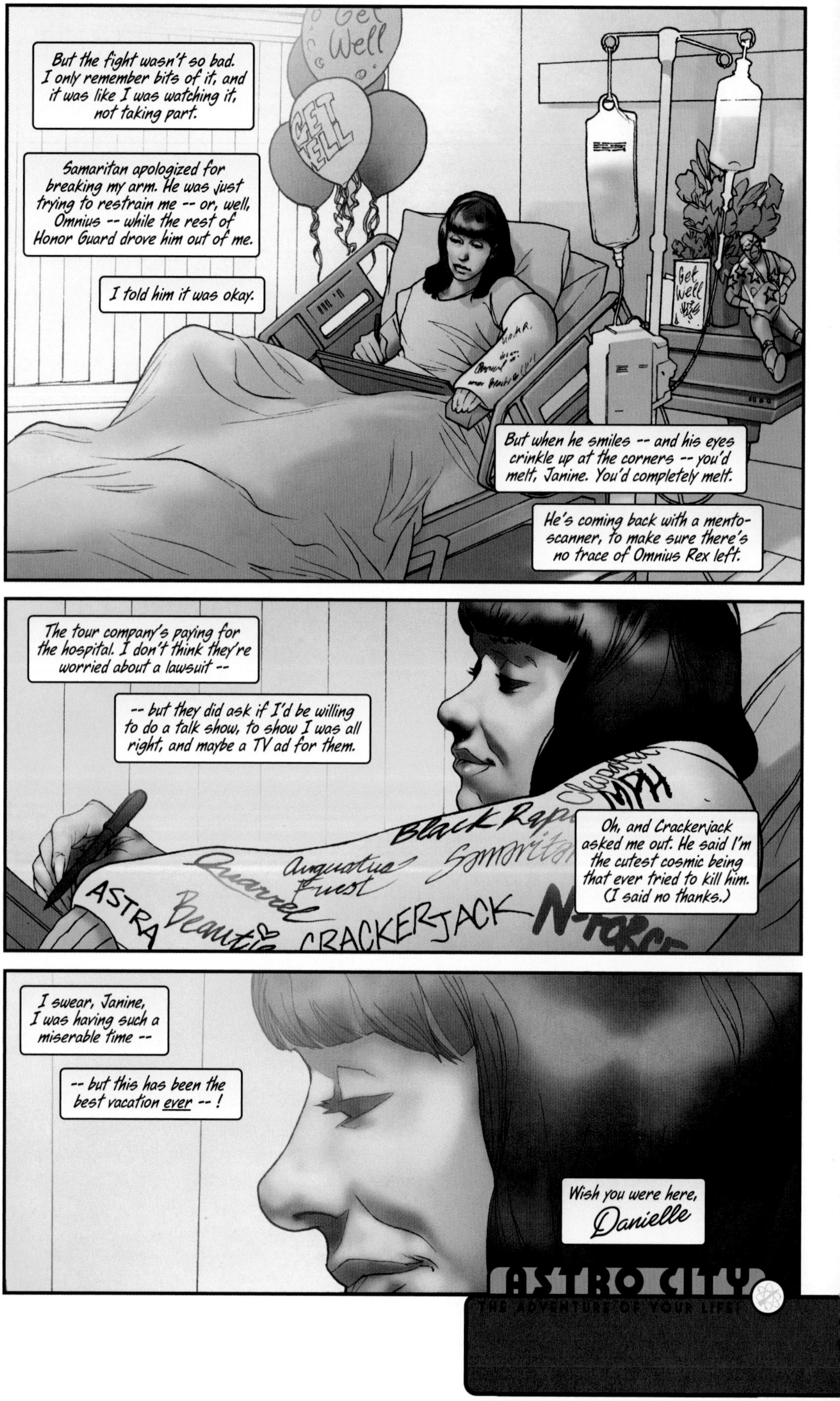

Get Well
GET WELL
But the fight wasn't so bad. I only remember bits of it, and it was like I was watching it, not taking part.
Samaritan apologized for breaking my arm. He was just trying to restrain me -- or, well, Omnius -- while the rest of Honor Guard drove him out of me.
I told him it was okay.
Get Well
But when he smiles -- and his eyes crinkle up at the corners -- you'd melt, Janine. You'd completely melt.
He's coming back with a mento-scanner, to make sure there's no trace of Omnius Rex left.
The tour company's paying for the hospital. I don't think they're worried about a lawsuit --
-- but they did ask if I'd be willing to do a talk show, to show I was all right, and maybe a TV ad for them.
Oh, and Crackerjack asked me out. He said I'm the cutest cosmic being that ever tried to kill him. (I said no thanks.)
MPH
Quarrel
ASTRA
CRACKERJACK
I swear, Janine, I was having such a miserable time --
-- but this has been the best vacation ever -- !
Wish you were here,
Danielle
ASTRO CITY
THE ADVENTURE OF YOUR LIFE!

For Elegance and Comfort...

YOU'LL ALWAYS FIND A WARM WELCOME AT

The ASTRO CITY
CLASSIC

Between City Center and Old Town.
*When you're at the Classic, you're in the heart
of Astro City. It's our pleasure to offer you
unparalleled access and so much more.*

- *Oversized rooms* •
- *Award-winning design* •
- *Fitness center* •
- *Wireless internet* •
- *Five-star restaurants* •

THE ASTRO CITY CLASSIC • *By any measure... a classic.*

From the Falls to the Heights

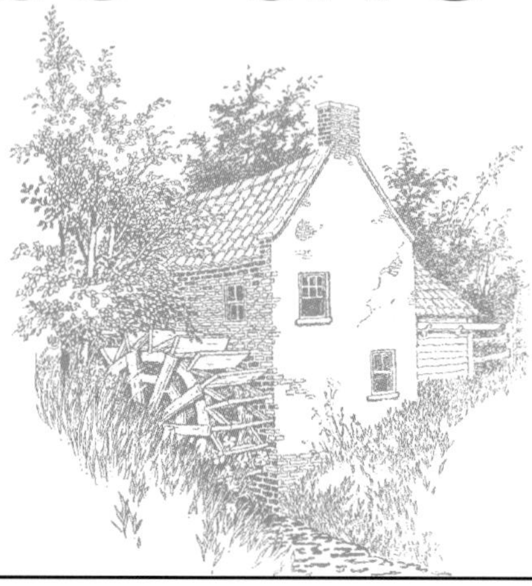

A Brief History of Astro City • by **Elliot Mills**

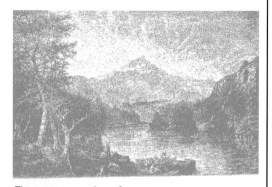

The deep and muddy ruts of covered wagons headed west can still be seen at the Romeyn Falls Historical Center, preserved under glass, an ever-present reminder of the humble beginnings that birthed a great city.

It was one of those wagons, carrying a man named Romeyn—Hannes, perhaps, or Josepus; history does not agree on his first name—that started it all. A cartoonist and engraver, either Dutch or Italian, he reportedly came to America after offending a wealthy and powerful patron. Unable to find work he found agreeable in the Eastern cities, he pushed west, his sights set on a new life as a farmer in California. After a broken axle halted his westward journey at the base of Mount Kirby, sometime in the late 1840s, he was left destitute, without funds or prospects. According to area lore, he carried with him hardware for a water-driven mill, and built what was intended to be a small and temporary operation at the falls feeding the Wildenberg River, hoping to earn enough to re-supply himself and continue on his journey.

He never left.

He never married, either, which may explain why so little is known of him. Irascible and uncommunicative, he worked at his mill, enlarging it in time to the version seen at the Historical Center, and spent his waning years producing paintings and engravings capturing the wild and natural beauty of his surroundings, many of which are on display at the Patterson Museum of Art.

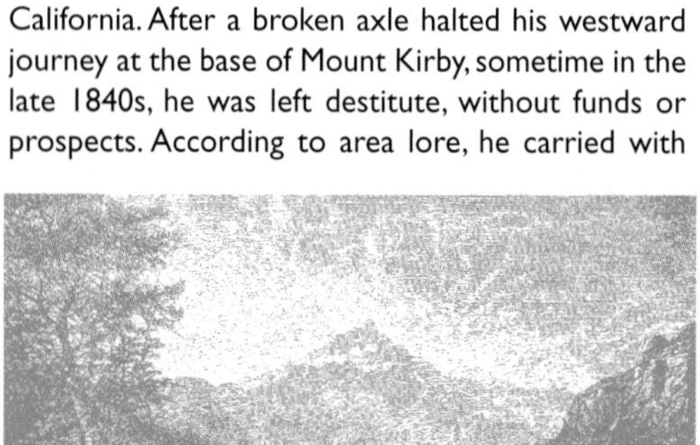

This page: a sampling of engravings by Hannes (or Josepus?) Romeyn.

A small community sprung up around his mill, mainly Scandinavian and Northern European immigrants, like Romeyn exhausted from the trip west, trying their hand at supplying those who still had the money and drive to push on. Farming, ranching, hunting, trapping and more supported the settlers, and supplied the raw materials for the goods they sold in the riverside marketplace.

In time, Romeyn's small mill and its bitter, silent miller, like the grain of sand around which an oyster forms a pearl, became the center of a thriving commercial district, supporting farms and ranches

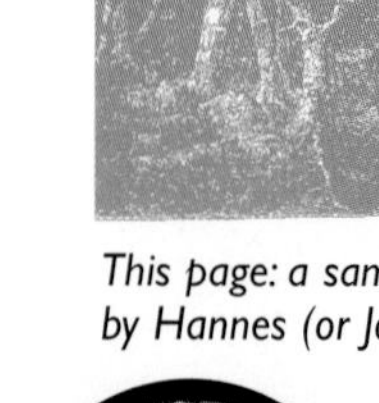

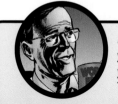

***Elliot Mills** began reporting for the Astro City Rocket forty-five years ago, and has been managing editor for the last thirteen years. A Pulitzer Prize winner and author of the memoir* Through Shining Eyes, *few know the city as well as he does.*

on both sides of the Wildenberg. In 1852, the area was incorporated as the town of Romeyn Falls.

For some years thereafter, Romeyn Falls had a reputation as a wide-open town, often lawless, but just as often witness to a mysterious sense of poetic justice. Outlaw bands occasionally ran roughshod over the area—but never for long. And legends sprang up, of a trapper-hero named Johnny

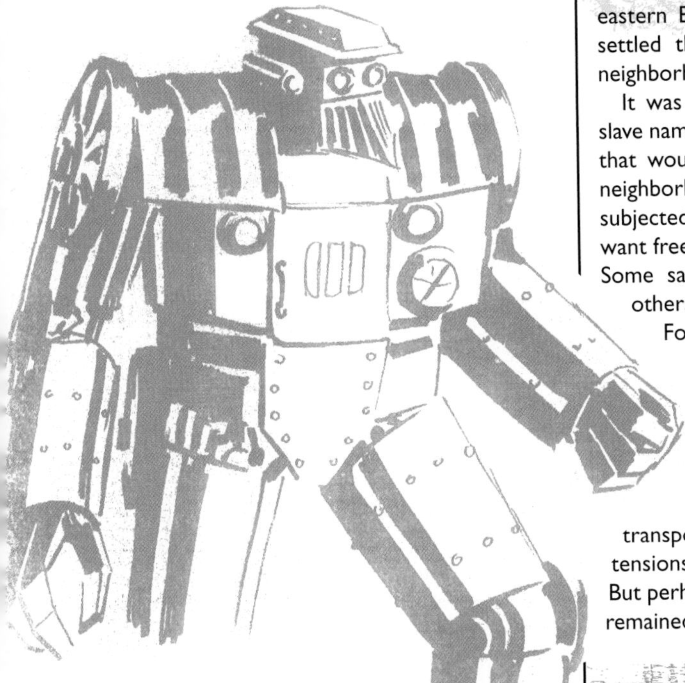

The earliest known drawing of Ironhorse the Human Locomotive (c. 1864). Artist unkown.

Lightfoot, a half-Indian woman known only as Palomino, and more. The Lightning Kid, subject of the recent Val Kilmer film, spent most of his career in and around Romeyn Falls.

And of course, in the 1860s, when the railroad came to the area, the first sightings of Ironhorse, the Human Locomotive, were reported, protecting both the trains themselves from would-be bandits, and Chinese laborers from the railroad bosses. Whether the Ironhorse occasionally glimpsed today is the same being is a matter of considerable debate, but his existence in the Old West is not.

But frontier days gave way to growth and maturity, and before long, Romeyn Falls was less Western town and more young city, a mercantile hub between the mountains and the plains. In 1869, Cardinal Enzio Grandenetti, one of Astro City's most significant citizens, arrived in town with plans to built a great cathedral that would outshine the spires of the Rockies themselves, serving the growing populace and glorifying God. Though the cathedral itself was never completed—it sprawls over fourteen blocks of Old Town today, and is run by the city as a museum—it changed the complexion of the city, bringing in the eastern European laborers and stonemasons who settled the eastern slopes on Mount Kirby, the neighborhood now known as Shadow Hill.

It was around this time, as well, that a former slave named Hiram Baker broke ground on the farm that would become the nucleus of the Bakerville neighborhood. Baker, like so many others, was subjected to racist harassment by those who didn't want free blacks in the area, but he held his ground. Some said he was protected by voodoo magic, others said it was simply the spirit of the town. For whatever reason, he and the other freedmen who settled around him thrived.

In the latter days of the 19th century, Romeyn Falls' history was similar to that of other cities in the area, as transportation interests grew in importance and tensions between farmers and cattlemen increased. But perhaps some of its former "wide-open" nature remained—something certainly happened in 1887,

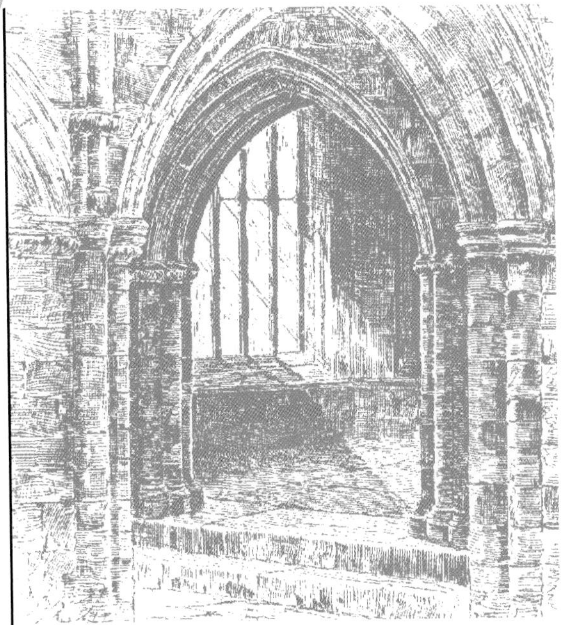

One of Enzio Grandenetti's early drawings, during the planning of his great cathedral. Top of page: another Romeyn engraving.

A Brief History of Astro City

when the slaughterhouse district on the western shore of the Gaines River burned. Contemporary accounts, elaborated on in fanciful dime novels, tell of the attack of the "Howling Dead," a ghostly stampede of bison and countless Indian warriors, staved off by a rare alliance of heroes, the composition of which varies from telling to telling but generally includes Ironhorse and is cited as responsible for the death of Johnny Lightfoot.

That wild night seemed to spell the end of Romeyn Falls' "mystery history," at least for a time. There are stories of undercover government agents and daring thieves, but few stories of superhuman forces outside the confines of Shadow Hill. It wasn't until 1919, in the wake of World War I, that Air Ace, often cited as Astro City's first true superhero, debuted. Thought to be "Whit" McAleer, a veteran of trench warfare who gained the ability to fly after being exposed to an experimental German gas attack, he bravely defended the city against the similarly-airborne Escadrille Gang, capturing the public imagination and winning the admiration of millions nationwide. Questions about his connection to the Cornerstone Club, a group of influential businessmen, remain speculative and unanswered.

Air Ace's brief but shining career seemed to crack open the gates of mystery, and slowly, the costumed population of Romeyn Falls began to grow. From the

Romeyn Falls, 1905. Engraving by Felton Dirks.

so-called Hawk of the Alleyways to the masked Chinese warriors known as the Five Fists, the Roaring Twenties roared with a different tone in the ever-more bustling city. Even Prohibition seemed to spawn larger-than-life crusaders, as bootleggers and racketeers seeking to establish a beachhead in Romeyn Falls found themselves opposed by the Cloak of Night, a shadowy vigilante who struck and vanished without warning or trace.

By the mid-1930s, of course, the Astro-Naut made his first appearance, and as the fires of war ignited in Europe, a virtual cornucopia of heroes appeared, from the night-prowling Lamplighter to the celebrated All-American and Slugger the Junior Dynamo. who [**BRIEF HISTORY** continued on p. 46]

Air Ace: from the famous 1920 Swinnerton painting that became an international sensation.

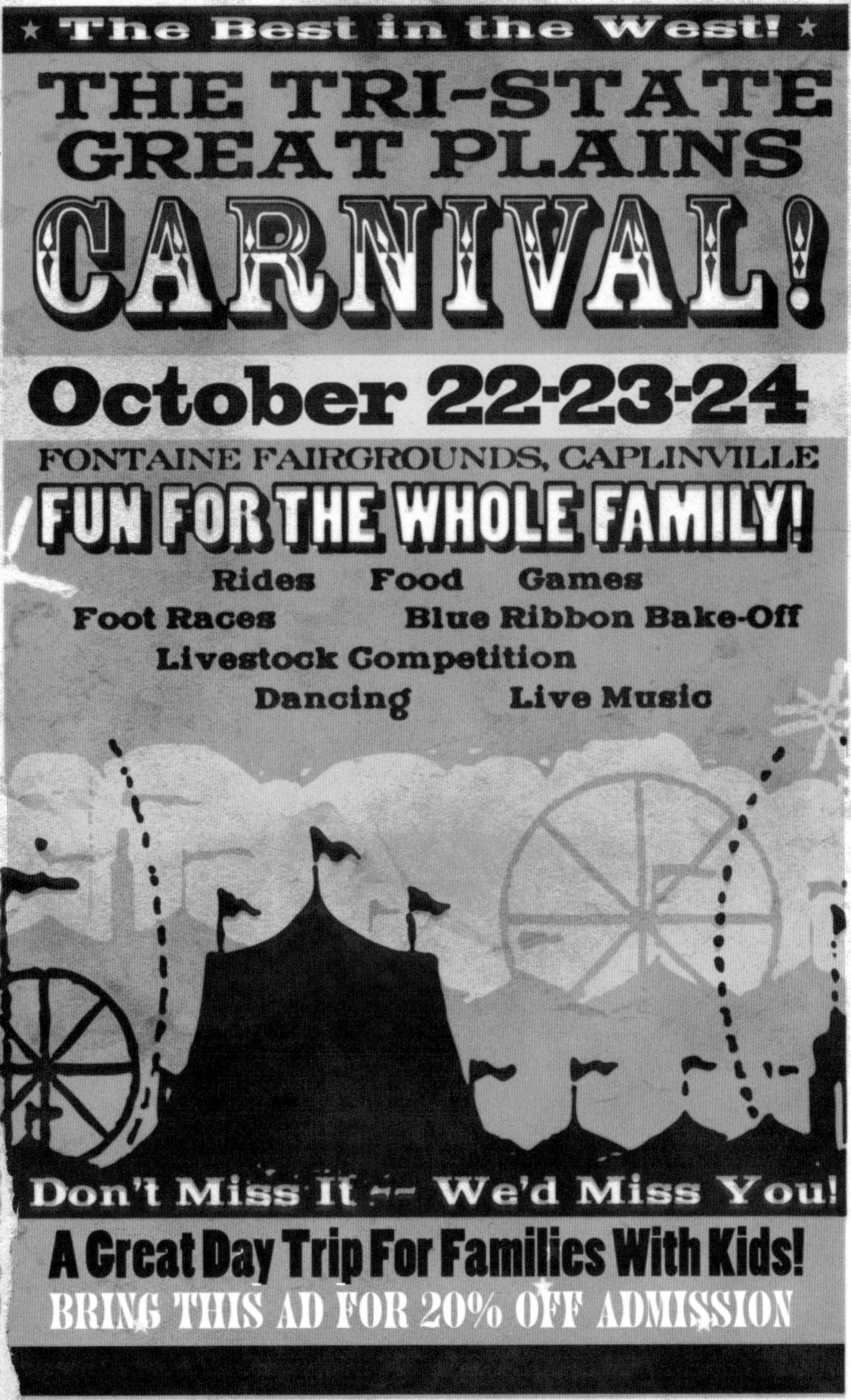
★ The Best in the West! ★
THE TRI-STATE
GREAT PLAINS
CARNIVAL!
October 22-23-24
FONTAINE FAIRGROUNDS, CAPLINVILLE
FUN FOR THE WHOLE FAMILY!
Rides Food Games
Foot Races Blue Ribbon Bake-Off
Livestock Competition
Dancing Live Music
Don't Miss It -- We'd Miss You!
A Great Day Trip For Families With Kids!
BRING THIS AD FOR 20% OFF ADMISSION

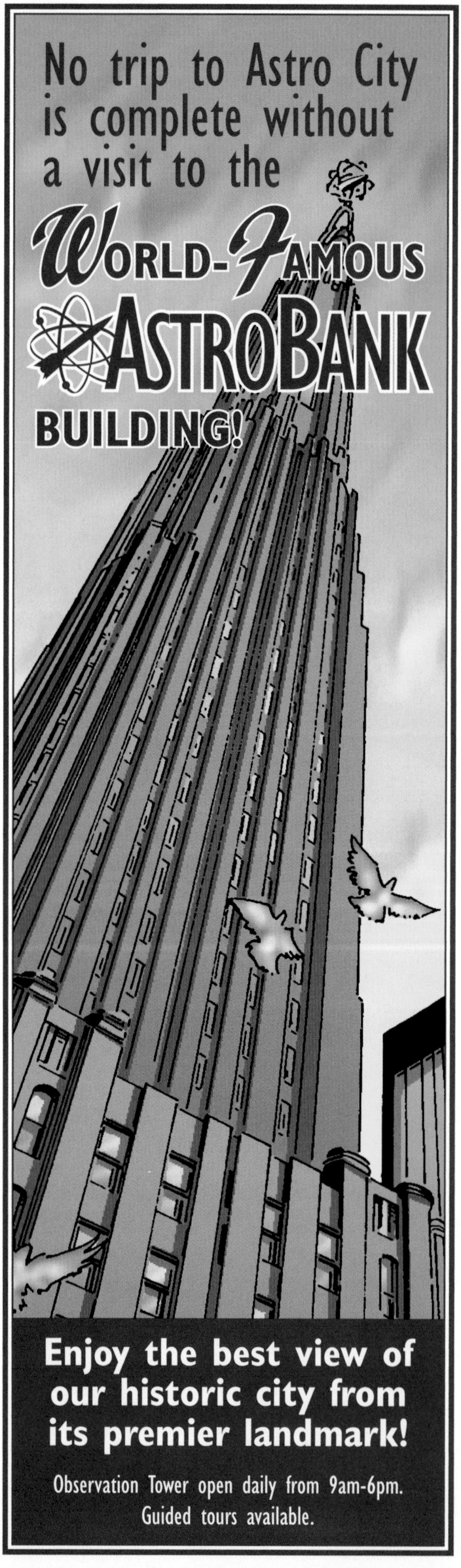
No trip to Astro City is complete without a visit to the
WORLD-FAMOUS
ASTROBANK
BUILDING!
Enjoy the best view of our historic city from its premier landmark!
Observation Tower open daily from 9am-6pm.
Guided tours available.

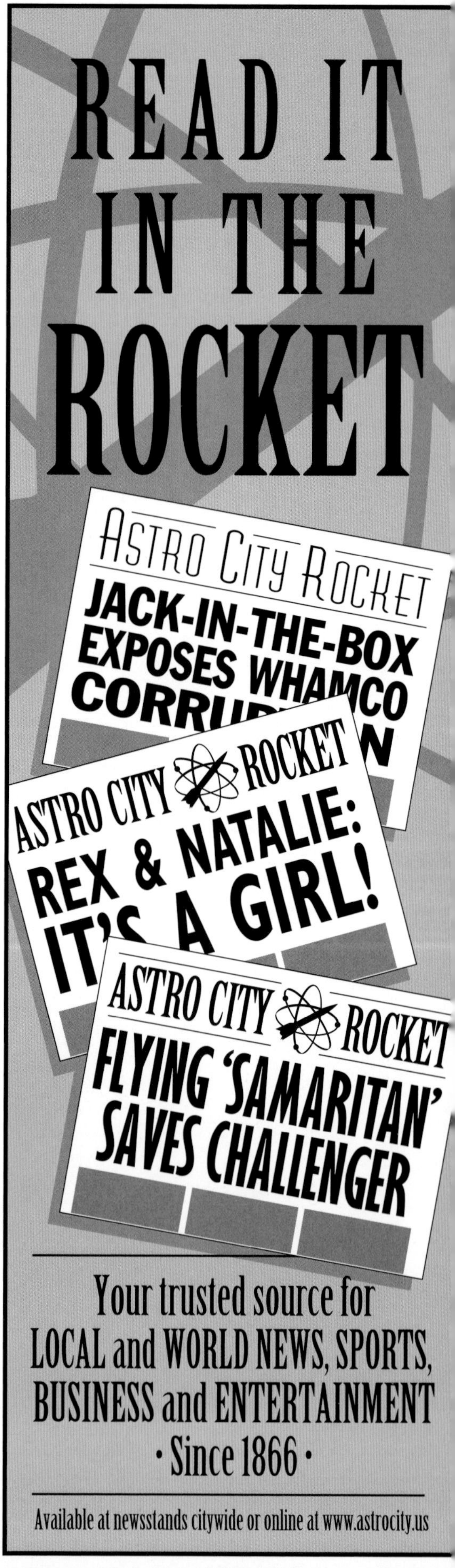
READ IT IN THE ROCKET
ASTRO CITY ROCKET
JACK-IN-THE-BOX EXPOSES WHAMCO CORRU
ASTRO CITY ROCKET
REX & NATALIE: IT'S A GIRL!
ASTRO CITY ROCKET
FLYING 'SAMARITAN' SAVES CHALLENGER
Your trusted source for LOCAL and WORLD NEWS, SPORTS, BUSINESS and ENTERTAINMENT
• Since 1866 •
Available at newsstands citywide or online at www.astrocity.us

Astro City's Neighborhoods

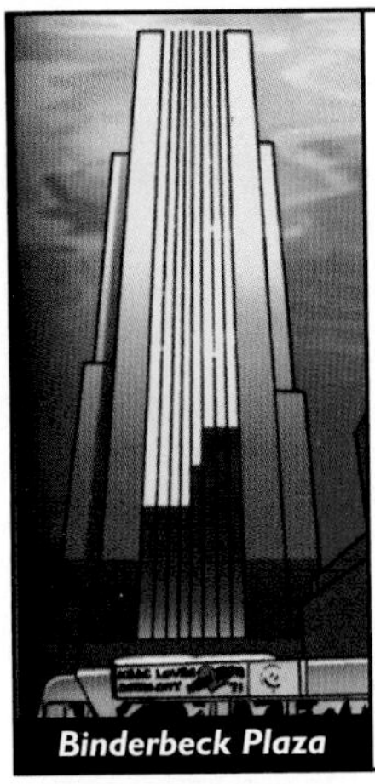

Binderbeck Plaza

"America's City of Heroes." "The Sentinel City." "The City of Wonders." Astro City has many nicknames—and even more neighborhoods. At first glance, it can be overwhelming—why is Kiefer Street in Shadow Hill and Kiefer Square in South Chesler? what's the difference between Derbyfield and Derbyville?—but break it up into small portions, and you'll do fine.

Here, we'll run it all down for you.

CITY CENTER - The heart of the city, home to the gleaming, modern skyscrapers that most people think of when they think of Astro City. This is the area most heavily rebuilt after the war, where most of the city's office workers toil. Once a Dutch neighborhood, it's now home to Binderbeck Square, the city's shopping and dining mecca, as well as Dedication Park and Museum Row, where you'll find the Sprang Museum of Popular Advertising and more.

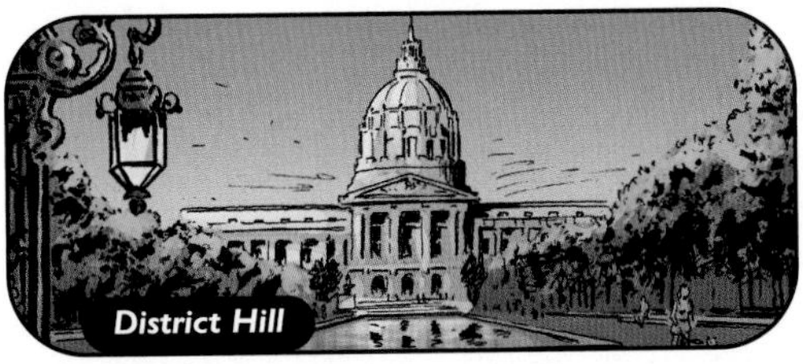

District Hill

OLD TOWN & DISTRICT HILL - South of City Center, Old Town reflects the character and traditions of Old Romeyn Falls, having been spared the devastation that transformed the city in the late Forties. Here, you'll find the sprawling Grandenetti Cathedral, as well as Iger Square, where blue-collar families and gentrifying young movers and shakers mix and mingle with Astro City's bohemian arts community. South of Old Town, wedged snugly between the Gleason Bridge and Bakerville, sits District Hill, home to City Hall and many of the city's civic structures.

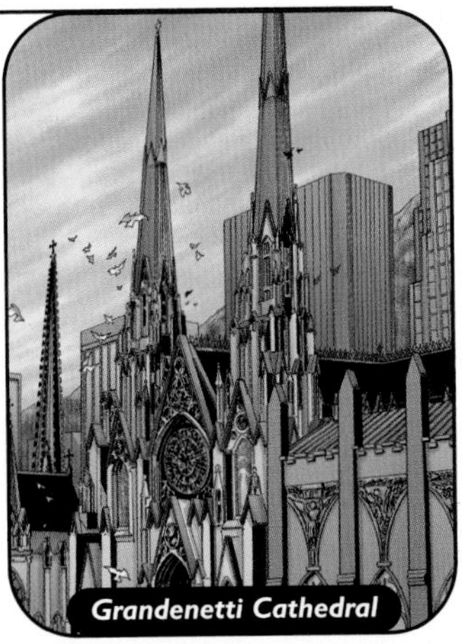

Grandenetti Cathedral

SHADOW HILL - An Eastern European ethnic enclave, Shadow Hill is heaven for any visitor who likes charming (or cluttered!) curiosity shops, spicy pirogues or fresh, flavorful *itafses* just out of the oven. Night falls early here, though, and Shadow Hill's mystic and mysterious reputation keeps most non-residents away after dusk. Brave souls venture up at dawn, to catch the Hanged Man, the Hill's eldritch guardian, wrapping up his nightly rounds.

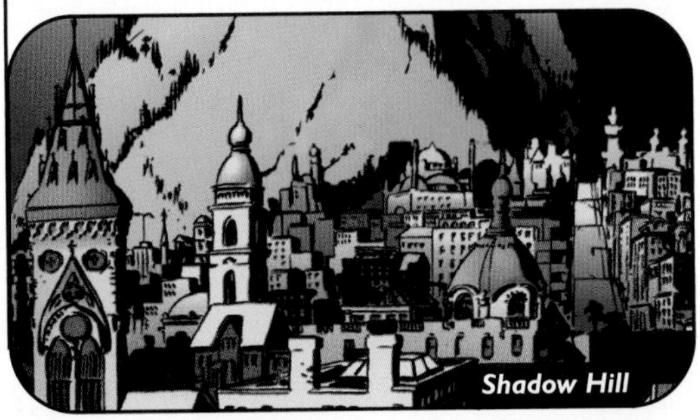

Shadow Hill

Astro City's Neighborhoods

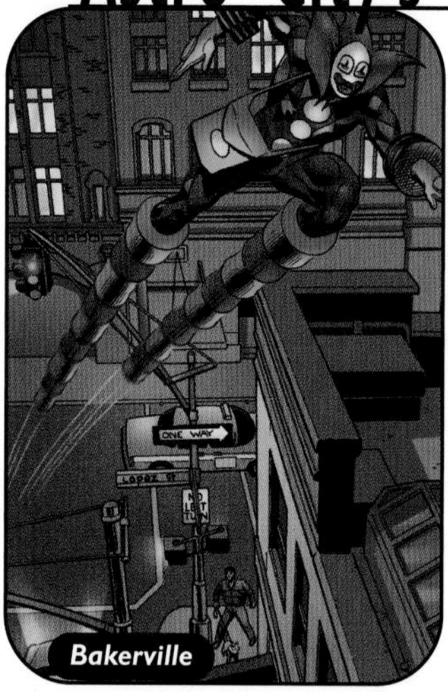
ONE WAY
Bakerville

BAKERVILLE - The longtime home to much of Astro City's African-American community, Bakerville is emerging from a troubled era, as Mulberry Street, the central artery, gets a facelift, and the recently-completed renovation of the New Carthage Theatre brings a thrilling return to Bakerville's 1930s-1950s elegance, when it was home to the hottest nightspots in the city. Bakerville also claims Centennial Park on the Wildenberg River, home to the annual Astro City Jazz Festival.

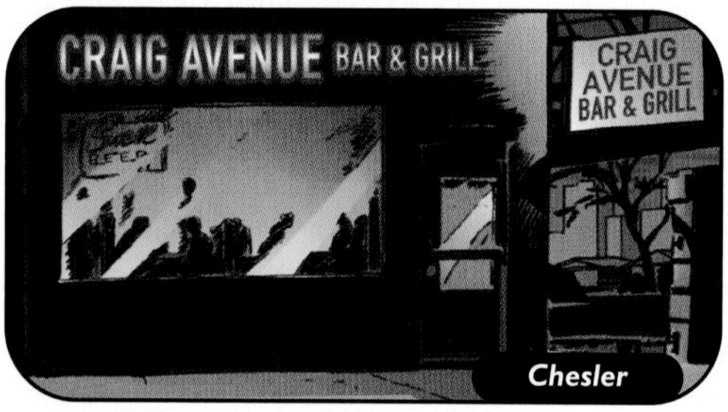
CRAIG AVENUE BAR & GRILL
CRAIG AVENUE BAR & GRILL
Chesler

CHESLER - Derisively nicknamed "The Sweatshop" by residents, Chesler has seen generations of low-income families pass through the small textile houses and warehouses that dot the neighborhood or trek across the Outcault Bride to work at the Goodman-Donenfeld factories, from Irish to Polish to Hispanic families depending on the decade. Dismissed by many as "the city's eyesore," Chesler's neighborhood bars and riverside eateries offer a distinctive atmosphere for the adventurous visitor.

THE FOOTHILLS - Kanewood, Gibson Hills and Patterson Heights rise above Center City on the southern shoulders of Mount Kirby. Home to Astro City's wealthy, rich and super-rich respectively, the Foothills communities offer spectacular architecture (including Patterson Mansion) and even more spectacular views. The Romeyn Falls Historical Center and the falls themselves can be found just north of Gibson Hills, tucked between Mount Kirby and the Wildenberg River.

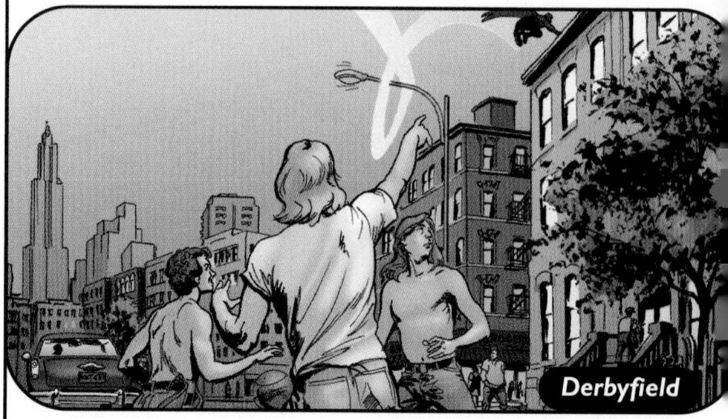
Derbyfield

NORTHSIDE - Rensie Avenue, where traditional kosher butchers and pickle men share space with trendy vintage-clothing shops and used bookstores, divides Fass Gardens and Derbyfield. These two bedroom communities house many of the young white-collar workers and elderly retirees of the city, and offer a cornucopia of funky shopping, dining and clubbing choices. Derbyville, by the way, is an ambitious lower-income housing project in Derbyfield, one that has seen prouder days.

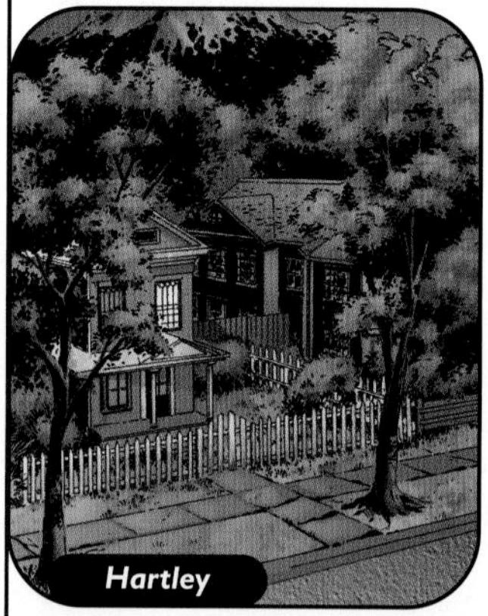
Hartley

HARTLEY - Crossing the Gaines River, we hit Astro City's largest area of suburban sprawl, where the white-picket-fence set sleeps, commutes, works and shops. There are enchanting enclaves here as well, from Craftsman*[**NEIGHBORHOODS** continued on p. 67]*

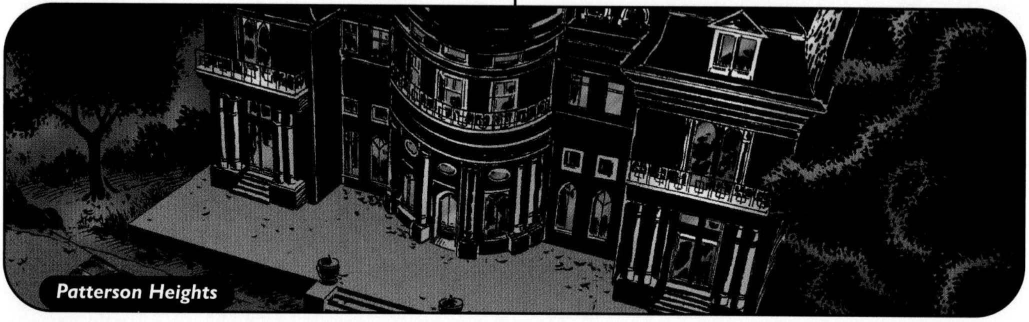
Patterson Heights

DINING GUIDE

with ***Eaton Runn,***
food critic for Current Magazine

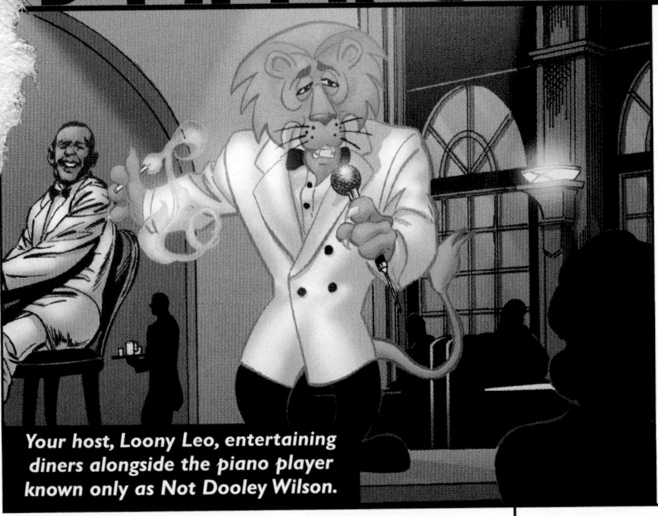

Your host, Loony Leo, entertaining diners alongside the piano player known only as Not Dooley Wilson.

Great chefs offer you the finest cooking from around the world—and beyond! Bon appetit!

FEATURED REVIEW:

LOONY LEO'S

Where else can you tuck into a juicy, perfectly-cooked steak to the tinkling melody of Forties standards, surrounded by movie posters and advertising art selling everything from Postum to a family sedan called the Liberator, all hosted by a baggy-eyed, gruff-voiced cartoon lion in an immaculate white tuxedo? Only in Astro City.

Loony Leo's is a theme restaurant, of course, but for all that, it's an experience no visitor to Astro City should miss. Built around the history and personality of classic cartoon star Loony Leo, who was accidentally brought to life during a 1946 conflict between the Gentleman and Professor Borzoi, it deliberately evokes the sort of manly, wood-paneled-and-dimly-lit joint you'd expect from a Warner Bros. thriller, where men were men, the cigar smoke was thick, and women wore strapless evening gowns and long gloves, and were probably played by Rita Hayworth. But there's no cigar smoke here, of course, and it's surprisingly kid-friendly, thanks to the presence of a living cartoon lion, familiar from a zillion afternoons in front of the Motorola, asking you how you're enjoying the crab cakes and making wry, understated jokes.

Leo's history, from his early cartoons to the live-action novelty films he made after manifesting in the real world due to a "belief ray," is well-represented around the restaurant, and the ongoing banter between Leo, a co-owner of the business, and his acerbically-witty piano player, make the evening a memorable one. [Understandably absent are any references to Leo's controversial involvement in the tragic 1957 death of Corliss McBride, which led to him dropping out of the public eye for well over a decade.]

So how's the food? Well, as you might expect from a restaurant run by a carnivore, you can't go wrong with any of the beef dishes—from the juicy T-bone steak to the tender, succulent ribs to the hearty Beef Wellington, there's nowhere west of the Mississippi that can compete. Poultry and fish dishes are less impressive, though still tasty—the grilled swordfish is particularly good—and the few pasta dishes are indifferent at best. The roasted new potatoes are crisp and perfectly seasoned, though the vegetables were overcooked. No visit to Leo's, however, would be complete without a slab of the chocolate buttermilk cake with Leo's house-made ice cream.

There is consistently talk of franchising Loony Leo's, but unless they find a way to duplicate Leo himself, I can't imagine it working. So make sure to see him in his natural habitat.

34 Binderbeck Square East. Lunch, M-F, dinner, 7 days. Moderate.

Goscinny's

15 Troisfontaines Ave. Open for dinner 7 days; lunch Tues-Fri; brunch, Sat-Sun. Expensive.

An Astro City landmark since 1959, Goscinny's reflects the joie de vivre and hearty regional fare of Brittany, and boasts unparalleled service. Try the chilled Breton lobster soup with cucumbers and black olives, followed by a delicious haddock brandade with roasted fillets of rougade, and Kouing Amman (a tower of ultra-thin pastry leaves filled with butter and sugar), before ending the evening with a glass of fine 25-year-old Calvados. The atmosphere is a winning blend of candlelit romance and airy Continental elegance.

Beefy Bob's

47 area locations. Open 7 days. Inexpensive.

We know, we know, it's a fast-food burger joint you can find in almost any town in America, and increasingly, the world. But if you're hopelessly addicted to the Double Cheesy-Beef, the brain-freezing shakes or the smiling face of Melvin the Interrupting—*moo moo moo!*—Cow, you may want to make a pilgrimage to the chain's first location, on the corner of Goodwin St. and Gonzalez Ave., where the menu is exactly what you expect but the décor hasn't changed since 1963.

[***DINING*** *continued on p. 62*]

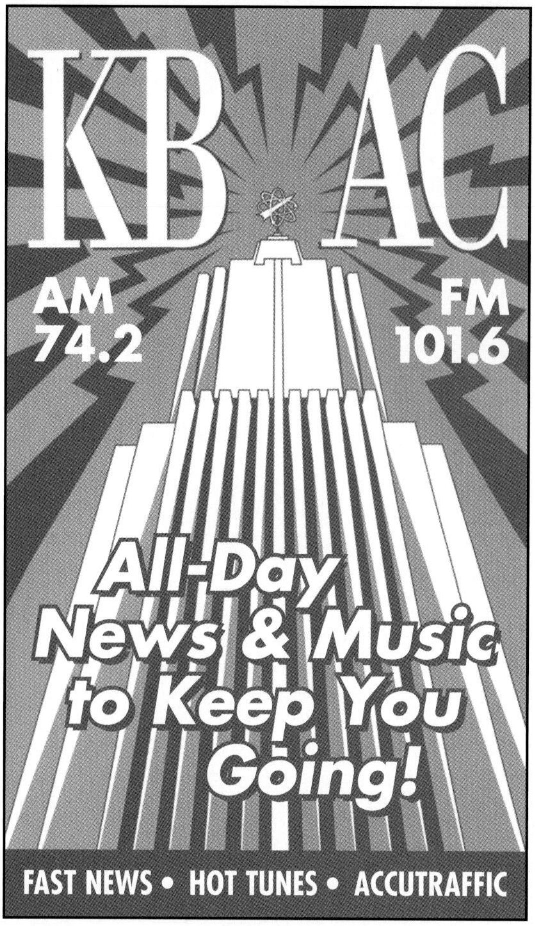
KBAC
AM 74.2
FM 101.6
All-Day News & Music to Keep You Going!
FAST NEWS • HOT TUNES • ACCUTRAFFIC

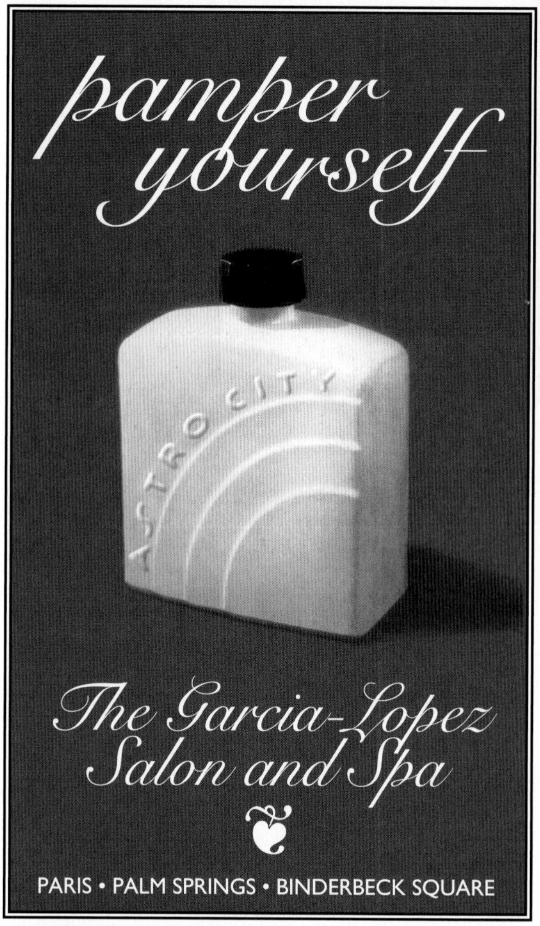
pamper yourself
ASTRO CITY
The Garcia-Lopez Salon and Spa
PARIS • PALM SPRINGS • BINDERBECK SQUARE

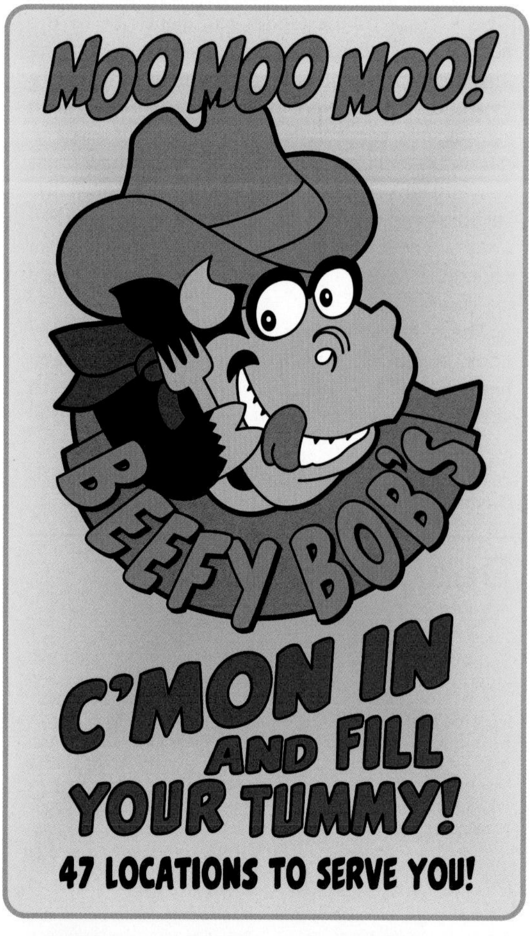
MOO MOO MOO!
BEEFY BOB'S
C'MON IN AND FILL YOUR TUMMY!
47 LOCATIONS TO SERVE YOU!

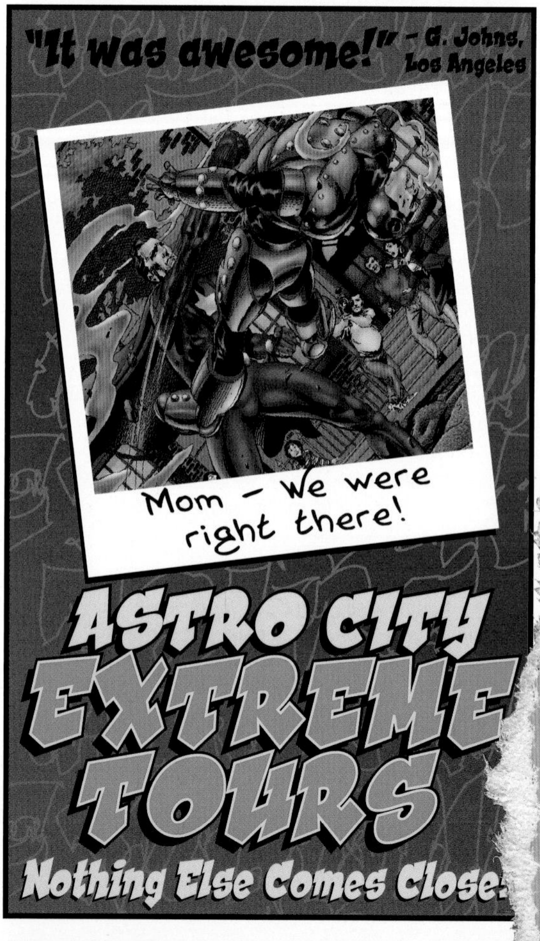
"It was awesome!" - G. Johns, Los Angeles
Mom - We were right there!
ASTRO CITY
EXTREME TOURS
Nothing Else Comes Close

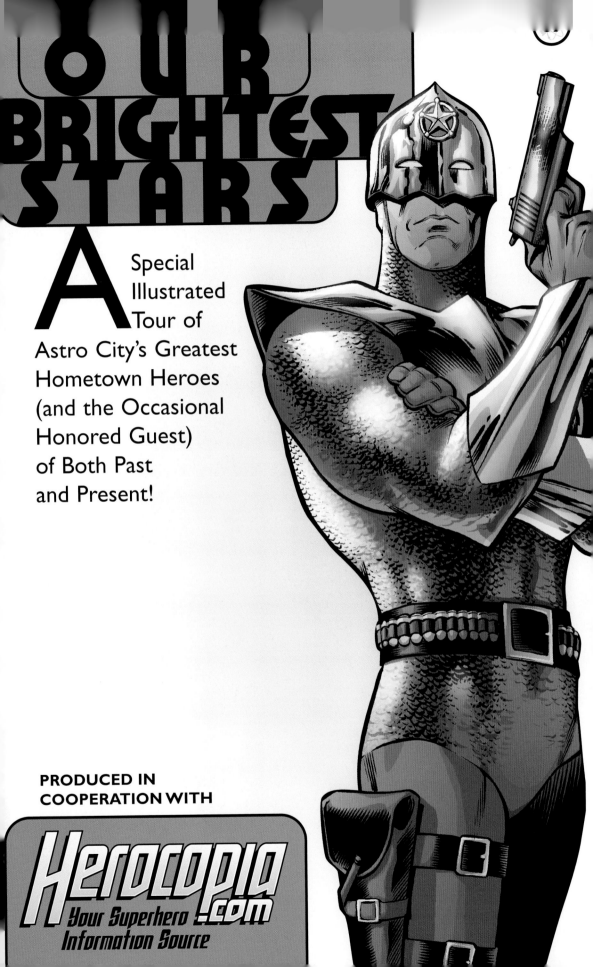

OUR BRIGHTEST STARS

A Special Illustrated Tour of Astro City's Greatest Hometown Heroes (and the Occasional Honored Guest) of Both Past and Present!

PRODUCED IN
COOPERATION WITH

Herocopia.com
Your Superhero
Information Source

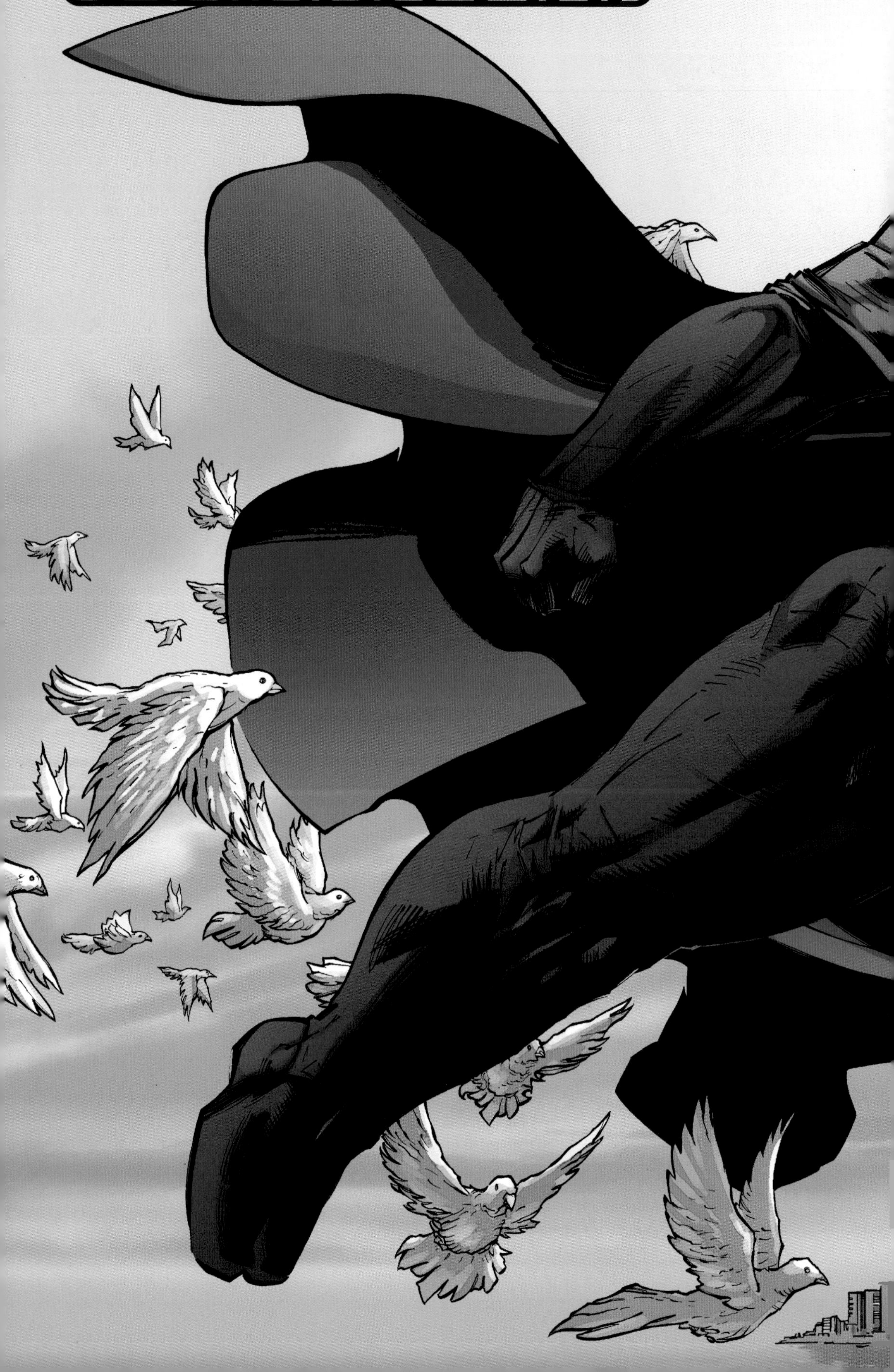

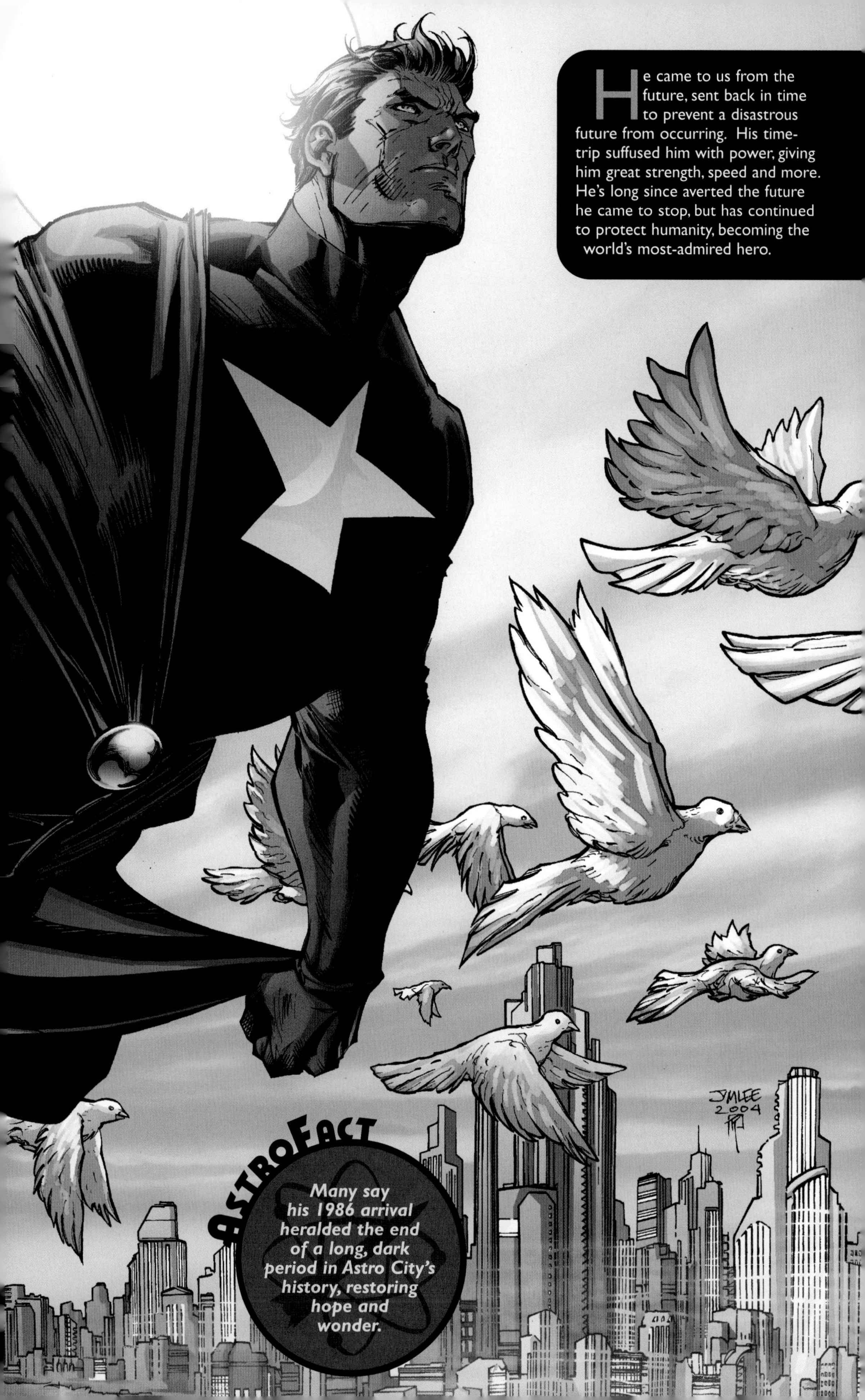
He came to us from the future, sent back in time to prevent a disastrous future from occurring. His time-trip suffused him with power, giving him great strength, speed and more. He's long since averted the future he came to stop, but has continued to protect humanity, becoming the world's most-admired hero.
JMLEE 2004
AstroFact
Many say his 1986 arrival heralded the end of a long, dark period in Astro City's history, restoring hope and wonder.

HONOR GUARD

Founded in Astro City in 1959 by the size-changing Max O'Millions, Honor Guard has become the world's preeminent alliance of heroes. Its current roster (pictured here with frequent ally Winged Victory) includes Beautie, the N-Forcer, the Black Rapier, Cleopatra, Samaritan, Quarrel and MPH.

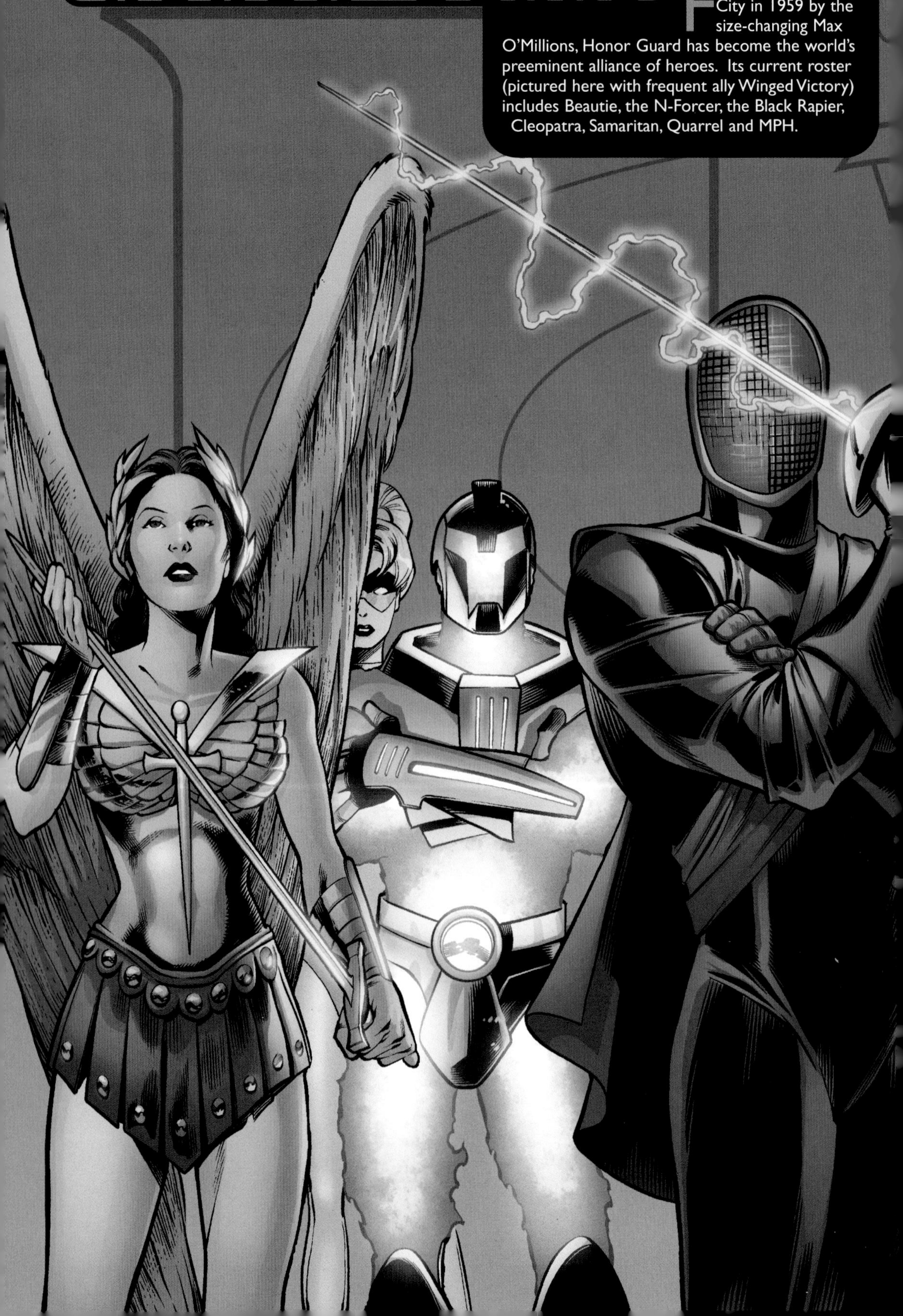

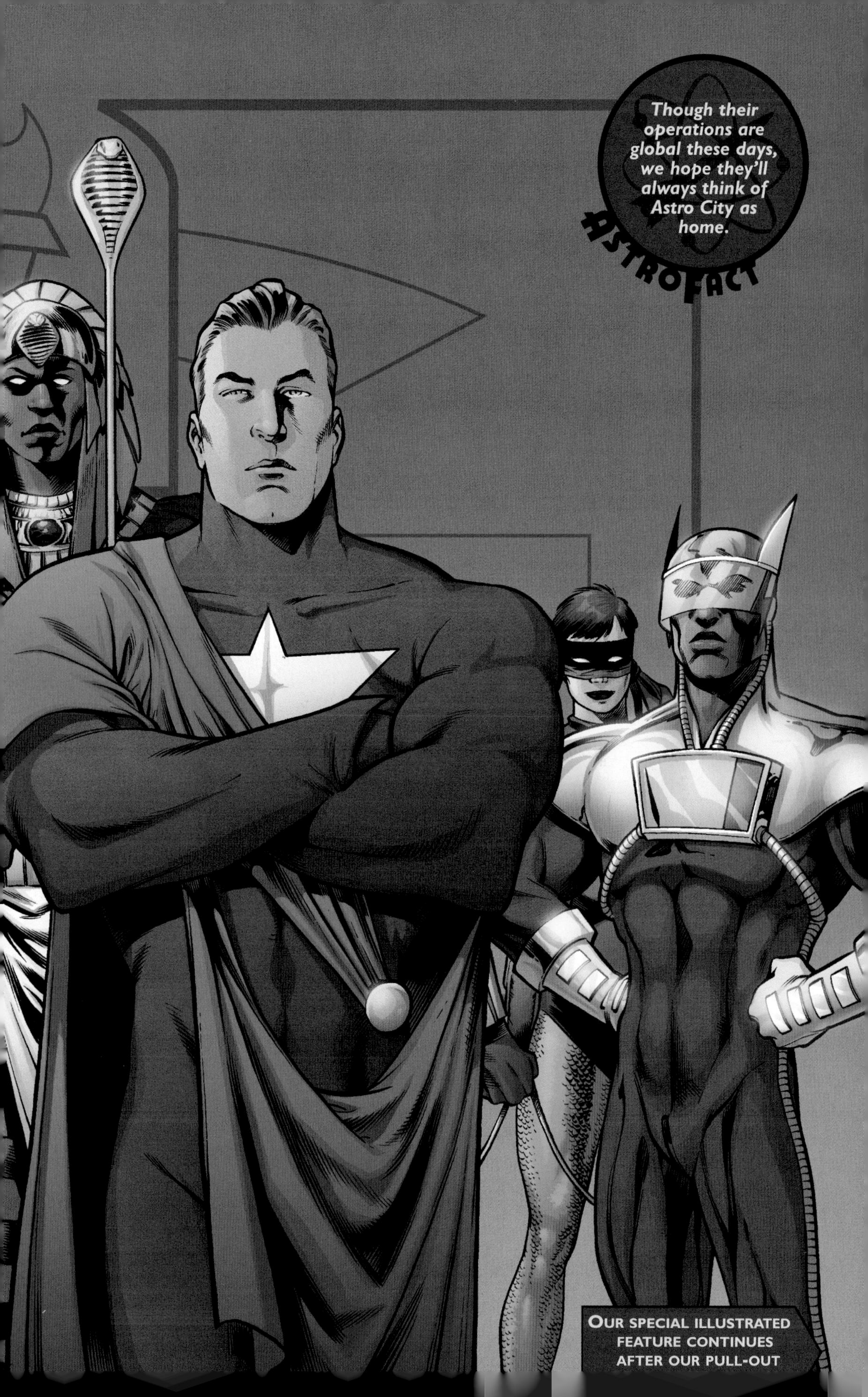
Though their operations are global these days, we hope they'll always think of Astro City as home.
ASTROFACT
OUR SPECIAL ILLUSTRATED FEATURE CONTINUES AFTER OUR PULL-OUT

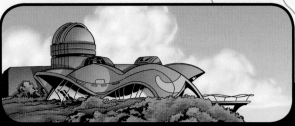

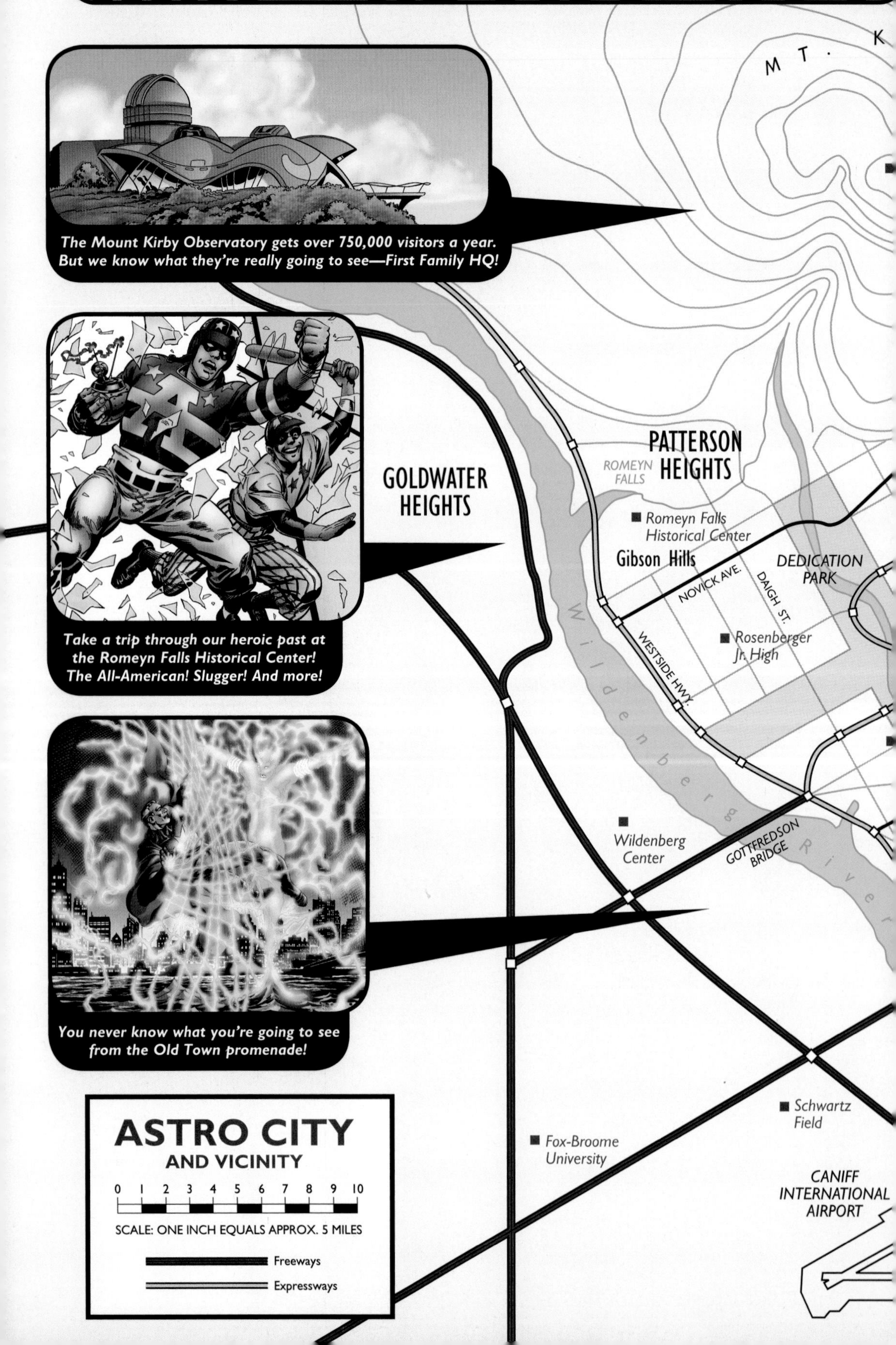

The Mount Kirby Observatory gets over 750,000 visitors a year. But we know what they're really going to see—First Family HQ!

Take a trip through our heroic past at the Romeyn Falls Historical Center! The All-American! Slugger! And more!

You never know what you're going to see from the Old Town promenade!

M T . K

PATTERSON HEIGHTS

ROMEYN FALLS

GOLDWATER HEIGHTS

■ Romeyn Falls
Historical Center

Gibson Hills

DEDICATION PARK

NOVICK AVE.

DAIGH ST.

WESTSIDE HWY.

■ Rosenberger
Jr. High

■ Wildenberg
Center

GOTTFREDSON BRIDGE

W i l d e n b e r g   River

■ Fox-Broome
University

■ Schwartz
Field

CANIFF
INTERNATIONAL
AIRPORT

ASTRO CITY
AND VICINITY

0 1 2 3 4 5 6 7 8 9 10

SCALE: ONE INCH EQUALS APPROX. 5 MILES

━━━━━ Freeways

═════ Expressways

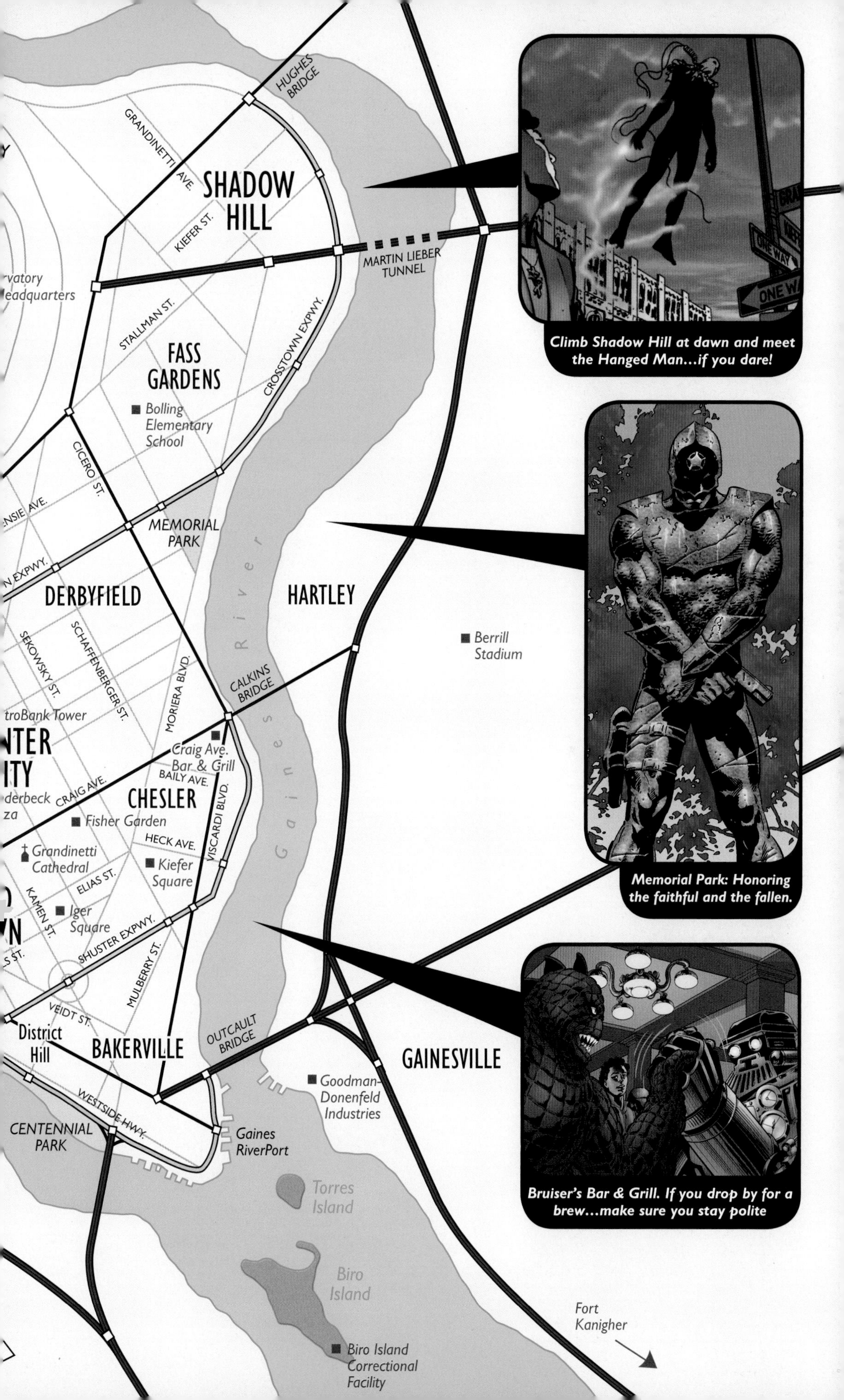
HUGHES BRIDGE
GRANDINETTI AVE.
SHADOW HILL
KIEFER ST.
MARTIN LIEBER TUNNEL
rvatory
eadquarters
STALLMAN ST.
FASS GARDENS
CROSSTOWN EXPWY.
Bolling Elementary School
CICERO ST.
NSIE AVE.
MEMORIAL PARK
N EXPWY.
DERBYFIELD
HARTLEY
Gaines River
Berrill Stadium
SEKOWSKY ST.
SCHAFFENBERGER ST.
MORIERA BLVD.
CALKINS BRIDGE
troBank Tower
NTER
ITY
Craig Ave. Bar & Grill
BAILY AVE.
derbeck
za
CRAIG AVE.
CHESLER
VISCARDI BLVD.
Fisher Garden
HECK AVE.
Grandinetti Cathedral
Kiefer Square
ELIAS ST.
KAMEN ST.
Iger Square
SHUSTER EXPWY.
S ST.
MULBERRY ST.
VEIDT ST.
District Hill
BAKERVILLE
OUTCAULT BRIDGE
GAINESVILLE
Goodman-Donenfeld Industries
WESTSIDE HWY.
CENTENNIAL PARK
Gaines RiverPort
Torres Island
Biro Island
Biro Island Correctional Facility
Fort Kanigher
ONE WAY

Climb Shadow Hill at dawn and meet the Hanged Man…if you dare!

Memorial Park: Honoring the faithful and the fallen.

Bruiser's Bar & Grill. If you drop by for a brew…make sure you stay polite

JACK IN THE BOX

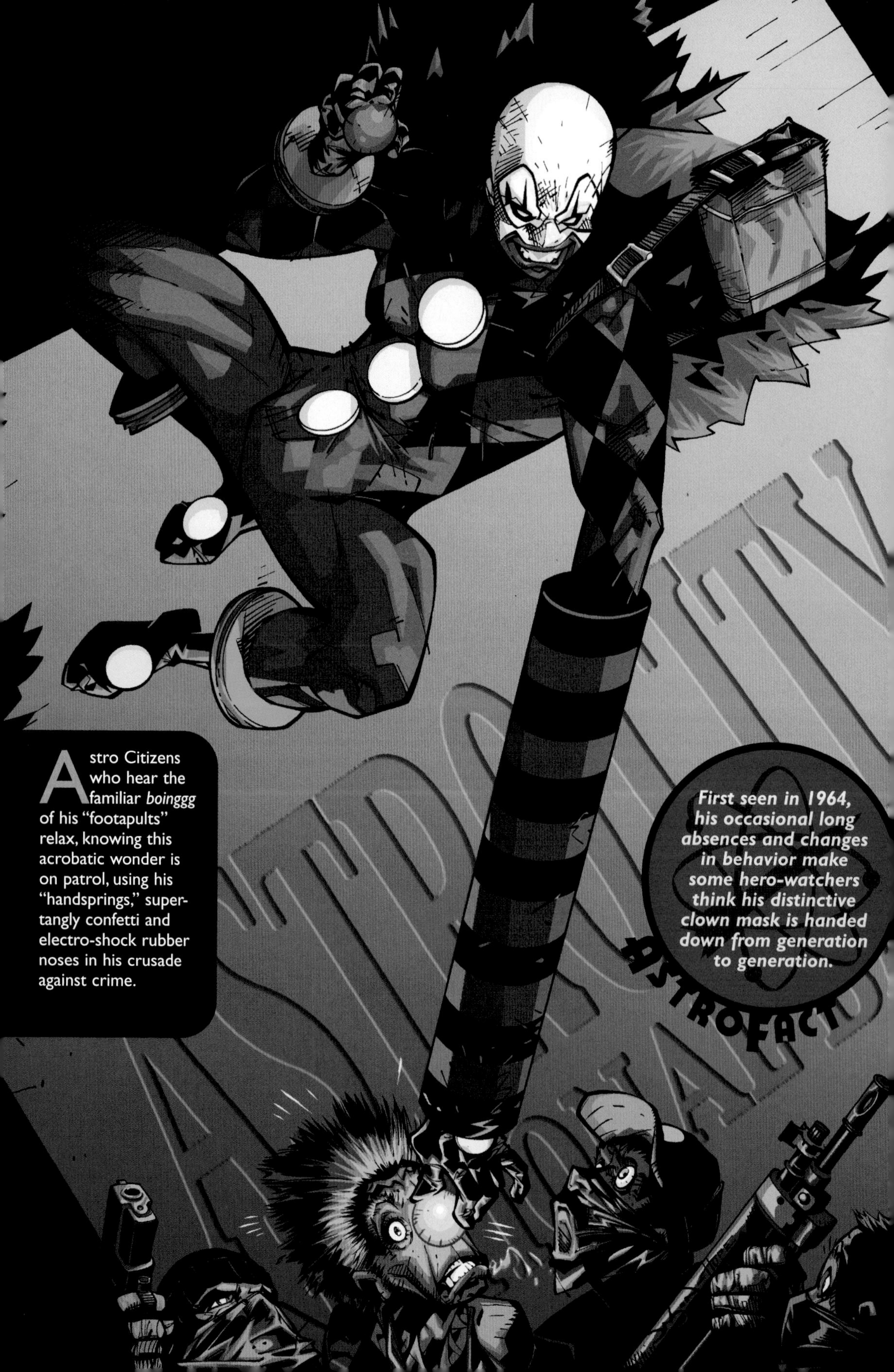

Astro Citizens who hear the familiar *boinggg* of his "footapults" relax, knowing this acrobatic wonder is on patrol, using his "handsprings," super-tangly confetti and electro-shock rubber noses in his crusade against crime.

ASTROFACT

First seen in 1964, his occasional long absences and changes in behavior make some hero-watchers think his distinctive clown mask is handed down from generation to generation.

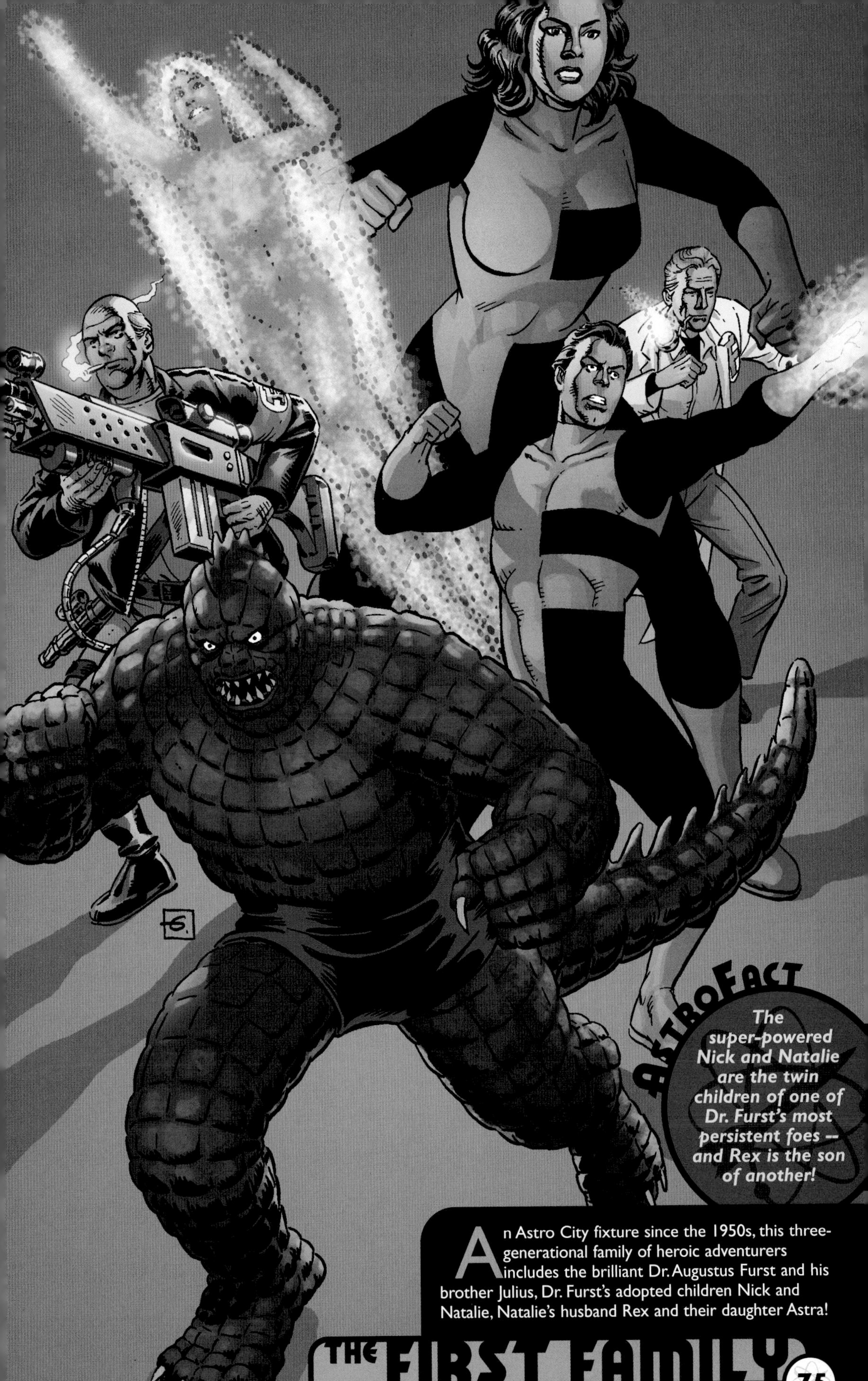

ASTROFACT

The super-powered Nick and Natalie are the twin children of one of Dr. Furst's most persistent foes -- and Rex is the son of another!

An Astro City fixture since the 1950s, this three-generational family of heroic adventurers includes the brilliant Dr. Augustus Furst and his brother Julius, Dr. Furst's adopted children Nick and Natalie, Natalie's husband Rex and their daughter Astra!

THE FIRST FAMILY

OUR BRIGHTEST STARS

WINGED VICTORY

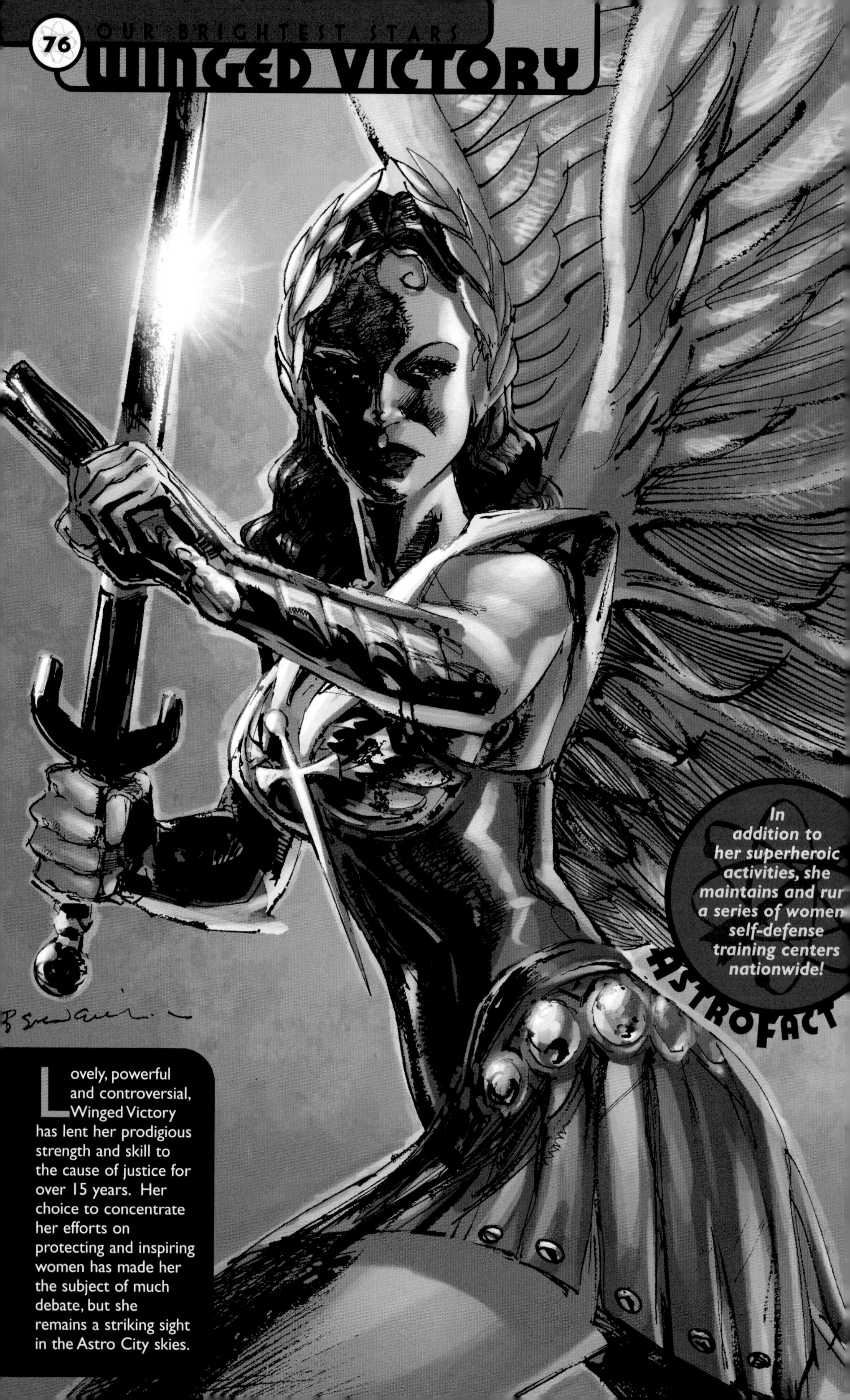

In addition to her superheroic activities, she maintains and rur a series of women self-defense training centers nationwide!

ASTROFACT

Lovely, powerful and controversial, Winged Victory has lent her prodigious strength and skill to the cause of justice for over 15 years. Her choice to concentrate her efforts on protecting and inspiring women has made her the subject of much debate, but she remains a striking sight in the Astro City skies.

THE N-FORCER

The longtime corporate symbol of N.R.-stics, Inc. (and before at of Nicholls-Royce ectronics), the -Forcer has been rotecting Astro City d the world for over ur decades, wearing a ccession of armored its that transform his ody into "n-force."

ASTROFACT

Some reports say the N-Forcer is a single, long-lived individual, others that the suit is piloted by an elite and private brotherhood of heroes.

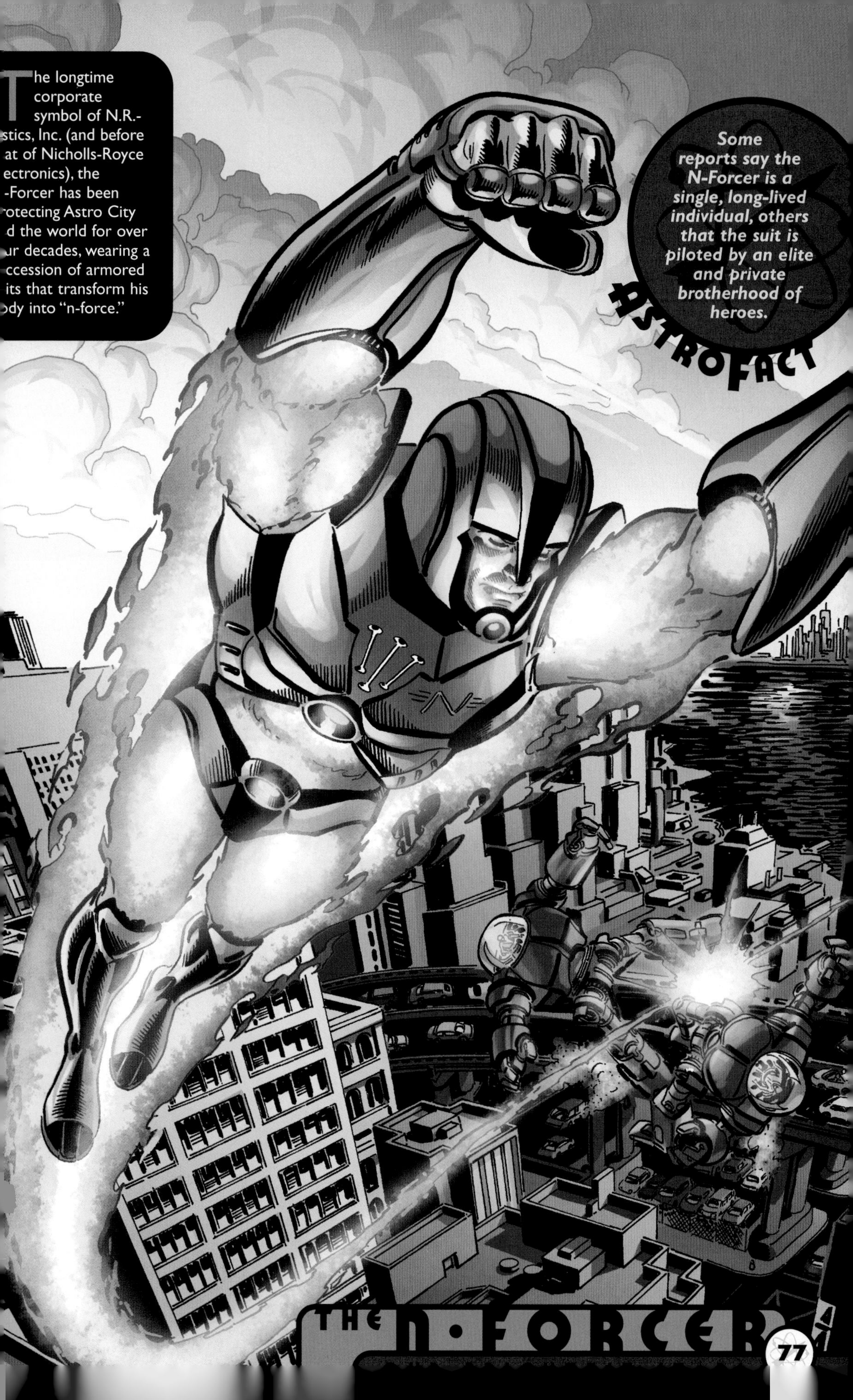

CLEOPATRA

There have been at least two Cleopatras wielding the mighty "sun-staff of Ra" in the cause of justice and peace, one in the 1950s and 1960s, the other in more recent times. Whether there have been more, and what their connection is to the historical Cleopatra, no one knows.

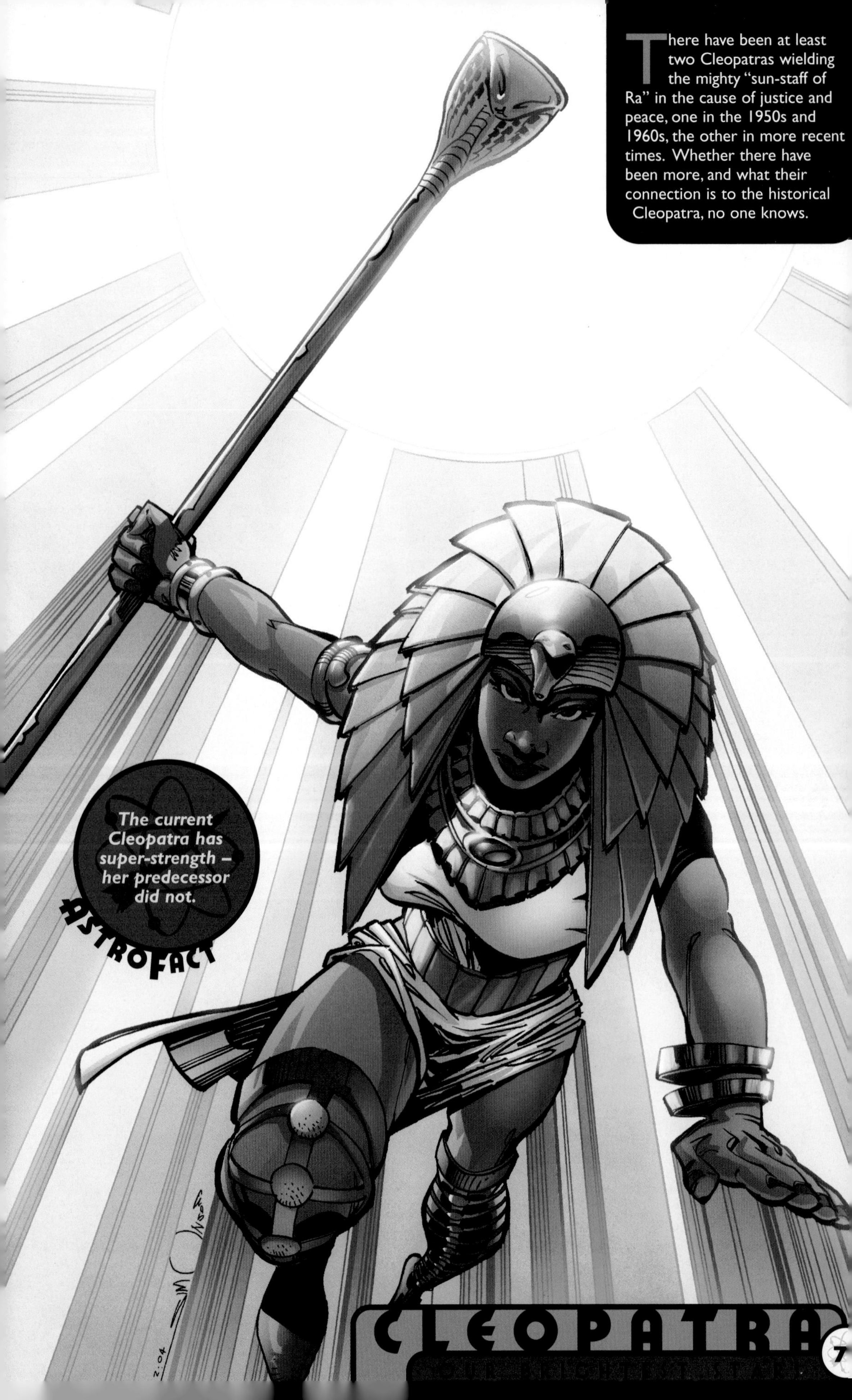

ASTROFACT

The current Cleopatra has super-strength – her predecessor did not.

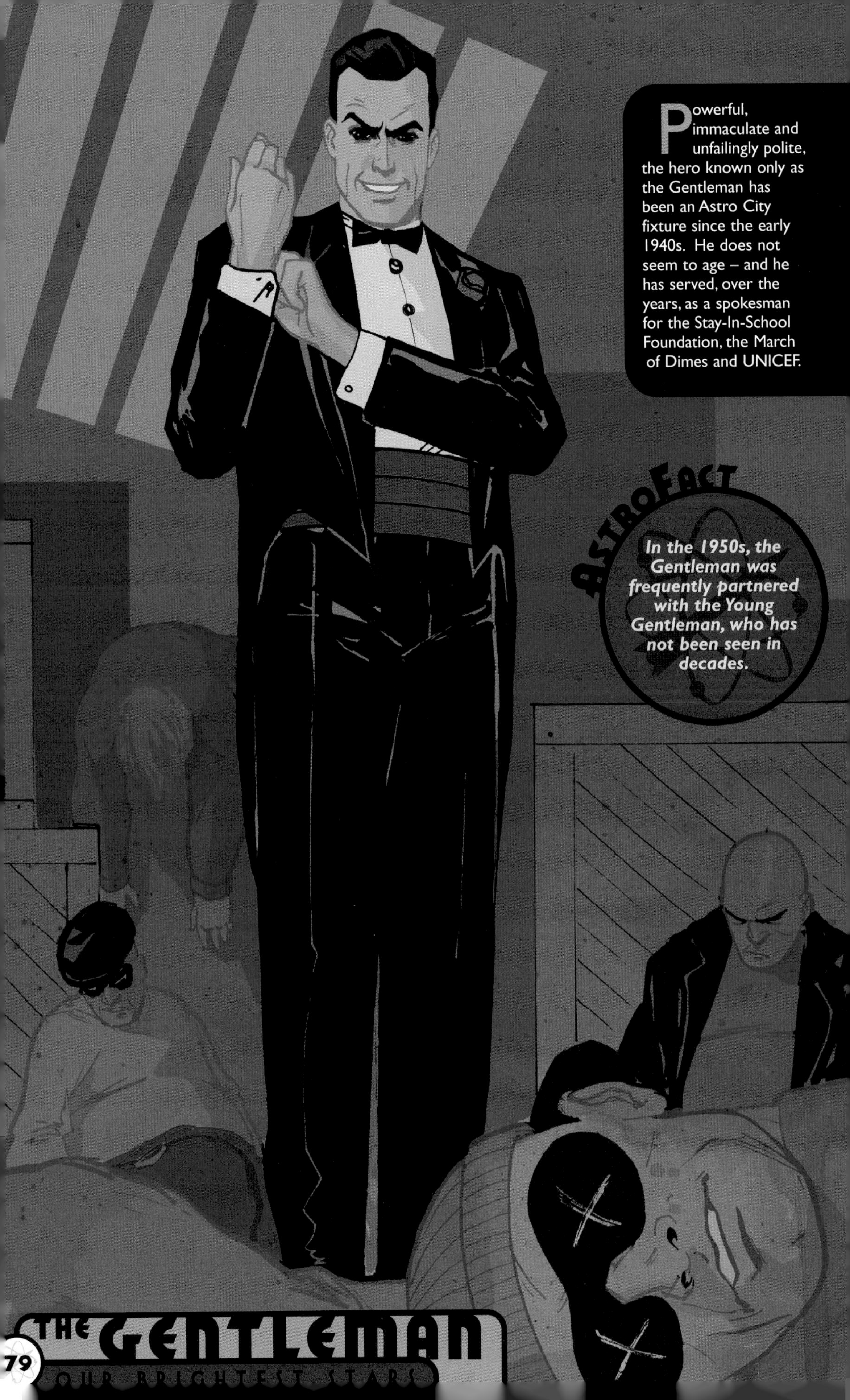

Powerful, immaculate and unfailingly polite, the hero known only as the Gentleman has been an Astro City fixture since the early 1940s. He does not seem to age – and he has served, over the years, as a spokesman for the Stay-In-School Foundation, the March of Dimes and UNICEF.

AstroFact

In the 1950s, the Gentleman was frequently partnered with the Young Gentleman, who has not been seen in decades.

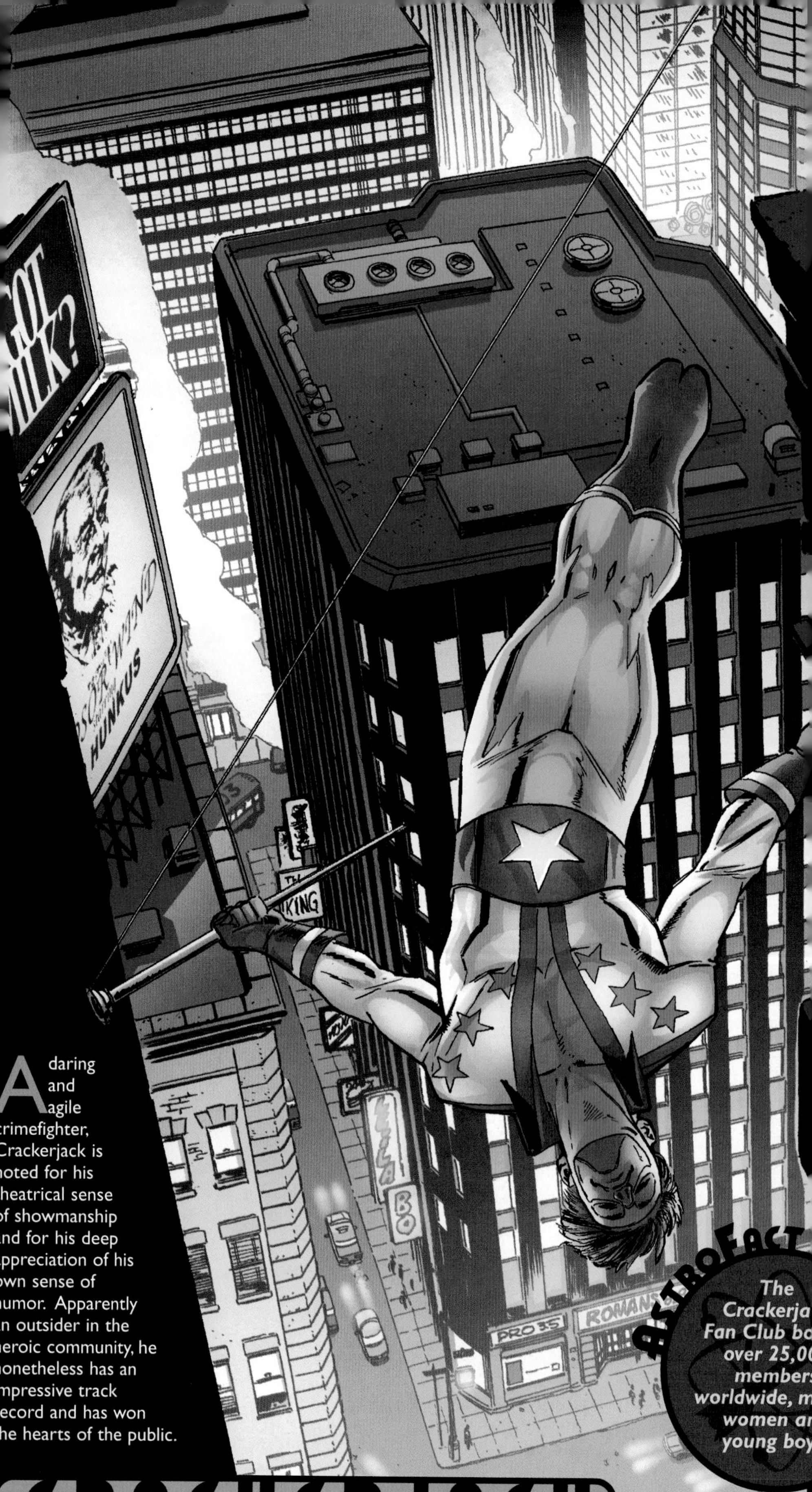
GOT MILK?
HUNKUS
KING
BO
PRO 35
ROWANS
LW 04

A daring and agile crimefighter, Crackerjack is noted for his theatrical sense of showmanship and for his deep appreciation of his own sense of humor. Apparently an outsider in the heroic community, he nonetheless has an impressive track record and has won the hearts of the public.

ASTROFACT

The Crackerja Fan Club bo over 25,0 members worldwide, m women ar young boy

CRACKERJACK

NIGHTINGALE AND SUNBIRD

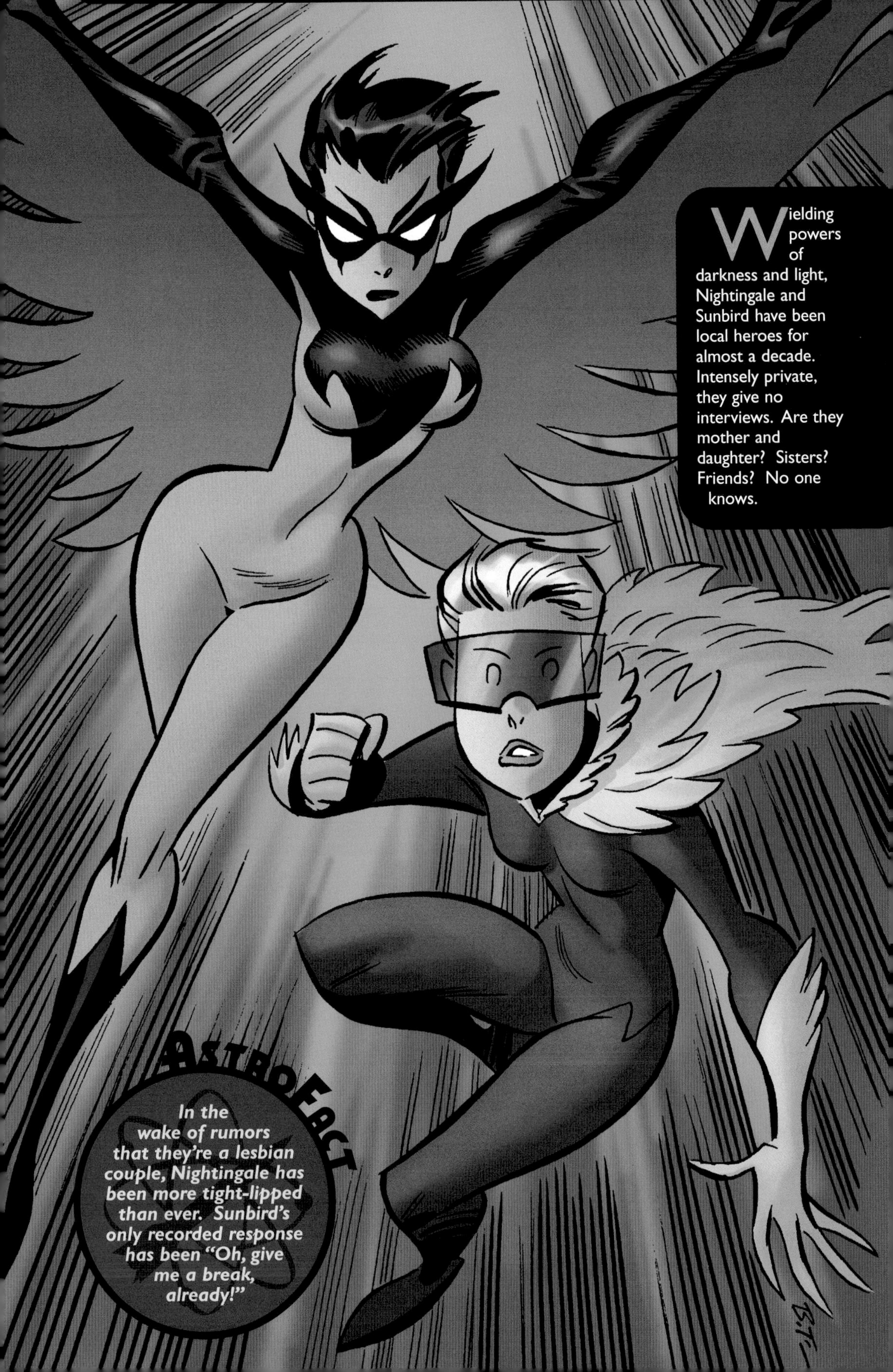

Wielding powers of darkness and light, Nightingale and Sunbird have been local heroes for almost a decade. Intensely private, they give no interviews. Are they mother and daughter? Sisters? Friends? No one knows.

ASTROFACT

In the wake of rumors that they're a lesbian couple, Nightingale has been more tight-lipped than ever. Sunbird's only recorded response has been "Oh, give me a break, already!"

THE CROSSBREED

The Crossbreed believe their powers to be gifts from God, to be used in His service. Led by the enigmatic, storm-casting Noah, the Crossbreed include the leonine Daniel, the rock-shaping Peter, the winged, angelic Mary, the giant David and the sonic-powered Joshua.

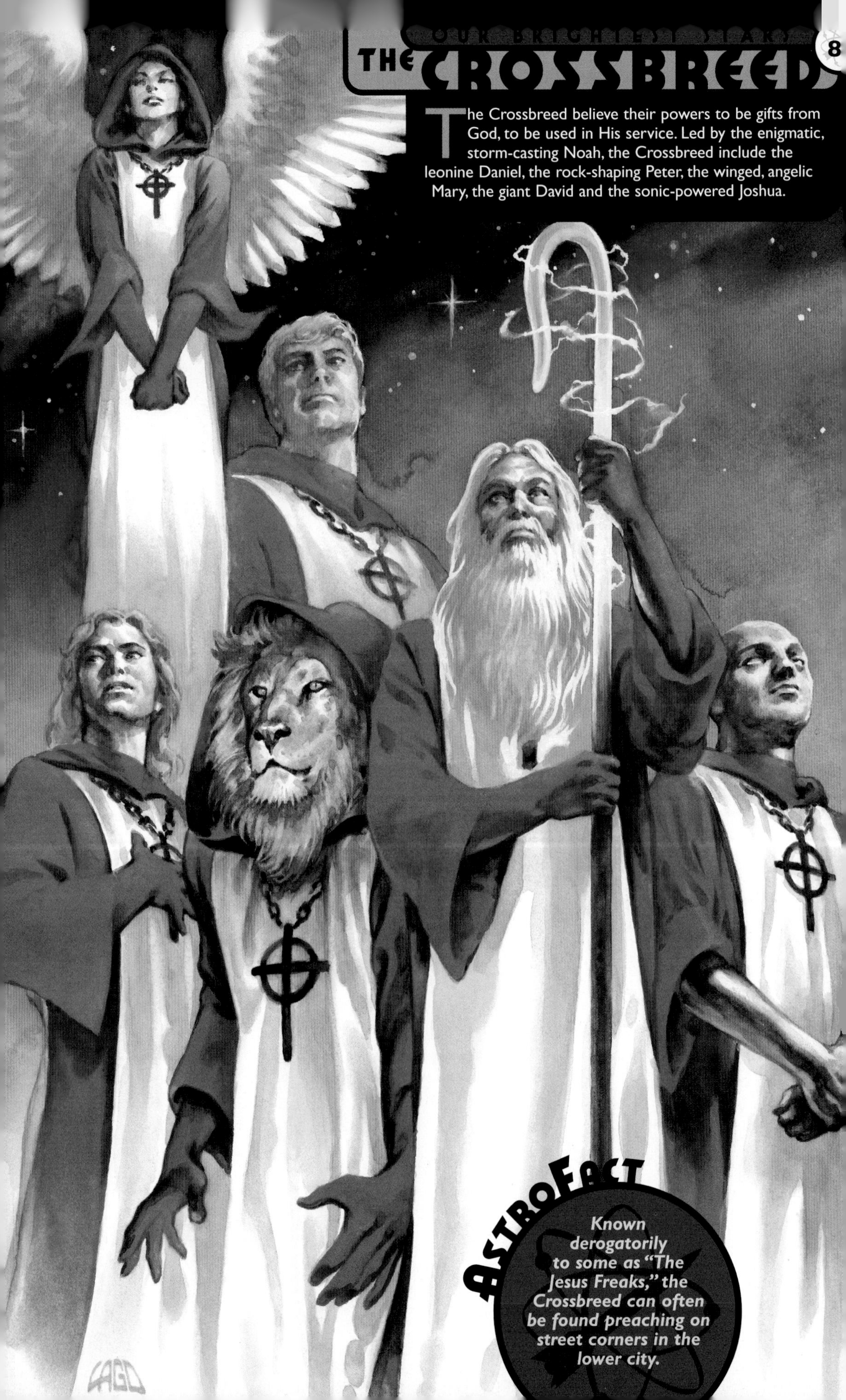
LAGO

AstroFact

Known derogatorily to some as "The Jesus Freaks," the Crossbreed can often be found preaching on street corners in the lower city.

THE FLYING FOX

Astro City's newest crimefighting figure, the Flying Fox is apparently unpowered, but an extremely skilled and tenacious fighter. The roar of her aero-cycle has become a familiar sound in the Northside.

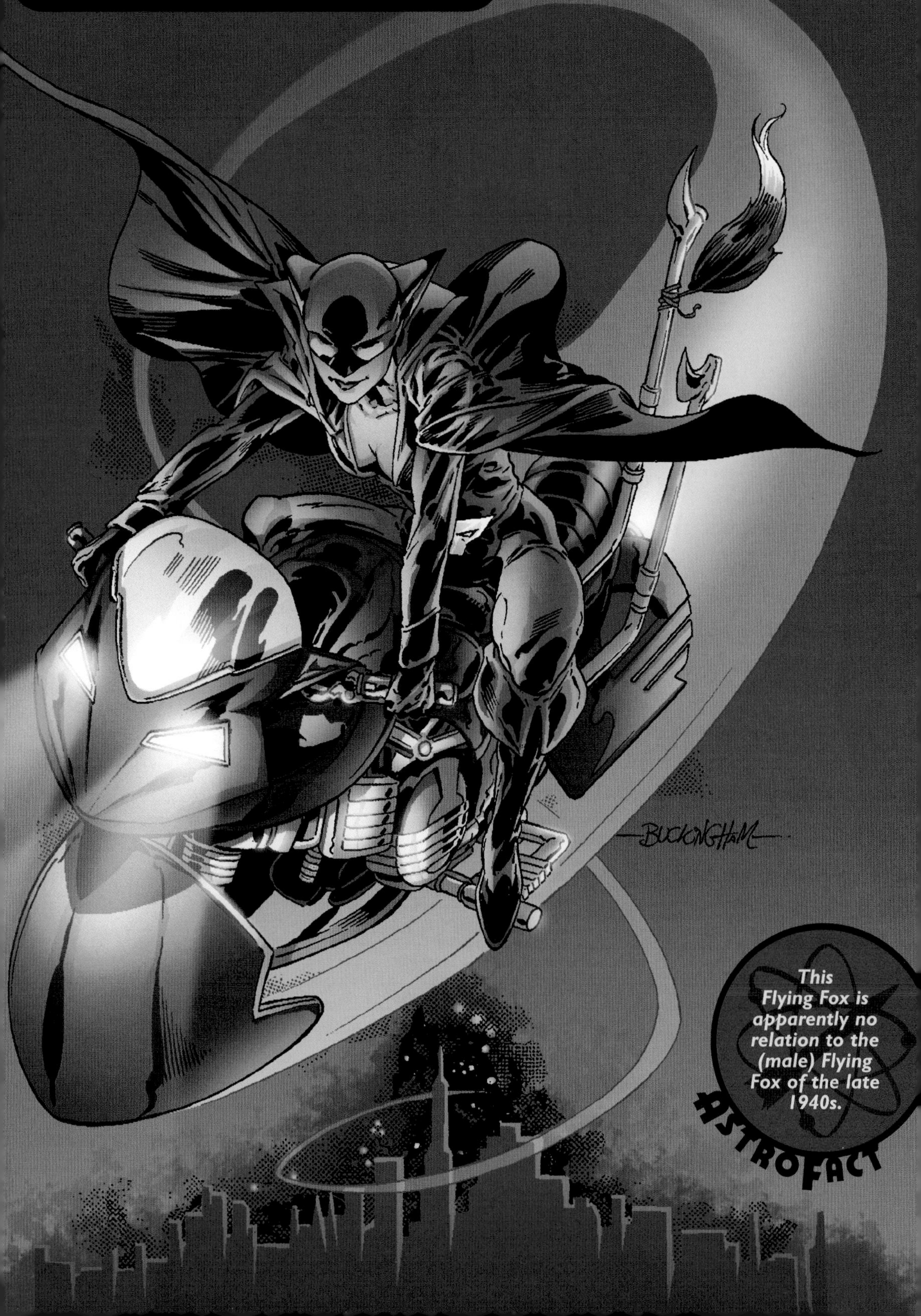
BUCKINGHAM

ASTROFACT

This Flying Fox is apparently no relation to the (male) Flying Fox of the late 1940s.

THE LIVING NIGHTMARE

A violent, destructive physical manifestation of society's fears, the Nightmare is not often considered a hero – but for two periods, mentally controlled by a heroic Marine pilot, he has been turned into a force for good, and a member of Honor Guard. We extend hope that someday, this could be a permanent change.

ASTROFACT

The tentacles on the Nightmare's head are said to be fear receptors, and he has occasionally been defeated by blocking or modifying his access to the fear around him.

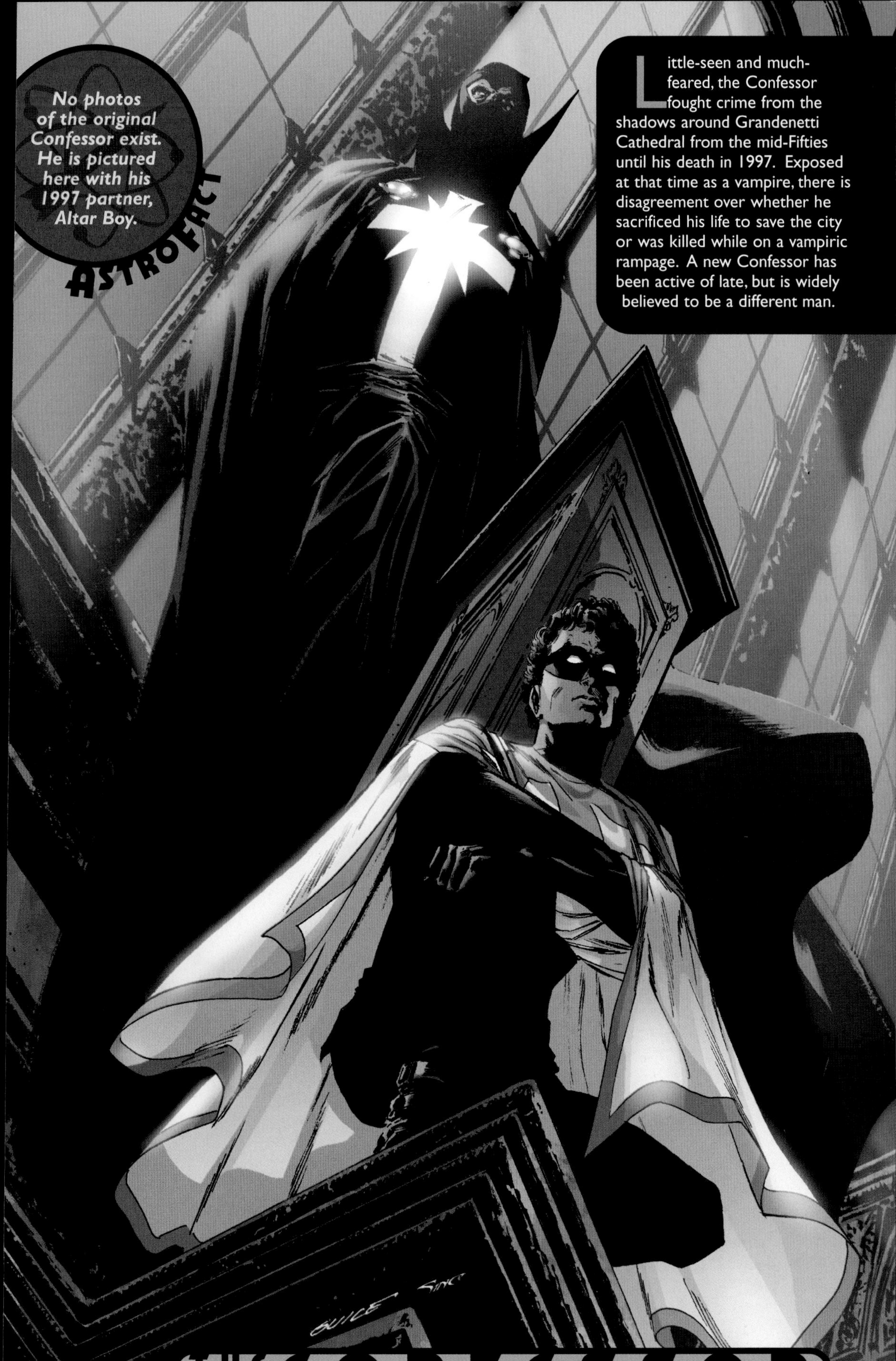

ASTROFACT

No photos of the original Confessor exist. He is pictured here with his 1997 partner, Altar Boy.

Little-seen and much-feared, the Confessor fought crime from the shadows around Grandenetti Cathedral from the mid-Fifties until his death in 1997. Exposed at that time as a vampire, there is disagreement over whether he sacrificed his life to save the city or was killed while on a vampiric rampage. A new Confessor has been active of late, but is widely believed to be a different man.

THE CONFESSOR

THE BLUE KNIGHT

Is he the ghost of a murdered policeman, returned from the grave for vengeance? Or a hi-tech vigilante, performing his "mystic" tricks through gadgetry? All we can say for sure is that the Blue Knight's war on organized crime began in 1974, causing some to hail him as an instrument of harsh justice and some to decry him as a serial killer.

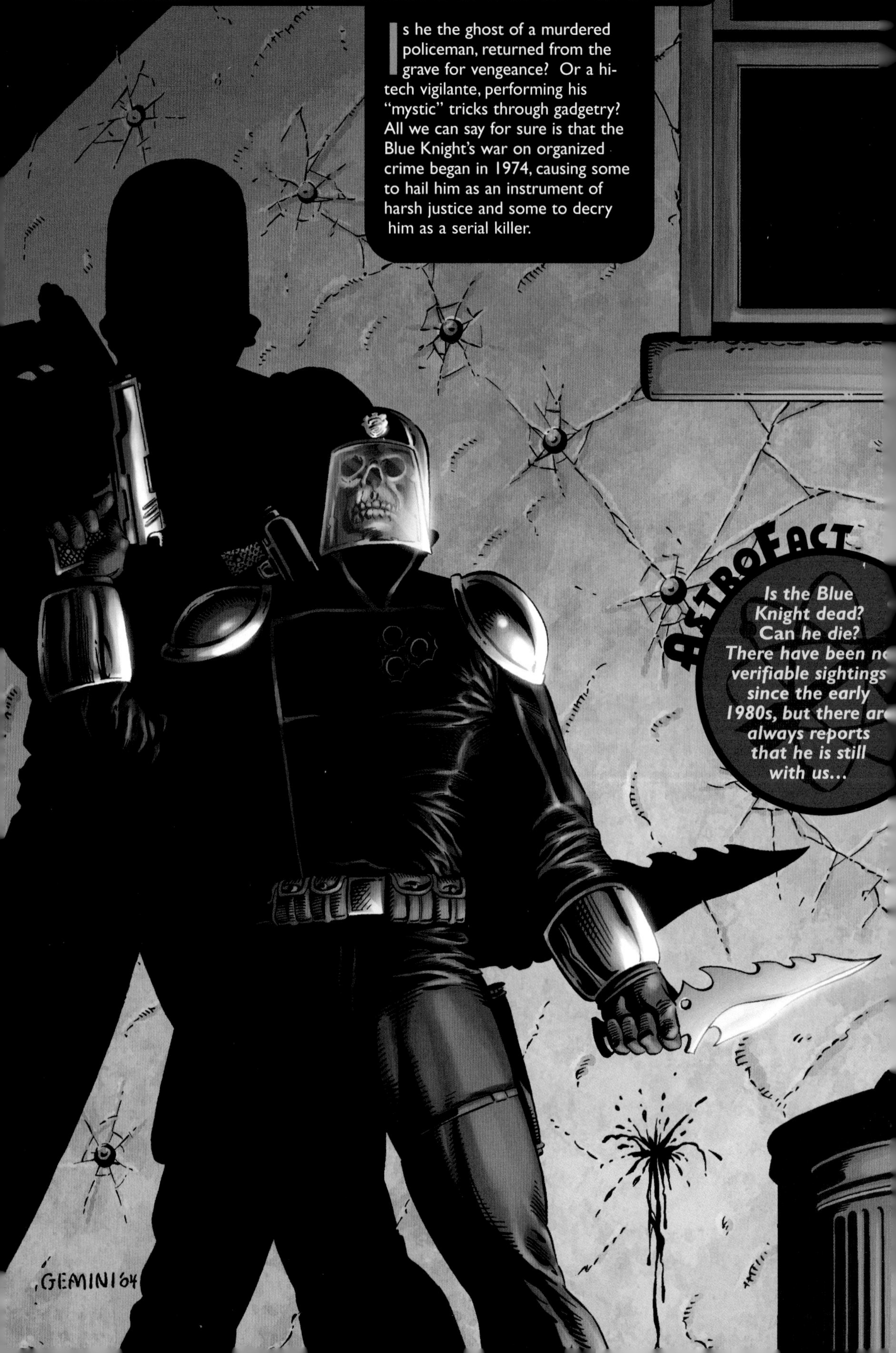
GEMINI'04

ASTROFACT

Is the Blue Knight dead? Can he die? There have been no verifiable sightings since the early 1980s, but there are always reports that he is still with us...

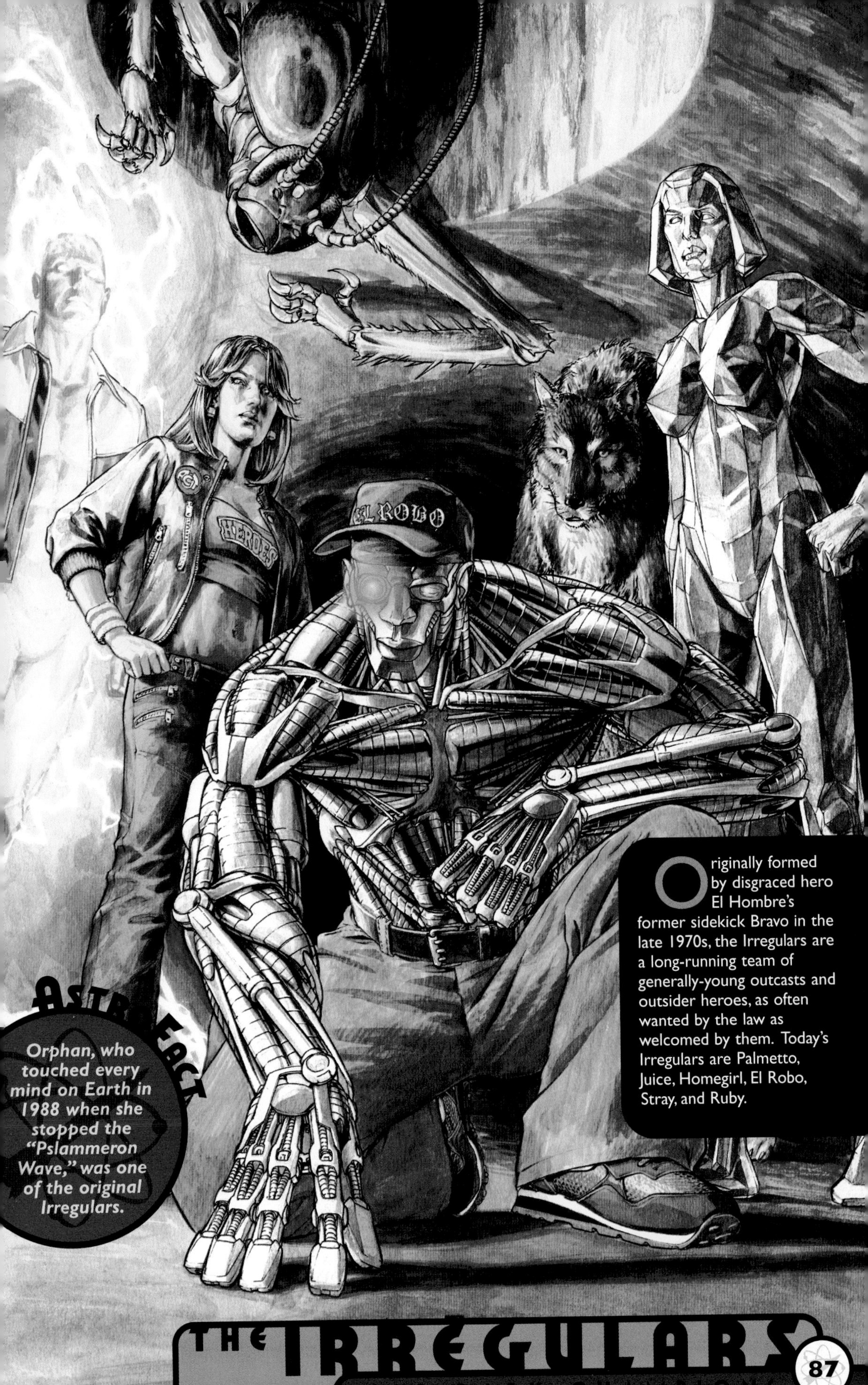

Originally formed by disgraced hero El Hombre's former sidekick Bravo in the late 1970s, the Irregulars are a long-running team of generally-young outcasts and outsider heroes, as often wanted by the law as welcomed by them. Today's Irregulars are Palmetto, Juice, Homegirl, El Robo, Stray, and Ruby.

Astro Fact

Orphan, who touched every mind on Earth in 1988 when she stopped the "Pslammeron Wave," was one of the original Irregulars.

THE IRREGULARS

OUR DARK CHAMPIONS

THE HANGED MAN

The eerie, eldritch protector of Shadow Hill. Little is known of his origins or history, only that he wields enormous power and has protected his community for over a century, becoming a familiar if unsettling figure in times of crisis.

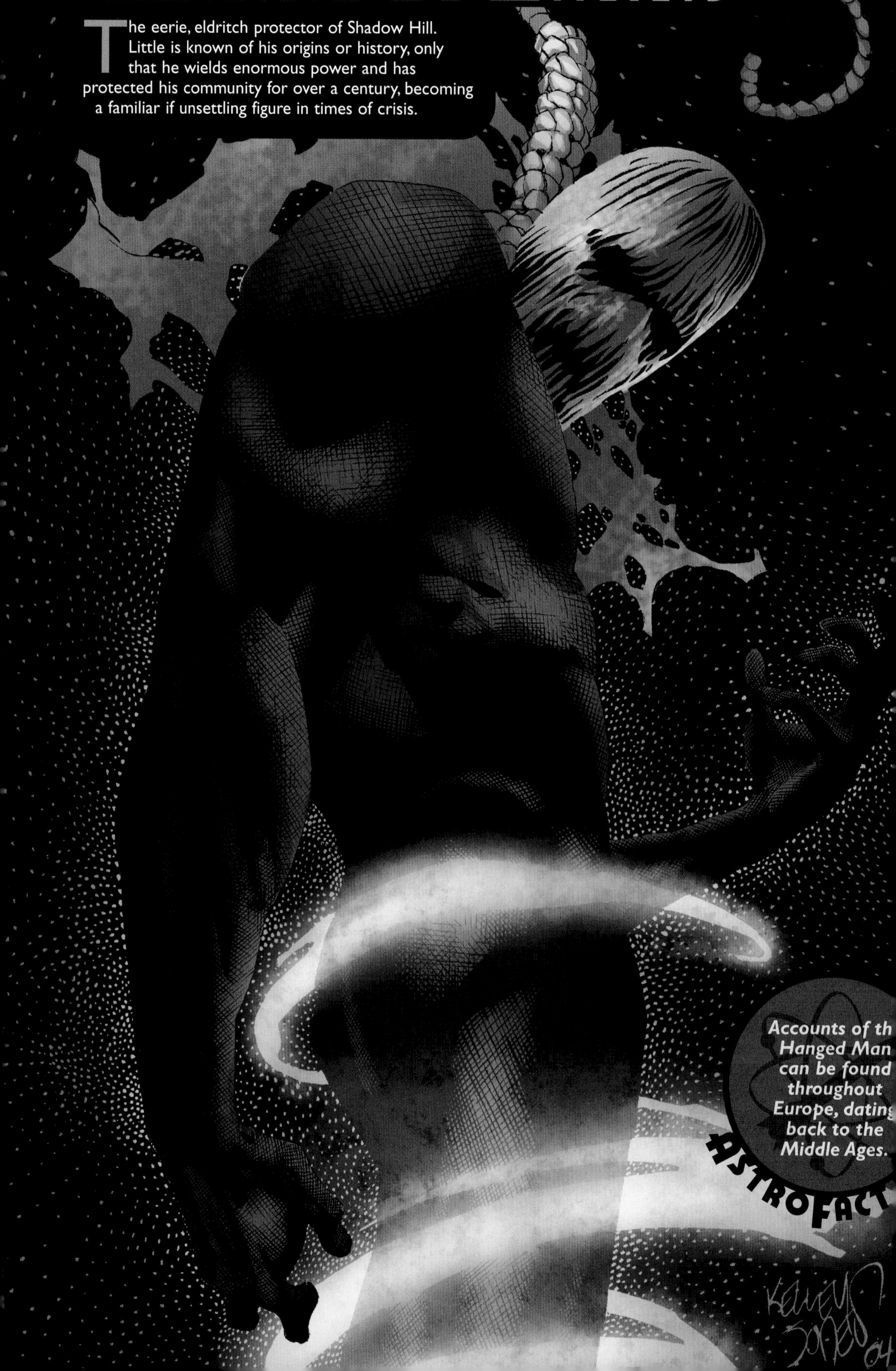

ASTROFACT

Accounts of th Hanged Man can be found throughout Europe, dating back to the Middle Ages.

The first super-powered champion to truly capture the public imagination and popularize the idea of the "superhero," Air Ace was a World War I soldier and aviator, given the power of flight through exposure to an experimental gas attack. Returning home to a troubled city, he took up the mantle of hero, and history was made.

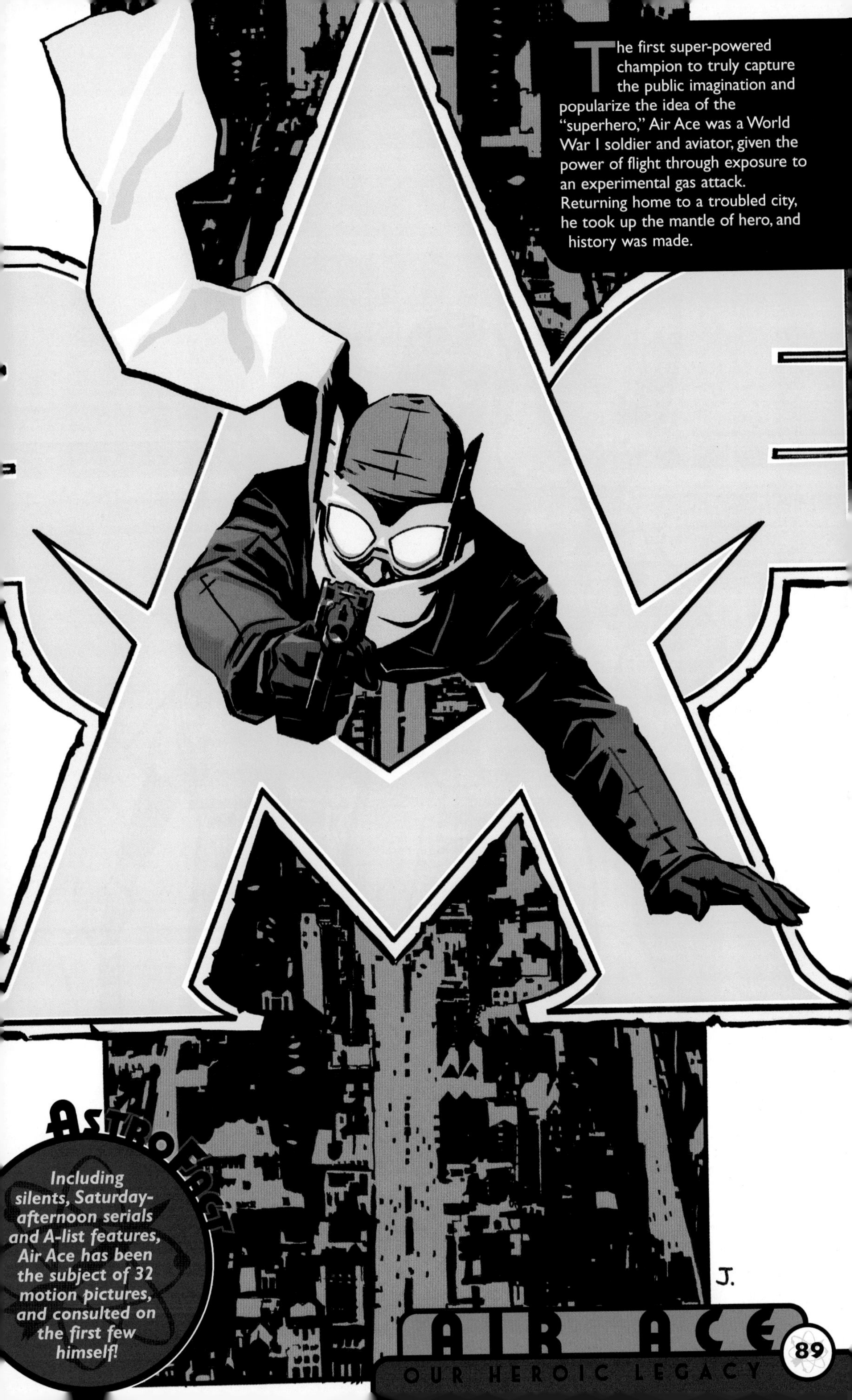
J.

AstroFact

Including silents, Saturday-afternoon serials and A-list features, Air Ace has been the subject of 32 motion pictures, and consulted on the first few himself!

THE ALL-AMERICAN

A patriotic hero of World War II and beyond, the All-American was Johnny Appleton, gridiron hero, transformed by his scientist uncle's experiments into an athletic paragon. Fighting the good fight in Europe and at home, the All-American eventually lost his life to a sniper's bullet in Korea.

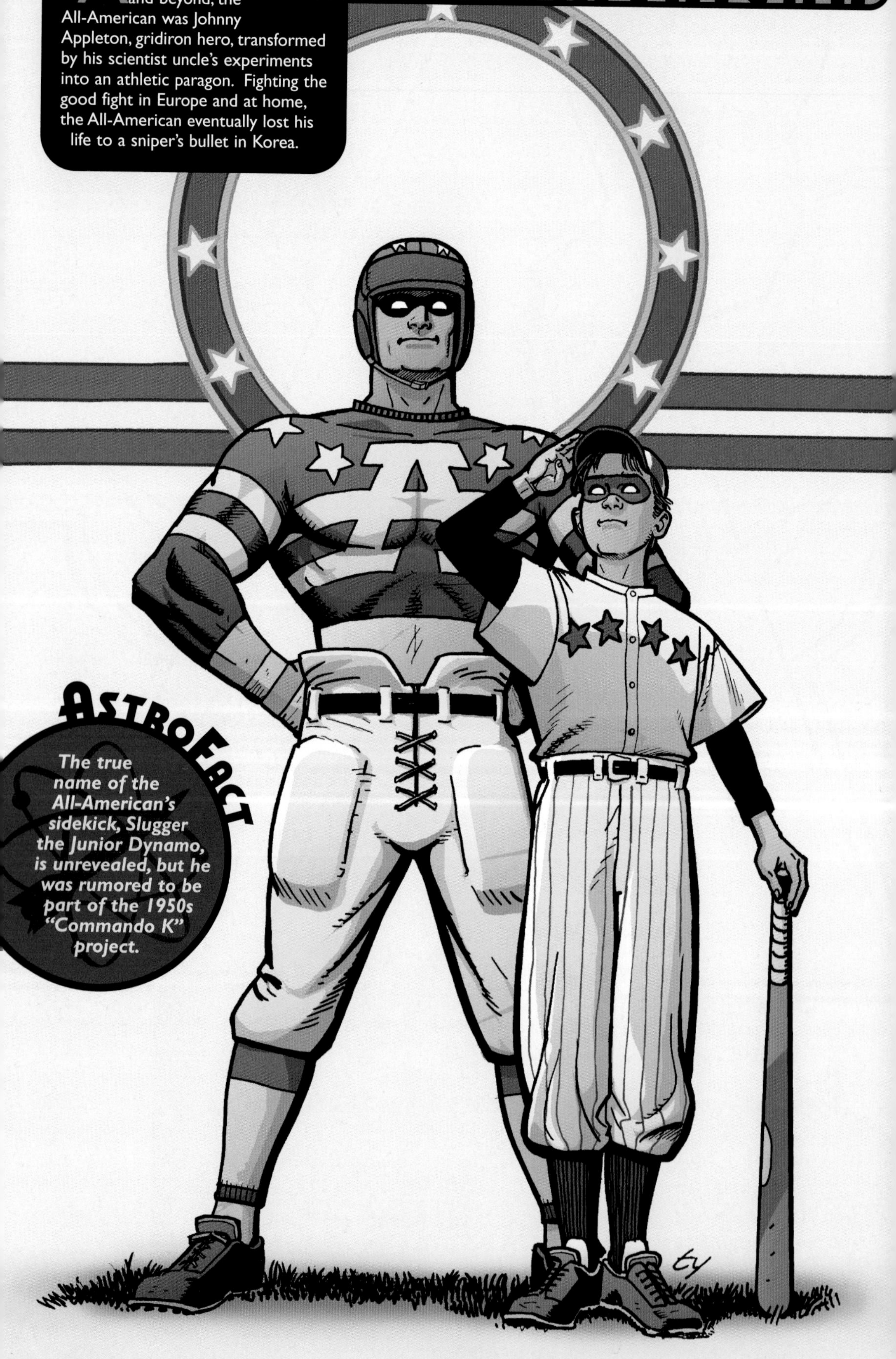

AstroFact

The true name of the All-American's sidekick, Slugger the Junior Dynamo, is unrevealed, but he was rumored to be part of the 1950s "Commando K" project.

OLD SOLDIER

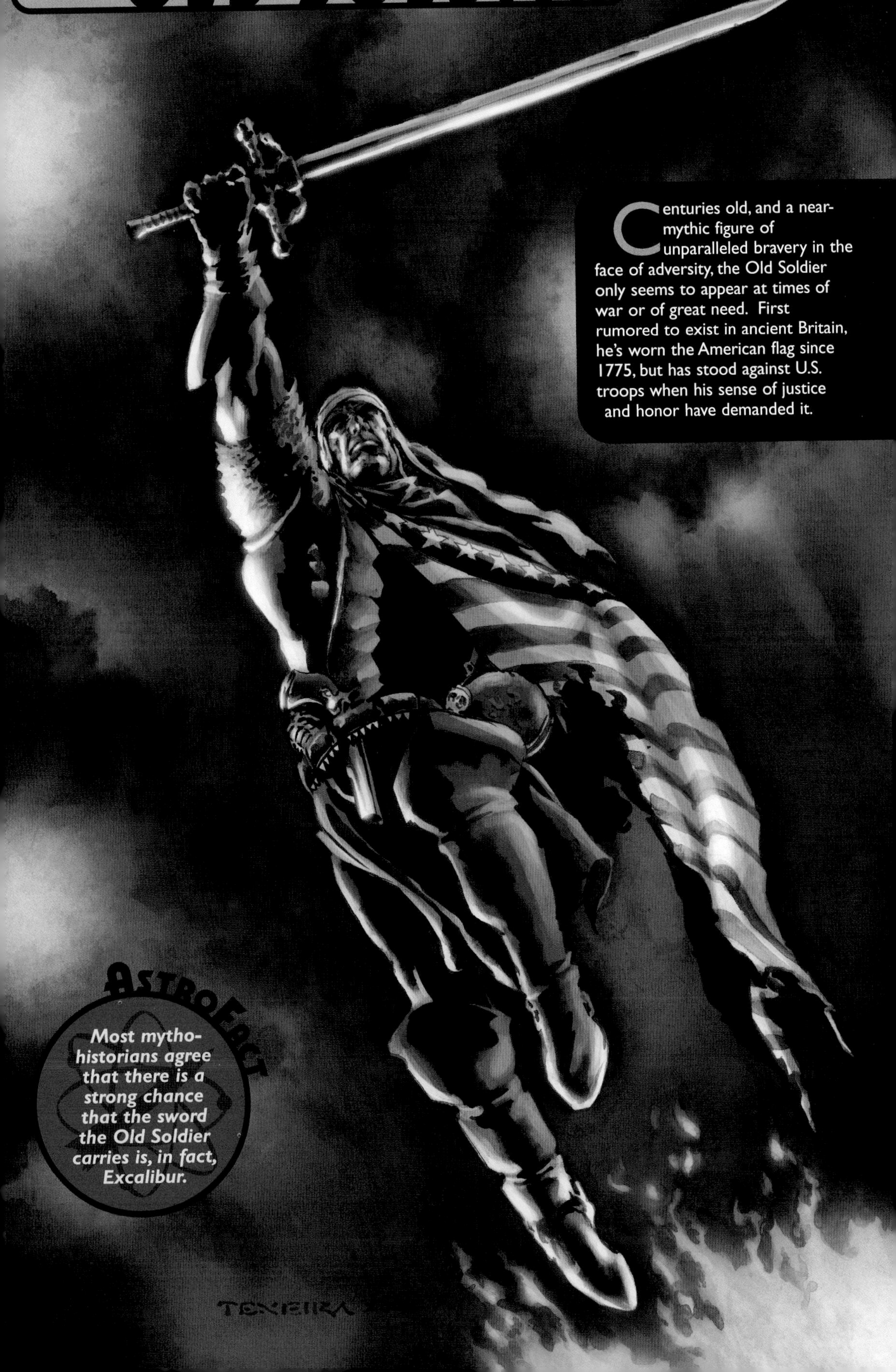
TEXEIRA

Centuries old, and a near-mythic figure of unparalleled bravery in the face of adversity, the Old Soldier only seems to appear at times of war or of great need. First rumored to exist in ancient Britain, he's worn the American flag since 1775, but has stood against U.S. troops when his sense of justice and honor have demanded it.

AstroFact

Most mytho-historians agree that there is a strong chance that the sword the Old Soldier carries is, in fact, Excalibur.

THE BLACK BADGE

Thought by many to have been K.O. Carson, ex-boxer and policeman, the Black Badge began fighting crime in Astro City's Bakerville neighborhood in the 1950s, when he felt that traditional law-enforcement wasn't serving the black community fairly. He retired in 1972.

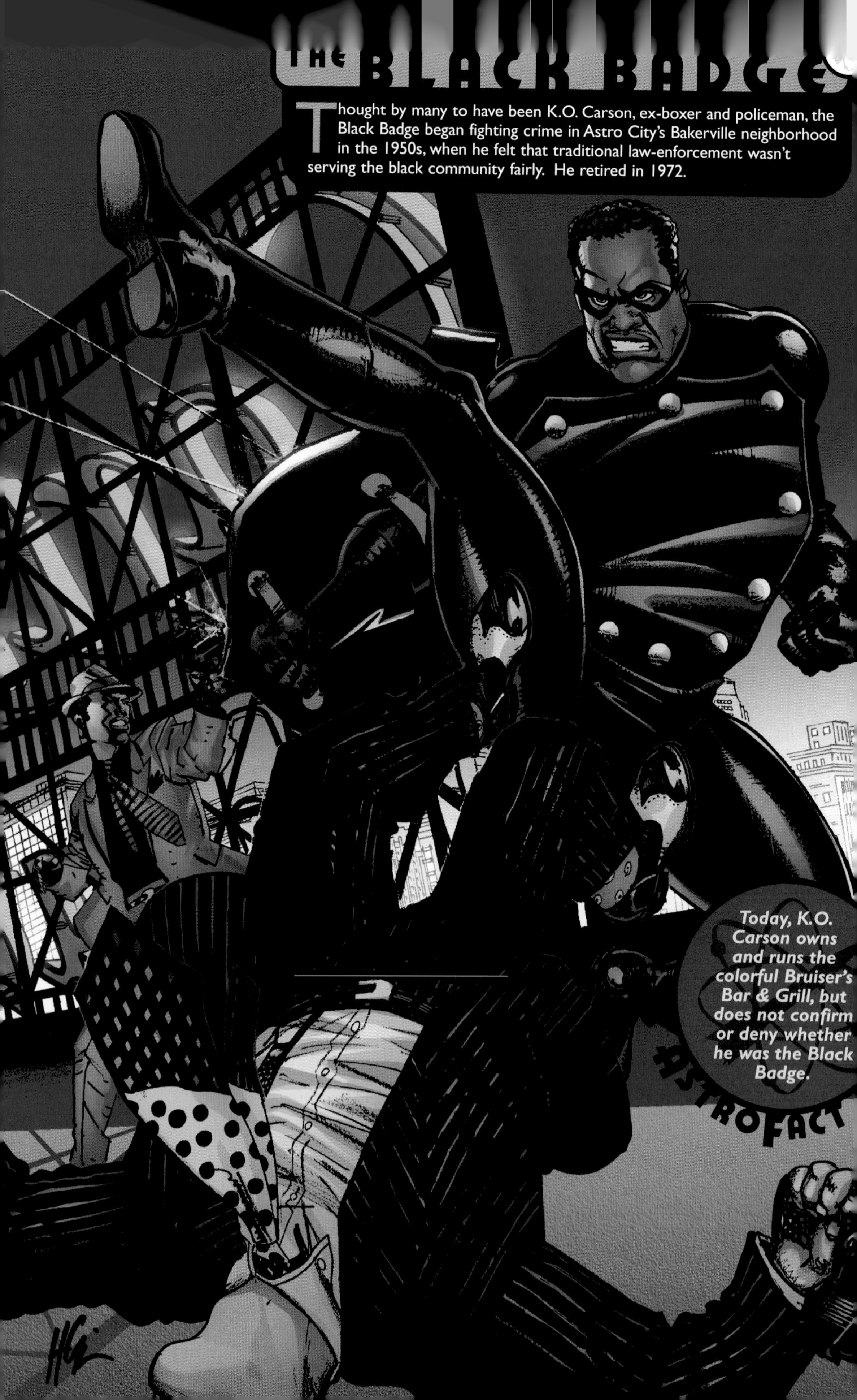
ASTROFACT
Today, K.O. Carson owns and runs the colorful Bruiser's Bar & Grill, but does not confirm or deny whether he was the Black Badge.

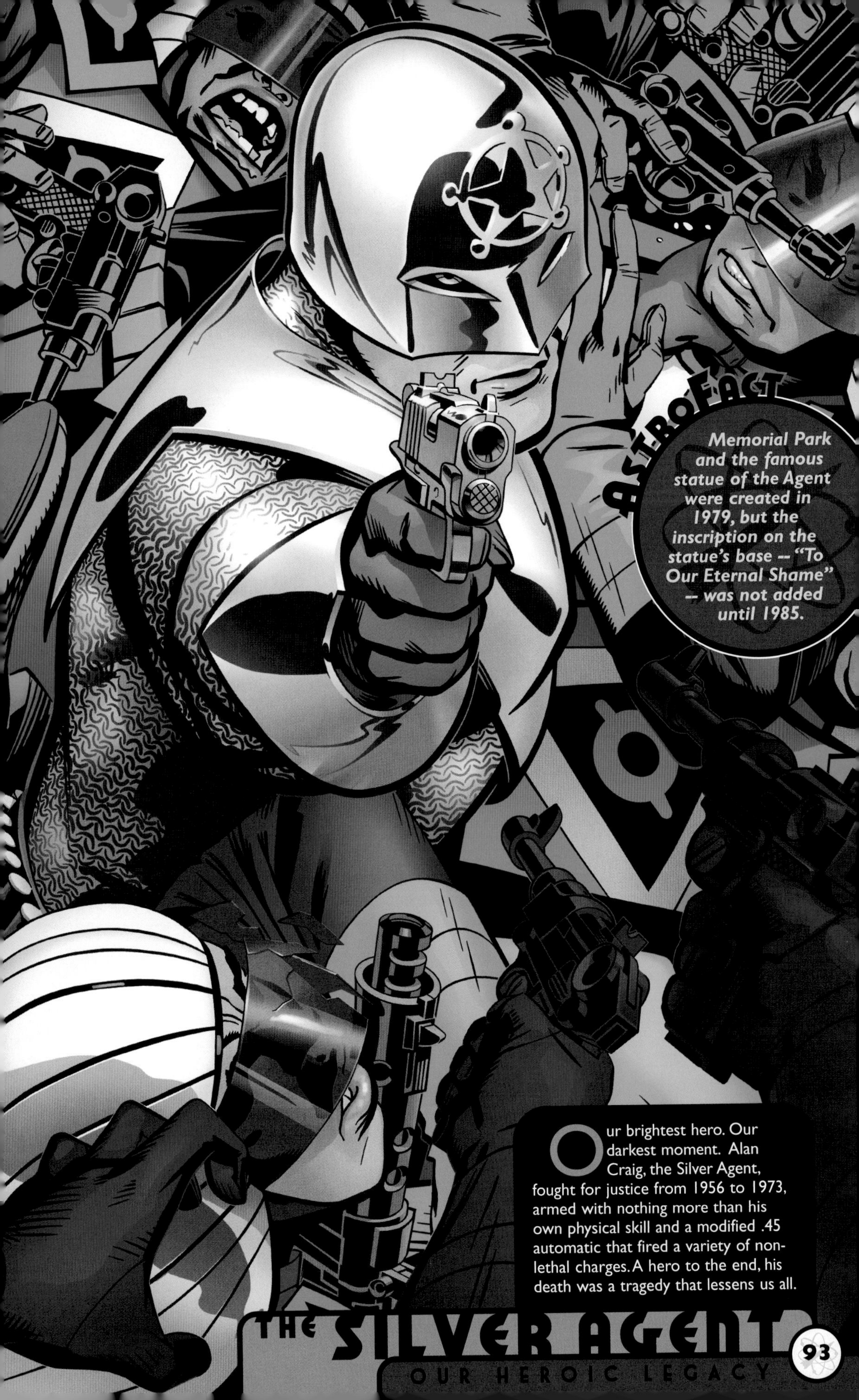

ASTROFACT

Memorial Park and the famous statue of the Agent were created in 1979, but the inscription on the statue's base -- "To Our Eternal Shame" -- was not added until 1985.

Our brightest hero. Our darkest moment. Alan Craig, the Silver Agent, fought for justice from 1956 to 1973, armed with nothing more than his own physical skill and a modified .45 automatic that fired a variety of non-lethal charges. A hero to the end, his death was a tragedy that lessens us all.

THE SILVER AGENT

Though he was with us only briefly, from 1961-1965, Atomicus burns bright in our memory. Born in a nuclear reactor in Fort Kanigher's Atomic Research Lab, there have been many guesses as to why he appeared, but no firm answers. We're just glad he was with us for a time, and wish him the best, wherever he might be now.

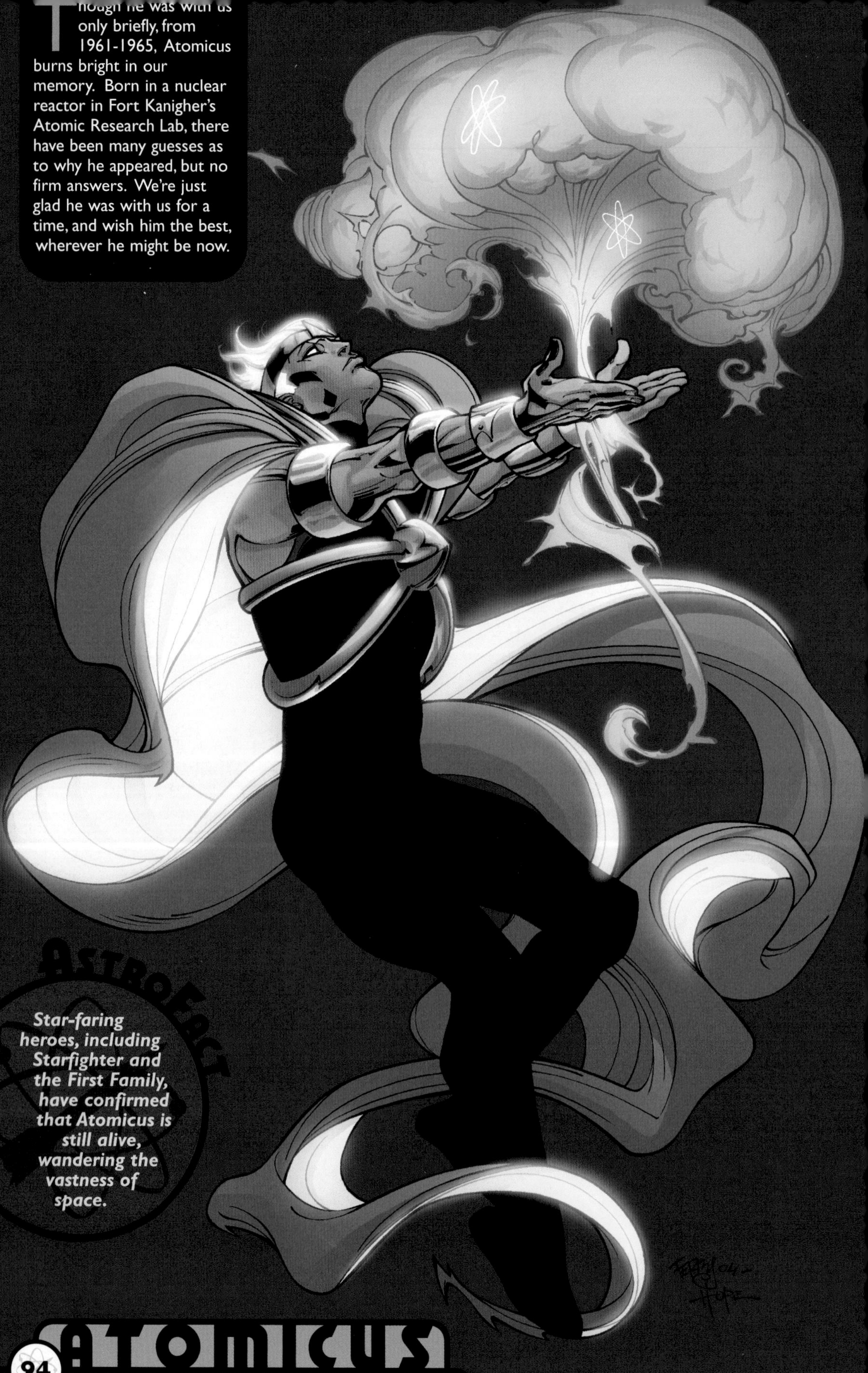

AstroFact

Star-faring heroes, including Starfighter and the First Family, have confirmed that Atomicus is still alive, wandering the vastness of space.

ATOMICUS

OUR HEROIC LEGACY

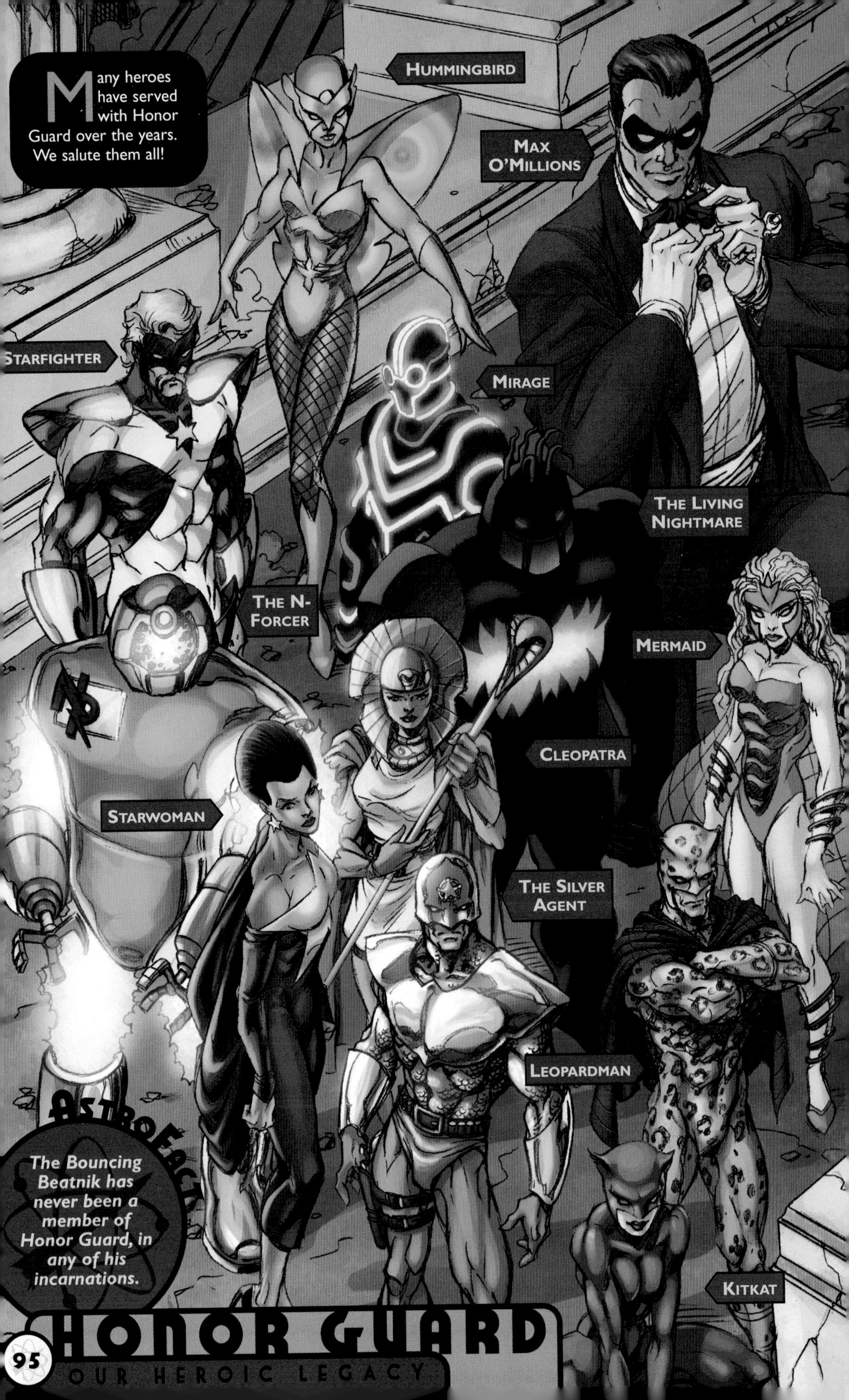

Many heroes have served with Honor Guard over the years. We salute them all!
HUMMINGBIRD
MAX O'MILLIONS
STARFIGHTER
MIRAGE
THE LIVING NIGHTMARE
THE N-FORCER
MERMAID
CLEOPATRA
STARWOMAN
THE SILVER AGENT
LEOPARDMAN
ASTROFACT
The Bouncing Beatnik has never been a member of Honor Guard, in any of his incarnations.
KITKAT
HONOR GUARD
OUR HEROIC LEGACY

SUPERSONIC

As powerful as a jumbo jet and as swift as a military fighter plane, Supersonic battled America's enemies from 1958-1982, tackling mobsters, enemy agents, aliens and more, on Earth and beyond. Connected in some way to Hillman-Holdaway Aircraft in Phoenix, Arizona, he fought in and for Astro City on numerous occasions.

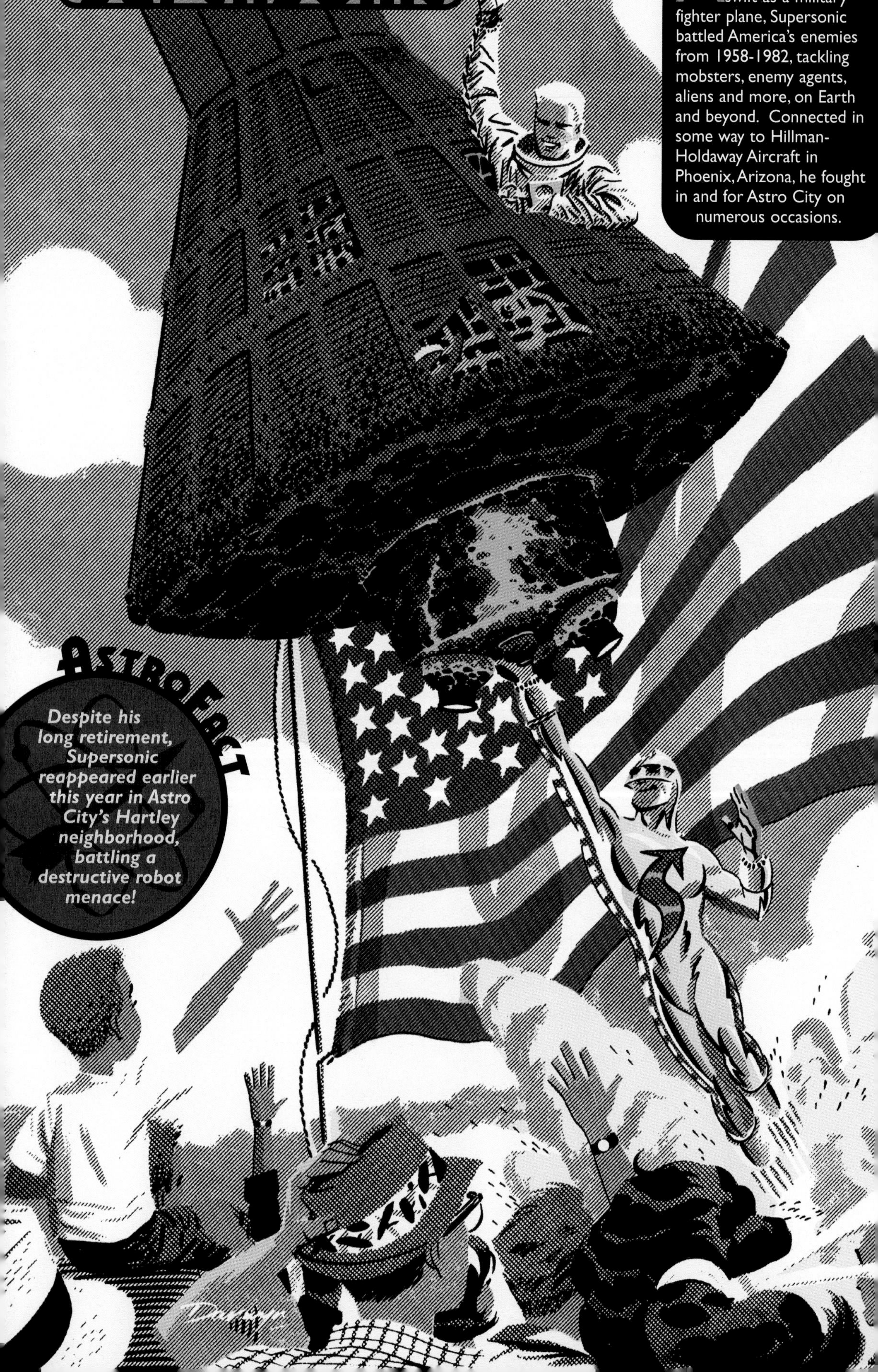

ASTROFACT

Despite his long retirement, Supersonic reappeared earlier this year in Astro City's Hartley neighborhood, battling a destructive robot menace!

ASTROCITY
A VISITORS GUIDE
HAS BEEN BROUGHT TO YOU BY

"Having A Wonderful Time…"

Kurt Busiek - writer
Brent Anderson - breakdowns
Ben Oliver - finished art & color
John Roshell and Comicraft's Rob Steen - letters

"Our Brightest Stars" artists:

Samaritan • **Jim Lee & Richard Friend**
Honor Guard & Intro Page • **Carlos Pacheco & Jesús Merino**
Jack-in-the-Box • **Jason Pearson & Sandra Hope**
The First Family • **Dave Gibbons**
Winged Victory • **Bill Sienkiewicz**
The N-Forcer • **Jerry Ordway**
Cleopatra • **Walter Simonson**
The Gentleman • **Phil Noto** *(art & colors)*
Crackerjack • **Lee Weeks**
Nightingale & Sunbird • **Bruce Timm**
The Crossbreed • **Ray Lago** *(painted art)*
The Flying Fox • **Mark Buckingham**
The Living Nightmare • **Simon Bisley**
The Confessor & Altar Boy • **Jackson Guice**
The Blue Knight • **Jim Starlin & Al Milgrom**
The Irregulars • **Gene Ha,** *colors by* **Art Lyon**
The Hanged Man • **Kelley Jones**
Air Ace • **John Paul Leon** *(art & colors)*
The Old Soldier • **Mark Texeira**
The Black Badge • **Howard Chaykin**
The Silver Agent • **Michael Golden** *(art & colors)*
Atomicus • **Pascal Ferry & Sandra Hope**
Honor Guard *(former)* • **Tom Grummett**
Supersonic • **Darwyn Cooke** *(art & colors)*
Winged Victory • **John Romita, Sr.**

All gallery pages colored by **Alex Sinclair**, except where noted.

Special thanks to **Andy Serwin** and **Carolyn Sliney**
for bibliographical and gastronomical assistance.

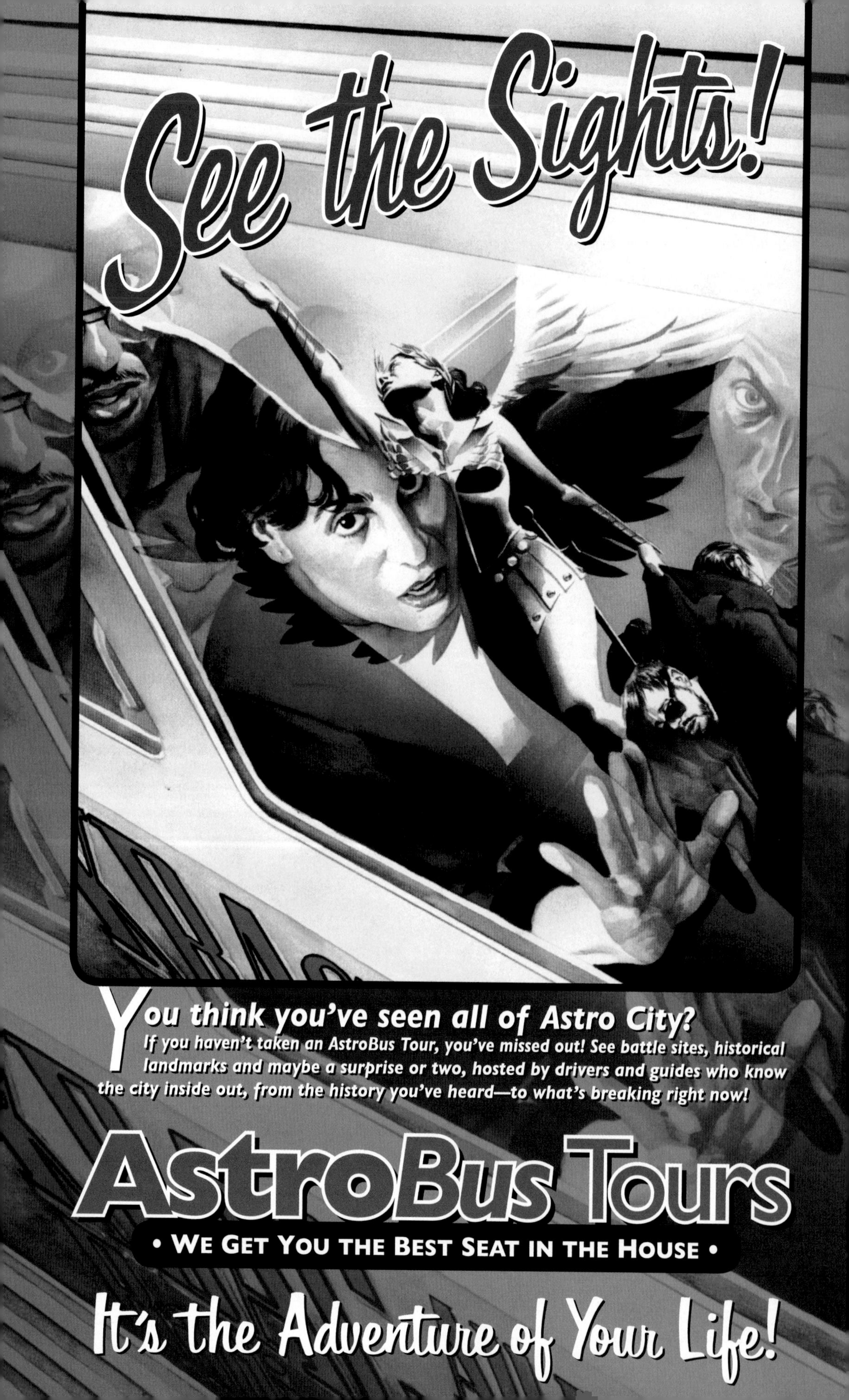
See the Sights!
You think you've seen all of Astro City?
If you haven't taken an AstroBus Tour, you've missed out! See battle sites, historical landmarks and maybe a surprise or two, hosted by drivers and guides who know the city inside out, from the history you've heard—to what's breaking right now!
AstroBus Tours
• We Get You the Best Seat in the House •
It's the Adventure of Your Life!

SKETCHBOOK

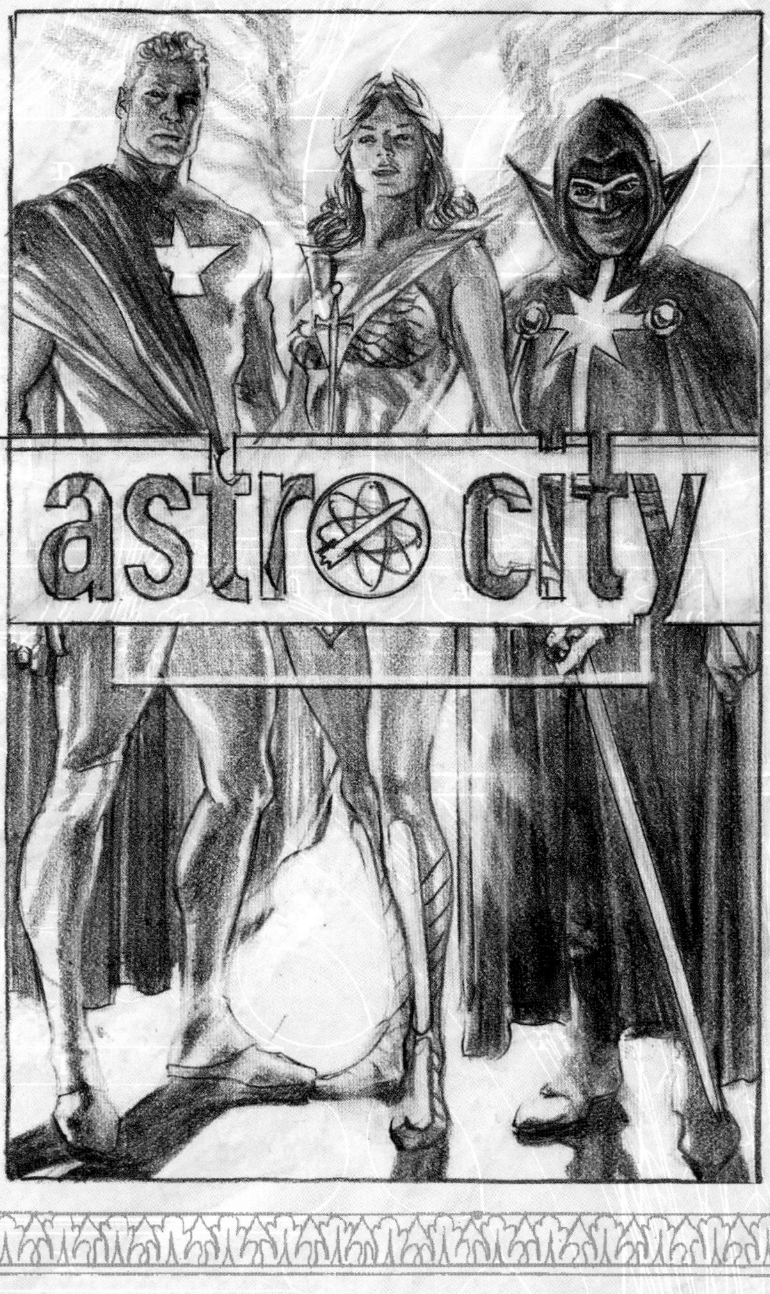
astro city

"WINGED VICTORY
COMPOUND AIDE
UNIFORM"
AC v3 #6
10-30-12

"WINGED VICTORY
COMPOUND AIDE
UNIFORM"
AC v3 #6
10-30-12
Ver2 lowcut
11-1-12

"WINGED VICTORY
COMPOUND AIDE
UNIFORM"
AC v3 #6
10-30-12
Ver2 lowcut
11-1-12

"WINGED VICTORY
COMPOUND AIDE
UNIFORM"
AC v3 #6
10-30-12
Ver2 lowcut
11-1-12

H E R O I

abstract
functionality
of zips

cowl-neck
sweater
UV Aide
rev. 11-2-12

jacket
contrast +
seamless body
shape

"WINGED VICTORY
COMPOUND AIDE
UNIFORM"
AC v3 #6
10-30-12
Ver2 lowcut
11-1-12

"WINGED VICTORY
COMPOUND AIDE
UNIFORM"
AC v3 #6
10-30-12
Ver 5
11-21-12

"WINGED VICTORY
COMPOUND AIDE
UNIFORM"
AC v3 #6
10-30-12
Ver 5
11-21-12

"WINGED VICTORY
COMPOUND AIDE
UNIFORM"
AC v3 #6
10-30-12
Ver 5
11-21-12

"WINGED VICTORY
COMPOUND AIDE
UNIFORM"
AC v3 #6
10-30-12

ver 5

11-21-12

rev. 11-23-12

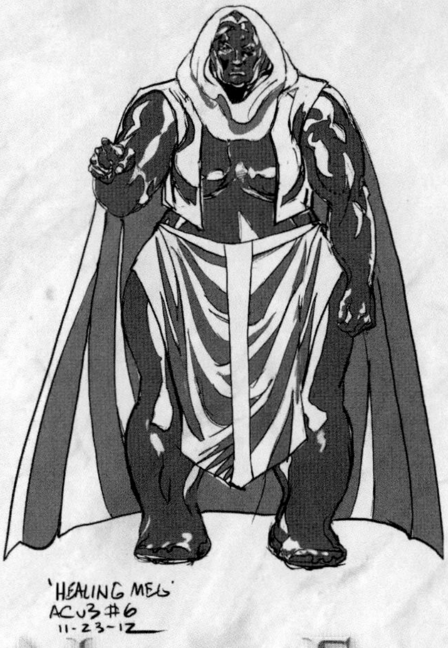
'HEALING MEG'
ACv3 #6
11-23-12

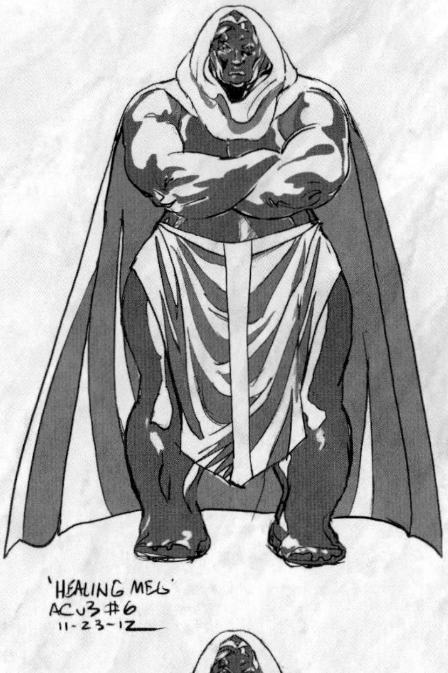
'HEALING MEG'
ACv3 #6
11-23-12

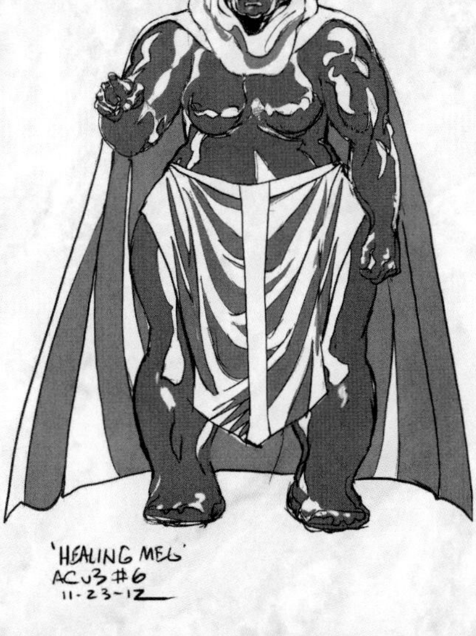
'HEALING MEG'
ACv3 #6
11-23-12

OPPOSITE: WE SPENT A LOT OF TIME DESIGNING WINGED VICTORY'S **SUPPORT STAFF.** THEY KEPT COMING OUT TOO PARAMILITARY FOR A WOMEN'S SHELTER, UNTIL WE SETTLED ON THE COWL-NECKED SWEATER AND DARK LEGGINGS, WITH THE INSIGNIA USED (FOR AIDES WITH LONG ENOUGH HAIR) AS A HAIR CLIP.

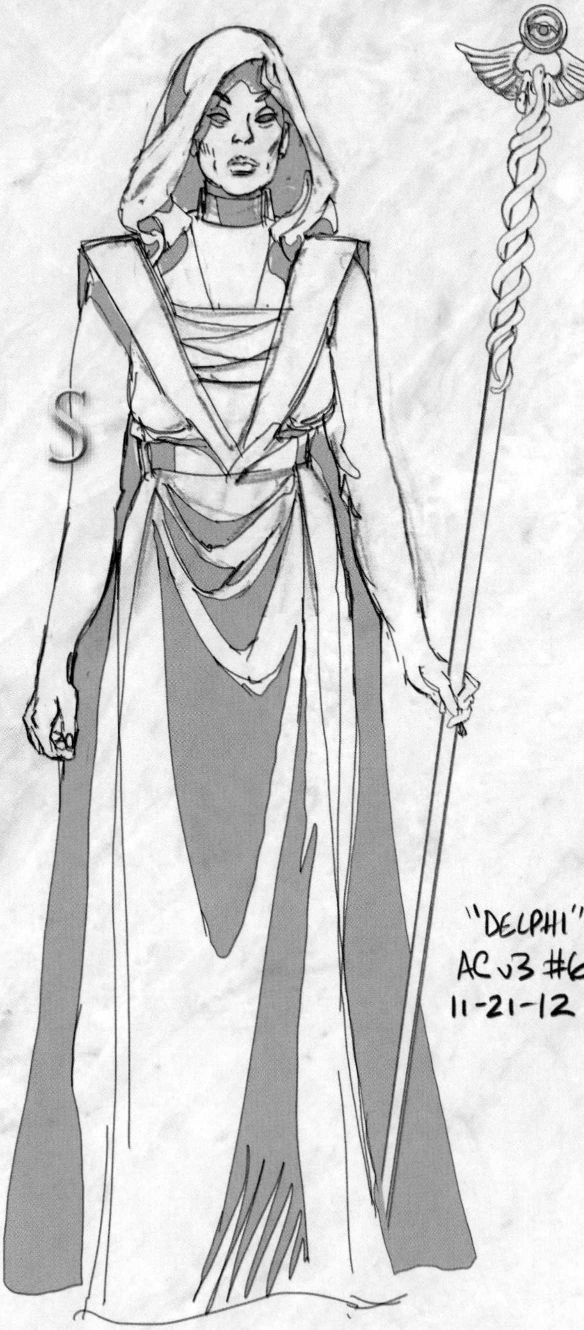
"DELPHI"
AC v3 #6
11-21-12

LEFT: WE WANTED **HEALER MEG** TO LOOK LIKE A BRONZE FERTILITY STATUE COME TO LIFE, SQUAT AND BULKY. AT FIRST, BRENT THOUGHT TO GIVE HER A VEST, BUT I SUGGESTED THAT IF SHE WAS BARE-BREASTED, IT WOULD FIT THE INTENT BETTER...NOT TO MENTION UNNERVING POOR TEENAGE JOEY.

ABOVE: **DELPHI,** THE SEER, CAME OUT JUST RIGHT ON BRENT'S FIRST TRY.

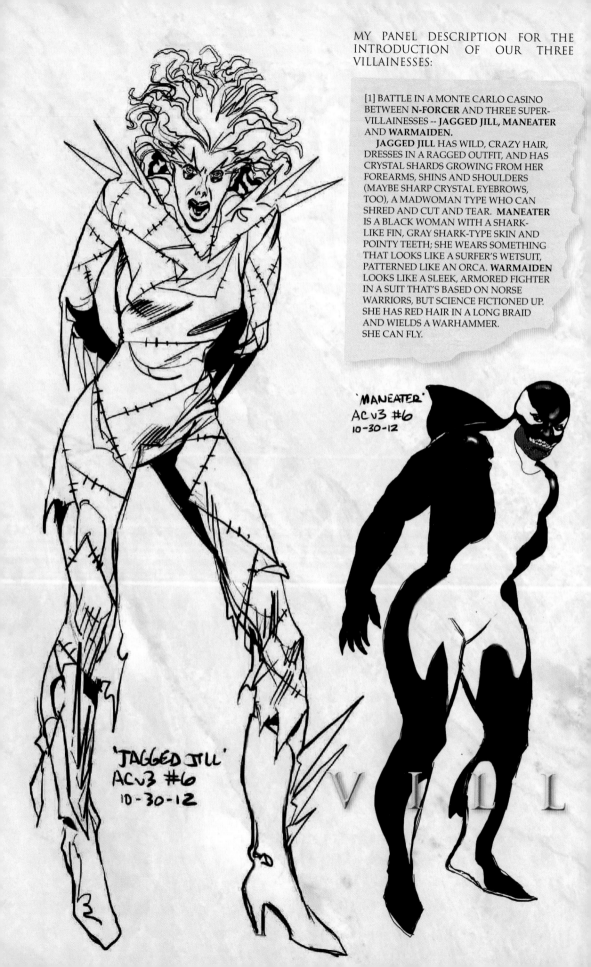

MY PANEL DESCRIPTION FOR THE INTRODUCTION OF OUR THREE VILLAINESSES:

[1] BATTLE IN A MONTE CARLO CASINO BETWEEN **N-FORCER** AND THREE SUPER-VILLAINESSES -- **JAGGED JILL, MANEATER** AND **WARMAIDEN.**

JAGGED JILL HAS WILD, CRAZY HAIR, DRESSES IN A RAGGED OUTFIT, AND HAS CRYSTAL SHARDS GROWING FROM HER FOREARMS, SHINS AND SHOULDERS (MAYBE SHARP CRYSTAL EYEBROWS, TOO), A MADWOMAN TYPE WHO CAN SHRED AND CUT AND TEAR. **MANEATER** IS A BLACK WOMAN WITH A SHARK-LIKE FIN, GRAY SHARK-TYPE SKIN AND POINTY TEETH; SHE WEARS SOMETHING THAT LOOKS LIKE A SURFER'S WETSUIT, PATTERNED LIKE AN ORCA. **WARMAIDEN** LOOKS LIKE A SLEEK, ARMORED FIGHTER IN A SUIT THAT'S BASED ON NORSE WARRIORS, BUT SCIENCE FICTIONED UP. SHE HAS RED HAIR IN A LONG BRAID AND WIELDS A WARHAMMER.
SHE CAN FLY.

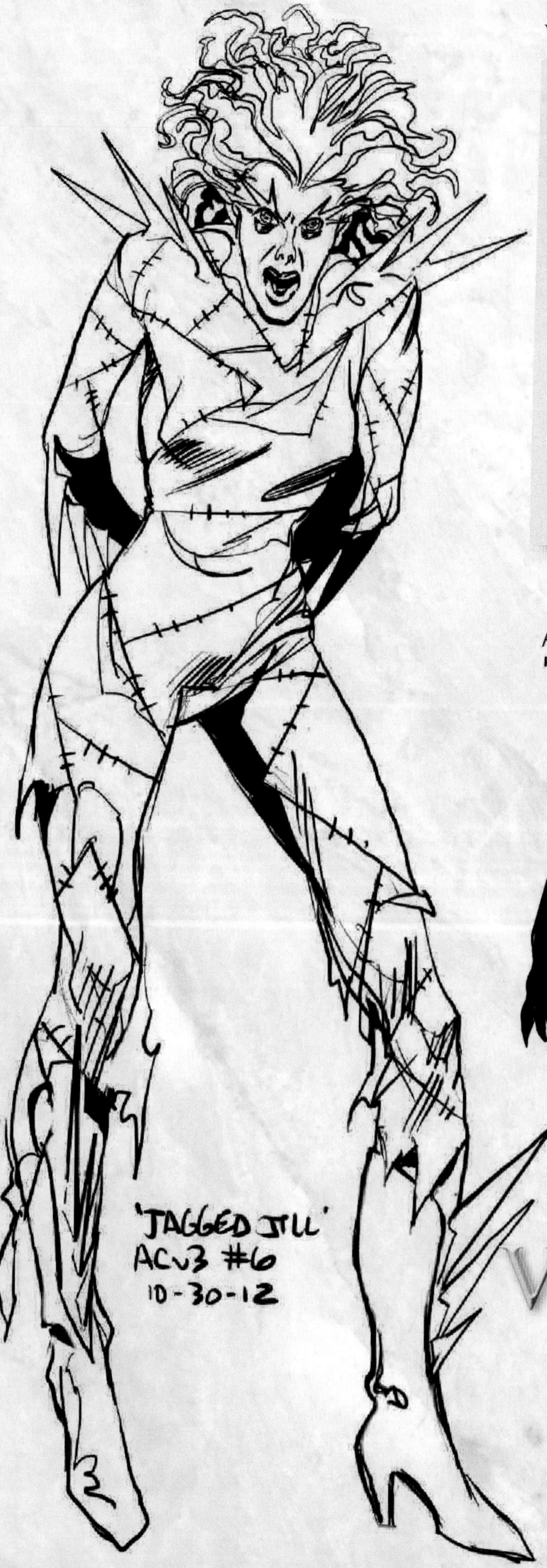
'JAGGED JILL'
ACv3 #6
10-30-12

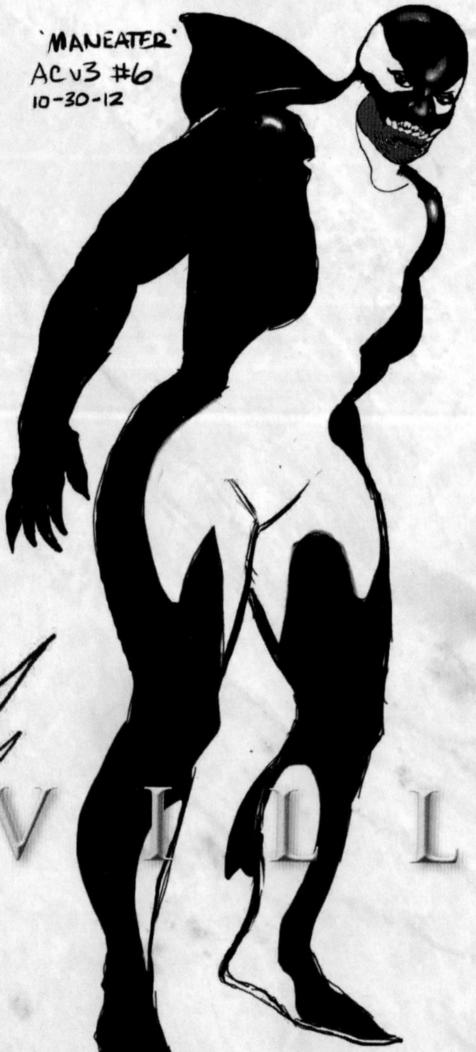
'MANEATER'
ACv3 #6
10-30-12

JAGGED JILL (WHOSE HAIR, AT LEAST, WAS INSPIRED BY THAT OF COMICS GREAT JILL THOMPSON) AND **MANEATER** (OPPOSITE) CAME OUT LOOKING GREAT ON THE FIRST ATTEMPT. BUT **WARMAIDEN** LOOKED A LITTLE TOO MUCH LIKE MARVEL'S THOR IN HER FIRST INCARNATION...

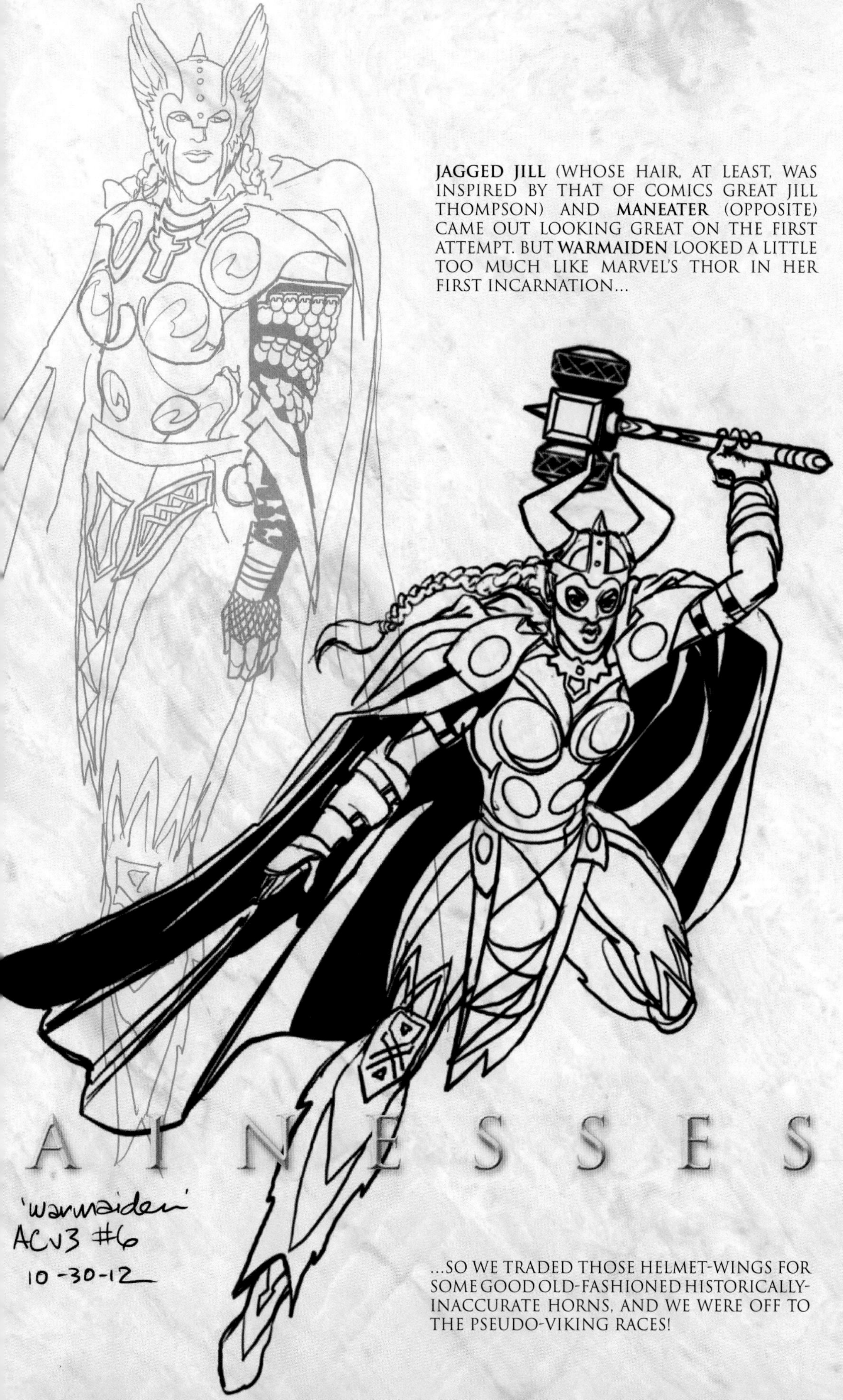
AINESSES
'warmaiden'
ACv3 #6
10-30-12

...SO WE TRADED THOSE HELMET-WINGS FOR SOME GOOD OLD-FASHIONED HISTORICALLY-INACCURATE HORNS, AND WE WERE OFF TO THE PSEUDO-VIKING RACES!

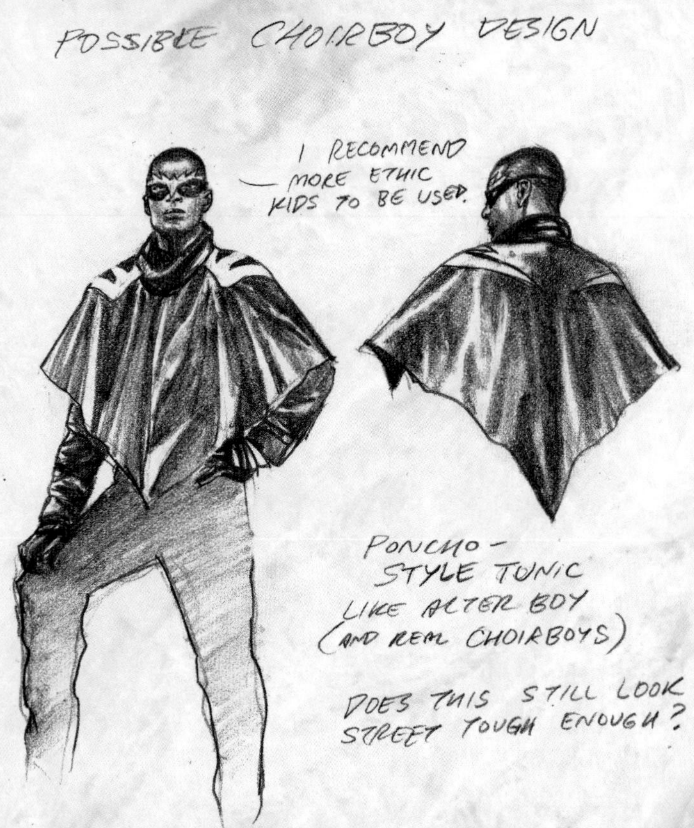
POSSIBLE CHOIRBOY DESIGN
I RECOMMEND MORE ETHIC KIDS TO BE USED.
PONCHO-STYLE TUNIC LIKE ALTER BOY (AND REAL CHOIRBOYS)
DOES THIS STILL LOOK STREET TOUGH ENOUGH?

BRENT HAD DONE A DESIGN FOR THE **CHOIRBOYS**, BUT WHEN IT TURNED OUT THEY'D BE APPEARING ON THE COVER OF NO.9, ALEX WANTED TO TAKE A HAND AT REWORKING THEM. HERE, WE CAN SEE HIS IDEA FOR WHAT THEY COULD LOOK LIKE...

C H O I R B

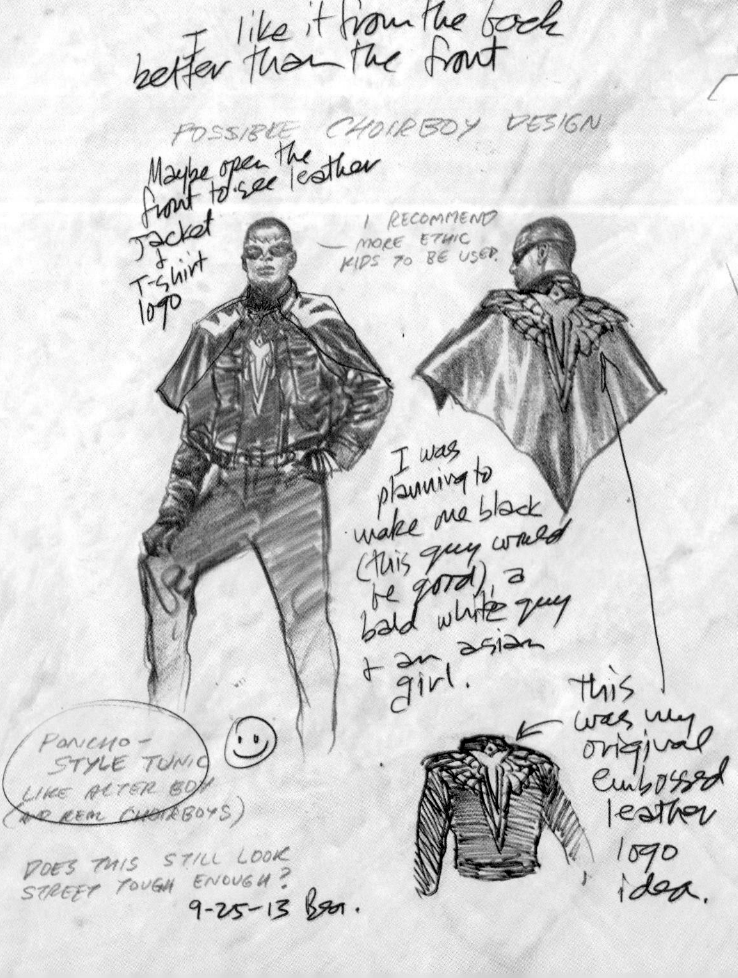
I like it from the back better than the front
POSSIBLE CHOIRBOY DESIGN
Maybe open the front to see leather jacket & T-shirt logo
I RECOMMEND MORE ETHIC KIDS TO BE USED.
I was planning to make one black (this guy would be good), a bald white guy & an asian girl.
This was my original embossed leather logo idea.
PONCHO-STYLE TUNIC LIKE ALTER BOY (AND REAL CHOIRBOYS)
DOES THIS STILL LOOK STREET TOUGH ENOUGH?
9-25-13 Bren.

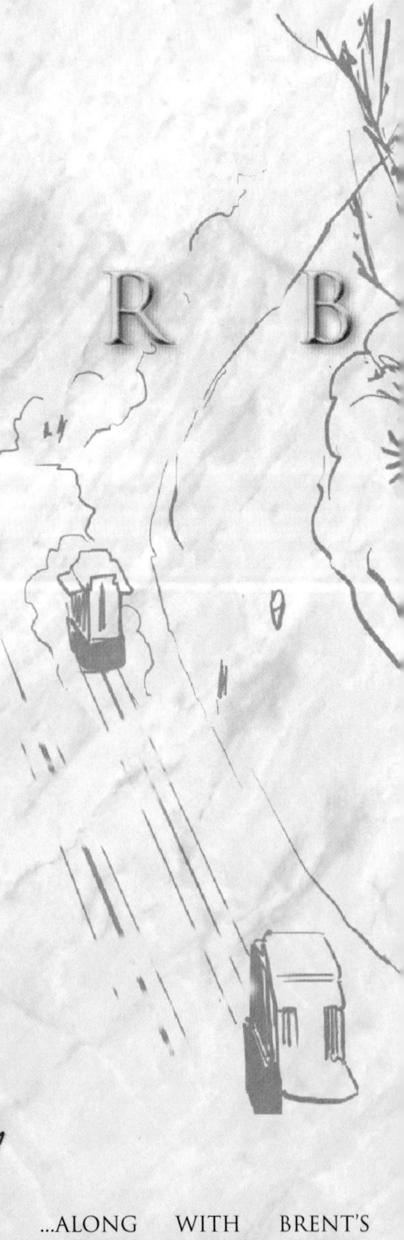

...ALONG WITH BRENT'S IDEAS FOR MODIFICATIONS.

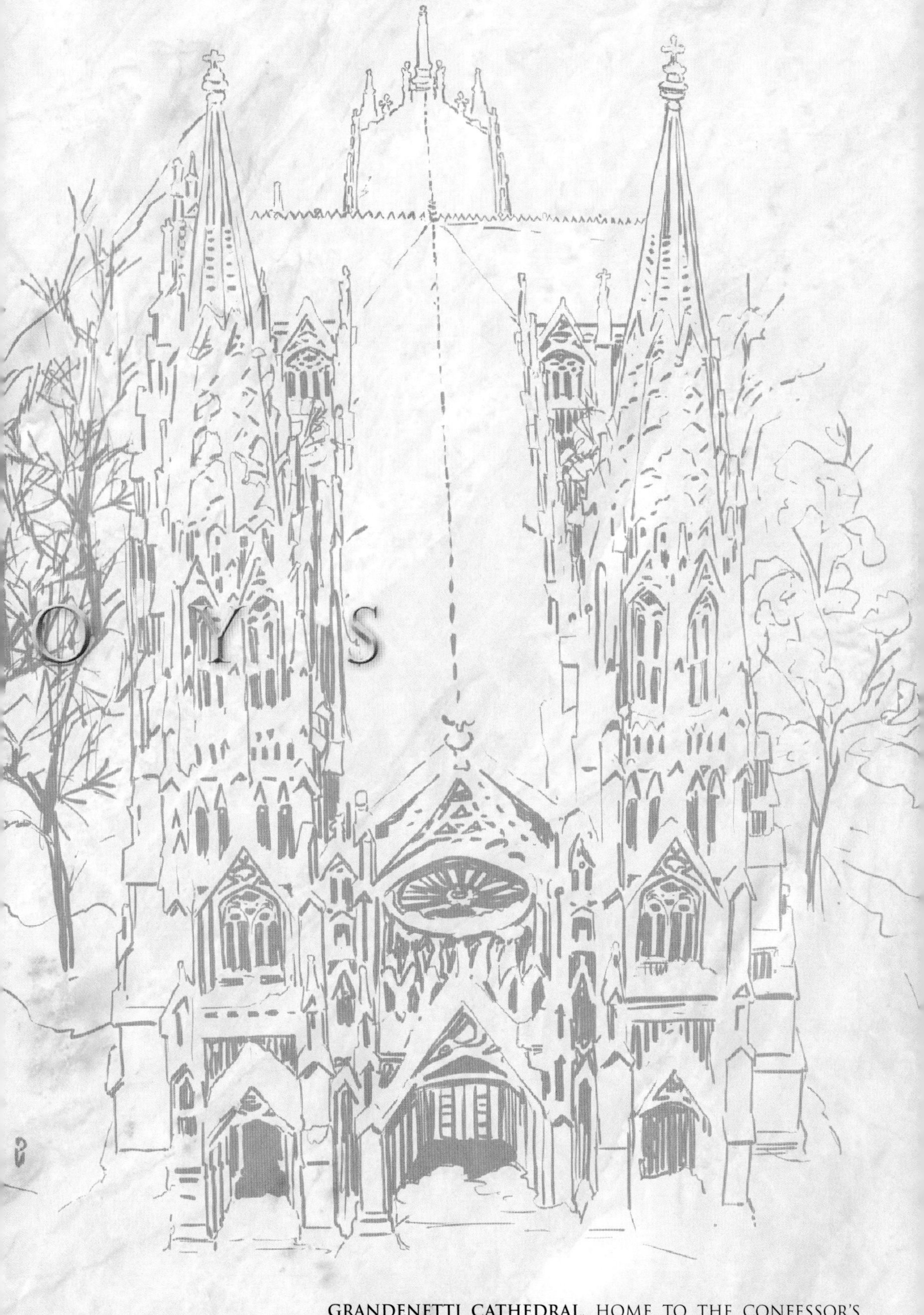

GRANDENETTI CATHEDRAL, HOME TO THE CONFESSOR'S LAIR AND A RECURRING SETTING WE'VE BEEN USING IN THE BOOK FOR YEARS NOW. MAYBE SOMEDAY WE SHOULD SHOW YOU THE BITS OF IT TOURISTS ACTUALLY GET TO SEE...

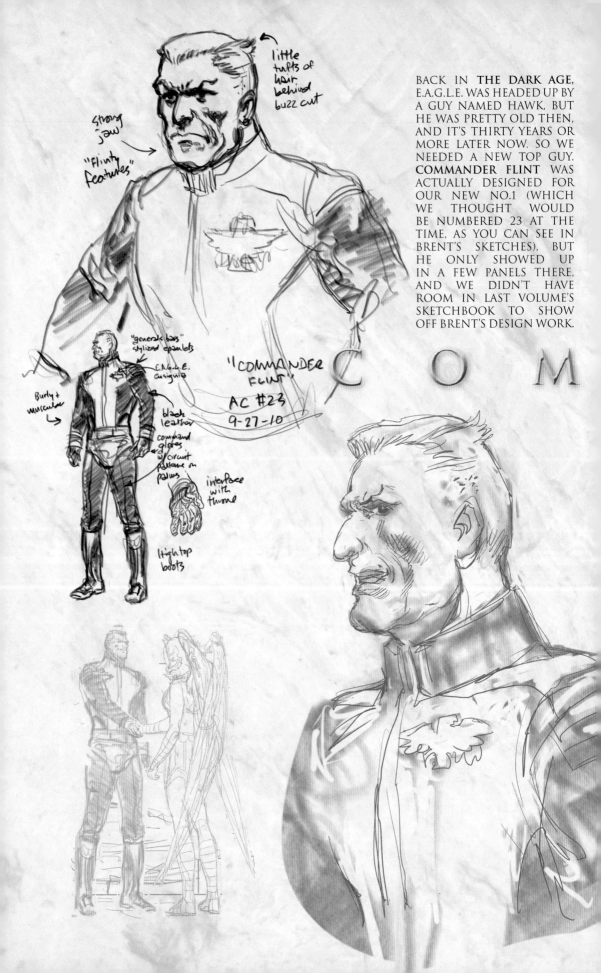

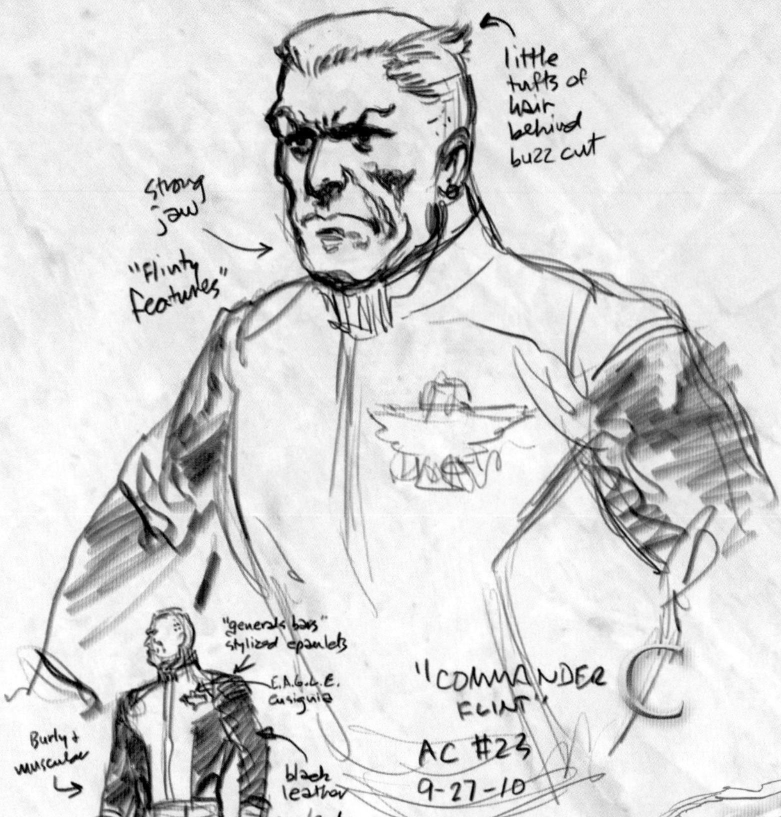
little tufts of hair behind buzz cut
strong jaw
"Flinty features"
"COMMANDER FLINT"
AC #23
9-27-10

BACK IN **THE DARK AGE,** E.A.G.L.E. WAS HEADED UP BY A GUY NAMED HAWK, BUT HE WAS PRETTY OLD THEN, AND IT'S THIRTY YEARS OR MORE LATER NOW. SO WE NEEDED A NEW TOP GUY. **COMMANDER FLINT** WAS ACTUALLY DESIGNED FOR OUR NEW NO.1 (WHICH WE THOUGHT WOULD BE NUMBERED 23 AT THE TIME, AS YOU CAN SEE IN BRENT'S SKETCHES), BUT HE ONLY SHOWED UP IN A FEW PANELS THERE, AND WE DIDN'T HAVE ROOM IN LAST VOLUME'S SKETCHBOOK TO SHOW OFF BRENT'S DESIGN WORK.

C O M

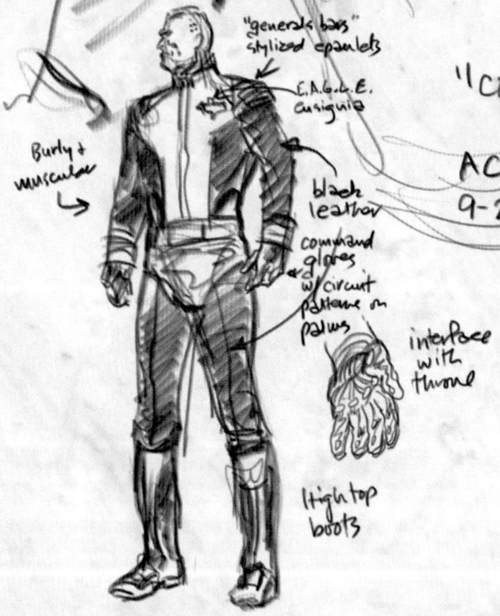
"generals bars" stylized epaulets
E.A.G.L.E. insignia
Burly + muscular
black leather
command gloves w/ circuit patterns on palms
interface with throne
high top boots

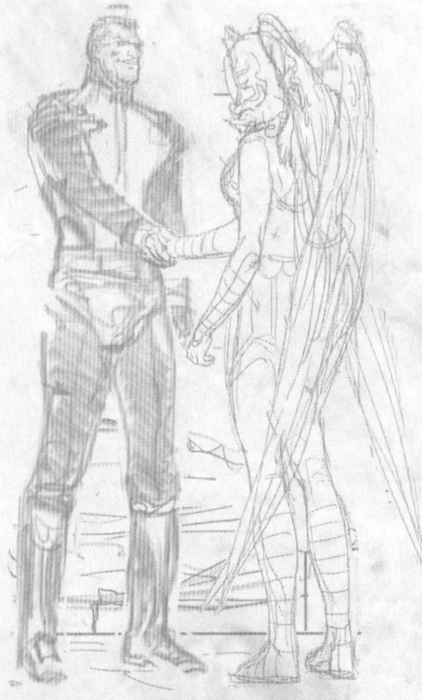

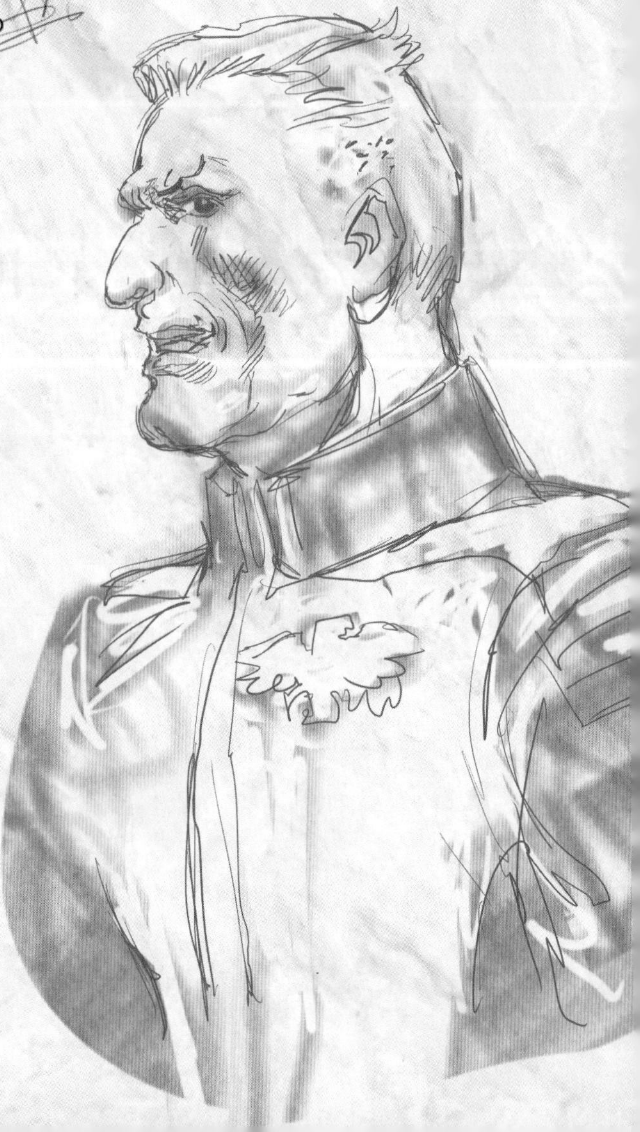

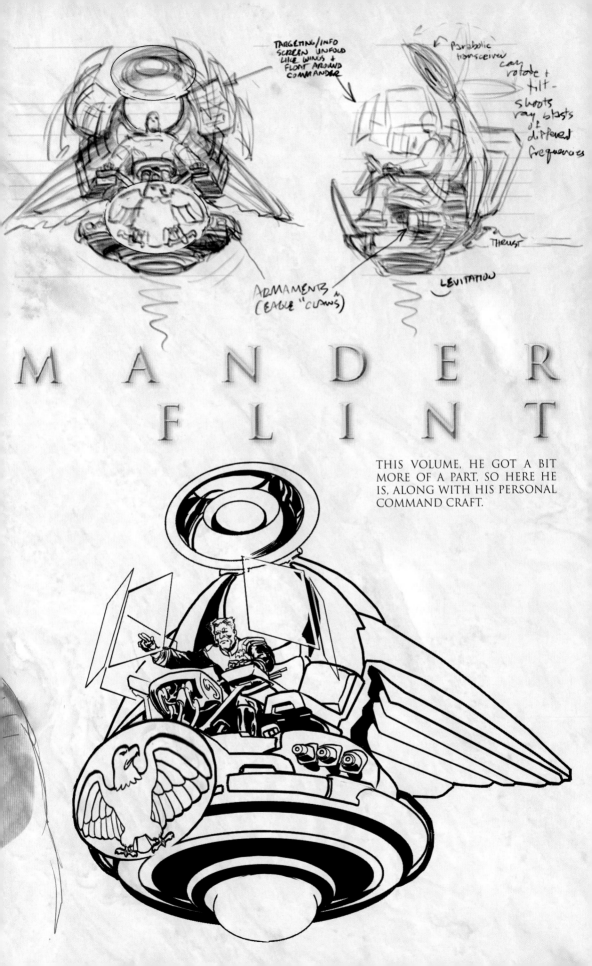

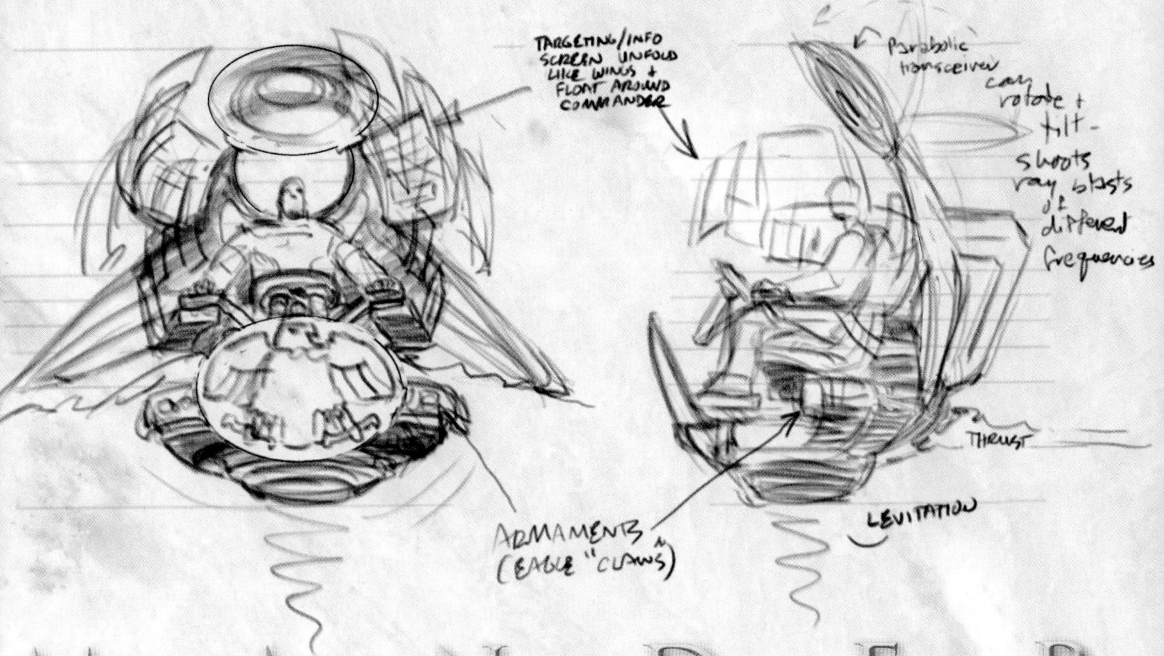
TARGETING/INFO SCREEN UNFOLD LIKE WINGS + FLOAT AROUND COMMANDER
Parabolic transceiver can rotate + tilt - shoots ray blasts of different frequencies
THRUST
ARMAMENTS (EAGLE "CLAWS")
LEVITATION

MANDER FLINT

THIS VOLUME, HE GOT A BIT MORE OF A PART, SO HERE HE IS, ALONG WITH HIS PERSONAL COMMAND CRAFT.

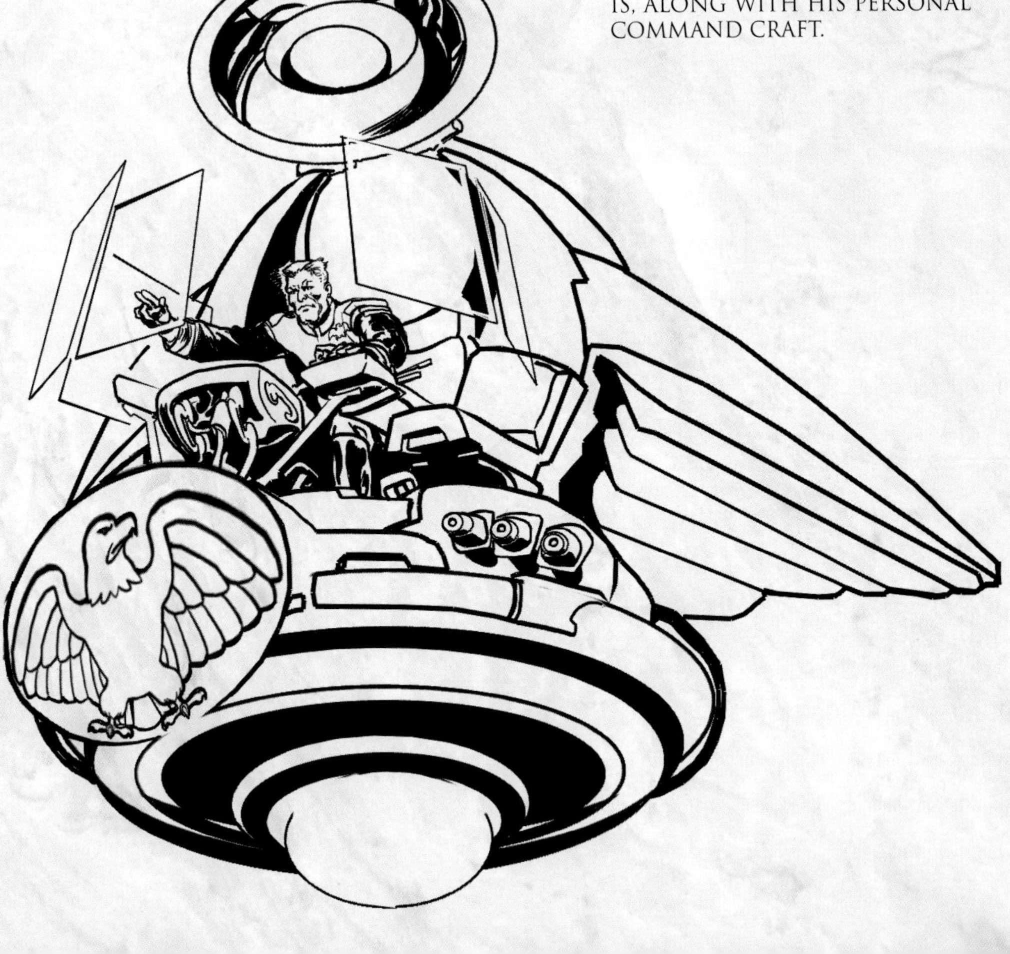

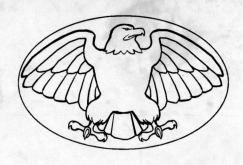

MORE **E.A.G.L.E.** GADGETRY, COURTESY OF VEHICULAR DESIGNMASTER BRENT ANDERSON.

ONE OF THE WAYS WE TRY TO MAKE ASTRO CITY FEEL LIKE A LIVING, BREATHING WORLD WITH A DEVELOPING, COMPLEX HISTORY IS TO MAKE SURE EVEN THE CHARACTERS AND CONCEPTS WHO SHOW UP OVER AND OVER AGAIN GET UPDATED NOW AND THEN. SAMARITAN AND WINGED VICTORY MAY CHOOSE TO STICK WITH THE SAME COSTUME DESIGN FOR YEARS (AND THEY LOOK SO GOOD, WHY WOULDN'T THEY?), BUT A GROUP LIKE E.A.G.L.E. IS GOING TO INTRODUCE NEW AND IMPROVED TECHNOLOGY OVER TIME, SO WE'D BETTER KEEP UP WITH THEM.

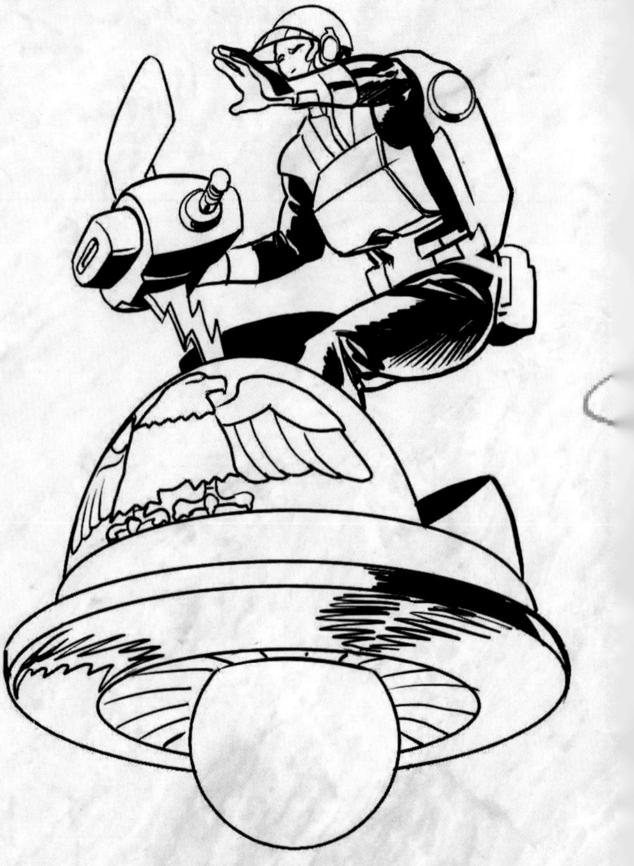

E.A.G.L.E.

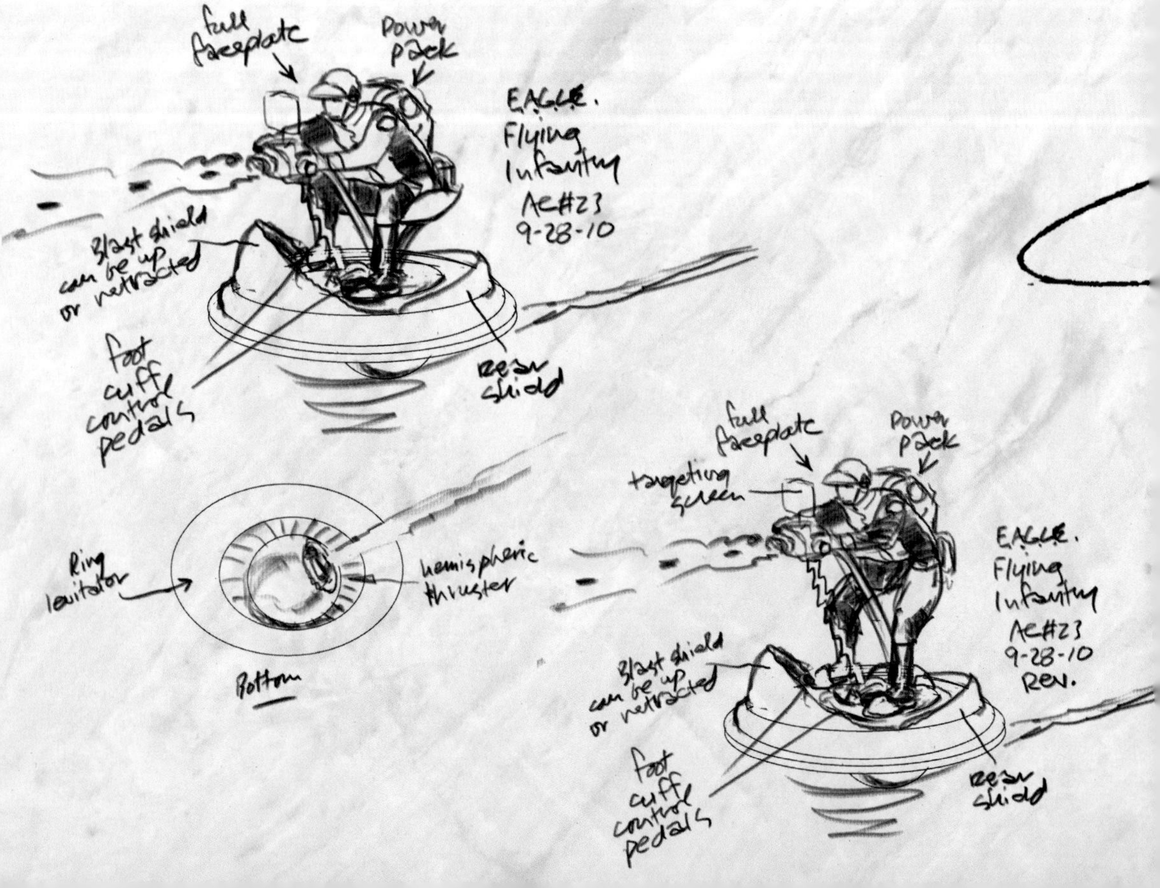
full faceplate
power pack
E.A.G.L.E.
Flying Infantry
AC#23
9-28-10
Blast shield can be up or retracted
foot cuff control pedals
rear shield
Ring levitator
hemispheric thruster
Bottom
full faceplate
power pack
targeting screen
E.A.G.L.E.
Flying Infantry
AC#23
9-28-10
Rev.
Blast shield can be up or retracted
foot cuff control pedals
rear shield

VEHICLES

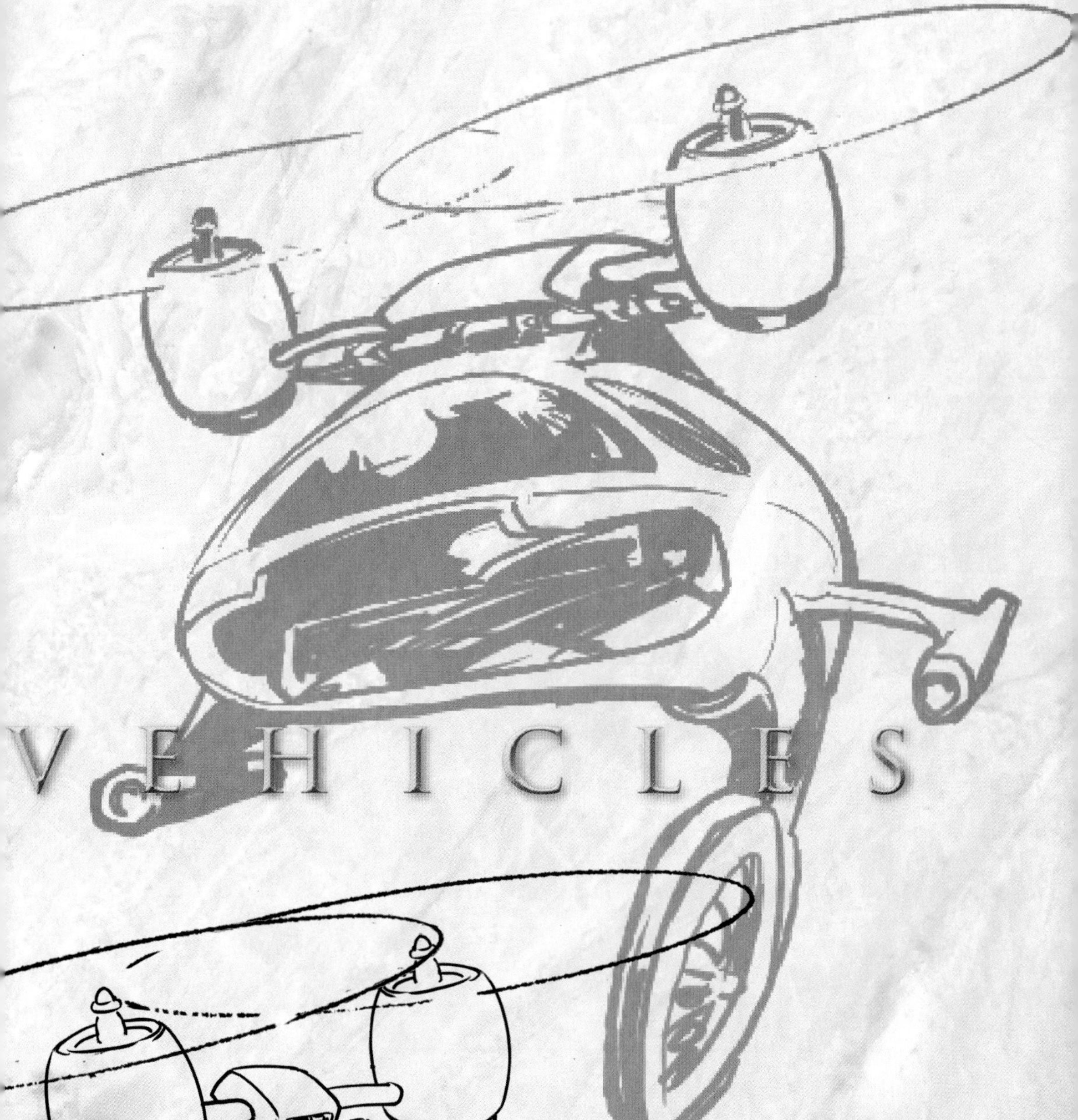

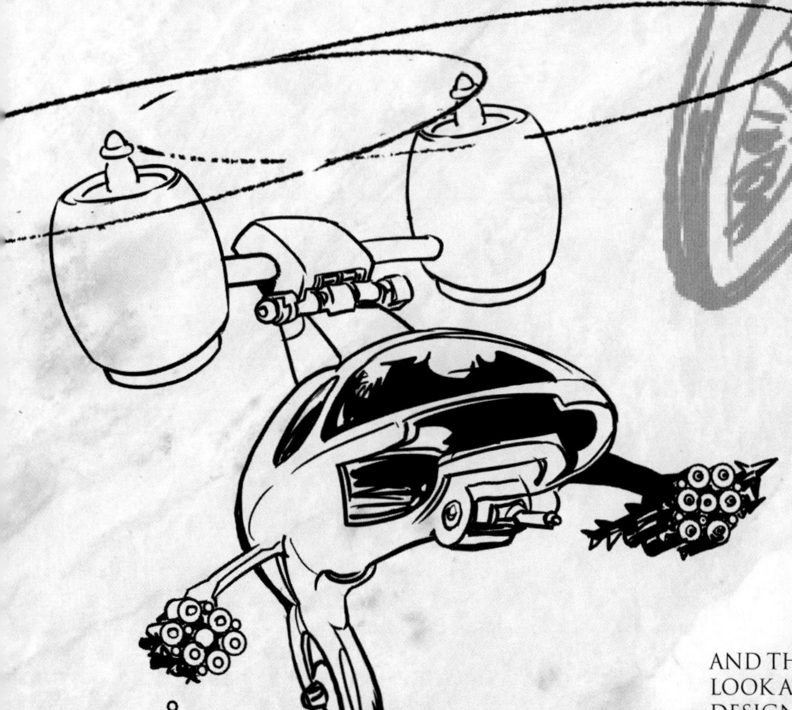

AND THAT FINISHES OFF ANOTHER LOOK AT THE BEHIND-THE-SCENES DESIGN OF OUR FAIR CITY!

—KURT BUSIEK

DON'T MISS THE REST OF THE ASTRO CITY SERIES:

astro city
life in the big city
KURT BUSIEK • BRENT ANDERSON • ALEX ROSS

KURT BUSIEK'S
Astro City
BUSIEK • ANDERSON • BLYBERG
SINCLAIR • ROSS • COMICRAFT
Confession
Introduction by NEIL GAIMAN

Kurt Busiek's
ASTRO CITY
Family Album
BUSIEK • ANDERSON • BLYBERG
ROSS • SINCLAIR • COMICRAFT
Introduction by Harlan Ellison

HOMAGE COMICS
KURT BUSIEK'S
Astro City
The TARNISHED ANGEL
COMPLETE AND UNABRIDGED
Introduction by FRANK MILLER

ASTRO CITY
LOCAL HEROES

ASTRO CITY
BROTHERS & OTHER STRANGERS
BUSIEK
ANDERSON
ROSS
SINCLAIR
COMICRAFT

ASTRO CITY
BROTHERS IN ARMS
BUSIEK
ANDERSON
ROSS
SINCLAIR
COMICRAFT

astro city
SHINING STARS
BUSIEK ANDERSON ROSS SINCLAIR COMICRAFT

astro city
through open doors
KURT BUSIEK • BRENT ANDERSON • ALEX ROSS

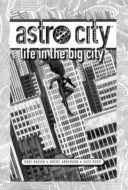

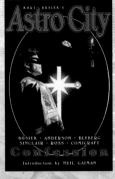

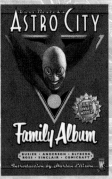

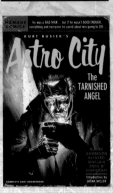

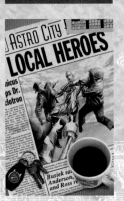

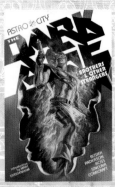

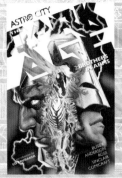

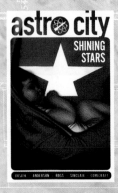

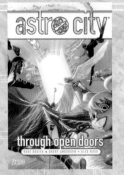

ABOUT THE CREATORS

KURT BUSIEK BROKE INTO COMICS IN 1982, SELLING STORIES TO BOTH DC AND MARVEL WITHIN WEEKS OF FINISHING COLLEGE. SINCE THEN, HE'S BEEN AN EDITOR, A LITERARY AGENT, A SALES MANAGER AND MORE, BUT IS BEST KNOWN AS THE MULTIPLE-AWARD-WINNING WRITER OF ASTRO CITY, MARVELS, SUPERMAN, CONAN, ARROWSMITH, SUPERSTAR, SHOCKROCKETS AND MANY OTHERS. HE LIVES IN THE PACIFIC NORTHWEST WITH HIS FAMILY.

BRENT ANDERSON BEGAN WRITING AND DRAWING HIS OWN COMICS IN JUNIOR HIGH SCHOOL, AND GRADUATED TO PROFESSIONAL WORK LESS THAN A DECADE LATER. HE'S DRAWN SUCH PROJECTS AS KA-ZAR THE SAVAGE, X-MEN: GOD LOVES MAN KILLS, STRIKEFORCE: MORITURI, SOMERSET HOLMES, RISING STARS AND, OF COURSE, ASTRO CITY, FOR WHICH HE'S WON MULTIPLE EISNER AND HARVEY AWARDS. HE MAKES HIS HOME IN NORTHERN CALIFORNIA.

ALEX ROSS WORKED ON TERMINATOR: THE BURNING EARTH AND CLIVE BARKER'S HELLRAISER BEFORE HIS BREAKOUT SERIES, MARVELS, MADE HIM AN OVERNIGHT SUPERSTAR. SINCE THEN, HE'S PAINTED, PLOTTED AND/OR WRITTEN SUCH SERIES AS KINGDOM COME, SUPERMAN: PEACE ON EARTH, JUSTICE, EARTH X, AVENGERS/INVADERS AND PROJECT SUPERPOWERS, AND WON OVER TWO DOZEN INDUSTRY AWARDS.

ALEX SINCLAIR HAS COLORED VIRTUALLY EVERY DC COMICS CHARACTER IN EXISTENCE, AND MORE BESIDES. BEST KNOWN FOR HIS AWARD-WINNING WORK WITH JIM LEE AND SCOTT WILLIAMS, HE'S WORKED ON SUCH BOOKS AS BATMAN: HUSH, SUPERMAN: FOR TOMORROW, BLACKEST NIGHT, BATMAN & ROBIN, ASTRO CITY, JLA, IDENTITY CRISIS, ARROWSMITH AND MORE.

WENDY BROOME WAS A LONGTIME MEMBER OF THE COLORING STAFF AT WILDSTORM STUDIOS, BEFORE GOING FREELANCE IN 2004. SHE'S MADE A SPECIALTY OF COLORING LARGE-CAST BOOKS, INCLUDING WILDCATS 3.0, THE AUTHORITY, GEN13, THE END LEAGUE, THUNDERCATS, WETWORKS AND TOP10 AS WELL AS PITCHING IN AS NEEDED ON ASTRO CITY.

JOHN G. ROSHELL JOINED COMICRAFT IN 1992, HELPING PROPEL THE LETTERING/DESIGN STUDIO TO ITS DOMINANT POSITION IN THE INDUSTRY. AS SENIOR DESIGN WIZARD, HE'S LETTERED THOUSANDS OF COMICS PAGES, ALONG WITH CREATING LOGOS AND FONTS, DESIGNING BOOK EDITIONS AND MORE. HE ALSO WRITES THE SERIES CHARLEY LOVES ROBOTS, WHICH APPEARS IN ELEPHANTMEN.

RICHARD STARKINGS DIMLY REMEMBERS WORKING ON SOME BATMAN PROJECT... THE KILLING JOKE? PEOPLE INSIST THAT HE DID LETTER IT WITH A TOOL NOT UNLIKE A COMPUTER... BUT TOO MANY LATTES AND BRITISH CHOCOLATE HAS WIPED HIS RECOLLECTIONS OF ANYTHING PRIOR TO ILLUSTRATOR 5. HE CURRENTLY WRITES ELEPHANTMEN.

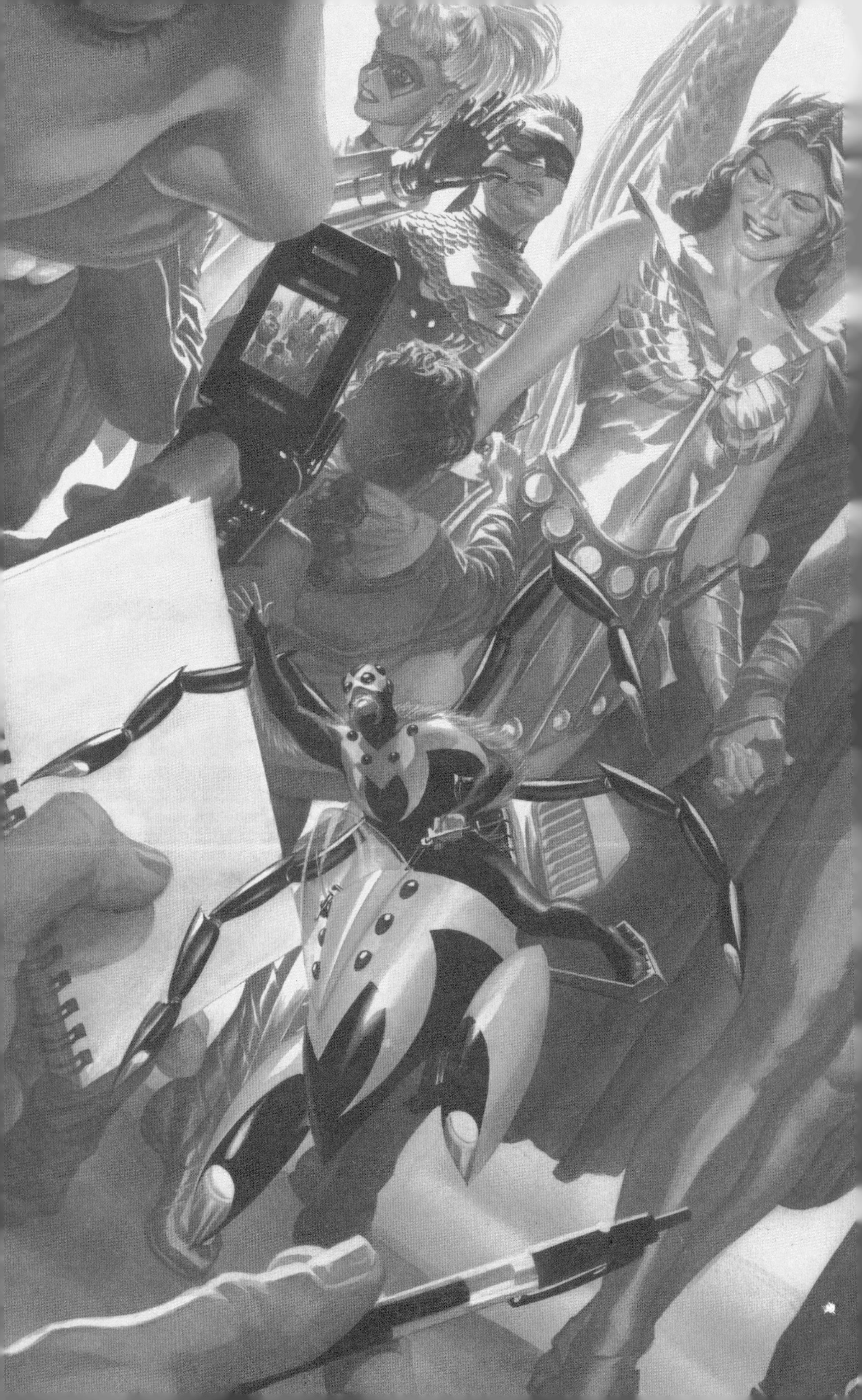